Data Communications and Distributed Networks

THIRD EDITION

Data Communications and Distributed Networks

Uyless D. Black

Bell Atlantic Education Services

PRENTICE HALL, Englewood Cliffs, New Jersey 07632

Library of Congress Cataloging-in-Publication Data

Black, Uyless D.
   Data communications and distributed networks / Uyless D. Black. --
3rd ed.
      p.   cm.
   Includes bibliographical references and index.
   ISBN 0-13-203464-6
   1. Data transmission systems. 2. Computer networks.
3. Electronic data processing--Distributed processing.   I. Title.
TK5105.B576 1993
004.6--dc20   92-28935
                                                          CIP

Acquisitions editor: Bill Zobrist
Production editor: Bayani Mendoza de Leon
Cover designer: Ben Santora
Copy editor: Brenda Melissaratos
Prepress buyer: Linda Behrens
Manufacturing buyer: Dave Dickey
Editorial assistant: Danielle Robinson

First edition published under the title of
Data Communications, Networks, and Distributed Processing

 © 1993, 1987, 1983 by Prentice-Hall, Inc.
A Simon & Schuster Company
Englewood Cliffs, New Jersey 07632

10 9 8 7 6 5 4 3 2 1

ISBN 0-13-203464-6

Prentice-Hall International (UK) Limited, *London*
Prentice-Hall of Australia Pty. Limited, *Sydney*
Prentice-Hall Canada Inc., *Toronto*
Prentice-Hall Hispanoamericana, S.A., *Mexico*
Prentice-Hall of India Private Limited, *New Delhi*
Prentice-Hall of Japan, Inc., *Tokyo*
Prentice-Hall of Southeast Asia Pte. Ltd., *Singapore*
Editora Prentice-Hall do Brasil, Ltda., *Rio de Janeiro*

TRADEMARK INFORMATION

IBM is a registered trademark of
International Business Machines
Corporation.

DEC is a registered trademark of Digital
Equipment Corporation.

Intel is a registered trademark of Intel
Corporation.

Xerox is a registered trademark of Xerox
Corporation.

NCP, SDLC, and BSC are trademarks of
International Business Machines
Corporation.

This book is dedicated to Ken Sherman,
a friend and mentor
who encouraged me many years ago
to begin writing about computer networks.

Contents

Preface

The idea for the first edition of this book originated in several data communications seminars that I conducted for a number of U.S., Canadian, and European firms. Some of the seminar participants expressed difficulty in finding a reference on data communications that included presentations on network software, protocols, and data bases. The dominant wish appeared to be for a book that described these concepts and practices in non-theoretical terms. In approaching my first edition, I examined the offerings available in the industry and came to the conclusion that there were many excellent references on the subject but they were beyond the grasp of the uninitiated, concentrated on one specific aspect of the topic, or were overly general. Therefore, my goal in writing this book was to provide a practical yet detailed explanation of the data communications system networks with highlights on software and data bases.

The task proved to be very challenging because the subject matter is not simple. I decided to write the book using as few formula and as little scientific jargon as possible. I also have tried to provide sufficient technical detail to remove the mystery and confusion that often surround these topics.

I prepared and refined these approaches and ideas with many seminar participants, with my business associates, and with many of my clients. After concluding that I could reach my goal of practicality and technical clarity, I committed the project to prose and pen. I hope the result will be valuable to the reader.

The third edition of this book incorporates many changes that have occurred in the industry since the original publication in 1983 and the second edition in 1987. I have added new material in all of the chapters and have also deleted material that was outdated. The majority of new material reflects new standards such as some of the IEEE

802 LAN standards and some of the CCITT ISDN standards. Also included are updates
to the industry as reflected in frame relay and broadband ISDN.

The book also contains additional material on distributed systems and internetworking. Most of this material emphasizes the (a) internetworking of personal computers
and (b) client-server operations.

As with the original book, this edition is intended for both the beginner and the
more advanced reader. The first three chapters should be read by the beginner.

ACKNOWLEDGMENTS

I have many organizations and individuals to thank for their contributions to this book.
As with the first two editions, the IBM Corporation provided the background information
for the case study on line loading and design. The staff at the Bell Atlantic Education
Services (BAES) has provided considerable support to me during this effort. Jeff Mandel
of Ascom Timeplex has also been very helpful and supportive. Janet Herbert and Fay
Napert have been most helpful in providing support for my lectures at Digital. My thanks
to Jeanne Malin for her fine work on the index. My thanks also to my wife Holly, who
provided support for this project.

Uyless D. Black

Data Communications
and Distributed Networks

1

Introduction

PURPOSE OF DATA COMMUNICATIONS SYSTEMS AND NETWORKS

During the past several years, there has been an increasing recognition within business and academic circles that certain nations have evolved into information societies. These countries now rely heavily on knowledge and information to spur economic growth. Many leaders today believe the generation of information has provided the foundation needed to increase the efficiency and productivity of a society. The use of information has lowered the costs of producing society's goods and has increased the quality of these products. The computer has been the catalyst for this information revolution.

To gain an appreciation of the statements of business and academic leaders, one need only examine selected segments of society to understand what the computer has done to provide this vital information.

- The many benefits from space exploration would not be available if the computer did not exist to process the millions of data elements used to guide space vehicles in their probe of the solar system.
- Transportation reservations systems (airline, hotel) and the nation's highly efficient methods of distributing goods are made possible through the computer.
- Some industries have significantly lowered the costs and increased the quality of their manufactured goods through the use of automated processes and computerized robots.

- Office tasks requiring a handful of people would require hundreds of workers if office automation were not available.

- Oil exploration, energy conservation, defense measures, and medical research and development are all dependent on the computer's ability to store and process information.

The computer has provided the foundation for the information society, but it is often a scapegoat for society's problems. One can read stories daily of the problems supposedly created by the computer, and the reader has probably had similar negative experiences. Yet, for all its perceived shortcomings, the computer and its contribution to our information society have made our lives immeasurably more pleasant and affluent. Like it or not, we have become dependent on the computer.

The information society is also based on data—the raw resource that comprises information. The essence of automation and the information society is the processing, manipulation, and creation of data to provide something intelligible—information.

This powerful capability is strengthened by the use of data communications systems. The systems provide for the transport of data and information between and among the computers. Data communications provides the connections to computers located in the far reaches of a country and the world. The computer facilities are tied together by data communications components, forming a network of automated resources to support the many functions of a business or organization.

Data communications is a vital part of the information society because it provides the infrastructure allowing the computers to communicate with one another. An airline reservation system uses data communications to link the reservation offices to the computer. The space flights and the space shuttle use data communications systems to send data to and from the rockets and the command centers on earth. Office workers are dependent on networks to provide the use of data files and computers to different departments in an organization.

Thus, data communications systems are an integral part of our lives. They provide the foundation for our information society. Many people do not recognize how pervasive the systems are in our economy and social activity. Yet the importance of data communications systems is so great that we should understand more about the field. The layperson can benefit from knowing their characteristics and uses. The computer professional should understand data communications and networks in order to take advantage of their capabilities and avoid the pitfalls associated with their misuse. This book attempts to provide the necessary information for both the professional and the layperson.

THE PURPOSE OF DATA COMMUNICATIONS SYSTEMS

Even though the many components that comprise data communications systems and distributed networks may appear to be complex, the purpose of this technology is very simple: the transport of user data between and among user machines. All aspects of data communications are designed to meet this one goal.

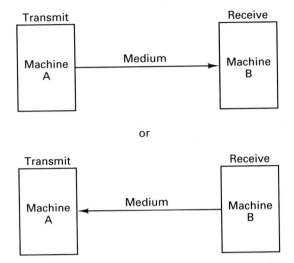

Figure 1-1. Components of a data communications system.

The user machines are typically computers, workstations, and terminals. From the standpoint of the data communications system, it makes no difference what type of machine is sending and receiving the data. It could be a large-scale IBM mainframe computer or a small Apple Macintosh computer. The purpose remains the same.

The Components

Regardless of how complex a data communications system may seem, it is really quite simple if an examination is made of its basic components. Three components are required in a data communications system. There must be a transmitting device, a receiving device, and some type of medium to carry the data between the transmitting and receiving devices (see Figure 1–1).

The transmitting device can take may forms. It may be a user computer or a specialized communications device such as a modem or multiplexer.

This same concept holds true for the receiving device. It may be a user computer, or a receiving modem, or a receiving multiplexer.

The medium may also take many forms. It may be copper wire that carries electrical signals that represent the user data. It may be a radio wave that is altered in various ways to represent data. It might even be an optical fiber in which light signals are changed in accordance with certain conventions to represent the user data.

If the many parts of a data communications system are examined, it will be discovered that they fit into one of these three basic components.

THE ADVENT OF COMPUTER-BASED DATA COMMUNICATIONS SYSTEMS

In the early days (in this industry, early 1960s) a central computer was used to support most organizations. The costs to build computers in those days were eronmous; hardware was very expensive, as was the operating system software. It made good sense for relatively unintelligent (dumb) user workstations to be located near the customer's working facilities and access the computer through remote communications lines.

However, things changed rapidly. In a few short years, significant progress was made in (a) increasing the speed of central processing units (CPUs) and (b) decreasing the cost to design and manufacture them. As the computer communications industry matured in the past few years, it has been recognized that while certain operations are well suited to operating in a centralized environment and obtaining the computational power and the ''intelligence'' of the central computer software, for many applications it makes no sense at all to incur the delay and throughput overhead of running the jobs to a central site.

For these reasons, distributed networks have come to the forefront of the industry. In the early 1980s, *distributed networks* was a buzzword. It was a term that struck the imagination of many people in the industry because it was a unique idea. Today, the idea of distributed networks is quite commonplace. Indeed, this author hesitated in even naming the book *Distributed Networks*. In today's environment, *data communications systems* almost implies distributed networks.

Distributed networks came about because of the ability of users to purchase workstations, terminals, and computers with extraordinary computational power and extraordinary intelligence. From the standpoint of an end user, it made little sense to send vast amounts of data and transactions to a central processor for service. Rather, the key concept of distributed communications in networks is for the work to be performed at the local computer, if possible, and for coordination of activities to be performed at a central site, if needed.

Of course, we should not forget that not every workstation has the computational power of a Cray machine. Consequently, most organizations take the rational approach of placing a certain amount of intelligence and distribution into remote devices and relying on the conventional and classical ''mainframe'' to perform these tasks that require computational power and intelligence beyond that of the distributed sites.

Evolution of Data Communications Systems

Data communications systems (using computers) came into existence shortly after the computer became widely used in organizations. In order to obtain the services of the computer, users simply walked to the room where the computer was located (designated as the computer room) and submitted a request for the computer to perform a service (see Figure 1–2(a)). This request was called a *job*. The computer accepted the user's job, performed its operations, and returned the results on hard-copy printouts. This process was called a *batch run* (and it is still widely used).

As the use of computers grew, it became inefficient for all users to walk to the computer room, submit their job, and return to get the results. Consequently, computer-based terminals were built and placed in user work spaces within a building. This approach allowed users to submit their job from each office (see Figure 1–2(b)).

This system required that the terminal be connected to the computer through some type of communications medium in order for the user to transmit and receive traffic to

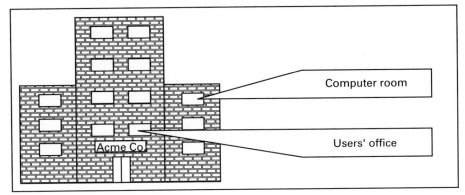

(a) Users took jobs to the computer room and picked up the
results (Batch Runs)

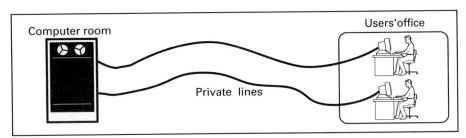

(b) The computer was then accessed by users with
terminals (Time Sharing)

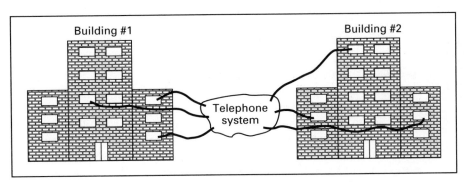

(c) "Remote users" eventually access the computer (Remote
Time Sharing)

Figure 1–2.   The advent of modern data communications systems.

and from the computer. Typically, private communications lines were wired between
the computer and the workstations to meet this requirement. This approach also allowed
many users to share the computational power of the increasingly powerful computers.

This concept is known as *timesharing*. The term means that multiple users are sharing the facilities of the machine by taking turns (albeit very fast turns) in obtaining the computer services.

As organizations grew and the need for the computer grew, it became necessary to share the computer with other users in different buildings. The simple private lines would not suffice, because an organization (a) did not have the means to place wire between buildings and/or (b) regulations would not permit it. The solution was to utilize the widely used telephone system to transport this traffic. Even though the telephone system was designed for voice traffic, various techniques were employed to send data through the telephone system (see Fig. 1–2(c)). This became known as remote time-sharing and is still a prevalent form of data communications.

NETWORK TOPOLOGIES

Communications networks are designed to facilitate the sharing of resources as well as to reduce communications costs, increase throughput, and decrease delay of services. Consequently, the topology (shape) of the network is an important consideration. The topologies of networks take many forms. The major topologies are explained in this section.

A common topology for many networks is the star topology. As shown in Figure 1–3(a), each station is connected through a point-to-point link to a central site. This site (called a hub or switch) assumes the responsibility for routing the traffic between the stations. With this approach, the stations have the impression that they are communicating on a dedicated line when an intermediate site, or sites, is involved.

The star topology is widely used in networks that are based on private branch exchanges (PBXs) and message switches. Typically, the stations attached to this network do not have responsibility for major communications tasks. These tasks remain the responsibility of the central hub. However, such a topology does pose risks because of the vulnerability of failure of the central switch.

The ring topology shown in Figure 1–3(b) has been used in local area networks (networks typically housed within a building or a campus) for many years. Each station is attached to the ring and receives all messages on the ring. Therefore, this network is a broadcast technology in that one station broadcasts to all. Each station must examine a destination address that resides in the message passing on the ring. If the message is destined for this station, it copies the traffic. If not, it ignores it.

The ring is usually unidirectional. That is, the traffic passes in one direction around the ring. Although, as we shall see later in this book, many ring networks now use two rings to the bidirectional transfer of traffic.

The bus topology shown in Figure 1–3(c) is similar to the ring topology in that it is a broadcast network and all stations receive all messages, which are discarded if they are not for that station. In this network, however, the traffic is passed in both directions through the medium. A sending station introduces signals onto the channel, and these signals are propagated into each direction. Because of this approach, a bus topology

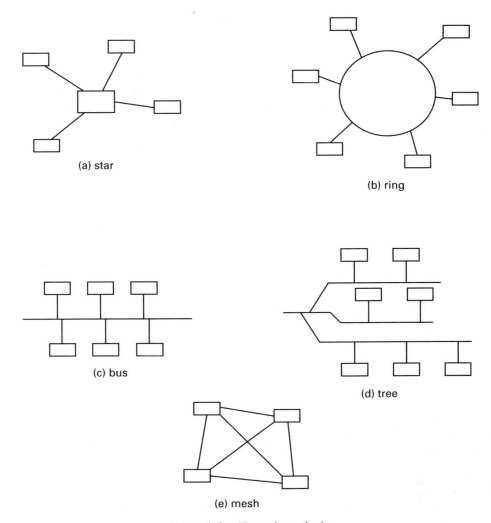

(a) star

(b) ring

(c) bus

(d) tree

(e) mesh

Figure 1–3. Network topologies.

prevents more than one station from sending at a time (the signals would interfere with one another). Consequently, a convention (a communications protocol) must be devised for the sharing of this line on a one-by-one basis.

The tree topology is also a widely used approach in a data communications network. It is similar to the bus topology except that the transmission medium is divided into several wires or cables (see Figure 1–3(d)).

The mesh topology in Figure 1–3(e) is used in some networks that do not have a large number of nodes involved. It is so named because each station is connected to every other station. The approach is useful for systems that need full connectivity. It provides very fast response time. Additionally, the stations need not have extensive protocols, because the switching functions are nil. However, meshed networks are quite

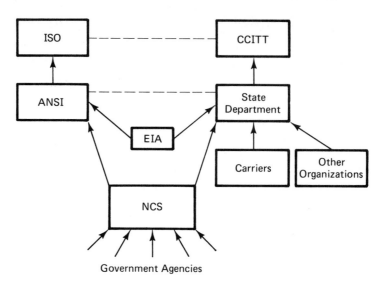

Figure 1–4. Data Communications Organizations.

expensive because with each addition of a station, a communications line must be attached to every other station in the network. For that reason, meshed networks have seen rather limited use in the industry.

Before delving into the details of data communications and networks, it should prove useful to examine some of the major organizations in this industry (see Figure 1–4).

ORGANIZATIONS IN THE INDUSTRY

The U.S. communications industry has been dominated by AT&T. However, unlike many countries, the United States has opened communications to competitive offerings, and in recent years the industry has become quite diverse. In other countries, the communications industry remains more highly regulated and is dominated by the countries' governments through an organization commonly known as the PTT (Postal, Telegraph, and Telephone Administration).

Since January 1, 1984, AT&T has undergone radical changes, primarily in the divestiture of the local Bell Operating Companies (BOCs). These companies now operate as independent entities from AT&T (more about this later).

The United States has one of the most reliable and efficient public communications systems in the world today. Over 30% of the telephones in the world are in the United States.

The future of communications in the United States will be greatly dependent on the action of Congress, the courts, and the regulatory agencies. Many people believe a sound communications infrastructure for the 1990s is as important as the communications links (canals, railways, roads) were to the United States in previous times. Our future in this vital industry is greatly dependent on the political and legal decisions that are being made today.

Carriers

The basic communication services in the United States, such as connections to homes and offices and long-haul lines, are provided by carriers. In earlier days, these organizations were called common carriers because certain industries (railroad, shipping) provided a common service for all people without discrimination and at a reasonable cost. These carriers provide the lines that link the computers in a network. Initially, the "common" carriers were given monopoly powers because Congress believed competition (with redundant services) made little sense. The wire communications industry grew up as a common carrier service. It was treated as a part of land transportation because the telegraph wires were constructed on railroad rights-of-way.

The best-known communications carriers are the telephone companies. They number well over 1,000 in the United States, although only 250 have more than 5,000 customers. Each telephone company serves a specific area under a franchise from a municipal or state government. Interstate communications are regulated by the Federal Communications Commission (FCC).

Today, the local telephone companies are called local exchange carriers and long-distance companies are called interexchange carriers.

VAN.   The value-added network (VAN) is also a creation of the FCC and, like the specialized common carrier, it is an industry unique to the United States. In 1976 the FCC ordered all common carriers to eliminate restriction on resale and shared use of their services and thus provided for the genesis of the VAN. The value-added carrier will often lease the backbone communications facilities from an exchange carrier. The VAN then augments the facilities with additional capabilities (i.e., adds a value) and offers these combined services to the public. Packet-switching network vendors are an example of value-added networks.

Federal Communications Commission

The FCC is responsible for the regulation of interstate radio, television, telegraph, and telephone communications and foreign-related communications. The FCC was created by the Communications Act of 1934 and is authorized to regulate the carrier industry. Prior to 1934, the Interstate Commerce Commission regulated wire communications.

All proposed interstate services must be reviewed and approved by the FCC. Intrastate services are under the auspices of state or municipal governments. Carriers file an application (tariff) for the new service. The tariff describes the service, the price of the service, and the reason for offering the service. Tariffs, once filed and approved, can be used by other carriers. The approved tariff also acts as an agreement between the carrier and the user.

International Record Carriers

International record carriers (IRCs) provide for transborder data communications between countries through ''gateway'' facilities. The carrier lines connect to the IRC lines at the gateway points. Profits are usually shared by a consortium of the companies in accordance with bilateral international agreements. The IRC role is changing; the companies are moving into domestic communications, and other organizations are moving into the IRC arena.

Transborder data flow is an issue of increasing concern among countries. To provide guidelines for transborder data flow and to establish legal protections, the Organization for Economic Cooperation and Development Guidelines Governing the Protection of Privacy in Transborder Data Flows for Personal Data was formed in 1980 to assess the issue of privacy *vis-à-vis* free exchange of information. In addition, in 1981 the Council of New York Convention for the Protection of Individuals with Regard to Automatic Processing of Personal Data was formed to address specifically the issue of privacy with regard to personal data.

International Organizations

INTELSAT.   The International Telecommunications Satellite Organization (INTELSAT) is an organization of over 100 countries. Its purpose is to share in the development and use of satellite systems. INTELSAT was formed in 1964 and has been very successful in meeting its goals. The Early Bird system and the INTELSAT satellites are examples of INTELSAT activities. INTELSAT's first satellite was operational in 1965 and had 240 voice channels. Recent INTELSAT satellites have a capacity for thousands of voice-type circuits and television channels.

CCITT.   The Comité Consultaif Internationale de Télégraphique et Téléphonique (CCITT) is a standards body under the International Telecommunications Union, an agency of the United Nations. The CCITT is the primary organization for developing standards on telephone and data communications systems among participating governments. It is an influential body responsible for the development of standards such as X.21 and X.25. U.S. membership on CCITT comes from the State Department at one level (the only voting level); a second level of membership covers private carriers such as AT&T and GTE; a third level includes industrial and scientific organizations; a fourth level includes other international organizations; and a fifth level includes organizations in other fields that are interested in CCITT's work.

The United States has established several CCITT-related study groups. Study Group A addresses the regulatory aspects of international communications, including telegraph operations, telex service, tariffs, public networks, and many aspects of telephony. Study Group B concentrates its efforts on telegraph transmission, equipment specifications, and telegraph signaling. Study Group C studies international telephone operations and Study Group D addresses problems relating to international data transmission service and international data networks.

ISO. The International Standards Organization is a voluntary organization consisting of national standards committees of each member country. The ISO coordinates its activities with CCITT on common issues. It is a fourth-level, or D class, member of CCITT. ISO has produced several well-known standards, such as high-level data link control (HDLC). The organization has a number of subcommittees and groups working with CCITT and the American National Standards Institute (ANSI) to develop standards for encryption, data communications, public data networks, and the well-known Open Systems Interconnection (OSI) model.

European Organizations

ECMA. The European Computer Manufacturers Association was founded by a number of European computer manufacturers in 1960. It promulgates its own standards, although it also participates in the ISO and IEC committee meetings. The ECMA goal is to develop standards that provide transparent connections between different vendors machines. It does not manufacture hardware or software even though the companies themselves are hardware and software vendors.

CEN/CENELEC. This organization is a combination of European Committee for Standardization (CEN) and the European Committee for Electro-technical Standardization (CENELEC). The organization has been quite influential in the publication of documents to address incompatibilities among the national bodies in Europe. CEN/ CENELEC also participates in many other committees in Europe such as the European Community (EC).

IEC. The International Electro-technical Commission is composed of committees that define standards dealing with electronic and electrical operations. Each country is represented on IEC. Typically, the ISO and IEC agree to cover all areas of standardization, with IEC usually covering lower-layer electrical standards and ISO providing standards for other aspects of data communications standards.

American National Standards Institute

The ANSI is a voluntary standards body in the United States and is a member of the ISO. It develops standards itself and accepts standards proposals from other organizations in the United States. ANSI activities are extensive. In addition to standards on programming languages, such as COBOL and FORTRAN, ANSI has several committees and groups working with communications standards as well. Its body, ANSC X3 (American National Standards Committee 3), and subcommittees provide the organization and mechanism for members to develop communications standards in conjunction with the ISO groups. The Appendix depicts the relationships of ANSI and ISO bodies. ANSI cooperates with CCITT through the State Department's Industry Advisory Group (IAG), which was created to allow ANSI and other standards groups more participation in CCITT issues.

These organizations are becoming more influential as more people recognize the value of standards. As one noted industry leader said, it is economically ridiculous and philisophically inane for each company to build its "own railroad gauge." We will see later how important the international standards have become in the United States, and we will also learn how these standards work in a communications system and a network. Figure 1–4 summarizes the relationships of the international organizations.

Electronic Industries Association

The Electronic Industries Association (EIA), a national trade association, is also very influential in developing standards in North American countries. The EIA work focuses primarily on electrical standards. Their more notable efforts include EIA-232-D and EIA-449. Subsequent chapters discuss the EIA standards.

The Institute of Electrical and Electronics Engineers

The Institute of Electrical and Electronics Engineers (IEEE) has assumed the worldwide lead for the development and publication of local area network (LAN) standards. IEEE sometimes acts as the representative for the United States on ISO and IEC committees. IEEE publishes a widely used set of specifications dealing with the LAN standards. They are called the IEEE 802 standards.

National Communications System

The National Communications System (NCS) is responsible for U.S. government standards administered by the General Services Administration (GSA). Those government agencies having large telecommunications facilities belong to the NCS, which works closely with these agencies as well as EIA, ANSI, ISO, and CCITT in fostering national and international standards. NCS is also responsible for preparing emergency plans for the nation's communications facilities.

National Institute of Standards and Technology

The National Institute of Standards and Technology (NIST) is part of the Department of Commerce. It is responsible for making recommendations to the president concerning federal data-processing and communications standards. NBS issues data-processing guidelines for federal agencies called Federal Information Processing Standards (FIPS) and telecommunications standards called the Federal Telecommunications Standards Program (FTSP).

The Internet Activities

One of the most successful and increasingly influential bodies for setting standards for data communications systems falls within the Internet arena. The overall authority for these activities rests with the Internet Activities Board (IAB). It consists of several task forces and groups, all of which work to define new protocols for the Internet as well as refine and improve existing protocols. The best-known standards resulting from the Internet activities are the widely used Transmission Control Protocol/Internet Protocol (TCP/IP), which are discussed in several parts of this book.

The Telephone System

The telephone system is still the most frequently used media for data communications systems and networks. The system is designed as a highly distributed multilevel switching hierarchy. At the bottom of the hierarchy is the user instrument, commonly the telephone, which is attached by two copper wires (local loops) to the phone company's local (central or end) office. Since each subscriber has a local loop connection, it can be seen that a considerable investment exists in this part of the network. The other offices in the telephone hierarchy are switching centers responsible for routing calls through the system based on the dialed number and the traffic load of other calls in the network. The switching is accomplished through computers and/or electromechanical devices.

The switching offices are connected by trunk circuits. Each local office also connects by toll-connecting trunks to an associated toll office (or toll center) servicing a particular region of the country. The higher-level offices form a network through intertoll trunks to provide for routing of calls between regions.

SUMMARY

The ability for computers to communicate effectively with one another rests largely on the use of standardized procedures between and among different vendors. The many benefits of computers and networks is enhanced greatly through the work being performed by national and international standards organizations and user groups. The major bodies for setting standards in the data communications industry rest with the ISO and the CCITT. Nevertheless, scores of other bodies have established standards within their own interest and specialty, and all contribute to the work of the ISO and CCITT.

2

Overview of a Data Communications Network

INTRODUCTION

This chapter introduces the major components that reside in a data communications network. Packet switches, terminals, front-end processors, and modems are introduced in this chapter as well as the concepts of broadcast and switched networks. In addition, this chapter defines and contrasts local area networks (LANs) and wide area networks (WANs). The concepts of internetworking are also introduced in this chapter as well as packet-switching networks. This chapter serves as an overview to these components. Subsequent chapters will delve into more detail on each specific component.

NETWORK TRANSFER CAPACITY

Data are transmitted between machines using bit sequences to represent codes. The speed of the data transmission is described in bits per second (or bit/s). Typical speeds of data communications systems are shown in Table 2–1. Later chapters discuss the reasons (and trade-offs) for the channel bit rates.

    The data communications world is fairly slow relative to the computer world. The slow speeds stem from the fact that computers usually communicate through the telephone line, which was the most convenient and readily available path when the industry developed computers and began to interface them with terminals and other computers in the 1960s. The telephone channel is not designed for fast transmission between high-speed computers, but for voice transmission between people, which does not require the

TABLE 2–1   LINK SPEEDS AND USES

Typical speed in bits/s	Typical uses
0–600	Telegraph, older terminals; telemetry
600–2,400	Human-operated terminals; personal computers
2,400–19,200	Applications requiring fast response and/or throughput; some batch and file transfer applications
32,000–64,000	Digital voice; high-speed applications; some video
64,000–1,544,000	Very high speed for multiple users; computer-to-computer traffic; backbone links for networks; video
greater than 1,544,000	Backbone links for networks; high-quality video; multiple digital voice

speed associated with data transmission. The point is explained in considerable detail in later chapters.

NETWORK TYPES

Data communications networks consist of (logically enough) data communications components. Typically, these components are called a network when several to many of these components operate together for the sharing of resources. The information is exchanged between these components through switches or other means of transporting traffic across the media.

A good analogy to the data network is the telephone network because the telephone network performs a service to a telephone user in the same manner the data network performs a service for the data communications user (usually a computer user).

Public and Private Networks

Networks may be classified as private or public. Private networks, as their name implies, are owned and managed by an enterprise and used only by the enterprise. In contrast, a public network (while owned by an enterprise) "rents" its network to the public. Again, the analogy of the telephone system is relevant here. As an example, AT&T, Sprint, and MCI are public telephone interexchange carriers who rent their services to whoever is willing to pay the fees charged for the services.

Switched and Broadcast Networks

Networks can be classified as a broadcast network or a switched network. Broadcast networks are distinguished by what is known as one-to-many transmission characteristics. This means that one communications device transmits to more than one device.

This idea is found in commercial television and radio broadcasting where one station sends to many receivers. Broadcast networks are widely available in networks in which the machines are in close proximity because it is relatively easy to send the signal to all stations on a limited number of media. In addition, broadcast is quite popular in satellite transmissions, wherein the satellite station transmits traffic to (potentially) thousands of receivers.

In contrast to broadcast networks, a switched network is not designed to transmit on a one-to-many relationship. An individual transmission is sent to the physical device (called a switch) wherein the switch determines how to route the data further. This approach does not mean that a switched network could not use broadcast topology (which indeed it can). Rather, it may not be economically nor technically feasible to send traffic to all parties in a switched network.

Local and Wide Area Networks

Until recently, it has been relatively easy to define wide area networks and local area networks and to point out their differences. It is not so easy today because the terms *wide area* and *local area* do not have the meanings they once had. For example, a local area network in the 1980s was generally confined to a building or a campus where the components were no more than a few hundred or a few thousand feet from each other. Today LANs may span scores of miles.

Nonetheless, certain characteristics are unique to each of these networks. A WAN is usually furnished by a third party. For example, many WANs are termed *public networks* because the telephone company or a public data network owns and manages the resources and sells these services to users. In contrast, a LAN is usually privately owned. The cables and components are purchased and managed by an enterprise.

LANs and WANs can also be contrasted by their transmission capacity (in bit/s).

Wide Area Networks (WANs)

- Multiple user computers connected together
- Machines are spread over a *wide* geographic region
- Communications channels between the machines are usually furnished by *a third party* (for example, the telephone company, a public data network, a satellite carrier)
- Channels are of relatively *low capacity* (measuring throughput in kilobits per second, kbit/s)
- Channels are relatively *error-prone* (for example, a bit error rate of 1 in 100,000 bits transmitted)

Local Area Networks (LANs)

- Multiple user computers connected together
- Machines are spread over a *small* geographic region
- Communications channels between the machines are usually *privately owned*
- Channels are of relatively *high capacity* (measuring throughput in megabits per second, Mbit/s)
- Channels are relatively *error-free* (for example, a bit error rate of 1 in 10^9 bits transmitted)

Figure 2–1.   Local and wide area networks.

Most WANs generally operate in the Kbit/s (kilobit per second) range, whereas LANs operate in the Mbit/s (megabit per second) range.

Another feature that distinguishes these networks is the error rate (the frequency of transmission line-induced errors). WANs are generally more error prone than LANs due to the wide geographic terrain over which the media must be laid. In contrast, LANs operate in a relatively benign environment because the data communications components are housed in buildings where humidity, heat, and electrical controls are controlled.

Figure 2–1 summarizes the major features of local and wide area networks.

NETWORK COMPONENTS

As depicted in Figure 2–2, a data communications network must have a communications medium; for example, a telephone communications line, a dedicated line, or a LAN channel. Thereafter, the other components vary, depending on the needs of the organization. Certainly, computers are part of the data communications network because the purpose of the network is to transport data between these machines. Most networks also utilize local area networks as well as long-distance communications lines.

Many organizations today also have installed multiplexers (MUXs) in their networks. This machine allows more than one DTE (data terminal equipment) to share the communications line and can result in substantial savings by decreasing the number of lines used. In Figure 2–2, two terminals are sharing one communications link to the host machine through the use of these multiplexers. This figure is a simple illustration. A multiplexer can support hundreds of devices.

Many installations also install servers in their communications systems. The purpose of the server is to perform support functions for workstations or to provide database and printer services that the workstations do not have the "intelligence" to perform.

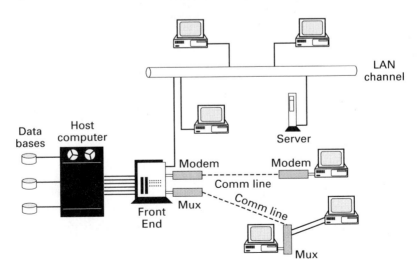

Figure 2–2. The major components of a data communications system.

Some computer systems today also contain a front-end processor. The purpose of this machine is to off-load communications tasks from the host computer, thus freeing the host computer to devote its CPU cycles to user applications and data-base operations. Even though this figure shows the use of a front-end processor, many organizations choose not to install these machines.

Since the purpose of a data communications system is to transport data between users and user devices, the data bases are a significant component in the process. For example, the amount and frequency of the data transferred affect the ''load'' on the data communications components.

Figure 2–2 also shows a local area network. Most user organizations today have installed a LAN or several LANs. The LAN can be attached to a front-end processor. Alternatively, the host computer can be directly attached with a LAN. Typically, functions are further off-loaded from the host computer with the use of data-base servers, terminal servers, and other support machines that are operating on the LAN. Consequently, communications between terminals on a network and the servers occur without requiring the use of host computer resources. In most instances, the front-end processor is not aware of many of the activities occurring on the LAN.

The LAN topologies vary widely in the industry, with Ethernet and token ring-type networks dominating the field. This example shows an Ethernet-type LAN, wherein the LAN devices are attached to a single channel (such as a coaxial cable or a twisted-wire pair). As we learned in Chapter 1, this type of LAN uses a bus topology.

If the workstations and other computers are located more than a few hundred feet from the front end or the host computer, modems are used to terminate the communications line with the host computer and remote workstation. In some installations, modems are not used, but modemlike devices (such as line drivers) will provide the signaling interface. A modem is used if the communications line uses analog signaling. A line driver is used if the line uses digital signaling.

As discussed earlier, in many installations, the user devices do not utilize the full capacity of the communications line. Consequently, multiplexers are installed to permit users to share the line. Although not shown in Figure 2–2, the MUX may use modems if the communications line is analog. Otherwise, the MUX uses a line driver (or a similar device) to achieve digital transmission and reception. Analog and digital systems are discussed in the next chapter.

Connecting Networks

As organizations have increased the use of data communications systems and LANs, it has become necessary to attach some of the LANs together to share the resources of the servers and the host computers.

For the attachment of these LANs, an additional component is needed. Its generic name is an internetworking unit (IWU), as shown in Figure 2–3, this component relays the traffic between the local networks and may also provide protocol conversion functions if the networks' protocols differ.

It may not be necessary to install an IWU, because many organizations choose to attach each LAN to the host computer or the front-end processor and then use these two

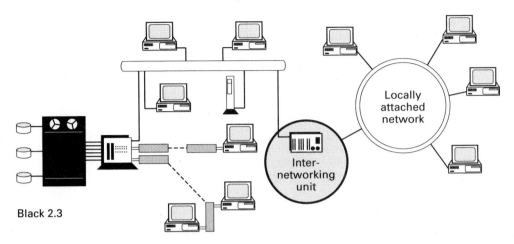

Black 2.3

Figure 2–3. Connecting networks with internetworking units.

devices to relay the traffic between the LANs. Nonetheless, the host/front-end processor still performs IWU services.

The IWU is called by many terms in the industry. Some individuals prefer the name *bridge*, others use the term *router*, still others use the term *gateway*. There is even a term to describe a unit that uses a mix of bridge and router, which is called a brouter. Whatever the term used, the component is still involved in relaying traffic between networks. Discussions in later chapters will define these terms more concisely.

For widely dispersed organizations, the wide area network becomes a very important component in the communications system. WANs can be interfaced to the host computer in a number of ways. One common approach is to dedicate a connection into a front-end processor (or the host directly) for the communications line to the WAN. Another approach is to use one of the interfaces of the LAN internetworking unit to provide the interface into the WAN. The communications lines between the host computer or the LAN IWU can be dedicated or dial-up lines; they may be either digital or analog lines.

Figure 2–4 shows the use of a device known as a data circuit-terminating equipment (DCE) at the front end and the IWU. The DCE could be a modem for connection to analog lines or a digital service unit (DSU) if digital lines are employed.

As shown in Figure 2–5, the WAN interface is usually provided with a packet switch. The packet switch interfaces to the host computer or the organization's IWU. For longer distances between the network and the host system, the packet switch also requires modems or DSUs for its connection into the line. The number of lines between the packet switch and the user organization's machine is usually determined by the amount of throughput required. It is not unusual to have more than one line attached for purposes of backup (in case problems occur on one of the communications links).

Within the network itself, other packet switches are employed to provide for the relay of traffic through the network to the final destination. The communications lines inside this network are typically high-capacity digital lines operating in the 56 kbit/s to

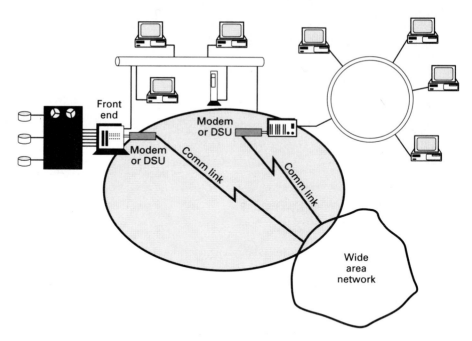

Figure 2–4.   Connecting wide area networks.

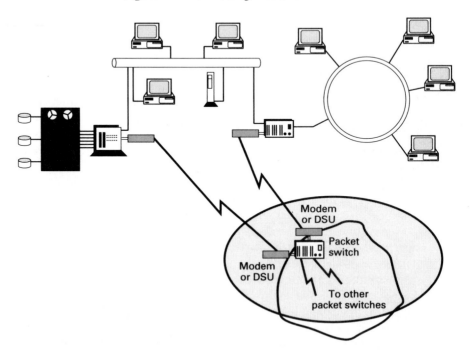

Figure 2–5.   Packet switches and wide area networks.

1.544 Mbit/s range or higher. Increasingly, these lines are using optical fiber that provide higher data rates (even in the gigabit range).

Physical Interfaces

A discussion of the major components in a data communications network is not complete until an examination is made of the interface between the modem/DSU/multiplexer and the front-end processor/IWU/packet switch (see Figure 2–6).

    This interface is important because it defines the cabling and connectors that are used to "plug" the two machines together. Moreover, this interface defines the type of signaling that is to occur (the voltages, speed, and so on). In most installations this connection is achieved through several pairs of wire that are attached to plugs commonly called pins. The reader is probably quite familiar with this plug, since it exists in all terminals and workstations. The most commonly used interface for providing this interconnection between the data communications equipment and the modems, multiplexers, or DSUs is known as EIA-232-D.

    However, be aware that this interface specification does not define the type of signaling that occurs between the modems, multiplexers, DSUs, or LANs. This signaling is left to other protocols and standards that are not shown in this figure.

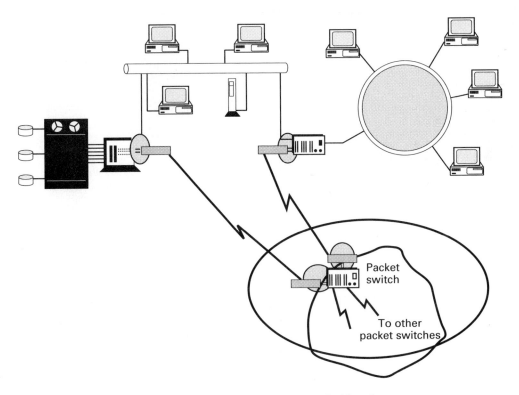

Figure 2–6. The physical interfaces.

SUMMARY

Data communications networks contain many different and varying components. The fundamental component to any network is the communications medium. Additionally, since the purpose of a data communications network is to convey data between computers, computers are an essential part to the network. The components in a communications network are chosen to best meet the needs of the users' requirements. In addition, the components chosen will depend on whether the organization requires LANs or WANs and whether the organization chooses to use analog or digital facilities.

Many components in a data communications network have been standardized through international agreements between the standards' bodies. This is an increasing trend and can only result in simpler networks and decreased costs to the enterprise.

3

Data Communications Systems Operations

INTRODUCTION

This chapter expands the material in Chapter 2 and introduces several key terms and concepts associated with data communications systems. The chapter is intended to serve as a general introduction to basic signaling concepts, modulation techniques, and transmission rates. In addition, the reader is provided with an introduction to the use of data communications codes as well as how machines are synchronzied to each other's transmission. The more experienced reader may choose to skip this chapter and proceed to the next. However, the beginner in data communications is encouraged to read the entire chapter.

HOW DATA ARE TRANSMITTED

Since the purpose of computers, data communications, and networks is to process data into information, a discussion of how data are represented on these media is in order. Data are stored inside a computer and transmitted on a communications system in the form of binary digits, or bits. The digits are either 1s or 0s and are coded in accordance with the binary (base 2) number system.

The binary bits inside a computer are represented by the level of polarity of electrical signals. A high-level signal within a storage element in the computer could represent a 1; a low-level signal, a 0. These elements are strung together to form numbers and characters, such as the number 6 or the letter A, in accordance with established codes.

Data are transmitted along the communications path (often the telephone network) between computer-oriented devices using electrical signals and bit sequences to represent numbers and characters. In some instances, the data representation may be by light signals, as in optic fibers (more on this topic later). The bit representations depict user data and control data. The control data are used to manage the communications network and the flow of the user data.

Figure 3–1 depicts how the data move from a sending computer device, through the communications medium, and into a receiving computer device. The reader should be aware that the binary data code is converted to base 10 for human consumption when it is displayed on terminals and printouts.

Throughout this book, the term *bits per second* (bit/s) is used to describe a transmission speed. The term refers to the number of binary bits per second that are transferred through a communications path or component. If a 2,400 bit/s line uses an 8-bit code to represent a number or character, then the character per second rate is 300 (2,400/8 = 300). The majority of communications speeds are quoted in bit/s rates.

It should be emphasized that a bit traveling down a communications path, as in Figure 3–1, is actually a representation of the electrical/electromagnetic or optical state of the line for a certain period of time. The bit 1 may be depicted by placing a negative voltage on the line for a few fractions of a second, and a 0 could be represented by a low-level signal positive voltage for the same period of time.[1]

Transmission Characteristics

A general knowledge of the characteristics of electrical transmission is essential if the reader is to gain an understanding of data communications. Line capacity, error control techniques, communications software, and many other network components are all analyzed and designed around the capabilities and limitations of electricity.

As Figure 3–1 shows, data are transmitted on a communications channel by the alteration of an electrical signal to represent 1s and 0s. The electrical signal state manifests itself by either the signal level or some other property of the complex electrical signal. The movement of the signal over its transmission path is referred to as *signal propagation*. On a wire path, signal propagation is a flow of electrical current. Radio transmission between computer sites without the use of wires is accomplished by emitting an electrical signal that propagates as an electromagnetic wave.

We know that all matter is composed of basic particles that may contain an electrical charge. Some of these particles, *electrons* and *protons*, have negative and positive polarity, respectively. The particles group themselves in an orderly fashion to form atoms; the negative and positive charges attract each other to create the stability in the atom. An electrical current flow is generated by the introduction of an electric charge at one end of the communications path or conductor. For example, placing a negative

[1]The following notations are used in this book: 0.001 = 1 millisecond (ms); 0.000001 = 1 microsecond (µs); 0.000000001 = 1 nanosecond (ns). Also, 1,000 = kilo (k); 1,000,000 = mega (M); 1,000,000,000 = giga (G).

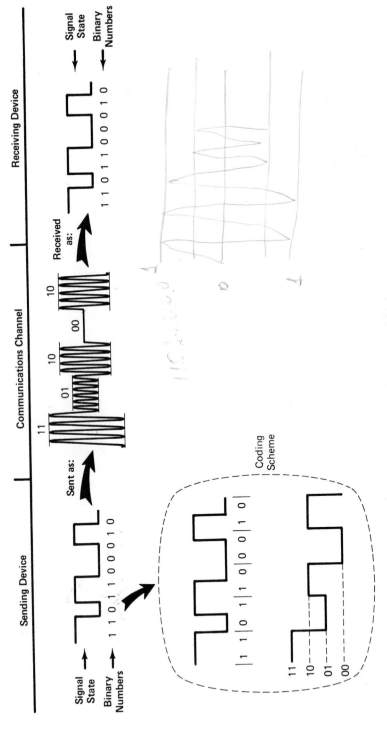

Figure 3–1. Transmitting data.

25

charge at the transmitter end of a conductor repels the negatively charged electrons in the path toward the other end, thus creating a current (that is, a flow of electricity). In essence, electrical current (and a data communications signal) is the movement of these electrons down a conductor path.

Most signals on a communications channel consist of oscillating wave forms as shown in Figures 3–1 and 3–2(a). The oscillating signal has three characteristics that can be varied in order for it to convey computer-generated data (amplitude, frequency, and phase). The amplitude or voltage is determined by the amount of electrical charge inserted on the wire. Figure 3–1 shows this voltage can be set high or low depending on the binary state, that is, a 1 or a 0.

Another characteristic of electricity is the power or strength as measured in watts. The signal power determines the distance the signal can travel or propagate on a wire communications circuit.

The term *baud* is another commonly used term in data communications. This term describes the rate of change of the signal on the line, that is, how many times (per second) the signal changes its pattern. As a simple example, in Figure 3–1, the sending device assembles the bits into groups of two and then modifies the oscillating wave form (that is, changes the signal state) to one of four amplitudes to represent any combination of 2 bits (00, 01, 10, 11). In this example, the bit transfer rate across the communications

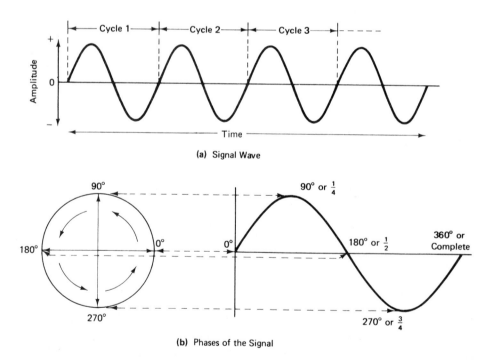

(a) Signal Wave

(b) Phases of the Signal

Figure 3–2. Oscillating signal.

path is twice the baud (or rate of signal change). Most modems today use up to 8 bits per baud to achieve greater signal transfer capacity.

The process in Figure 3–1 is called *modulation*. This term means that the data stream changes or modulates the signal on the communications path (channel or link).

The signal is also distinguished by its frequency, or number of complete oscillations of the wave form in a given time. Frequency is measured in oscillations per second. The electrical industry has defined the unit of 1 hertz (Hz) to mean one oscillation per second.

Another term used to describe frequency is *cycles per second* (cps). The frequency of the wave has no relation to the amplitude. Signals can have many different combinations of the two. The *amplitude* indicates the signal level and the amount of negative or positive voltage, while the *frequency* indicates the rate (in hertz) of the signal oscillation.

The *phase* of the signal describes the point to which the signal has advanced in its cycle. In Figure 3–2(b), the phases of the signal are identified as the beginning of the cycle, 1/4 of the cycle, 1/2 of the cycle, 3/4 of the cycle, and the completion of the cycle. The wave can also be labeled with degree markings like that of a sine wave or a 360° circle. The *sine wave* is so named because the wave varies in the same manner as the trigonometric sine function. The sine wave is derived from circular motion. The amplitude of the wave increases to a maximum at 90°, in the same manner that the sine of an angle of rotation increases to a maximum of 90°. Since a complete cycle represents a 360° rotation around the circle, 1/4 of a cycle point represents a phase value of 90°. The use of trigonometry to describe the electrical signal has proved very valuable for engineers.

The wave in Figure 3–2(b) depicts the signal at its maximum strength at two points in the cycle. One-half of the cycle is represented by a positive voltage and the other one-half by a negative voltage. The changing voltage state results in electrical charges changing their direction of flow down the wire circuit. The voltage continuously varies its amplitude and periodically reverses its polarity. The nature of the charge is the only difference. The strength, either positive or negative, is the same at the two peaks in the cycle.

The alternating nature of the signal voltage determines the direction of the current flow on a transmission wire. For example, a negative voltage at the transmitting end of the wire will repel the negative particles (electrons) of the conductor wire toward the receiving end, thus creating the direction of the current. On the other hand, the positive voltage will attract the charges back to the transmitter. The reader may recognize this form of signaling by the term *alternating current* (ac).

The information rate of a data signal on a path between computers is partially dependent on the amplitude, frequency (or frequencies), and phase of the signal. As Figure 3–1 shows, the information rate in bits per second (bit/s) depend on how often a signal changes its state. We will see later that the alteration of the amplitudes, frequencies, and phases of the signal will provide a change of state on the line, thus permitting a 1 to 0 or 0 to 1 representation with the change. The binary 1s and 0s are coded to represent the characters and numbers of user data messages flowing on the network between the computers.

Analog transmission.　　The signal just described is called an analog signal because of its continuous, nondiscrete characteristics. This form of transmission was not designed to convey the discrete binary numbers that are found in computers. It is widely used, however, because analog facilities such as the telephone system were readily available when data communications networks were developing.

The local telephone line is designed to carry voice, which is analog in nature. The human voice sends out analog wave forms of sound. The signals are actually oscillating patterns of changes in air pressure—in effect, air vibrations. These mechanical vibrations act on the telephone microphone and are converted into electrical voltage patterns that reflect the characteristics of the speech pattern.

The analog voice signal is not one unique frequency, nor is the electrical signal. Rather, the voice and its signal on a telephone line consist of wave forms of many different frequencies. The particular mix of these frequencies is what determines the pitch and sound of a person's voice. Many phenomena manifest themselves as a combination of different frequencies. The colors in the rainbow, for instance, are combinations of many different lightwave frequencies; musical sounds consist of different acoustic frequencies that are interpreted as higher or lower pitch. These phenomena consist of a range or band of frequencies.

The human ear can detect sounds over a range of frequencies from around 40 to 18,000 Hz. The telephone system does not transmit this full band of frequencies. The full range is not needed to interpret the voice signal at the receiver. Due to economics, only the frequency band of approximately 300 to 3,300 Hz is transmitted across the path (the actual range is slightly larger). This is one reason why our voice conversations sound different on a telephone line.

Bandwidth.　　The range of transmission frequencies that can be carried on a communications line is referred to as the *bandwidth* of the line. Bandwidth is a very important ingredient in data communications because the capacity (stated in bits per second) of a communications path is dependent on the bandwidth of the path. If the telephone channel were increased from a bandwidth of about 3 kilohertz (kHz) (300 to 3,300 Hz) to 20 kHz, it could carry all the characteristics of the voice. This also holds true for transmitting data; a better data transmission rate can be achieved with a greater bandwidth.

The effect of bandwidth was demonstrated by several individuals, notably Shannon, Fourier, and Nyquist. Fourier demonstrated that the sum of a minimum number of sine-wave frequencies (whose frequencies, f, were integral multiples; for example, f, 2f, 3f, . . . nf) were required to represent a signal. This is shown in Figure 3–3. The state of the line is changing 2,000 times per second; in other words, the signal change rate is 2,000 baud. A limited bandwidth of 500 Hz is insufficient to distinguish the signal accurately. As the bandwidth increases, the digital levels are more accurately portrayed.

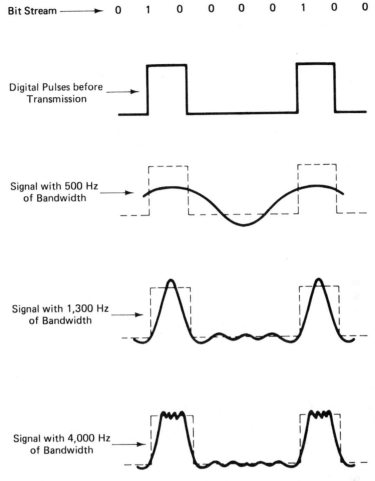

Bit Stream ⟶ 0 1 0 0 0 0 1 0 0

Digital Pulses before Transmission ⟶

Signal with 500 Hz of Bandwidth ⟶

Signal with 1,300 Hz of Bandwidth ⟶

Signal with 4,000 Hz of Bandwidth ⟶

Figure 3–3. Effect of bandwidth.

The greater the bandwidth, the greater the capacity. This statement is explained by Table 3–1. The electronic frequency spectrum ranges from the relatively limited ranges of the audio frequencies through the radio ranges, the infrared (red light) ranges, the visible light frequencies, and up to the X-ray and cosmic ray band. The importance of the higher frequencies can readily be seen by an examination of the bandwidth of the audio-frequency spectrum and that of microwave or coaxial cable transmission media. The bandwidth between 10^3 and 10^4 is 9,000 Hz (10,000 − 1,000 = 9,000), which is roughly the equivalent to three 3,000-Hz voice-grade lines. The bandwidth between 10^7 and 10^8 (the HF and VHF spectrum) is 90,000,000 Hz, which is theoretically the equivalent of 30,000 voice-grade lines. While a somewhat simple example, this does demonstrate that the telecommunications industry is moving to technologies utilizing the higher radio frequencies because of the greater bandwidth capabilities.

TABLE 3-1   THE FREQUENCY SPECTRUM

Approximate Frequency	Name	Use
10^3	—	Telephone voice frequencies
10^4	VLF	Telephone voice frequencies with higher-speed modems
10^5	LF	Coaxial submarine cables; some high-speed batch data transfer
10^6	MF	Land coaxial cables; AM sound broadcasting
10^7	HF	Land coaxial cables; shortwave broadcasting
10^8	VHF	Land coaxial cables; VHF sound and TV broadcasting
10^9	UHF	UHF TV broadcasting
10^{10}	SHF	Short-link waveguides; microwave broadcasting
10^{11}	EHF	Helical waveguides
10^{12}	—	Infrared transmission
10^{13}	—	Infrared transmission
10^{14}	—	Optic fibers; visible light
10^{15}	—	Optic fibers; ultraviolet
10^{19}–10^{23}	—	X-rays and gamma rays

Period and wavelength.   The amount of time for a cycle duration is called the *period*. A signal of 2,400 Hz has a cycle period of 0.000416 second (1 sec/2,400 = 0.000416). The period T is calculated as 1/F, where F is the frequency in hertz. The important point to remember is the higher the frequency the shorter the period. This has implications for the use of certain types of communications paths and the selection of data rates for network equipment.

The wavelength and frequency are inversely proportional to each other. The higher the frequency, the shorter the wavelength, as proved by the formula: WL = S/F, where WL = wavelength, S = speed of signal propagation (usually quoted as 180,000 miles/second for radio propagation), and F = frequency of signal in hertz. The wavelength of the signal is an important factor in network equipment selection, protocol design, and response time analysis. Later we will learn how signal period and wavelength affect these important decisions in a data communications system, especially in satellite communications.

Other wave forms.   Another common approach in sending binary values is through the use of a symmetrical square wave. Figure 3-4 depicts this mode of transmission. The square wave represents a voltage that is switched *instantaneously* from positive to negative polarity. The square wave is an excellent mode for the transmission of digital data, since it can represent only the binary states of 0 and 1, with its positive and negative values.

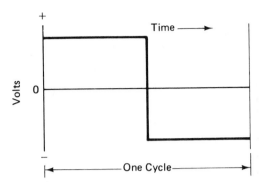

Figure 3–4. Square wave.

DC signals. Many communications systems do not use the analog (ac) form of transmission. A simpler approach is direct-current (dc) transmission. DC signals resemble the symmetrical square wave in that they can take only the discrete values of 1 and 0. However, the dc transmitter does not use the oscillating wave form, but an on–off pulse of electrical energy. In addition, the dc signal is transmitted as it is, without being superimposed on any other signal or frequency. An ac signal is often modified to "ride" other frequencies for purposes of efficiency, speed, and transmission distance. Many systems with limited distance requirements do not need the more powerful (and expensive) ac transmission scheme and, therefore, utilize dc signaling. The reader should remember that the sinusoid wave form, as in the symmetrical square wave, is the type of transmission needed for long-distance data communications lines. While both dc and ac signals can be made to carry digital bit streams, the ac mode is used for long-haul transmission. Later discussions will explain this topic further.

The "ancient" telegraph is an example of dc signaling. The key of the telegraph instrument is a switch that, when depressed by an operator, closes a circuit and places a voltage on the sending end of the line. The voltage produces a current that flows down the line and is detected at the receiver as a pulse. The receiver converts the pulse of current into a short audible tone. In earlier systems, the transmitted current activated at the receiving site an electromagnet powered by a battery. The electromagnet pulled or repelled the key (closed or opened the circuit) in accordance with the transmitted signal. The mechanical movement of the key produced audible clicks, and the clicks established a pattern of code. The length of time the key is depressed provides the dot and dash signals of the famous Morse code.

Transmission capacity, speed, and delay. The transmission capacity, stated in bits per second (bit/s), of a communications system is quite important because response time and throughput for the user applications running on a computer depend on the capacity of the system. For example, a 4,800-bit/s line will provide twice the capacity of a 2,400-bit/s line and will result in increased throughput and better response time. From this statement, one might reasonably pose the following scenario: Let an engineer design a very fast transmitter that changes the signal state (baud) on the line very rapidly. Assuming a bit can be represented with each baud, one could then achieve a very high bit rate. Within certain limits, this can indeed be achieved. However, limits do exist and pose finite restrictions on the transmission rate.

The telephone network is designed to carry voice, which is a low-bandwidth signal. Adequate voice fidelity requires a frequency spectrum of about 3 kHz. The frequency spectrum for voice-grade circuits does not allow for a high rate of bits per second to be transmitted.

The limiting factors on transmission capacity are the bandwidth, signal power, and noise on the conductor. An increased signal power can indeed increase the line capacity and also provide for greater distance for the propagation of the signal. However, excessive power may destroy components in the system and/or may not be economically feasible. Many years ago, a transatlantic communications line was rendered useless because excessively high voltage signals were used.

The noise on a line is a problem that is inherent to the line itself and cannot be eliminated. Noise (called thermal, Gaussian, white, or background noise) results from the constant, random movement of electrons on the conductor and provides a limit to the channel capacity. The hiss you hear on a telephone line is such a noise. Any electrical conductor is a source of noise. The power of the noise is proportional to the bandwidth, so an increased bandwidth will also contain additional noise. An electronic technique known as *filtering* is used to reduce the added noise.

One of the fundamental laws in communications is Shannon's law. Shannon demonstrated the finite limits of a transmission path with the following formula:

$$C = W \log_2 (1 + S/N)$$

where   C = maximum capacity in bps
         W = bandwidth
         S/N = ratio of signal power (S) to noise power (N)

If the reader studies this formula, it will be evident that increasing bandwidth, increasing signal power, or decreasing noise levels will increase the allowable bit/s rate. However, changing these parameters may be physically or economically prohibitive. A voice-grade line with a 1,000-to-1 signal-to-noise ratio yields a maximum allowable 25,900-bit/s rate.[2] The theoretical limit imposed by Shannon's law is actually much lower in practice. Due to errors occurring in a transmission, it is usually not desirable to push Shannon's law to its limit. For example, the 25,900-bit/s rate might require such short bit times (for example, 1 sec/25,900 = 0.00004 bit time) that a small imperfection on the line could cause bit distortion. We will learn later that the signal state itself can be made to represent more than 1 bit and will provide some relief to the imposition of Shannon's law.

One method to increase the signal-to-noise ratio is to place more signal amplifiers on the line. Amplifiers strengthen the signal periodically as it travels down the communications path. Since noise is constant throughout the line, the location of the amplifiers must not be spaced too far apart to allow the signal power to fall below a certain

[2] James Martin, *Telecommunications and the Computer.* Englewood Cliffs, N.J.: Prentice-Hall, 1976, p. 304.

level. However, while frequent spacing of amplifiers improves the S/N ratio, it can also be quite costly. Moreover, the amplifiers must be carefully designed to minimize the amount of noise that is amplified along with the signal.

A circuit can actually carry a much greater signal rate than 25.9 kbit/s through a technique called *digital transmission*. However, digital transmission entails the use of higher bandwidths and more frequent spacing of digital repeaters (the digital equivalent of an analog amplifier). Digital transmission need not have as high a S/N ratio, since Shannon's law shows that a relatively small increase in bandwidth offsets a much greater decrease in the S/N ratio.

Practically speaking, many people associated with data communications and networks are not interested in *why* a limited capacity exists, but *what* the limit is. The engineer's task is to determine the limits and convey this information to other people, who then use the engineer's information to design and configure the network.

The range of options and costs for obtaining different speeds of lines varies greatly. The choice inevitably revolves around the user needs and the costs to meet those needs. Table 3–2 shows some available ranges of transmission speeds, as well as some typical user applications that utilize the transmission speeds. It can be seen that a wide range of options exists, and that a 9.6 kbit/s rate is inadequate for many types of transmissions.

Transmission or propagation delay of the signal is yet another consideration for

TABLE 3–2 RANGE OF TRANSMISSION REQUIREMENTS

Type of Transmission	Typical Number of Bits	Transmission Time at 9.6 kbit/s (sec)
A page or a full CRT screen of text (uncompressed)	$1-4 \times 10^4$	1–4
Facsimile image, black and white, two-tone (compressed)	$2-6 \times 10^5$	20–60
Full-page, three-color image, high quality (heavily compressed)	$2-10 \times 10^6$	200–1000
A 20-cm floppy disk, single-sided, double-density	5×10^6	500
A 720-m reel of computer tape (type 6250 BPI) or two medium-sized disk units (IBM 3310)	1×10^9	100,000 (29 hours)
One second of digitized telephone speech at pulse-code modulation	6.4×10^4	7
One second of digitized telephone speech (heavily compressed)	2.4×10^3	0.25
One second of Picturephone (moving video image)	6.3×10^6	660

From ''Assessing the New Services'' by Thomas Mandey, *IEEE Spectrum*, October 1979.

the engineer as well as the user. Propagation delay depends on several factors, such as the type of circuit and the number and type of intermediate points between the transmitter and receiver. A good rule of thumb is that a transmission over a path with coaxial cables and microwave travels at approximately 130,000 miles/sec. However, the velocity of the signal varies considerably with frequency. For instance, a typical telephone toll line (19 gauge) can operate at approximately 110,000 miles/sec at 10 kHz and 125,000 miles/sec at 50 kHz. The speeds are slower than the theoretical speed of 186,000 miles/sec due to the frequencies and certain electrical characteristics in the cable. Additional and significant delays may be encountered as the message moves through a network into and out of intermediate stations. However, the primary transmission delays are experienced on the path itself; the intermediate components, such as switches and computers, while causing delays, usually operate at very high speeds (in nanoseconds or billionths of seconds). Of course, storing the message at these stations on disk or tape introduces considerably more delay.

Is a transmission speed of 130,000 miles/sec sufficient? After all, a theoretical 3,000-mile line across the United States would require only 0.023 sec (3,000 miles/ 130,000 miles/sec = 0.023 sec) for the signal to reach its destination. (Remember, additional delays may result from other intermediate components.) The answer to the question is that it depends on the user requirement and the user application. For example, a delay of 0.023 sec to several seconds may be sufficient for message transfers between human operators yet insufficient in an environment where two computers are multiprocessing a distributed data base. The effect of a 23-millisecond (ms) wait time can be quite costly in terms of computer processor time and can create serious data-base synchronization problems. Later, we will examine the effect of propagation delay on satellite links.

Asynchronous and Synchronous Transmission

Figure 3–5 provides an illustration of a simple transmission process. The transmitted bits are actually consecutive intervals of time and are measured by a sensing and timing mechanism at the receiving site. The start bit precedes the data character and is used to notify the receiving site that data are on the path (start bit detection). The path or line is said to be idle prior to the arrival of the start bit and remains in the idle state until a start bit is transmitted. During the idle state, current is flowing on the line. The low signal state of start initiates mechanisms in the receiving device for sampling, counting, and receiving the bits of the data stream (bit counter). The data bits are represented as current for the mark signal (binary 1) and no current for the space signal (binary 0).

The user data bits are placed in a temporary storage area, such as a register or buffer, and are later moved into a terminal or computer for further processing. Stop bits, consisting of one or more mark signals, provide for a time lapse in which the mechanism in the receiving site (of older equipment) can readjust for the next character. Following the stop bits, the signal returns to idle level, thus guaranteeing that the next character will begin with a 1 to 0 transition. If the preceding character had been all 0s, the start

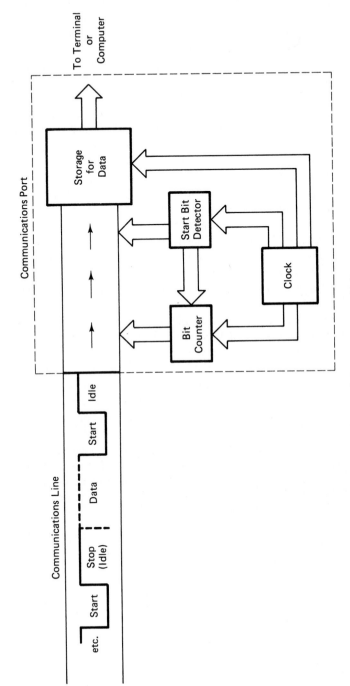

Figure 3-5. Asynchronous transmission process.

bit detection would become confused if a stop bit were not present to return the voltage to a high or idle level.

This method is called *asynchronous transmission* due to the absence of continuous synchronization between the sender and receiver. This allows a data character to be transmitted at any time without regard to any previous timing signal; the timing signal is a part of the data signal. Asynchronous transmission is commonly found in machines or terminals such as teletypes or teleprinters and low-speed computer terminals. Many personal computers use asynchronous transmission. Its value lies in its simplicity.

An important component of any communications system is the clocking device. Its purpose is to continuously examine or sample the line for the presence or absence of the predefined signal levels. It is also used to synchronize all internal components. The device can be compared to any type of timing device in that its speed is dependent on how fast it can change state from a "tick" to a "tock." Notice that the clock is connected to other components to maintain consistent timing of all parts.

The sampling clock actually samples the communication line at a much faster rate than the arriving data. For example, if the data were arriving at 2,400 bit/s, the timing mechanism might sample at 19,200 times per second, or eight times the bit/s rate. The faster sample time enables the receiving device to detect the 1 to 0 or 0 to 1 transition very quickly and, thus, keeps the sending and receiving devices more closely synchronized.

The importance of the sampling rate is evident in Figure 3–6. The bit time on a line of 2,400-bit/s rate is 0.000416 sec (1 sec/2,400). A sampling rate of only 2,400 times per second might sample at the beginning of the bit or at the end of the signal. In both cases, the bit is detected. However, it is not unusual for a signal to change slightly and remain on the line for a shorter or longer duration. A slow sampling rate may fail to sample the change of state of the line at the proper time and, as a signal "drifts," it is likely to lead to the end station not receiving the bits correctly.

For the reader who wishes more detailed information on asynchronous systems, refer to Appendix 3A at the end of this chapter.

A more efficient method, *synchronous transmission*, is distinguished by the existence of a separate clocking signal at the sending and receiving stations. The synchronous scheme is shown in Figure 3–7. The entire data field is now surrounded by control bits. These bits are usually called flags or preambles. They are used to notify the receiver

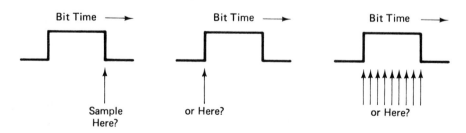

Figure 3–6.   Bit sampling.

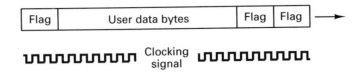

Figure 3–7. Synchronous transmission process (on short-distance circuits).

that a message is arriving. On short-distance circuits, a separate channel can be used to provide the timing signals between the devices.

As in the asynchronous mode, the receiving device searches for the unique bit pattern of the flags, but uses a locally generated clocking signal to determine when and how often to sample the incoming signal. The timing signal provides the means to synchronize the clocking devices at the sending and receiving devices. Once the devices are synchronized, they are usually very stable. The clocks may drift some, but a common oscillator clock is accurate to 1 part in 100,000, so an oscillator sampling at 2,500 times per second would stay "in sync" several seconds. A better method to provide synchronization is to devise special codes to represent the binary data streams that provide for periodic resynchronization. These codes are called clocking codes.

The flag/preamble must be distinguished from user data to allow the receiver to search for this signal. Vendors may use different bit streams to represent the signal. A common approach is to use an 8-bit value of 01111110 to represent a flag.

BASIC TERMS AND CONCEPTS

Frames, Headers, and Codes

The electrical signals and bit sequences on the line are transmitted in the form of a frame (see Figure 3–8). The frame is a logical unit of user data, control data, or both. The frame usually contains the following elements (or fields):

- *User data:* Consisting of one or many fields, user data are created by a terminal operator at a keyboard or are the output of a computer program. They are usually associated with an application such as accounts receivable or inventory control.
- *Flags:* Explained in preceding section.
- *Address field:* Contains unique numbers or letters that identify the transmitting and receiving stations on the link.
- *Control characters:* Provide a means to keep the frames flowing in the proper order.
- *Error check:* Used to verify a successful, error-free transmission.

The bit sequences for the characters depend on the particular code set. A wide variety of codes is available today. The earliest codes used in data communications were designed for telegraphic transmission. For example, the Morse code consists of dots and

Flag	Error check	Data	Control	Flag	→

Figure 3–8. Typical frame format for synchronous transmission.

dashes in a particular sequence to represent characters, numbers, and special characters. The dots and dashes represent how long the telegraph operator presses the key on the transmitter.

In the early 1970s, the industry developed many 5-bit codes. The Baudot code is an example of a 5-bit code that is still used today, although not in modern systems.

Many codes evolved from the Morse and Baudot codes. Today the more prevalent codes in use are the Extended Binary Coded Decimal Interchange Code (EBCDIC) and the American National Standard Code for Information Interchange (ASCII). EBCDIC is widely used in IBM architecture. It is an 8-bit binary code and thus provides for 256 possible characters in the code set (2^8). Figure 3–9 shows the EBCDIC code structure.

The code in Figure 3–9 can be interpreted as follows: bits 1 through 4 are described in the column heading and bits 5 through 8 are described in the row entries. The com-

Bits (8765) \ (4321)	0000	0001	0010	0011	0100	0101	0110	0111	1000	1001	1010	1011	1100	1101	1110	1111
0000	NUL	SOH	STX	ETX	PF	HT	LC	DEL			SMM	VT	FF	CR	SO	SI
0001	DLE	DC$_1$	DC$_2$	DC$_3$	RES	NL	BS	IL	CAN	EM	CC		IFS	IGS	IRS	IUS
0010	DS	SOS	FS		BYP	LF	EOB	PRE			SM			ENQ	ACK	BEL
0011			SYN		PN	RS	UC	EOT					DC$_4$	NAK		SUB
0100	SP										c	.	<	(	+	|
0101	&										!	$	*	)	;	¬
0110	–	/										,	%	–	>	?
0111											:	#	@	,	=	''
1000		a	b	c	d	e	f	g	h	i						
1001		j	k	l	m	n	o	p	q	r						
1010			s	t	u	v	w	x	y	z						
1011																
1100		A	B	C	D	E	F	G	H	I						
1101		J	K	L	M	N	O	P	Q	R						
1110			S	T	U	V	W	X	Y	Z						
1111	0	1	2	3	4	5	6	7	8	9						□

PF — Punch Off
HT — Horizontal Tab
LC — Lower Case
DEL — Delete
SP — Space
UC — Upper Case

RES — Restore
NL — New Line
BS — Backspace
IL — Idle
PN — Punch On
EOT — End of Transmission

BYP — Bypass
LF — Line Feed
EOB — End of Block
PRE — Prefix (ESC)
RS — Reader Stop
SM — Start Message
Others — Same as ASCII

Figure 3–9. EBCDIC code.

bination of these bits reveals the code within the table. The code represented in Figure 3–10 is interpreted by bits 1 through 4 shown as a row entry and bits 5 through 7 shown as column entries.

ASCII is the most extensively used code for data transmission (see Figure 3–10). It is a 7-bit code with one additional bit added for error-detection purposes. The code was first developed in 1963 and has become a standard.

The figures also show that certain bit configurations of the 7-, or 8-bit codes are used to represent more than one character. Some of the codes represent control signals for the communications system. For example, the EBCDIC code of 00101110 represents the control function ACK, which is used to acknowledge the receipt of a frame across a communications path. The use of different codes in a communications system obviously presents compatibility problems. Code translation packages are available to allow communications devices that do not have the same code set to communicate with each other.

American

National Standard Code

for

Information Interchange

				7	0	0	0	0	1	1	1	1
\multicolumn{4}{c	}{Bits}	6	0	0	1	1	0	0	1	1
4	3	2	1	5	0	1	0	1	0	1	0	1
0	0	0	0		NUL	DLE	SP	0	@	P	\	p
0	0	0	1		SOH	DC1	!	1	A	Q	a	q
0	0	1	0		STX	DC2	''	2	B	R	b	r
0	0	1	1		ETX	DC3	#	3	C	S	c	s
0	1	0	0		EOT	DC4	$	4	D	T	d	t
0	1	0	1		ENQ	NAK	%	5	E	U	e	u
0	1	1	0		ACK	SYN	&	6	F	V	f	v
0	1	1	1		BEL	ETB	'	7	G	W	g	w
1	0	0	0		BS	CAN	(	8	H	X	h	x
1	0	0	1		HT	EM	)	9	I	Y	i	y
1	0	1	0		LF	SUB	*	:	J	Z	j	z
1	0	1	1		VT	ESC	+	;	K	[	k	{
1	1	0	0		FF	FS	'	<	L	\	l	:
1	1	0	1		CR	GS	–	=	M	]	m	}
1	1	1	0		SO	RS	.	>	N	∧	n	~
1	1	1	1		SI	US	/	?	0	–	o	DEL

Figure 3–10. ASCII code.

Communications Sessions between User Applications

The communications flow between two components in a network is called a *session*. The session can take several forms. For example, a session can exist between two operators at two terminals in the network, between computers, or between two software programs—either applications (payroll, accounts receivable, etc.) or network control programs. Other forms of sessions can exist as well. Whatever the form, sessions are ultimately established to serve the end user, such as a terminal operator or an applications program.

Sessions utilize the information in the headers (or other parameters) of frames. For example, a data-base retrieval request from a terminal operator at site A would provide a header in the message that identified an address of site B, the data-base location, or some other kind of identifier, such as type of data. As the frame is passed through the network, the header is examined and the proper resources are identified and allocated to service the request. The more advanced networks now provide for a layering structure of the sessions and a layering of the communications logic to provide the resources. Chapter 9 discusses the layering concept in more detail.

Line Characteristics

The transmission path or line provides the media for the data exchange between users. This exchange includes session establishment, the exchange of user messages, and session termination. In addition to the electrical attributes of the path, other characteristics play an important role in the performance and design of the communications system. Later chapters will cover the types of paths used in a network (for example, microwave, satellite). This section discusses the following characteristics of a communications channel:

- Point-to-point and multidrop (multipoint) configurations
- Simplex, half-duplex, duplex arrangements
- Switched and leased lines

Point-to-point and multidrop configurations. A point-to-point line connects two stations [see Figure 3–11(a)]; a multidrop line has more than two stations attached [see Figure 3–11(b)]. The selection of one of these configurations is dependent on several factors. First, a point-to-point arrangement may be the only viable choice if a prolonged dedicated user-to-user session is necessary. Second, the traffic volume between two users may preclude the sharing of the line with other stations. Some computer-to-computer sessions require a point-to-point arrangement. Third, two users may be the maximum number involved in the process.

A multidrop arrangement is commonly used in situations where low-speed terminals communicate with each other or a computer. The line is shared by the stations, thereby providing for its more efficient use.

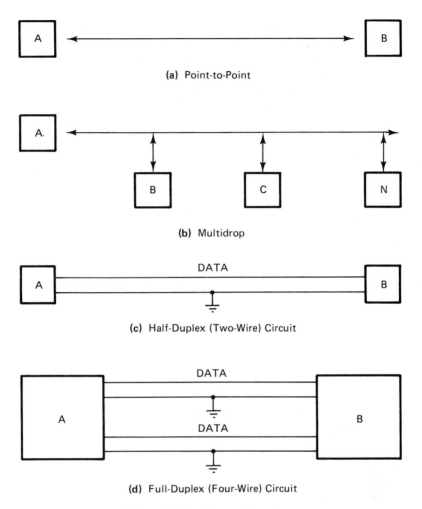

Figure 3–11. Line configurations.

　　Multidrop lines require the use of more elaborate controls than do point-to-point lines. The stations on the multidrop path must be supervised to provide for the allocation and sharing of the line. Sessions must be interleaved and priorities must be established for the more important sessions. Data link controls are used to control the flow of messages in these sessions.

　　Simplex, half-duplex, and duplex arrangements.　　These terms are often subject to more than one interpretation. They usually refer to the manner in which message traffic flows across the line. Another less common interpretation is the number of physical paths involved in the transmission. We will discuss both of these interpretations.

Traffic flow. A simplex transmission provides for the movement of frames across the path in one direction only. The sender cannot receive and the receiver cannot send. A commercial radio broadcast is one example of a simplex transmission. The scheme is used in numerous applications. For instance, environmental filtering and sampling systems often use a simplex arrangement wherein the sampled data from water or air is transmitted in one direction only to a computer for analysis.

Half-duplex transmission provides for movement of data across the line in both directions, but in only one direction at a time. Human-operated keyboard terminals commonly use this approach. Typically, a message sent to the terminal requires the operator to decipher the message, enter an appropriate response, and send the reply. The terminal and the other station ''take turns'' using the line; the sending station waits for a response before sending another message. Half-duplex is also called two-way-alternate transmission (TWA).

Duplex transmission (also called full-duplex) provides for simultaneous, two-way transmission between the stations. Multipoint lines frequently use this approach. For example, station A sends traffic to the central computer at the same time the computer sends traffic a message to station B. Duplex transmission permits the interleaving of sessions and user data flow among several or many stations. Full-duplex is also called two-way-simultaneous transmission (TWS).

Physical path. Unfortunately, the physical lines or paths are sometimes described as half-duplex or duplex circuits. Figure 3–11(c) depicts a half-duplex configuration. This arrangement provides for two conductors, but only one is used for message exchange. The second conductor is a return channel or common ground to complete the electrical circuit. This circuit is more accurately called a *two-wire circuit.*

A duplex (or full-duplex) circuit is shown in Figure 3–11(d). In this case, four conductors are used to provide two data transmission paths and two return channels. This circuit is more accurately called a *four-wire circuit.*

The reader should note that a two-wire circuit does not necessarily mean that the traffic flow across the circuit is half-duplex.

Switched and leased lines. The use of switched lines is well known to all of us because we use such facilities to make telephone calls. The dial-up telephone uses the public telephone exchange. The switched line is a temporary connection between two sites for the duration of the call. A later call to the same site might use different circuits and equipment in the telephone system. The leased line is a permanent connection between sites and does not require a dial-up to obtain the communications path. The path is configured and connected to alleviate dialing (addressing) the site in the network. The advantages and disadvantages of switched and leased lines are as follows:

- A switched line requires several seconds to complete a call and obtain a connection. User needs may dictate the use of leased lines wherein no dial-up delay is encountered.

- Leased lines can provide for better performance and fewer errors. First, the leased lines can be monitored and ''conditioned'' to perform better because the connection does not change. Second, some switching systems introduce noise into the line and the noise sometimes distorts the data.

- Low-volume traffic users usually benefit from using switched lines due to the greater costs of leased facilities. Periodic use of a line favors the dial-up approach of leased lines.
- The switched lines are quite flexible. A failed circuit requires only that a user redial into the public network. A leased line failure requires more effort and entails additional delays to recover.

The choice between leased and switched facilities is a very important consideration for an organization. An analysis of traffic volume, peak loads, response time, and throughput performance is a prerequisite to making rational decisions about the use of leased or switched lines.

Use of the Telephone Network

The following section will give the reader an idea of how the telephone system provides the facilities for a call. Our illustrations are simplifications but sufficient to understand the process.

Figure 3–12 shows some of the components in the local telephone and in the end office. The telephone has switches (SH for switch hooks) that are kept open by the phone's weight in the telephone cradle. As long as the phone is "on hook," the open switches do not provide an electrical connection to the telephone office. When an individual picks up a phone, the SH switches are closed. This "off hook" condition is detected in the central telephone office by the closed SH switches allowing a flow of dc current to the end office. A computer or other devices can "call" the office by activating off-hook through circuitry.

The end office has an electronic detector that scans the incoming local loop lines. At approximately every 100 ms, a line is scanned for the off-hook condition of a dc current flow.

The central office has several switches that it uses to establish the call. Upon detecting the dc current flow from the local subscriber, the office places a dial tone on the line by closing the S1 switch. This permits a tone of 480 Hz to be sent to the caller's telephone. Upon receiving the dial tone, the subscriber (or computer) is alerted to dial a number. The number is then entered by a rotating dial, or pressing the touch-tone buttons. The computer can also perform the dial-up operations.

The signals arrive at the local telephone office, and the call is passed to the local toll center. Computers are used to route the call through the telephone system. Upon receiving a dialed number, the computer examines routing tables to determine which path should be used. If the call is in another area of the country, the logic will determine the proper path to the remote toll center. The call may be routed and switched through several levels of toll centers.

In a matter of seconds, the call arrives at the receiver's local central office. This office scans the appropriate local loop to determine if it is busy. The central office can

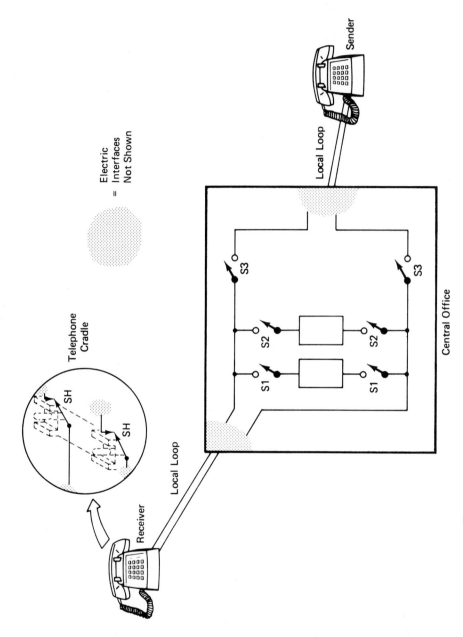

Figure 3–12. Establishing a call.

44

so determine by checking for the absence or presence of dc current flow. The end office will close switch S2 to activate the ringing mechanism in the called party's telephone. S2 closure permits the sending of a 20-Hz signal to the telephone.

If the called telephone is taken off-hook to answer the ring (thus connecting the current flow to the end office), the ringing signal is removed by opening S2. The connection is then completed by closing S3. A switched call between cities typically passes through four to nine switching centers.

SUMMARY

Users communicate on communications networks through either analog or digital signaling. With the use of analog signaling, telephone circuits are typically employed, requiring the use of modulation techniques. The interpretation of the traffic between machines on a communications system is achieved through the use of control fields called headers. These headers provide identification of the transmitter and receiver and services such as sequencing and error detection. In many communications systems predefined codes are used to define certain services and control functions. The codes are standardized by a number of organizations in the industry.

These communications occur through point-to-point or multipoint line configurations with various arrangements available to achieve simplex, half-duplex, and duplex transmission. The lines can also be arranged for dedicated service with leased lines or dial-up service with switched lines.

APPENDIX 3A. ASYNCHRONOUS OPERATIONS

This appendix continues the discussion on asynchronous systems that began earlier in this chapter. As we learned, asynchronous communications have been in existence for many years. They are attractive because the asynchronous components are not complex and are relatively inexpensive.

Asynchronous systems owe their existence to several events that transpired in the telegraph industry many years ago. Early communications systems employed a transmitter and a teleprinting system. These early machines printed onto a paper tape. The tape was printed based on receiving electrical impulses that represented a character code. These signals set a circumferential wheel in a particular position (to a desired character) and the printing occured by contacting the character with the paper tape.

In early systems the code used for transmission was the famous Morse code. But it proved to be too complex for data communications systems because of its variable length. Consequently, the industry adopted a fixed-length code supposedly devised by John Maurice Emile Baudot. Baudot developed what is now known as the Baudot code while working in the French telegraph service in the 1870s. Baudot's code is now known as International Telegraph Alphabet #1. The code most people associate with Baudot code is actually the International Telegraph Alphabet #2, which was devised by Donald Murray.

As shown in Figure 3A–1, the "Baudot code" is a 5-bit code (although during the development of this code the term *bits* was not in use) with 2^5 characters (32). Two characters are used to shift the printer into a letters of figures to provide for more character variation.

The term *baud* or *baud rate* describes the signaling intervals on a line and was named after Emile Baudot.

A decision to use a preliminary signal called the start bit to synchronize the teleprinter with the incoming transmission stream was an elegantly simple solution to a very vexing problem. Although it required some modifications to existing teleprinters, it formed the basis for many communications systems that still exist today. We will see how this works shortly.

An asynchronous communications channel is said to be in an idle state with high voltage. This is also known as the MARK condition, and is represented with a logical 1. A negative pulse is represented as logical zero, and is known as a SPACE. Asynchronous traffic is sent from the least to most significant bit. In Figure 3A–2, the international alphabet character B is sent as bits 10011.

Asynchronous transmission is cost-effective for low-speed and low-volume transmissions such as those from keyboard entry terminals. For larger volumes, synchronous transmission is more efficient.

Hex	Binary	LETTERS Shift	FIGURES Shift	Hex	Binary	LETTERS Shift	FIGURES Shift
0	00000	Blank	Blank	10	10000	T	5
1	00001	E	3	11	10001	Z	+
2	00010	LF	LF	12	10010	L	)
3	00011	A	-	13	10011	W	2
4	00100	Space	Space	14	10100	H	reserved
5	00101	S	'	15	10101	Y	6
6	00110	I	8	16	10110	P	0
7	00111	U	7	17	10111	Q	1
8	01000	CR	CR	18	11000	O	9
9	01001	D	WRU	19	11001	B	?
0A	01010	R	4	1A	11010	G	reserved
0B	01011	J	BELL	1B	11011	FIGS	FIGS
0C	01100	N	,	1C	11100	M	.
0D	01101	F	reserved	1D	11101	X	/
0E	01110	C	:	1E	11110	V	=
0F	01111	K	(	1F	11111	LTRS	LTRS

Character 5 is an apostrophe; OC is a comma, Shifted F, G, and H positions are reserved for national usage.

Figure 3A–1. International Alphabet #2.

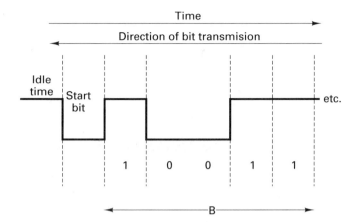

Figure 3A–2.   The asynchronous start bit.

As figure 3A–3 shows, asynchronous transmission incurs a 25% overhead with the start/stop bits. A protocol using synchronous formats incurs an overhead of only 4.6%. The decreased overhead of synchronous formats must be weighed against the more expensive circuitry to support it.

The start bit solved the sender/receiver synchronization problem by placing a synchronization bit (the start bit) just before the first bit of each character. This bit allowed the receiver to align itself to the signal.

While the start bit adds a significantly enhanced feature to data communications systems, it does not solve one very vexing problem: bit corruption on the communications channel. Is this a significant problem? In many communications systems it is (because the communications channel is not designed for data, but rather for voice that has a high tolerance for errors such as impulse noise and cross talk).

The problem with asynchronous systems (discussed thus far) is illustrated in Figure 3A–4. The character B is transmitted without problems, but the next succeeding synchronization signal (the start bit) is damaged on the communications channel. Consequently, the next zero bit is interpreted as the start bit when in fact it is the first bit of the second character of the transmission from the letter L. Consequently, the receiver assumes that the first bit of the letter L begins with 1 when that is actually the second bit. Consequently, it interprets 4 bits of the letter L and the next space incorrectly as the letter D.

The problem stems from the fact that data are transmitted without any intervening idle time. Indeed, without some remedial action shown in this figure, subsequent characters would be damaged without any method of correcting them.

Asynchronous	*Synchronous (HDLC)*
2 (start/stop)/8 = .25	6 (bytes of control overhead) * 8 bits = 48 bits
	128 (bytes of data * 8 bits = 1,024 bits 48/1,024 = .046
25% Overhead	4.6% Overhead

Figure 3A–3.   Overhead comparison of asynchronous and synchronous protocols.

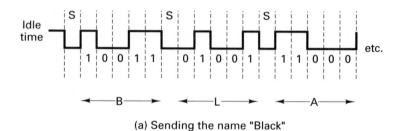

(a) Sending the name "Black"

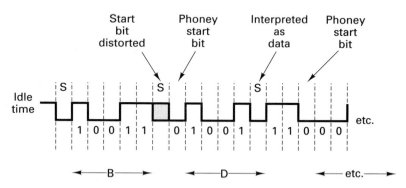

Figure 3A–4. An error in the start bit.

As shown in Figure 3A–5, asynchronous systems use an end-of-character signal (an end-of-character bit). This bit is known in the industry as the stop bit. With this addition, an asynchronous system reads the character (which in our example is the 5-bit code) and the stop bit. If bits become misaligned, the receiver is required to check that each arriving character and begins with a SPACE and ends with a MARK; otherwise, the character is discarded. The addition of the stop bit while enhancing asynchronous operations considerably was introduced before it was realized it solved this problem. In

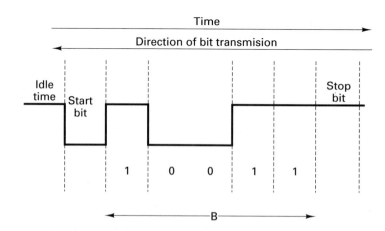

Figure 3A–5. Adding the stop bit.

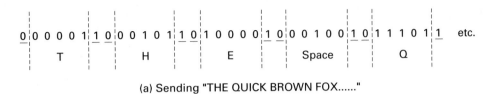

(a) Sending "THE QUICK BROWN FOX......"

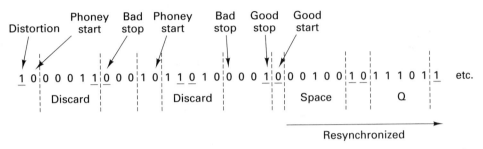

(b) An error and error recovery

Figure 3A–6.   Error and error recovery.

the early days, a period of idle time was inserted between characters to allow for the relatively slow teleprinter's mechanical gear to align itself and await the next character. These idle times became known as bit times, and they range today between 1-, 1-1/2-, and 2-bit times.

The asynchronous protocols are also called character-framing protocols. Perhaps a more accurate term is simply asynchronous, start/stop protocols.

The robustness of asynchronous transmission may not be evident from a superficial examination. However, consider the example in Figure 3A–6. The data stream transmitted across the communications channel is: "The quick brown fox jumped over . . ." The 5-bit coding for this phrase is shown in this figure. In Figure 3A–6(a), the bits are coded transmitted across from the right-hand side of the page to the left. The underlined numbers indicate the start and stop bits that are placed around each character.

In Figure 3A–6(b), the start bit of the character T is distorted. Therefore, the receiver assumes the next zero bit is the start bit. Thereafter it counts the next successive 5 bits, assuming these bits constitute a character. Upon receiving these 5 bits, it examines the next bit, assuming it to be a stop bit (a value of 1). However, this bit is the start bit for the letter H. Consequently, the receiver has not received a valid start/stop combination and it discards this erroneous character. It searches until it finds a 1 bit, then assumes the next 0 bit is the start. It then counts 5 more bits. Once again, it encounters a bad stop bit, and continues the examination until it finds the next 1, which happens to be the legitimate stop bit of the letter E. Consequently, the next bit is the legitimate start bit for the space character, and it is now resynchronized on the data stream.

While this example shows resynchronization occurring quite rapidly, with only the loss of word THE, it is by no means unusual. Indeed, the reader might wish to try an experiment by jotting down a phrase and showing a distortion occurring either at the stop or the start bit. It will be evident that resynchronization occurs rapidly.

4

Major Components in a Data Communications System

INTRODUCTION

This chapter examines the major components in a data communications system. It continues the introduction of this subject from Chapter 3 and describes the functions of machines such as modems, multiplexers, packet switches, as well as the transmission medium that conveys the traffic between these machines. The transmission medium covered in this chapter includes wire pairs, coaxial cable, satellite transmission, microwave, and optical fibers.

Comparisons are made between the different switching techniques used in the industry today with particular emphasis on packet switching.

THE TRANSMISSION PATH

The transmission path in a data communications system is known by several names: channel, link, line, trunk, circuit, and media. These terms are used interchangeably in this section of the book. The path for the movement of data between computer sites can take several different physical forms. This section describes the more prevalent methods in use today. The transmission characteristics of each path are explained.

Wire Pairs

Wires are described by their size. The sizing system in the United States is called the American Wire Gauge (AWG) System. The AWG System specifies the size of the round wire in terms of its diameter. Higher-gauge numbers indicate thinner wire sizes. The smaller the diameter of the wire, the greater its resistance to the propagation of a signal. Increased resistance results in a decreased bit rate across the communications path. At higher transmission frequencies, the signal tends to travel on the outside surface of the wire. A smaller wire provides less total surface for the radiating signal, resulting in an increased signal loss. A larger wire with a greater cross-sectional area allows for an increased signal intensity. The local subscriber loops (of the telephone system) are usually 22- to 26-gauge wire. Trunk and toll lines typically employ 19-gauge wires.

In the earlier part of the century, a pair of wires or three wires constituted the path for telegraphs and telephones. The wires typically provided for 12 separate transmissions circuits per pair. Wire pairs can still be seen in certain parts of the United States, primarily in the rural areas. The wires are openly suspended from telephone poles and connected to the poles with insulating points. The early facilities had 16 pairs on a pole, providing a capacity per route of about 200 separate transmissions. The wire is usually made of copper and steel. Open wire pairs have been replaced by other technologies because of attenuation (signal loss) and cross-talk (circuit interference) problems.

Wire "cables" have replaced most of the individual wire pairs. Several hundred of these wires are packaged into one cable. The wires are paired and twisted around each other to decrease certain electromagnetic problems. (Another term describing the technology is *twisted-wire pairs*.) The cables can contain hundreds of pairs. They provide for better performance than the open pairs but are still susceptible to cross talk. The cables are quite heavy and cumbersome; a 1-foot section of the cable containing 400 pairs weighs several pounds. Wire pair cables are usually laid under the streets, suspended from poles, or installed inside the ducts of buildings.

Microwave

Electromagnetic radiation was predicted by James Clark Maxwell as early as 1873, and in 1887 Heinrich Hertz actually produced radio waves. These waves are fields of force and are similar to light (both are radiations of electromagnetic energy), but radio waves are longer and more coherent in phase. The signals can be altered to carry information in the form of binary bits.

Electromagnetic radiation can be created by inducing a current of sufficient amplitude into an antenna whose dimensions are approximately the same as the wavelength of the generated signal. The signal can be generated uniformly (like a light bulb) or can be directed as a beam of energy (like a spotlight).

Microwave is a directed line-of-sight radio transmission (see Figure 4–1). It is used for wideband communications systems and is quite common in the telephone system. Television transmission also utilizes microwave transmission, because microwave transmission is above the 1 gigahertz (GHz) frequency band and provides the capacity required for video transmission. The high bandwidth gives a small wavelength, and the smaller the wavelength, the smaller one can design the microwave antenna. The antenna size has significant implications for distributed processing systems. The transmitting towers are spaced 20 to 30 miles apart. The transmitted radio beam is focused narrowly to the receiving antenna.

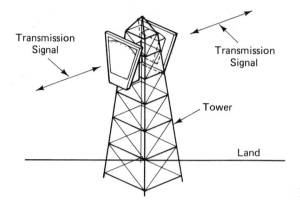

Figure 4–1. Microwave.

These towers can be seen throughout cities and the countryside. They have become a familiar landmark to the motorist. The antenna is also frequently placed on the rooftops of buildings.

Microwave is very effective for transmission to remote locations. Canada has one of the most extensive systems in the world, and the former Soviet Union has placed microwave systems in such remote areas as Siberia. Several U.S. companies' primary product line is the offering of voice-grade channels on their microwave facilities.

Coaxial Cables

Coaxial cables have been in existence since the early 1940s and are another very popular medium. They are used extensively in long-distance telephone toll trunks, urban areas, and local networks. The technology consists of an inner copper conductor held in position by circular spacers (see Figure 4–2). The inner wire is surrounded by insulation and covered by a protective sheath. The covering protects the conductor and prevents interference from signals of other coaxial cables.

Coaxial cables are designed to provide for greater bandwidth and faster bit rates than wire cables. Typical coaxial cable systems can carry from 3,600 to 10,800 voice-grade channels. As stated earlier, the use of higher frequencies on a wire pair is limited

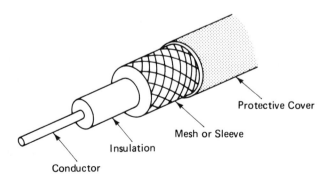

Figure 4–2. Coaxial cable.

because higher frequencies tend to produce a current flow on the outside portion of the wire. This phenomenon (the ''skin effect'') creates significant attenuation and cross-talk problems on uninsulated wires. The same holds true for coaxial cables: The current flows more on the outside of the wire at higher frequencies. However, the wire is encased in the shell, so the current is actually flowing in the inside of the outer shell and the outside of the inner wire. This approach allows for a system above the 60-megahertz (MHz) bandwidth (and 10,800 voice-grade circuits). The technology is somewhat limited due to repeater design and signal loss at higher frequencies.

Comparison of Wire-Pair Cable and Coaxial Cable

Twisted-pair cable is usually *balanced:* The two wires have the same ''electrical references'' to ground potential, and the current in each conductor is 180° out of phase with each other. This latter feature is attractive if other signals interfere, since radiated fields that are 180° out of phase tend to cancel each other. These twisted pairs exhibit relatively low signal loss (attenuation).

A coaxial cable is an *unbalanced* circuit. The center conductor carries the current and the sleeve acts as another conductor operating at ground potential (or ground return). The sleeve (also called a *shield*) prevents energy from radiating into the surrounding area. An unbalanced coaxial line experiences greater attenuation than balanced wire pairs, but it is easier to install and maintain.

A balanced transmission line must not collect moisture, which will change the electrical properties between the two lines, resulting in signal reflections and additional line losses. The line must also be kept clear of other conductors such as downspouts, rain gutters, and metal towers.

In contrast, coaxial cable has an outside shield at ground potential, so it can be mounted anywhere. A balanced line offers the lowest attenuation, but coaxial cable is still widely used because it is easy to install and has a large transmission capacity.

Satellite Communications

In 1945, Arthur C. Clarke, a well-known science-fiction writer, described in *Wireless World* the communications satellite technology as it exists today. Later, Clarke predicted satellite communications would create as profound an impact on the world as did the telephone. One may question the latter claim, but few people dispute the significance of satellite communications.

The technology is actually a radio relay in the sky. Satellite stations with transmitting and receiving antenna (transponders) are launched into orbit by rockets where they receive signals from transmitting stations on earth and relay these signals back to earth stations. Figure 4–3 illustrates this process.

Unique aspects of communications satellites.   Satellite communications are unique from other media for several reasons:

Figure 4–3.   Satellite transmission.

1. The technology provides for a large communications capacity. Through the use of the microwave frequency bands, several thousand voice-grade channels can be placed on a satellite station.
2. The satellite has the capacity for a broadcast transmission. The transmitting antenna can send signals to a wide geographic area. Applications such as electronic mail and distributed systems find the broadcast capability quite useful.
3. Transmission cost is independent of distance between the earth sites. For example, it makes no difference if two sites are 100 or 1,000 miles apart. If they are serviced by the same communications satellite, the signals transmitted from the satellite can be received by all stations, regardless of their distance from each other.
4. The stations experience a significant signal propagation delay. Since satellites are positioned about 22,300 miles above earth, the transmission has to travel to the satellite and return to the receiving earth station. A round-trip transmission requires a minimum of about 240 milliseconds (ms), and could be greater as the signal

travels through other components. This delay may affect certain applications or software systems.

5. The broadcast aspect of satellite communications may present security problems, since all stations under the satellite antenna can receive the broadcasts. Consequently, transmissions are often changed (encrypted) for satellite channels.

History of the technology.   Although satellite communications concepts have existed for many years, the ideas could only be implemented after the advent of space-age technology and solid-state electronics. The United States and the former Soviet Union lead in the development of the technology. The Soviet Union was first off the launching pad with its Sputnik I on October 4, 1957, and the United States followed shortly with Explorer I on January 1, 1958. Neither of these rockets carried communications satellites. The United States Army is credited with the first communications satellite (SCORE), which was launched December 18, 1958. The world's first commercial satellite, Early Bird, was orbited from Cape Kennedy on April 6, 1965. The WESTAR satellite launched by Western Union in 1974 was the first U.S. domestic satellite. COMSAT was credited with the first satellite communications system for ships at sea with the 1976 Marisat System.

Canada has also been a leader in communications satellite technology. As early as 1962, it launched the Alouette system and achieved the world's first geosynchronous domestic system with the Anik series orbits in 1972, 1973, and 1975. Canada has also pioneered satellites in the 14/12 GHz bandwidth—considerably greater in capacity than the 6/4 GHz that are commonly used today. Canada has benefited greatly from satellite communications—no other country has a population of 24 million people scattered over 5.9 million square miles. Due to Canada's extensive satellite system, fewer than 250,000 people cannot be reached through the technology.

The earlier satellites were passive. The U.S. satellites Echo I (launched in 1960) and Echo 2 (launched in 1964) merely reflected the transmitted signal (up-link signal) back to the earth station (down-link signal). The improvement in rocket technology and the smaller weight of solid-state electronics now provide for active satellites that receive a signal, amplify it, and retransmit it back to earth.

The earlier satellites were still not commercially viable. The limited rocket power could boost the satellite into orbits no greater than 6,000 miles above the earth. The low orbit resulted in the satellite moving faster than the earth's rotation and, as the satellite moved across the horizon, the earth station had to rotate its antenna. Eventually, the satellite would disappear and tracking would be passed to another earth station or satellite. The North Atlantic region would have required about 50 satellites for continuous coverage, a very expensive arrangement.

Many of the current satellites are in a geosynchronous orbit. They rotate around the earth at 6,900 miles/hour and remain positioned over the same point at 22,300 miles above the equator. Thus, the earth station's antenna can remain in one position, since the satellite's motion relative to the earth's position is fixed. Furthermore, a single geosynchronous satellite with nondirectional antennas can cover about 30% of the earth's surface. Geosynchronous satellites can achieve worldwide coverage (some limited areas in the polar regions are not covered) with three satellites spaced at 120° intervals from one another (see Figure 4–4).

The general public in the United States became aware of satellite technology in the mid-1970s when companies like Home Box Office (HBO) began to use the technology to beam remote events to its cable television affiliates. HBO's first offering was the "Thrilla in Manilla" heavyweight fight on September 30, 1975, between Muhammad Ali and Joe Frazier. The fight was transmitted live to 15,000 HBO subscribers in Florida and Mississippi.

Today, the typical satellite operates in the 6 and 4 GHz bands (the C band) for the up-link and down-link, respectively. The bandwidth can be divided in a variety of ways. Several have 12 channels, each using a bandwidth of 36 MHz, with a 4-MHz spacing between the channels. These channels are further divided into lower-speed circuits such as voice-grade channels. The voice-grade channels may be further divided to operate subchannels at speeds such as 1,200, 2,400, 4,800, or 9,600 bit/s.

Increasingly, satellites are using frequencies in the 11/12/14 GHz range (Ku band). The 30/20 GHz (K band) range will also be used. The 6/4 GHz bandwidths are also assigned to terrestrial microwave systems, and the use of the higher-frequency spectrums will eliminate what is now serious interference and signal congestion problems between microwave and satellite systems.

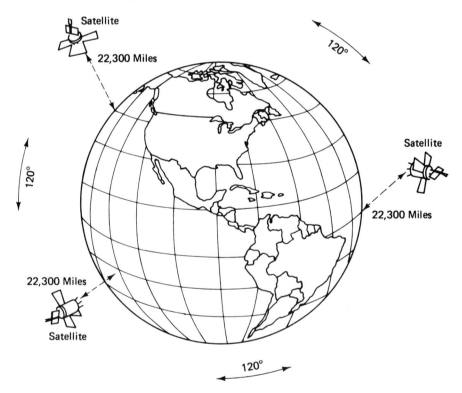

Figure 4–4. Geosynchronous satellites.

The 30- and 20-GHz satellites are also very attractive due to the spectrum/orbit problem. While ample space exists 22,300 miles above the earth for all the satellites, the satellites must be spaced apart in order to prevent radio interference from adjacent satellites. The 6/4 GHz requires about 4° (450 miles) of separation. The wavelengths of the 30/20 GHz satellites are more narrow, and thus the satellites can be placed more closely together, about 1° of arc apart. This is an important consideration because the 6/4 slots over the United States and Puerto Rico are already overcommitted. Satellites are now carrying antennas that operate both in the 6/4 and 16/12 GHz bands because these signals will not interfere with one another. The 14/12 and 30/20 bands also require smaller antennas because the wavelengths are shorter.

The 14/12 and 30/20 GHz bands are not without problems. The major obstacle to their use is their susceptibility to rain. The water and oxygen molecules in the rain absorb the electromagnetic energy. Attenuation of the higher frequencies with the shorter wavelengths is particularly severe. In contrast, the 6/4 GHz bands are relatively immune to rain. The problem is more severe for earth stations that are located farther away around the globe from the satellite stations, since these stations experience a greater "look angle," requiring the signal to travel through more atmosphere. The rain loss problem could be solved by boosting power in the satellites and in the earth stations, but this has not been cost-effective. Later we will examine some methods of solving the rain problem (see discussions on multiplexing).

Satellites may also experience solar eclipses [see Figure 4–5(a)]. During 23 days in spring and fall, the earth is aligned directly between the sun and the satellite station. Consequently, the solar cells that power the satellite must be strong enough not to deplete their energy. The satellite must also be designed to withstand the extremely cold temperatures when it is shielded from the sun. Solar eclipses range from 72 minutes on September 21 and March 21 down to a few minutes as the satellite moves farther away from the equinox.

A more noticeable problem is a sun transit [see Figure 4–5(b)]. When the satellite station is aligned directly between the earth station and the sun, the sun's rays travel directly into the earth station's antenna, which creates excessive thermal noise on the channel. This problem occurs twice a year for five consecutive days, lasting 10 minutes a day.

Future satellite efforts.   Satellite communications certainly represent one of the more powerful technologies in data communications today. The advances made in the use of higher frequencies will result in smaller and cheaper earth station antennas. The potential applications for satellite use will increase dramatically as smaller antennas are made available. Individual homeowners are now able to install small antennas (about 3 feet in diameter) for direct television communications with the satellites.

The impact on the telephone companies, their local loops, and on distributed processing are enormous. Carriers are now able to bypass completely the telephone company facilities to service large corporations, small businesses, and even private citizens. With thousands of satellites in orbit, the earth is indeed "shrinking" as worldwide communications become commonplace. A notable example is the teleport, now used throughout the world. The teleport consists of satellites shared by multiple users. For

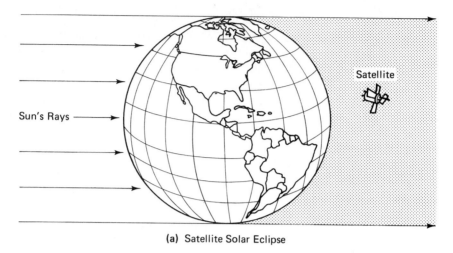

(a) Satellite Solar Eclipse

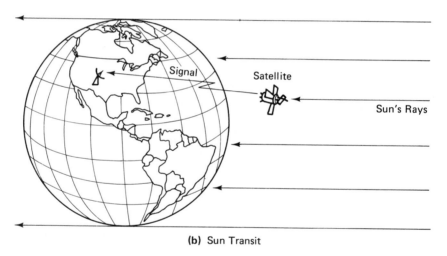

(b) Sun Transit

Figure 4–5.   Satellite transmission problems.

example, the users may be tenants in an office building within an industrial complex. The users of the teleport are linked to the satellite through cable, optical fibers, or microwave links. The idea is to share the high-capacity satellite channels in order to reduce users' overall communications costs. The teleport transmits all types of images (voice, data, facsimile, and video) with a wide diversity of data rates. The digital transmission speeds range from low speeds to 1.544 Mbit/s.

Optical Fibers

The use of light for sending messages has been in existence for hundreds of years. In ancient times, Greek armies transmitted coded light messages between their military units. In the 18th century, French scientists experimented with optical telegraph systems.

These efforts had limited success because light signals attenuate rapidly in the atmosphere. The use of light for transmitting data has gained considerable attention and support in the industry. However, rather than use the atmosphere to transmit the light, newer techniques make use of cables (optical fibers) for the transmission.

Without question, optical fibers have a bright future. There are several reasons for this statement:

1. Optical transmission has a very large information capacity in terms of bandwidth. The frequencies encompassing light-wave transmission are very high in the electromagnetic spectrum. The reader may recall that bandwidth is largely dependent on the frequency range. Optical fiber bandwidths in the range of 500 MHz are not unusual today; some researchers believe an optical fiber will carry 1,000 MHz; Bell Labs has successfully placed 30,000 simultaneous telephone calls on one optic fiber.

2. Optical fibers have electrically nonconducting photons instead of the electrons found in metallic cables such as wires or coaxial cables. This is attractive for applications in which the transmission path traverses environments that are subject to fire and gaseous combustion from electricity. Optical cables are not subject to electrical sparks or interference from electrical components in a building or computer machine room.

3. Optical fibers have less loss of signal strength than copper wire and coaxial cables. The strength of a light signal typically is reduced only slightly after propagation through several miles of optical fiber cable. Repeaters can be spaced as far as 20 to 30 miles apart. In contrast, North American standards on existing copper cables stipulate repeaters every 2.8 miles (a T1 carrier operating at 1.544 Mbit/s).

4. Optical fibers are more secure than cable transmission methods. Transmission of light does not yield residual intelligence around the cable. Residual electromagnetic energy is found in electrical transmission. Moreover, it is quite difficult to tap an optical fiber cable. (In fact, this is one of the disadvantages at the present time, due to the limitation of multipoint optical fiber lines.)

5. Optical fiber cables are very small (roughly the size of a hair) and very light weight. For example, 900 wire pairs pulled through 1,000 feet in a building would weigh 4,800 pounds. Two optical fibers pulled the same distance with protective covers (and much greater capacity) would weigh only 80 pounds.

6. Optical fibers are easy to install and operate in high and low temperatures.

7. Due to the low signal loss, the error rate for optical fibers is very attractive. For example, a typical error rate on an optical fiber is 10^{-9} versus 10^{-6} in metallic cables.

8. Semiconductor technology has been refined to provide transmitting and receiving devices for the system. The rapidly decreasing costs of solid-state chips have further spurred the optical fiber industry.

Methods of transmission. The light signal is transmitted down the optical fiber in the form of on/off pulses representing a digital bit stream. The waves travel through the core of the cable, bouncing off a layer called *cladding* (see Figure 4–6). The

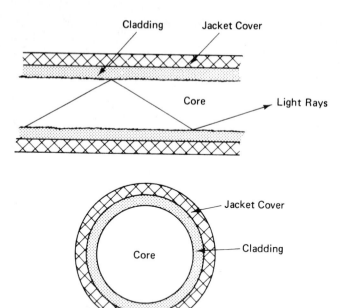

Figure 4–6. Optical fiber.

refracting of the signal is carefully controlled through the design of the cable and the receivers and transmitters. The light signal cannot escape the optic cable because the core's refractive index is higher than the cladding's refractive index. Thus, the light travels down the cable in a reflecting path.

The light signal source is usually a laser or a light-emitting diode (LED). The lasers provide for greater bandwidth and yield significantly greater capacity than other methods. For example, a wire-pair cable has a bandwidth distance parameter of 1 MHz/km; a coaxial cable has a 20-MHz/km parameter; and an optic fiber has a 400-MHz/km bandwidth distance parameter. The signal is emitted from microchips composed of semiconducting materials that transmit near infrared wavelength signals. Silicon photodetectors are used to receive the signals and convert the light ray to the original off/on electrical pulse for interface into the terminal, computer, or modem.

Several methods are used to transmit the fiber light rays through the fiber. In a *step index multimode* fiber [Figure 4–7(a)], the core and cladding interface is sharply defined. The light rays bounce off the interfaces into the core at different angles, resulting in different path lengths (modes) for the signal. This causes the signal to spread out along the fiber and limits the step index cable to approximately 35 MHz/km. This phenomenon is called *modal dispersion.*

A better approach, called *graded index multimode*, is to alter the cladding/core interface to provide different refractive indexes within the core and cladding [Figure 4–7(b)]. Light rays traveling down the axis of the cable encounter the greatest refraction and their velocity is the lowest in the transmitted signal. Rays traveling off axis encounter a lower refractive index and thus propagate faster. The aim is to have all modes of the

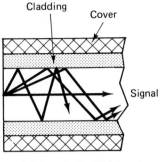

(a) Step Index Multimode

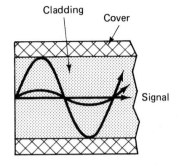

(b) Graded Index Multimode

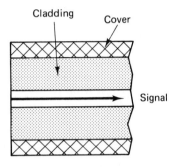

(c) Step Index Signal Mode

Figure 4–7. Types of fibers.

signal attain the same net velocity through the fiber in order to reduce modual dispersion. The approach can result in bandwidths of 500 MHz/km.

A *step index single mode* fiber goes one step further [see Figure 4–7(c)]. The core size, 8 micrometers (μm) in diameter, and core/cladding index allow for only one mode to propagate down the fiber. This approach provides for very high bandwidth and came into prominence with the development of single-mode lasers.

Optical transmission is also subject to spectral or chromatic dispersion. The light passing through the fiber is made up of different frequencies and wavelengths. The refractive index differs for each wavelength and allows the waves to travel at different net speeds. LEDs, with a wide wavelength spread, are subject to considerable spectral dispersion. Lasers exhibit a nearly monochromatic light (limited number of wavelengths) and do not suffer any significant chromatic dispersion.

Optical signal wavelengths near 1.33 μm all travel at about the same speed. However, shorter wavelengths result in the "red" part of the light traveling slightly faster than the "blue" part of the light. The opposite effect is found in wavelengths longer than 1.33 μm.

Optical signal loss can also occur. The cable itself can absorb or scatter light due to impurities that were introduced into the cable during manufacturing. An optimum wavelength to avoid chromatic dispersion is 1.33 μm; to avoid optical loss, a wavelength of 1.55 μm is preferable. A *completely* monochromatic laser (at 1.33 μm) would solve the problem, but a technically feasible and economically viable laser always exhibits some speed in wavelength.

Present and future users of optical fibers.   Companies throughout the world are migrating to the technology. Optical fiber modems and multiplexers are readily available from many vendors today, and many local area networks make extensive use of them. With a single cable pair capable of carrying 400 Mbit/s and/or over 6,000 simultaneous telephone calls, it is not difficult to understand the rapid emergence of optical fibers.

Submarine Cable

Submarine coaxial cable was introduced for transmission over bodies of water to replace or augment high-frequency radio schemes. The technology has been around since 1850, when a cable was laid across the English Channel. The first submarine cable in North America was laid in 1852 between New Brunswick and Prince Edward Island, and in 1858 the first transatlantic cable was laid.

One might question the viability of underwater cable in view of the extraordinary satellite communications technology. However, many consider the path attractive due to its costs, security, and absence of a long signal propagation delay. Submarine cable is also designed to perform without repair for 20 years; the average life of a satellite is less than half that time. The technology has been reliable with the exception of fishing boats occasionally damaging the line. Recent installations have the shallow-water cables buried, and this effort has provided much better reliability. Nevertheless, metallic, submarine cables are gradually being replaced by optical fibers.

Waveguides

Prior to the advent of optical fibers, waveguides were considered to be the upcoming technology for short-haul transmissions. The technology entails the transmission of radio waves through a tube. The tubes are designed to transmit waves of very high frequency and provide for very high data transfer rates. Until recently the tubes could not be sharply bent and were expensive to build. Waveguide tubes are used in certain limited situations; for example, as a feeder between a microwave antenna and the equipment on the ground. The technology is sound, fast, and reliable, but it cannot match the performance and flexibility of the optical fiber.

Several other transmission paths are available but are not used very much. High-frequency (HF) radio transmission was used extensively before satellite communications, although its error rate precluded any appreciable use for data transmission except for telegraph signals. Several organizations use meteor trail transmission. This technology relies on the reflection of radio waves off meteor trails.

Summary of Media Options

Today the prevalent technologies for data communications media are microwave, coaxial, and wire-pair cables. Use of communications satellites is growing rapidly and will continue to expand. Optical fibers are replacing much of the copper cable technology. The trend is toward integrated networks using a combination of technologies.

MODEMS

The digitally oriented computers and terminals often communicate with one another through the analog telephone facilities. Therefore, the digital messages must be translated into a form suitable for transmission across the analog network. The modem is responsible for providing the required translation and interface between the digital and analog worlds. The term *modem* is derived from (a) the process of accepting digital bits and changing them into a form suitable for analog transmission (modulation) and (b) receiving the signal at the other station and transforming it back to its original digital representation (demodulation). *Modem* is derived from the two words *modulator* and *demodulator*. Modems are designed around the use of a carrier frequency. The carrier signal has the digital data stream superimposed on it at the transmitting end of the circuit. This carrier frequency has the characteristics of the sine wave.

Voice transmission is also subject to the modulation–demodulation process. Transmission media such as microwave and coaxial facilities have much greater bandwidth ranges than the 3 kilohertz (kHz) used for voice transmission. Consequently, the 300-to 3,300-Hz speech band is often changed through modulation to "ride" a carrier signal of much higher frequency. Other voice transmissions are spaced approximately 4 kHz apart to modulate different carrier frequencies on the same physical circuit. Typically, 12 voice transmissions can be modulated to share one two-wire circuit. The computer-generated bit stream can, therefore, undergo two separate modulation processes, one by the local modem and the other by the telephone company. The section in this chapter on multiplexing explains telephone company modulation in more detail.

Modulation Techniques

Three basic methods of digital bit modulation exist today. Some modems use more than one of the methods. Each method impresses the digital data signal onto the analog carrier signal. The carrier is altered to carry the properties of the digital data stream. These modulation methods are called frequency, amplitude, and phase modulation.

Amplitude modulation.   Amplitude modulation (AM) modems alter the carrier signal amplitude in accordance with the modulating digital bit stream [see Figure 4–8(a)]. The frequency and phase of the carrier are held constant and the amplitude is raised or lowered to represent a 0 or 1. In its simplest form, the carrier signal can be switched on or off to represent the binary state. AM modulation is not often used by

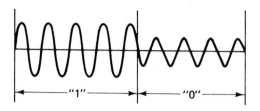

(a) Amplitude Modulation

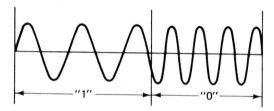

(b) Frequency Modulation

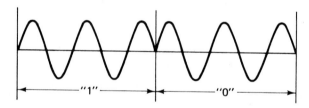

(c) Phase Modulation

Figure 4–8.   Modulation techniques.

itself due to transmission power problems and sensitivity to distortion. However, it is commonly used with phase modulation to yield a method superior to either FM or AM. This technique will be explained shortly.

Frequency modulation.   Figure 4–8(b) illustrates frequency modulation (FM). This method changes the frequency of the carrier in accordance with the digital bit stream. The amplitude and phase are held constant. In its simplest form, a binary 1 is represented by a certain frequency and a binary 0 by another.

Several variations of FM modems are available. One approach is the frequency shift key (FSK) modem using four frequencies within the 3-kHz telephone line bandwidth (see Figure 4–9). The FSK modem transmits 1,070- and 1,270-Hz signals to represent a binary 0 (space) and binary 1 (mark), respectively. It receives 2,025- and 2,225-Hz signals as a binary 0 (space) and binary 1 (mark).

The FSK modem can operate with a full-duplex data flow on half-duplex (two-

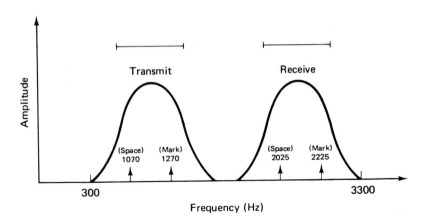

Figure 4-9. Frequency shift key modulation.

wire) or full-duplex (four-wire) facilities. The four frequencies permit the simultaneous sending and receiving of data within two channels. One channel is within the 300- to 1,700-Hz bandwidth and the other is within 1,700 to 3,000 Hz. FSK modems are typically asynchronous low-speed machines. Some full-duplex, dial-up personal computers utilize the FSK asynchronous modem. Others typically employ some form of phase modulation (in combination with AM), which has become the preferred method for modulation.

   Phase modulation.   Previous discussions of the sine wave described how a cycle is represented with degree markings to indicate the point to which the oscillating wave has advanced in its cycle. Phase modulation (PM) modems interrupt the continuous wave form and alter the phase of the signal to represent a 1 or 0 [see Figure 4–8(c)]. The common approach today is to compare the phase of the cycle in a current time period to the phase in a previous time period. This approach is called *differential phase shift keying* (DPSK).

Multilevel Transmission

At this point in our discussion, the reader may assume that the bit rate (bit/s) of a modem is comparable to the baud (recall that baud is the rate of signal change on the line). In low-speed modems (almost obsolete today), the baud is usually the same as the bit rate. To increase the bit rate across the limited bandwidth of the telephone channel, modem manufacturers frequently employ methods to represent more than 1 bit per baud. This technique is called *multilevel transmission*.

   Multilevel transmission partially solves the problem of the short bit times that result from the high baud. A bit rate of 9,600 bit/s requires a signal change every 104 μs (1 sec/9,600 = 0.000104). This short time is often insufficient for the modem to detect and interpret the data stream. However, multilevel modems can use a modulation rate of 1,200 baud and, by representing 2 bits per baud, achieve a 2,400 bit rate. Thus, multilevel modems achieve a higher bit rate per baud. The process is illustrated in Figure 4–10.

A common form of multilevel transmission is quadrature amplitude modulation (QAM). The QAM modem creates one of eight (or more) possible different bit conditions per baud by combining two AM levels with four PM changes. For example, the eight-level scheme allows 3 binary bits to be transmitted ($2^3 = 8$) with each baud. See Figure 4–10(a).

Practically speaking, limitations exist on how many times the signal can be divided and remain detectable at the receiving modem. While the lower baud provides more time for detection and interpretation, smaller increments in the differences between signal states make accurate data recovery more difficult. Moreover, a noise spike (or other imperfection) on a line with multilevel transmission will distort more bits than with a single-level modulation scheme. Although multilevel transmission leads to more complex and costly modems, the technique is effective and widely used.

Another way to view multilevel modulation is through its *constellation*, which depicts the various amplitude and phase combinations of a modem signal. Figure 4–10(b) shows the constellations of V.22*bis*, V.26*ter*, the Bell 208, and V.32 modems. The phase change is represented by a rotating vector moving from a point on a quadrant to another point. Figure 4–10(b) shows the V.22*bis* vector moving 90° (from point 2 to point 3). Also, the length of the vector represents the amplitude of the signal. In Figure 4–10(b), the V.22*bis* 90° phase change can be combined with an increase in amplitude from one level to another (from point 1 to point 2).

V.22*bis* provides a complex signal of 3 amplitude and 12 phase changes. Modems using V.22*bis* can operate at 2.4 kbit/s, full duplex on two-wire dial-up lines. V.22*bis* uses the split-stream technique discussed earlier.

V.26*ter* uses a very simple modulation scheme of four phase changes; yet it can achieve 2.4 kbit/s by a technique called *bandwidth sharing*. With this approach, a modem uses echo cancellation to cancel out the effects of its own transmission. Thus, the shared bandwidth means the modem uses only the signal from the other modem. The V.26*ter* modulation method provides a less error prone signal than V.22*bis*.

Other Modems

The short-haul or limited-distance modem (LDM) is used for transmissions of a few feet to approximately 20 miles. The distance is highly variable and depends on the operating speed, type of transmission path, and configuration of the telephone company facilities. Typical LDMs use wire pairs or coaxial cables, and some can operate at higher data rates (19.2 kbit/s to 1 Mbit/s.). The use of the short-haul modem requires the removal of certain analog equipment on the telephone line. These machines are attractive due to their simplicity and low cost. Dedicated circuits are required.

Line drivers are dc machines used to eliminate modems. Operating distances range from a few feet to several miles. The line driver is usually placed between two computer-related devices and replaces two modems (on short distances). These machines are also

Bit Combinations

$000 = A_1\phi_1$
$001 = A_2\phi_1$
$010 = A_1\phi_2$
$011 = A_2\phi_2$
$100 = A_1\phi_3$
$101 = A_2\phi_3$
$110 = A_1\phi_4$
$111 = A_2\phi_4$

Phase and Amplitude Signals

$\phi_1 = 0°$ Phase Shift
$\phi_2 = 90°$ Phase Shift — 4 Phases
$\phi_3 = 180°$ Phase Shift
$\phi_4 = 270°$ Phase Shift

A_1 = Low Amplitude
A_2 = High Amplitude — 2 Amplitudes

Combined Signals

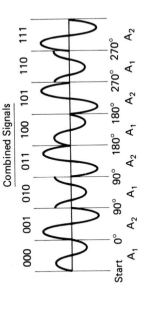

| | 000 | 001 | 010 | 011 | 100 | 101 | 110 | 111 |

Start | 0° | 90° | 90° | 180° | 180° | 270° | 270° |
A_1 | A_2 | A_1 | A_2 | A_1 | A_2 | A_1 | A_2

(a) Quadrature Amplitude Modulation

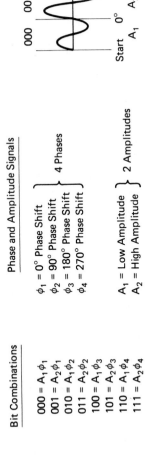

V.22 bis
(3 Amplitudes, 12 Phases)

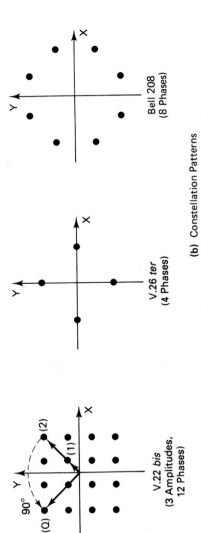

V.26 ter
(4 Phases)

Bell 208
(8 Phases)

V.32
(QAM or TCM)

(b) Constellation Patterns

Figure 4-10. Multilevel modulation.

Black 4.10

attractive due to their very low price. Typical distances and speeds for line drivers are as follows:

Speed (kbit/s)	Distance (ft)
1.2	25,000
2.4	17,500
4.8	12,500
7.2	10,250
9.6	8,800
19.2	6,300
38.4	4,450
50.0	3,870
56.0	3,675
72.0	3,200

A null modem is actually an EIA-232-D cable interface (discussed shortly) pinned to allow a direct connection between two devices when a modem is not required. Null modems provide no timing signals; consequently, they are used with asynchronous devices that derive their timing from start/stop bits.

A modem eliminator is used in situations where two synchronous devices (such as terminals, printers, plotters) are close together. The modem eliminator provides the interface and clocking for the devices.

Some people do not distinguish between a null modem and a modem eliminator. This writer uses the terms *null modem* as an interface for asynchronous devices and *modem eliminator* as an interface for synchronous devices. The exact use of the terms is somewhat irrelevant as long as the conversing parties use the same term to describe the same device.

Many other modemlike devices are available in the marketplace. Practically any device can now be manufactured for a user's specific needs.

Advances in Modems

Modem technology has improved dramatically in the past few years. Perhaps nowhere is this progress more evident than in the technology implemented in new modems called *trellis-coded modulation* (TCM).

Trellis is a forward-error correction process that can reduce errors on a typical telephone line by three orders of magnitude (e.g., from $1:10^3$ to $1:10^6$). The effect on throughput is remarkable. Previous discussions on the multilevel modems noted that the closer together the carrier signal states, the more the signal was distorted by noise. The close proximity of the constellation points makes it more difficult for the receiver to interpret them accurately. Such is not the case with a trellis-coded modem.

The scheme is based on the transmission of additional bits, which are calculated using the message bits. For example, each 6 user bits have two of those bits input into an encoder. The encoder produces 3 bits as its output. Thus, the user data stream carries 1 trellis bit for every 6 user bits.

The encoder provides for eight possible combinations (which are called states; $2^3 = 8$). However, the rules allow a transition from a given state to only one of four other states. A 7-bit trellis modem uses $2^7 = 128$ constellation points, which brings the points even closer together than a V.32 QAM modem [see Figure 4–10(b)]. However, only certain signal points (states) are valid.

The transmitted signal will likely be distorted and may arrive at the receiving modem with an invalid sequence of signal points *relative* to *previous* signal states. A conventional modem would interpret the signal erroneously. The receiving TCM modem discards spurious states and then selects the most logical and valid sequence closest to the one received. In other words, the receiver "guesses" the closest valid sequence (state). Chapter 5 provides more detailed information on this valuable technique.

Interface Standards

The Bell System, CCITT, the EIA, the computer industry, and other modem vendors have developed several standards defining how to interface the modems (the data circuit-terminating equipment, DCE) with the terminals or computers (the data terminal equipment, DTE). Acceptance of the standards has been instrumental in the ability to use equipment from different vendors.

EIA-232-D.   EIA sponsors the EIA-232-D standard, which is used extensively in North America. The CCITT publishes comparable standards. V.28 describes the electrical characteristics of the interface and V.24 describes the circuits' functions. Figure 4–11 defines the circuits of EIA-232-D. These circuits are actually 25-pin connections and sockets. The terminal pins plug into the modem sockets. All the circuits are rarely used; most devices utilize 12 or fewer pins.

The circuits perform one of four functions:

1. Data transfer across the interface
2. Control of signals across interface
3. Clocking signals to synchronize data flow and regulate the bit rate
4. Electrical ground

The functional descriptions of the circuits are listed next. The reader should be aware that several options exist on how to use some of these circuits. Each vendor's offering should be examined carefully.

> *Circuit AA Protective Ground:* Conductor is electrically bonded to equipment frame.
> *Circuit AB Signal to Ground:* Common ground for all circuits. This circuit has nothing to do with ground but is used as a voltage reference for the other circuits.

Pin No.	CCITT Equiv.	Circuit	Direction	Description	Interface Type													
					A	B	C	D	E	F	G	H	I	J	K	L	M	Z
1	101	AA	Both	Protective Ground	x	-	-	-	-	-	-	-	-	-	-	-	-	-
7	102	AB	Both	Signal Ground	x	x	x	x	x	x	x	x	x	x	x	x	x	x
2	103	BA	To-m	Transmitted Data	x	x		x	x	x	x	x		x		x	x	p
3	104	BB	To-T	Received Data			x	x	x	x	x	x	x	x	x	x	x	p
4	105	CA	To-m	Request to Send	x	x	x	x	x	x				x		x		p
5	106	CB	To-T	Clear to Send	x	x	x	x	x	x	x	x		x		x	x	p
6	107	CC	To-T	Data Set Ready	x	x	x	x	x	x	x	x	x	x	x	x	x	p
20	108.2	CD	To-m	Data Terminal Ready	d	d	d	d	d	d	d	d	d	d	d	d	d	p
22	125	CE	To-T	Ring Indicator	d	d	d	d	d	d	d	d	d	d	d	d	d	p
8	109	CF	To-T	Received Line Signal Detector	x	x	x	x	x	d	x	x	x	x	x	d	d	p
21	110	CG	To-T	Signal Quality Detector														p
23	111	CH/CI	Either	Data Signaling Rate Selector/Indicator							x							p
24	113	DA	To-m	Transmitter Signal Element Timing (DT/DCE)	s	s	s	s	s	s	s	s		s	s	s	s	p
15	114	DB	To-T		s	s	s	s	s	s	s	s		s	s	s	s	p
17	115	DD	To-T	Receiver Signal Element Timing (DCE)		s	s	s			s	s	s	s	s	s	s	p
14	118	SBA	To-m	Secondary Transmitted Data		s	s	s	s	s	x	x	x	x	x	x	x	p

Figure 4-11. EIA-232-D.

16	119	SBB	To-T	Secondary Received Data		x		x	x	x	x	p
19	120	SCA	To-m	Secondary Request to Send			x	x	x	x	x	p
13	121	SCB	To-T	Secondary Clear to Send		x		x	x	x	x	p
12	122	SCF	To-T	Secondary Received Line Signal Detector		x		x	x	x	x	p

Legend:

p To be specified by the supplier

- Optional

d Additional Interchange Circuits required for Switched Service

s Additional Interchange Circuits required for Synchronous Channel

x Basic Interchange Circuits, All Systems

m modem

T term

PIN Number 9 & 10 usually reserved for Modem testing

PIN Numbers 11/18/25 unassigned

Key to Columns:

A Transmit Only

B Transmit Only*

C Receive Only

D Full-Duplex* Half-Duplex

E Full-Duplex

F Primary Channel Transmit Only*/Secondary Channel Receive Only

G Primary Channel Receive Only/Secondary Channel Transmit Only*

H Primary Channel Transmit Only/Secondary Channel Receive Only

Key to Columns (Cont'd):

I Primary Channel Receive Only/Secondary Channel Transmit Only

J Primary Channel Transmit Only*/Half-Duplex Secondary Channel

K Primary Channel Receive Only/Half-Duplex Secondary Channel

L Full-Duplex Primary Channel*/Full-Duplex Secondary Channel* Half-Duplex Primary Channel/Half-Duplex Secondary Channel

M Full-Duplex Primary Channel/Full-Duplex Secondary Channel

Z Special (Circuits specified by Supplier)

*Indicates the inclusion of Circuit CA (Request to Send) in a One-Way Only (Transmit) or Full-Duplex Configuration where it might ordinarily not be expected, but where it might be used to indicate a nontransmit mode to the data communication equipment to permit it to remove a line signal or to send synchronizing or training signals as required.

Figure 4-11. EIA-232-D (*cont.*).

Circuit BA Transmitted Data: Data signals transmitted from DTE to DCE. This represents the user data. Data cannot be transmitted unless circuits CA, CB, CC, and CD are all activated.

Circuit BB Received Data: User data signals transmitted from DCE to DTE.

Circuits CA Request to Send: Signal from DTE to DCE. This circuit notifies DCE that the terminal or computer has data to transmit. Circuit CA is also used on half-duplex lines to control the direction of data transmission. The transition of off to on notifies the DCE to take any necessary action to prepare for the transmission. For example, in a polled environment, the Request to Send signal would initiate the sending of a carrier signal to the remote modem. The transition from on to off notifies the DCE that the DTE has completed its transmission.

Circuit CB Clear to Send: Signal from DCE indicating the DTE can transmit the data. The Clear to Send signal may be turned on after receiving a carrier signal from the remote modem. The use of CB varies from modem to modem and is used differently on half-duplex and full-duplex circuits.

Circuit CC Data Set Ready: Signal from DCE indicating the machine is (1) on hook (connected to channel on a switched line), (2) DCE is in data transmit mode (not test, voice, etc.), (3) DCE has completed timing functions and answer tones.

Circuit CD Data Terminal Ready: Signal from DTE indicating terminal or computer is powered up, has no detectable malfunction, and is not in test mode. Generally, CD is ON if it is ready to transmit or receive data. In a switched arrangement, a ring from the remote site will normally activate CD.

Circuit CE Ring Indicator: Signal from DCE indicates that a ringing signal is being received on a switched channel.

Circuit CF Receive Line Signal Detector: Signal from DCE indicating the DCE has detected the remote modem's carrier signal.

Circuit CG Signal Quality Detector: Signal from DCE to indicate that the received signal is of sufficient quality to believe no error has occurred.

Circuits CH and CI Data Signaling Rate Selector/Indicator: Signals from DTE and DCE, respectively, to indicate the data signaling rate for dual-rate machines. Some devices have the capability to transmit varying bit rates.

Circuit DA Transmitter Signal Element Timing: Signals from DTE to provide timing of the data signals being transmitted on circuit BA (Transmitted Data) to the DCE. The mark and space elements are indicated by this circuit. (See Chapter 2 for a description of mark and space.) DTE provides this signal; if the DCE provides timing, then circuit DB is used.

Circuit DB Transmitter Signal Element Timing: Signals from DCE to provide timing of the data signals being transmitted on circuit BA (Transmitted Data) to the DCE. Again, as in circuit DA, the mark and space elements are indicated by circuit DB. DCE provides this signal; if the DTE provides the timing, then circuit DA is used.

Circuit DD Receiver Signal Element Timing: Signals from DCE to provide timing to DTE of the data signals being received on circuit BB (Received Data).

In addition to these circuits, EIA-232-D defines five other circuits designated as secondary channels: SCA, SCB, SCF, SBA, and SBB. These pins can be used to implement the side channel modem transmission scheme described earlier in the chapter. The remaining circuits are used for testing and other vendor-specific functions.

The data flow across the EIA-232-D interface is illustrated in Figure 4–12. The use of half-duplex/full-duplex, leased line/switched line, or side channels determine the sequence and order of the activation of the circuits. This illustration depicts a half-duplex, private line configuration.

EIA-449. The EIA also publishes EIA-449, a significant improvement over EIA-232-D. The latter standard has several electrical specifications that limit its effectiveness. For instance, EIA-232-D is limited to 20 Kbit/s and recommends short distance cables

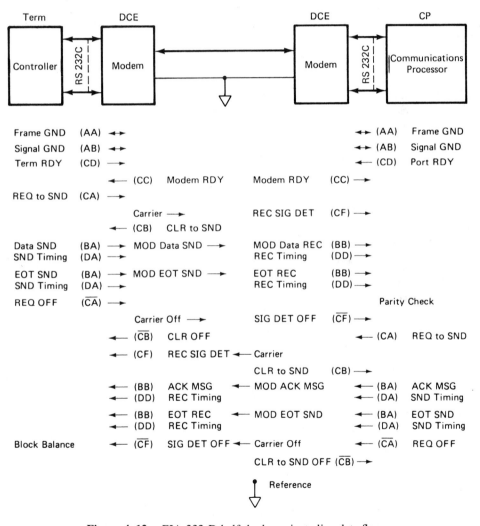

Figure 4–12. EIA-232-D half-duplex private line data flow.

between the components. It also presents a noisy electrical signal. EIA-449 provides 37 basic circuits with 10 additional circuits and other testing maintenance loops. It is compatible with recent CCITT and ISO standards. In addition, the EIA-449 specification establishes a bit rate of 2 Mbit/s and a greater distance between the machines (see Figure 4–13).

The additional 10 circuits are defined as follows:

Circuit SC Send Common: Connected to DTE to serve as a reference voltage for unbalanced receivers.

Circuit RC Receive Common: Connected to DCE to serve as a reference voltage at DTE for unbalanced receivers.

Circuit IS Terminal in Service: Signal to indicate if DTA is available. This prevents an incoming call from being connected to the DCE when DTE is busy. If DTE is out of service, this signal can make a port busy during a rotary hunt to that machine.

Circuit NS New Signal: Signal to alert master stations in a multipoint network when a new signal is about to begin. Signal is from DTE to DCE. Used to improve response time in multipoint polling networks.

Circuit SF Select Frequency: Signal used to select the transmit and receive frequencies of the DCE. Used in a multipoint circuit where the stations have equal status.

Circuit LL Local Loopback: Signal to check the local DTE/DCE interface. The signal also checks the transmit and receive circuitry of the local DCE.

Circuit RL Remote Loopback: Signal to check both directions through the common carrier path and through the remote DCE up to the remote DCE/DTE interface.

Circuit TM Test Mode: Signal from DCE to DTE that DCE is in test condition (conditions LL or RL).

Circuit SS Select Standby: Signal used to increase reliability by switching to a backup channel or to allow switching between alternate applications' transmissions.

Circuit SB Standby Indicator: Signal indicates whether DCE is set up to operate with the SC (select standby) circuit.

EIA-449 also provides standards to support the transition away from EIA-232-D. EIA has specified adapter configurations between EIA-232-D and EIA-449. The adapters are meant to be temporary until the EIA-232-D functions are replaced. Figure 4–14 illustrates the adapter configurations.

Several years ago, many people predicted that EIA-449 would replace EIA-232-D, and applications requiring more speed or a greater number of pins have migrated to EIA-449 and its companion high speed interface, EIA-422. However, EIA-449 and EIA-422 are still limited in use for a number of reasons:

- Previous commitment to and investment in EIA-232-D
- Larger pin connector is difficult to fit onto small machines

Circuit Name	MNEM	CAT	PIN No.	Circ. Class	Circuit Direct.	Usage Opt.	Nearest RS232 Equivalent
Signal Ground	SG	II	19	G	—	M	Signal Ground
*Send Common	SC	II	37	G	To DCE	M	—
*Receive Common	RC	II	20	G	From DCE	M	—
*Terminal in Service	IS	II	28	C	To DCE	O	—
Incoming Call	IC	II	15	C	From DCE	A	Ring Indication
Terminal Ready	TR	I	12,30	C	To DCE	S	Data Terminal Ready
Data Mode	DM	I	11,29	C	From DCE	M	Data Set Ready
Send Data	SD	I	4,22	D	To DCE	M	Transmitted Data
Receive Data	RD	I	6,24	D	From DCE	M	Received Data
Terminal Timing	TT	I	17,35	T	To DCE	O	Xmit Sig Element DCE
Send Timing	ST	I	5,23	T	From DCE	T	Xmit Sig. El Tim DTE
Receive Timing	RT	I	8,26	T	From DCE	T	Rec. Sig. El Timing
Request to Send	RS	I	7,25	C	To DCE	M	Request to sent
Clear to Send	CS	I	9,27	C	From DCE	M	Clear to send
Receiver Ready	RR	I	13,31	C	From DCE	M	Carrier Detect
Signal Quality	SQ	II	33	C	From DCE	O	Signal Quality Det.
*New Signal	NS	II	34	C	To DCE	O	—
*Select Frequency	SF	II	16	C	To DCE	O	—
Sig. Rate Selector	SR	II	16	C	To DCE	O	Data Sig Rate Select
Sig. Rate Indication	SI	II	2	C	From DCE	O	Data Sig Rate Select
*Local Loopback	LL	II	10	C	To DCE	O	—
*Remote Loopback	RL	II	14	C	To DCE	O	—
*Test Mode	TM	II	18	C	From DCE	M	—
*Select Standby	SS	II	32	C	To DCE	O	—
*Standby Indicator	SB	II	36	C	From DCE	O	—
Shield	—	II	1	G	—	O	—
Spares	—	II	3,21	—	—	O	—

Figure 4–13. EIA-449.

(a) circuits on the 37-pin main connector

Name			Pin		Class	Direction		Full Name
Signal Ground	SG	=	5	=	G	—	O	Signal Ground
Send Common	SC	=	9	=	G	To DCE	O	—
Receive Common	RC	=	6	=	G	From DCE	O	—
Sec. Send Data	SSD	=	3	=	D	To DCE	O	Secondary Transmit Data
Sec. Req. to Send	SRS	=	7	=	C	To DCE	O	Secondary Request to Send
Sec. Clear to Send	SCS	=	8	=	C	From DCE	O	Secondary Clear to Send
Sec. Rec. Ready	SRR	=	2	=	C	From DCE	O	Secondary Rec. Line Signal
Shield	—	=	1	=	G	—	O	—

(b) circuits on the 9-pin optional connector

Legend and Notes:

Circuit Classifications:
G = Ground or Common
D = Data
C = Control
T = Test

Circuit Category
I = Category I 20,000BPS
II = Category II 20,000BPS

Usage Options
M = Mandatory for all two-way communications channels
S = Additional circuits required for all switched channel
A = Additional circuits required for all switched channel with answering signaled across the interface.
T = Additional circuits required for synchronous primary channel
O = Optional circuits.

Other:
• = New circuits not contained in RS232 Standard

Figure 4–13. EIA-449 (*cont.*).

76

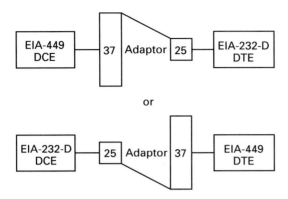

Figure 4–14. RS449 adaptor.

- Many applications do not need more speed and more channels
- Increased expense of EIA-232-D
- Recognition that another interface standard was being developed by CCITT for the ISDN (Integrated Services Digital Network)
- Forthcoming improvements to EIA-232-D with EIA-530

The reader can obtain more detailed information on these standards by writing to the Electronics Industry Association, Standards Sales Office, 2001 Eye Street NW, Washington, DC 20006. The EIA has several documents that provide very useful information on the DTE and DCE interface.

The Modem Market

Modem suppliers include hundreds of different models and types. It is estimated that the United States has over 5 million modems installed, but that the installation base will decline in the 1990s as users migrate to end-to-end digital networks.

Table 4–1 lists the more common EIA recommended interfaces and their counterparts from other organizations (if any). Table 4–2 lists the widely used Bell/AT&T modems and their CCITT equivalents. The Bell/AT&T modems are not always exactly equivalent to the CCITT specifications. For example, the Bell 103, 113, and 202 modems use different carrier frequencies from their CCITT counterparts.

The following list contains the major features available in modems today. The reader should be aware that the market is quite diverse; many variations of the features are available.

- Speed in bit/s (and multiple speeds)
- Leased line or dial-up
- Diagnostic capabilities
- Electrical interface types (EIA-232-D, etc.)
- Type (line driver, coupler, etc.)

TABLE 4–1 EIA AND RELATED STANDARDS

Series	Description	Related Standards
RS232-C	Interface between data terminal equipment and data communication equipment employing serial binary data interchange	CCITT V.24, V.28; ISO 2110
RS269-B	Synchronous signaling rates for data transmission	CCITT V.5, V.6, X.1; ANSI X3.1; FED-STD 1013; FIPS 22-1
RS334-A	Signal quality at interface between data terminal equipment and synchronous data communication equipment for serial data transmission	ANSI X3.24
RS363	Standard for specifying signal quality for transmitting and receiving data-processing terminal equipments using serial data transmission at the interface with nonsynchronous data communication equipment	None
RS366-A	Interface between data terminal equipment and automatic calling equipment for data communication	CCITT V.25
RS404	Standard for start–stop signal quality between data terminal equipment and nonsynchronous data communication equipment	None
RS410	Standard for the electrical characteristics of class A closure interchange circuits	None
RS422-A	Electrical characteristics of balanced voltage digital interface circuits	CCITT V.11, X.27; FED-STD 1020A
RS423-A	Electrical characteristics of unbalanced voltage digital interface circuits	CCITT V.10, X.26; FED-STD 1030A
RS449	General-purpose 37- and 9-position interface for data terminal equipment and data circuit-terminating equipment employing serial binary data interchange	CCITT V.24, V.54, X.21bis

TABLE 4-2 CCITT AND BELL/AT&T MODEM TYPES

Modem Type	CCITT Standard	Transmission Mode	Circuit Type	Sync/Async	Type of Modulation	Speed (bit/s)
103J/113D	V.21	FDX	2-W/Dial	Async	FSK	300
202S	V.23	HDX	2-W/Dial	Async	FSK	1200
202T	V.23	FDX	4-W/Leased	Async	FSK	1200
212A	V.22	FDX	2-W/Dial	Async or Sync	FSK 2PSK	300 1200
201C	V.26bis	FDX	2-W/4-W Dial/Leased	Sync	4PSK	2400
201B	V.26	FDX	4-W/Leased	Sync	4PSK	2400
208A	V.27bis	FDX	4-W/Leased	Sync	8PSK	4800
208B	V.27ter	FDX	2-W/Dial	Sync	8PSK	4800
209	V.29	FDX	4-W/Leased	Sync	16QAM	9600

79

- Bell and CCITT compatible
- Asynchronous or synchronous
- Voice/data
- Reverse channel
- Loopbacks
- Point to point, multipoint, or piggyback
- Automatic answer
- Modulation type (phase, frequency)
- Multilevel transmission
- Baud
- Half-duplex or duplex
- Line conditioning
- Distance of transmission

Summary of Modem Operations

Modems are the prevalent component used to interface user devices with the communications link. Modems are designed to modulate digital signals over an analog carrier and to demodulate the signal at the other end. In the past, the Bell modems were the de facto standards in North America and some other parts of the world. Today, the EIA DTE/DCE interface specifications and the CCITT V series modems have become the accepted standards throughout the industry.

SWITCHING

Modern-day networks consist of many components such as terminals and computers spread throughout buildings, cities, states, and nations. Many networks have hundreds of elements that, at any given time, must be able to establish a session and path with one another. It is obvious that a component cannot have a direct (point-to-point) connection to every other component. For example, a relatively small network of 500 components would require 124,750 individual interconnections [$n(n-1)/2$], where n is the number of components to be interconnected.

One solution to this problem is to place switches on the transmission path (as in Figure 4–15). The sites are not interconnected directly but effect the transmission first through a switch or switches and then to the receiving terminal, or computer. In Figure 4–15, site C communicates with site L by sending its transmission to the switch; the transmission contains an address in a message header. In the case of a telephone network, the telephone number acts as the address. The switch uses the address to determine which path to use to deliver the transmission. The switch substantially reduces the number of interconnection paths.

Figure 4–15 also depicts a hierarchical switching arrangement. Site N provides switching facilities for sites O, P, Q, and R; N transmits to switch S only for traffic

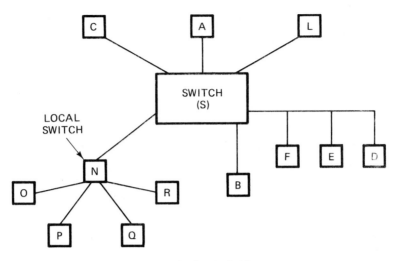

Figure 4–15. Switching.

needs outside its switching domain. Most switches also provide for the sharing of the path by multiple sites. For example, sites D, E, and F share one of the paths through a multidrop arrangement.

Circuit Switching

Circuit switching was designed initially as a direct electrical connection between two components. The telephone network is an example of circuit switching. The direct connection served as an open "pipeline," permitting the two end users to utilize the facility as they see fit—within bandwidth and tariff limitations. The hierarchical aspect of telephone switching and routing has been replaced in many parts of the world by a non-hierarchical system.

Crosspoints and staging.   Circuit switching is arranged in one or a combination of three architectures: (a) concentration (more input lines than output lines), (b) expansion (more output lines than input lines), and (c) connection (an equal number of input and output lines). In its simplest form, a circuit switch is an N × M array of lines that connect to each other at crosspoints (see Figure 4–16). In a large switching office, the N lines are input from the subscriber (terminals, computers, etc.) and the M lines are output to other switching offices.

Circuit switching is usually performed in more than one array or stage in order to reduce the number of crosspoints. If N lines are to be connected as in Figure 4–17, N^2 crosspoints are required. Clos demonstrated that multistaging switches are economical for networks when N > 16. Multistage networks are designed with fewer crosspoints, yielding a more economical arrangement. However, this approach usually allows for the blocking of a call. It is prohibitively expensive to implement a switch that handles *all*

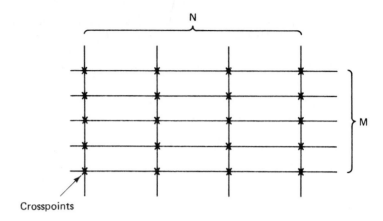

Figure 4-16. Crosspoints in a circuit switch.

calls. The telephone office uses several stages, and the path is selected through the switches to reduce the probability of a blocked call.

Circuit switching provides a path *only* for the sessions between data communications components. Error checking, session establishment, message flow control, mes-

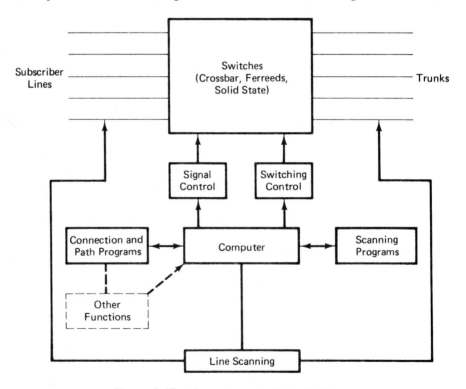

Figure 4-17. Computer-controlled switching.

sage formating, selection of codes, and protocols are the responsibility of the users. Little or no care of message traffic is provided in the circuit-switching arrangement. Consequently, the telephone network is often used as the basic foundation for a data communications network, and additional facilities are added by the value-added carrier, network vendor, or user organization. Subsequent examples of other switching technologies (for example, message and packet) often use circuit switching and then provide additional functions and facilities.

Circuit switching today is performed through time-division multiplexing (TDM) techniques. With this approach, a user is not provided direct connections through the network. Rather, slots of digitized voice traffic are sent through the network by exchanging the slots through the memory elements of the computer switch. TDM supports voice traffic well, because it guarantees the availability of the slots for each voice conversation. This requirement is essential, since digitized voice traffic cannot afford the variable delay that is found in some systems used with ''bursty'' data transmissions. We return to this subject later in the book when digital networks are examined.

Early switches.   Late-night movies provide a nostalgic example of an earlier form of circuit switching—the telephone switchboard operator. The operator, after requesting and receiving the number from the caller, plugged the proper cords and jacks into the switchboard to provide the direct connection. If the call were destined for a location outside the plugboard, the call would be routed to another switchboard operator. In this manner, the call would be switched through the network to the final destination.

The manual switchboard was largely replaced by the automatic exchange, a step-by-step switch called the Strowger switch. This technique operates on each dialed number by adjusting an electromechanical device to connect an incoming line to an outgoing line. The dialed number determines the physical position of one contact on a possible interface to one of 100 contacts or outgoing circuits. Each number moves the switch in a step-by-step fashion until the desired outgoing line is found. If the line is free, the caller is connected; if not, a busy signal is returned to the caller.

The Strowger switch is quite slow and subject to considerable electrical noise. The crossbar switch provided improvements over the Strowger switch and largely replaced the older technology. It also connects input lines to output lines but uses electromagnets to open or close vertical and horizontal bars to establish the physical connection.

The next major advance in circuit switching came with the introduction of common control. This technique avoids the time-consuming and cumbersome serial step-by-step process by first storing the dialed number and then using it to set up the circuit. Common control allows for more efficient use of switching logic and provides increased flexibility in altering telephone numbers.

Computer-controlled switching.   More recently, the computer has been used extensively to control circuit switches. The telephone companies and private branch exchange (PBX) manufacturers are replacing older systems with computer-controlled systems. For example, the electronic switching system (ESS) uses the computer to scan the lines through sensing devices that detect the on-hook or off-hook condition (see

Figure 4–17). The scanning information is read and stored by the computer, and the appropriate logic is executed to handle any changes in the status of the line.

Upon detecting that a line is off hook, the computer sends a dial tone to the subscribing instrument through the signaling modules. (The signaling module is used for other control signals such as ringing and busy.) The dialed number is received; connection and path analysis determines which trunk should be used to establish the required connection. Thereafter, the call is switched through the network hierarchy, eventually resulting in the receiving end office placing a ringing signal onto the receiving subscriber's line.

Computer-controlled circuit switching is distinguished by the following characteristics:

- Real-time data transmission is provided by the direct connection.
- Dial-up delay can be eliminated by the use of leased lines.
- User must provide all data communications functions such as message flow control and session establishments.
- Blockage can occur, in which case a busy signal is returned to sender.
- Transmissions are point to point.
- Once connection is established, any subsequent overload of the switch is invisible to the connected components.

Message Switching

Message switching is designed specifically for data traffic. As in circuit switching, the communications lines are connected to a switching facility, but the end users do not have a direct physical connection. Rather, the data message is transmitted to the switch, where it is stored on a queue for later delivery. The term *store-and-forward* is associated with message-switching networks.

Early message-switching networks, consisting of input messages to the "switch," were transcribed onto perforated paper tape. The tape messages were taken from one machine by an operator and manually carried to another machine for relay (switching) to an intermediate or final destination. In the 1960s, the author worked in a paper tape switching center aboard a U.S. Navy communications ship. During peak traffic periods, the backlog and queues of messages were almost overwhelming to the operators and managers. In one instance, the Gulf of Tonkin incident created a traffic backlog so immense that lower-priority messages were stored for days. Moreover, the manual handling of the paper tapes created inordinate delays and many errors.

Computers are now used for message switching. The messages are stored on disks. The computer programs read the incoming message header, decode the destination address, and route the message onto the proper communication line.

Computer-controlled message switching is distinguished by the following characteristics:

- Connection is not a direct, physical interface as in circuit switching.
- Data connections use variable slots if TDM is employed in contrast to circuit-switching systems where the TDM slots are guaranteed and predictable.
- Since the messages are stored onto a disk, tape, or drum device before transmission, real-time processing is usually not feasible.
- Storage of messages allows for adjustments to peak traffic periods. Lower-priority messages are queued for later transmission.
- The message switch usually provides for code and protocol conversions between different types of computers or terminals.
- Multiple line speeds are accommodated.
- Messages can be broadcast to all nodes in the network or a subset of nodes.
- The switch provides for care of message traffic; error checking, logging, and recovery procedures are part of the system capabilities.
- Priorities are allowed in the message traffic. The message switch can process higher-priority messages before lower-priority traffic.

While message switches provide for considerable flexibility, they do have some significant disadvantages because their centralized topology makes them subject to bottleneck and reliability problems. Consequently, today's modern data communications networks generally do not employ message switches in the network. The message switches may be connected to the network to perform store-and-forward services, electronic mail, or other applications.

Packet Switching

If one examines certain features of circuit and message switching, it becomes obvious that a combination of the two techniques provides a powerful tool for data communications: the low-delay mode of circuit switching and the routing power of message switching. Packet switching is intended to provide for low-delay processing and switching of data messages between computers or between terminals and computers. It was designed to provide optimum utilization of fixed long-distance circuits.

Packet switching is so named because a user's logical message is separated (disassembled) and transmitted in multiple packets. The packet contains user data and control data, all of which are switched as a composite whole. Each packet of the user data contains its own control and identification. The addressed packets occupy a transmission channel (or line) for the duration of the transmission only; the line is then made available for other users, terminals, or computers. The idea of the packet is to limit the packet size so that it does not occupy the line for extended periods. Moreover, packet switching supports user traffic based on demand and variable slots (variable-sized packets) are used to accommodate different types of user traffic loads. This approach works quite well for data transmissions in which transmissions are often bursty and of variable length. The technique is less suited to applications that require constant and predictable slots such as voice and video transmissions.

Instead of dedicating a port to one user, the system interleaves the bursts of traffic from multiple users across one port. The user perceives a dedicated port is being used when actually the user terminal or program is sharing a port with other users.

The major goals of packet switching are:

- To provide for statistical multiplexing capabilities of the channel and the port
- To smooth the asymmetrical traffic among multiple users
- To provide for fast response time to all users of the facility
- To provide for high availability of the network to all users
- To provide for distribution of risks and sharing of resources

When and When Not to Use Packet Switching

How does an organization know when to use or not to use packet-switching systems? With the preceding discussion in mind, one way to address this question is to compare the following four alternatives for connecting DTEs:

Public telephone dial-up system

Private, nonswitched channels

Public packet networks

Private packet networks

Organizations with relatively low data-transfer rates benefit from using public dial-up lines. If sessions between DTEs are short and the connections between the DTEs are local, the dial-up approach makes good sense if the user does not mind the dial-up delay and an occasional busy signal. Since dial-up charges are based on time and distance, infrequent and short-distance transmission favor the use of the public telephone system.

Private leased lines are used by organizations that experience heavy, constant traffic and/or cannot tolerate the delays of dial-up. The organization can use the permanently connected leased lines continuously. Moreover, companies that establish multidrop connections on their private channels usually benefit from using the leased channel option because the multidrops permit a more effective sharing of the channel.

Public packet networks (several of which are discussed in this chapter) are sometimes called value-added carriers (VACs) because they provide value-added services to their customers. For example, VACs lease lines from the telephone carrier, add packet switches and protocol converters to the lines, and sell the service to any customer willing to pay the fees. Organizations with low to medium traffic volumes can usually benefit from subscribing to a public packet network. Also, for organizations that are spread out over a large geographic area, the public packet network may be better economically, since most of the public packet carriers charge primarily on volume of traffic, not on the distance between user stations.

Many organizations have established private packet networks or private circuit-switched systems. There are several reasons for private systems. For medium to high traffic volumes, private networks are more cost-effective than dedicated private lines.

The reader should be aware that changing carrier offerings and tariffs require a careful analysis of the options vis-à-vis a company's needs. Moreover, the value-added aspects of packet networks could alter a user organization's decisions to favor a packet switching alternative.

Packet-swtiched networks switch user traffic based on a variety of criteria, generally referred to as *cost metrics* or *least-cost routing*. The name does not mean that routing is based solely on obtaining the least-cost route in the literal sense.

- Capacity of the link
- Number of packets awaiting transmission onto the link
- Load leveling through the network
- Security requirements for the link
- Type of traffic via-à-vis the type of link
- Number of intermediate links between the transmitting and receiving stations
- Ability to reach (connect to) intermediate nodes and, of course, the final receiving station

Whatever the least-cost criteria may be, the network designer's goal is to determine the least-cost, end-to-end path between any two communicating stations.

Even though networks vary in least-cost criteria, three constraints must be considered: (a) delay, (b) throughput, and (c) connectivity. If delay is excessive or if throughput is too little, the network does not meet the needs of the user community. The third constraint is quite obvious: The communications devices must be able to reach each other; otherwise, all other least-cost criteria are irrelevant.

The algorithms used to route the packets through the network vary. As we shall see in this chapter, some algorithms are set up at a central site or executed at each individual packet switch. They may provide a static, end-to-end path between the two users of the network, or they may route the traffic through different packet switches. We shall also see that they vary in how they adapt to changing network conditions. Some algorithms adapt only to failures, and some adapt as traffic conditions change.

The packet-switched network (see Figure 4–18) has multiple multiplexed routes available from each node in the network. The packets are routed across the paths in accordance with traffic congestion, error conditions, the shortest end-to-end path, and other criteria that are covered later in this discussion. In some networks, a user's individual packets are routed across different communications lines and later assembled as a logical message for presentment to the end user.

Packet switching has seen increasing use due to a number of factors:

- The alternate routing scheme gives the network considerable reliability. Failed switches or lines can be bypassed.

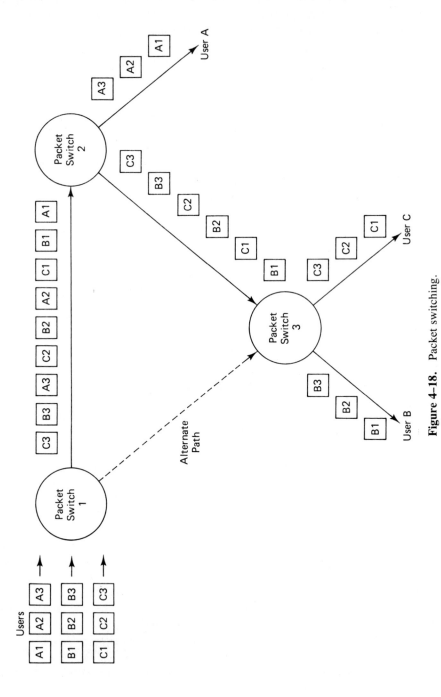

Figure 4-18. Packet switching.

88

- Packet-switching computers are designed for minimum delay between end users, usually fractions of a second.
- The technology can use the existing telephone network (for the path); the packet switches thus provide a value-added service for the end user.
- Packets containing a portion of user data are more secure than a message with a complete logical message.

The intermittent transmission of small packets allows a line and computer port to be shared by multiple users through time-division multiplexing. This idea is called a *logical* or *virtual channel* and is an integral part of X.25.

Packet switching is a complex undertaking. The switches must be highly reliable and very efficient. If routing decisions change as conditions change, the routing algorithms must maintain a steady-state condition of all network components. The network logic must adapt quickly to dynamic conditions that would cause suboptimal routing. Adaptation must be done uniformly over all affected nodes. Control is required to prevent packet saturation at busy nodes in the network.

Packetizing to reduce delay.   The size of a message, block, frame, or packet is a critical design factor in a network. The effect of packetizing and packet size can be seen in Figure 4–19. Referring to Figure 4–19(a), a message of length n bits is to be transported from node A, through nodes B and C, to the final destination, node D. The length of the message is such that, at time t + 5, all control and user data arrive at site B. At this node, they are checked for errors and relayed (assuming insignificant processing delay at the node) to node C. The data finally reach the end node D at t + 15.

In Figure 4–19(b), the message has been disassembled into four packets, each with its own control header. The packetizing results in an increased number of overhead bits in the headers, which also results in a longer transmission time to node B than in the example of Figure 4–19(a). Assuming no delay time between transmission of the four separate packets across one line, the four packets arrive at node B at time t + 8, which is 3 units of time slower than with the self-contained message block. However, notice that the first packet arrives at t + 2 and is checked for errors. Since it is a self-contained unit, it is immediately relayed to node C. In contrast, the longer message of Figure 4–19(a) cannot be relayed until all bits have arrived at node B and are checked for errors. As the four packets pass through node C, the delay is t + 10, the same delay as the self-contained message in Figure 4–19(a). Finally, at node D, the overall delay of the four packets is t + 12, or 3 units of time faster than the message transported in Figure 4–19(a).

Of course, packetizing experiences a point of diminishing returns. Inordinately small packets will increase the delay beyond that of longer user data blocks due to the large ratio of overhead bits to user bits (as well as saturating queues at the switching sites).

There is no such thing as a free lunch. The network packet switches must be designed to handle more individual "pieces" and must have the speed and capacity to

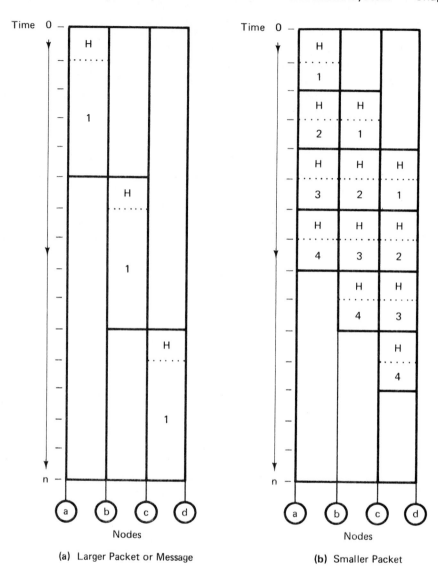

Figure 4-19. Packet size.

minimize queuing inside the machine. Most queueing systems cannot be loaded to over 70% of capacity, and the packet switches must be loaded even lower. Packet networks have control mechanisms to warn against traffic congestion that is building up. Others control congestion by limiting the number of packets that a user can have outstanding at one time. Still others require a sending site to obtain a "reservation" from the receiving site before a session is established.

Packet routing.   Routing algorithms are implemented using the concepts of static or adaptive routing. The static scheme provides a fixed path through the network based on criteria such as user session or packet type. The rationale for static routing is that a session usually requires transmission of multiple packets between the same user end points and a static end-to-end path achieves simplicity and seriality. The fixed, static path approach is also called *session-oriented routing.* The dynamic scheme is called *nonsession-oriented routing.*

Several variations of static routing exist. For example, alternate static routing provides for a first- or second-choice path based on line conditions, packet priority, type of user session, or other criteria. Once the path is established, it remains the same for the duration of the user session, unless problems occur. Another popular approach is to provide for routing control from a network control center. The center changes routing tables as conditions in the network change. Some implementations allow network management to establish routing the packets based on minimum cost, the shortest route, or minimum delay considerations. The decisions are input as parameters into the logic of the packet-switching computers.

Adaptive routing algorithms alter the route of packets in a dynamic manner, based on network conditions at any given instant. The routing decisions are typically based on obtaining performance information of adjacent switches and determining the readiness of the adjacent nodes to receive and relay the packets. The adjacency readiness information is obtained by sites exchanging tables with each other, usually every few seconds. These tables provide data to determine the optimum route out of the sending switch. The tables are updated by each node or by a central network control center. The former method is called *distributed route maintenance* and the latter is *centralized route maintenance.*

Another method of obtaining adjacency readiness information is for the sending switch to maintain data on the delays encountered in obtaining acknowledgments from receiving switches in the receipt of previously transmitted packets. Still another approach is for the packets themselves to contain delay information about the switches through which they pass. Lengthy delays alert the system to transmit the packet across another channel to other nodes.

Adaptive routing is a powerful, sophisticated approach and is used by several networks such as the Advanced Research Projects Agency (ARPA) network. However, the approach can lead to nonsteady-state conditions and must be carefully designed before implementation. Figure 4–20(a) shows why. Let us assume node D wishes to transmit a packet to node A, the final destination (FD). The arrows indicate the time unit delays experienced between adjacent nodes. The optimum path for the packet is D → C → B → A (NN means next node); the overall delay (OD) is 7 time units (D → C = 2, C → B = 2, B → A = 3). All other routes entail a longer delay. (Some routing algorithms determine the routing path based on the number of hops or intermediate nodes that must be traversed; this example does not use the hop method.)

Suppose, after the packet reaches the intermediate node C, the network conditions have changed such that, in Figure 4–20(b), the optimum route to node A is C → D →

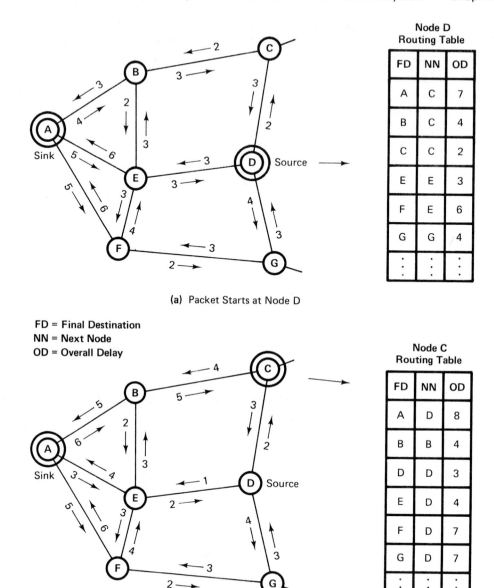

FD = Final Destination
NN = Next Node
OD = Overall Delay

Figure 4-20. Adaptive routing.

E → A. The packet is returned to its original site D without making any progress toward reaching its final destination. Adaptive routing techniques are refined enough to handle this kind of problem, but the techniques are complex and use resources at the packet switch. To solve our specific problem of the ''lost'' packet in this example, several vendors increment a count in the control header of the packet. Upon the count exceeding a threshold, the packet is given special handling by the network control center or by error-handling logic at the packet switch.

Packet-switching standards. The international standards organizations ISO and CCITT have developed standards for interfacing into a packet-switching network. In the United States, the Department of State, the common carriers, vendors, and national standards organizations have participated in defining these standards. One such standard, called X.25, defines the interface between DTE and DCE for terminals operating in the packet mode on data networks.

Packet Voice

It is only a matter of time before packet voice becomes a widely used technology. Voice packets can share a common channel just as data packets do today. The rationale for voice by packets is much the same as data by packets: to share the transmission and switching facilities.

Experiments and research thus far encourage optimistic predictions for using packet-switching networks for both voice and data. However, voice by the packet does present some problems. First, it is desirable to use existing packet networks for voice transmission to preclude building a redundant network. Data transmission is relatively intolerant of errors, so today's packet-switching protocols (such as X.25) assume the posture of correcting as many errors as possible. However, voice transmission is quite tolerant of occasional errors, and a lost, short speech segment would not affect the intelligibility of a conversation between two users. (On the other hand, a series of lost packets could possibly change the meaning of a conversation.)

Another problem pertains to the delay of the transmission of the packets through intermediate nodes of the network and the consequent delay of their arrival at the receiver. In data packet networks, packets encounter different delays, especially if they are traveling through a nonsession-oriented network. Voice reproduction requires a fixed rate of packet reconstruction and a fixed rate of *outplay* at the receiving end to the user. Since packets arrive at variable times, a packet must be delayed and buffered at the receiving site in order to allow the reassembling of any late-arriving packets. A point is reached, however, where late-arriving, nonarriving, or wandering packets simply must be ignored and the resultant output packets must be given to the end user. This can create gaps in a voice conversation if the delays become severe.

One approach to solve the delay problem is based on choosing a target *play-out* by an analysis of the network to determine when the majority of packets arrive. Upon passing the threshold, the packets are presented as output. Several approaches are under study to enhance this technique by dynamically adjusting the delay time based on network conditions at a particular period.

Private Branch Exchanges

The PBX switch is used extensively in offices. The PBX serves an individual private organization, provides telephone and data-switching capabilities within the building, and also connects outside to the common carrier facilities. The PBX user base has grown dramatically as computers have been placed in the PBX to provide for sophisticated functions such as call forwarding, automatic redial, and abbreviated dialing for speed calling. The computerized PBX (CBX) provides more functions than most users know how to utilize. It is now used to integrate voice/data transmission and to provide for local networking within a building.

MULTIPLEXING, LINE SHARING, AND COMPRESSION

A voice-grade communications line is capable of a 9.6-kbit/s rate using high-speed, multilevel modems. Theoretically, this type of line can transmit 17,280,000 bits in 30 minutes (1,800 seconds × 9,600 bits = 17,280,000). Yet many devices use only a small fraction of this line capacity. A keyboard terminal operated by a human typically sends and receives a few thousand bits during a 30-minute session with the computer. Assuming 4,000 eight-bit characters were exchanged during this period (a very fast typist!), the efficiency ratio of the total capacity of the 9.6-kbit/s line would be 0.0018 [(4,000 bytes × 8 bits per byte)/17,280,000 bit capacity = 0.0018]. This is a very poor use of an expensive component in the data communications system. Moreover, with the increasing use of faster lines operating at 56 kbit/s and 1.5 Mbit/s, the ratio is worse.

The solution is to provide more traffic (in user data streams) for the path. Since many applications use low-speed keyboard terminals as input into the network, the high-speed lines are given more work by placing more than one terminal device on the line. Increased work provides for better line utilization.

Multiplexing

Multiplexers accept lower-speed data streams from terminals and combine them into one high-speed data stream for transmission to the central site. At this site, a multiplexer demultiplexes and converts the combined data stream into the original multiple lower-speed terminal data streams. Since several separate transmissions are sent over the same line, the efficiency ratio of the path is improved (see Figure 4–21).

Frequency-division multiplexing.   In the previous decade, the most widely used multiplexing technique was frequency-division multiplexing (FDM). This approach divides the transmission frequency range (the bandwidth) into narrower bands (called subchannels). Figure 4–22(a) depicts the FDM scheme. FDM decreases the total bandwidth available to each terminal but, since the devices are low speed, the narrower bandwidth is sufficient for each device. The data transmissions from the attached devices are sent simultaneously across the path. Each device is allocated a fixed portion of the

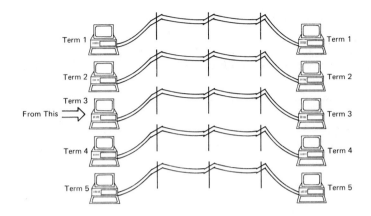

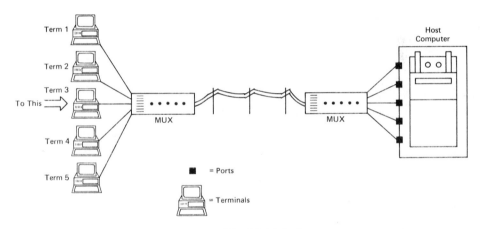

Figure 4–21.   Multiplexing.

frequency spectrum. For example, an ASR-33 teletype terminal usually requires a bandwidth of 170 Hz. Given this requirement, a voice-grade channel can accommodate 12 to 15 110-bit/s ASR-33 terminals.

The subchannels must be separated by unused frequencies (guard bands) to prevent overlapping signal interference. Therefore, the full 3-kHz telephone voice-grade bandwidth cannot be fully utilized. The guard bands exist to compensate for signal filters that do not sharply cut off the outside frequencies of the subchannel. Even with these guard bands, the contiguous channels will experience some cross interference (cross talk). Figure 4–23 shows several alternatives for dividing the 3-kHz spectrum.

FDM is often used in short-distance, multidrop arrangements. It is code transparent, and any terminal of the same speed can use the same subchannel after the subchannel is established. Multiplexer vendors have different requirements for connecting to their equipment, however, and the user should check for vendor variations. Most connections

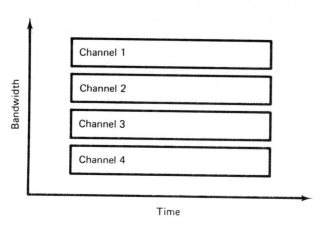

(a) Frequency Division Multiplexing (FDM)

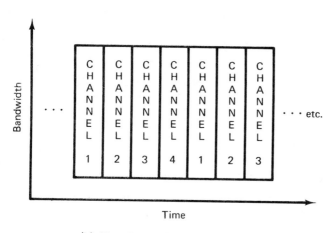

(b) Time Division Multiplexing (TDM)

Figure 4-22.   FDM and TDM.

to terminals are accomplished through the EIA-232-D connection. An FDM provides the modulation/demodulation within its own circuitry.

The common carriers' communications channels are grouped together in packages to take advantage of the greater bandwidths of coaxial cable, microwave, and satellite transmission schemes. The channels are subdivided by using frequency-modulation techniques. This is accomplished by a carrier frequency being generated for each channel; the separate carrier is required to translate and "carry" each device's signal. Each carrier channel is assigned a different frequency to prevent interference from other channels.

The process is illustrated in Figure 4-23. Each signal is placed onto (modulated) a carrier frequency. The carriers are generated by a central oscillating device, which also generates a pilot or reference signal. The pilot signal is used at the receiving end to provide a reference for demodulation and demultiplexing. The multiplexed signals travel

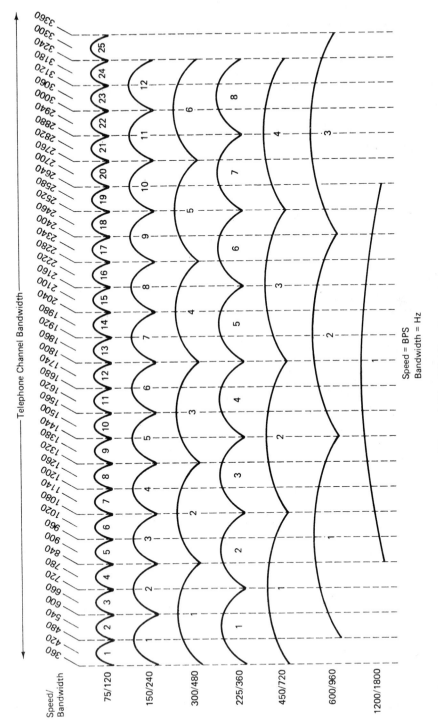

Figure 4-23. Dividing the spectrum.

Speed = BPS
Bandwidth = Hz

across the high-capacity communications link, arrive at the end site, and are then converted back to the original signals.

Figure 4–24 shows that signal filters are involved in the process. As stated earlier, filters suppress or eliminate certain unwanted frequencies by increasing the signal loss of those frequencies. Filters are necessary due to the nature of the output of modulation. For example, let us assume a voice-grade channel with a bandwidth of 300 to 3,300 Hz is to be modulated onto a carrier frequency of 60 kHz. The resultant output contains the basic carrier frequency and two modulated frequencies, an upper sideband, and a lower sideband:

Upper sideband: 60,300 to 63,300 Hz

Carrier frequency: 60,000 Hz

Lower sideband: 56,700 Hz to 59,700 Hz

Since it is necessary to carry only one of the sidebands, the filters are used to remove the unwanted band and perhaps the carrier signal as well. At the receiving end, the filters are also required, since the demodulation process also creates the sidebands.

Time-division multiplexing.   Time-division multiplexing provides a user the full channel capacity but divides the channel usage into time slots. Each user is given a slot and the slots are rotated among the attached user devices [see Figure 4–22(b)]. The

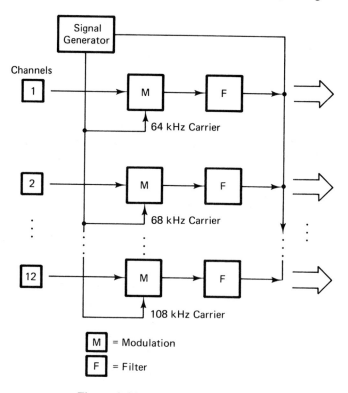

Figure 4–24. FDM carrier and filters.

time-division multiplexer cyclically scans the input signals (incoming data) from the multiple incoming points. Bits, bytes, or blocks of data are peeled off and interleaved together into frames on a single higher-speed communications line. TDMs are discrete signal devices and will not accept analog data.

TDMs operate in either a bit, byte, or block fashion. A bit TDM peels off 1 bit at a time. Each frame contains a bit from each sampled device. A typical bit interleaved TDM can handle 18 terminals on a voice-grade line. The character (or byte) interleaved TDM assembles an entire character or byte into the frame. The character MUX is generally more efficient, since it permits fewer overhead bits than a bit MUX. A character interleaved TDM can handle 29 subchannels within a voice-grade line. Block multiplexing is explained in the section on statistical multiplexing.

TDMs process binary, digital data; consequently, modems are required for interface into the common carrier analog network.

Isochronous multiplexing.   A TDM generally sends out signal pulses to the attached input devices to keep the data streams synchronized. The pulses are provided by a master clock in the multiplexer. Some communications lines have a large number of input devices operating with different physical transmission times and signal propagation delays. The isochronous MUX does not ''sync'' through the master clock but provides internal buffers for the time-independent data streams to store data. The buffers allow the data to arrive at random intervals where they are stored and later multiplexed out onto the high-speed side of the MUX. The buffers are ''elastic'' in that they can be expanded or contracted to accommodate dynamic traffic flows.

Statistical multiplexing.   The conventional TDM wastes the bandwidth of the communications line because the time slots in the frames are often unused. Vacant slots occur when an idle terminal has nothing to transmit in its slot. Statistical TDM multiplexers (STDMs) dynamically allocate the time slots (that is, the bandwidth) among active terminals; thus, dedicated subchannels (FDMs) and dedicated time slots (TDMs) are not provided for each port, and idle terminal time does not waste the line's capacity. It is not unusual for two to five times as much traffic to be accommodated on lines using statistical TDMs. Figure 4–25 shows a typical STDM configuration and a STDM data unit (frame).

In most statistical multiplexers, the length of the frames varies in accordance with the input data streams. These streams usually come from asynchronous start–stop terminals. The majority of statistical multiplexers support synchronous devices as well. Isochronous transmission is accepted on some vendor's models. The frames must contain information on which channels have transmitted data within the frame. Typically, each frame provides ''mapping'' (MAP) that tells which devices have data and the number of data bits or bytes in each frame. The frames also have headers, sequence numbers, and error-checking fields for purposes of identification and control.

Statistical multiplexers have evolved in a short time to become very powerful and flexible machines. Today, vendors sell machines that overlap the functions found in PBXs, message/packet switches, front ends, concentrators, and even satellite-delay

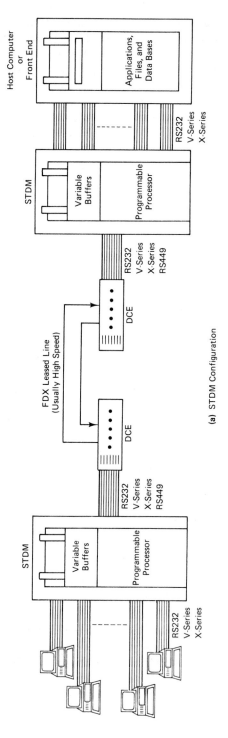

(a) STDM Configuration

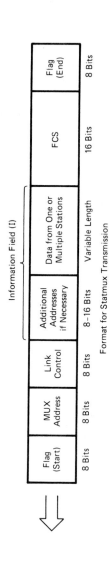

(b) STDM Frame

Figure 4–25. Statistical time-division multiplexing (STDM or STATMUX).

compensation units. STDMs have virtually taken over the FDM market and now offer serious competition to the TDMs. Statistical multiplexers also provide extensive error-checking techniques and buffer management, as well as data flow control. Some STDMs provide modulation circuitry for interfacing into analog networks. Otherwise, separate modems are required. Flow control is used to prevent the transmitting devices from sending data too fast into the multiplexer's buffers.

Statistical multiplexers are seldom beneficial in networks using full-duplex data flow protocols or in local networks where the organization owns the communications path. Nor will they be beneficial for applications with nonbursty, continuous traffic, since the STATMUX cannot interleave multiuser traffic if the line is continuously busy. Notwithstanding, these components should be given serious consideration by organizations using long-haul leased lines.

Multiplexed Common Carrier Systems

As stated earlier, the telephone companies and other carriers use frequency multiplexing extensively. For example, the telephone system provides a multiplexing hierarchy that multiplexes 12 sub-voice-grade channels into one voice-grade channel at the low-capacity end and up to 10,800 voice channels into a large-capacity link at the high-capacity end.

The AT&T/Bell hierarchy uses multiplexed groups. The channel group contains 12 voice-grade channels. The voice channels are spaced 4 kHz apart and occupy the 60- to 180-kHz range. In this system, only the lower sidebands are used, and the upper sidebands and related carriers are suppressed (filtered out). Five channel groups are then multiplexed onto a supergroup. The supergroup contains 60 voice-grade channels ($12 \times 5 = 60$). Ten supergroups are in turn multiplexed onto a master group, yielding a capacity for 600 voice-grade channels ($12 \times 5 \times 10 = 600$). Six master groups make up a jumbo group with 3,600 voice-grade channels ($12 \times 5 \times 10 \times 6 = 3,600$). At the upper level in the scheme is the jumbo group multiplexed, which is composed of three jumbo groups and 10,800 voice-grade channels ($12 \times 5 \times 10 \times 6 \times 3 = 10,800$), occupying a frequency range of 3,124 to 60,556 kHz. The common carriers also have facilities for digital multiplexing using the concepts of time-division multiplexing.

Multiplexing Satellite Signals

Modern satellite systems have adapted TDM concepts as a means to control and allocate resources to channel users. TDMA (time-division multiple access) is now used in systems throughout the world.

TDMA determines channel assignments based on the traffic: the number of connected voice data calls and the number of queued data connection requests. Each transponder on the satellite is managed by a *reference station* (REF), which allocates the time slots on the channel to the users assigned to the transponder.

Typically, assignments are made in response to user requests in earlier transmissions. For example, Satellite Business Systems (SBS) provides a control field in which users place their reservation requests. The reference station then assigns the channel slots on a periodic basis. Once assignments are made, the users comply and transmit within the assigned slots. At the same time, users place requests for subsequent slots in the control field for the reference station to analyze.

Concentrators

The term *concentrator* is often confused with *statistical multiplexer*. This is certainly understandable, since the functions of the two components often overlap. Strictly speaking, a concentrator has n input lines, which, if all input devices are active, would exceed the capacity of the m output line. Consequently, in the event excessive input traffic is beginning to saturate the concentrator, some terminals are ordered to reduce transmission or are not allowed to transmit at all. We also find this kind of function in STDMs and in communications front ends. The overlapping functions of multiplexers, concentrators, and front ends often make it difficult to apply any clear-cut definitions to the components.

Statistical multiplexers are used as a combination concentrator/front end to enable a computer connection (port) to communicate with multiple channels (see Figure 4–26). The stat MUX in this environment is called a *port concentrator*. The port concentrator is responsible for control of the line. It provides buffering, error detection, and line synchronization with the remote components.

The port concentrator often provides for dial-up access to the port(s). This allows a large number of terminals to contend for a limited number of ports at the computer. The more sophisticated concentrators (called *port selectors*) integrate dedicated and dial-up terminals. The port selector switches the devices to the available ports as required.

Data Compression

The transport of data across the communications path is an expensive process. Multiplexers, concentrators, and multipoint techniques allow for more efficient utilization of the expensive medium. Data compression provides yet another option by reducing the number of characters in a transmission.

Messages are comprised of a fixed number of bits coded to represent a character. The codes have been designed as fixed length because most computers require a fixed number of bits in a code to efficiently process data. The fixed-length format means that all characters are of equal length, even though all characters are not transmitted with equal frequency [Figure 4–27(a)]. For example, characters such as vowels, spaces, and numbers are used more often than consonants and characters such as a question mark.

One widely used solution is to establish a variable-length code for purposes of transmission. The most frequently transmitted characters (bytes) are "compressed" and represented by a unique bit set smaller than the conventional bit code [Figure 4–27(b)]. This data compression technique can result in substantial savings in communications costs.

Data compression techniques are classified as reversible and nonreversible; reversible techniques are further divided into semantic independent and semantic dependent procedures. Nonreversible techniques (often called *data compaction*) per-

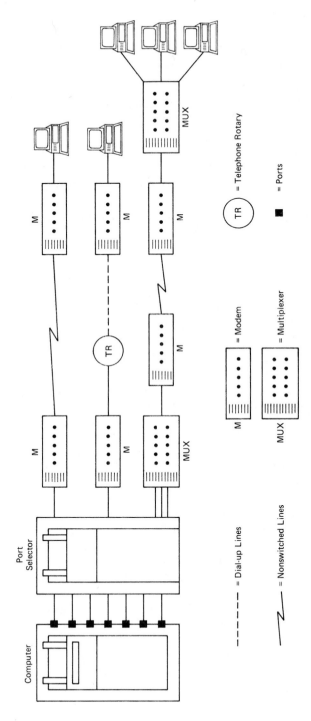

Figure 4-26. Port concentrators and selectors.

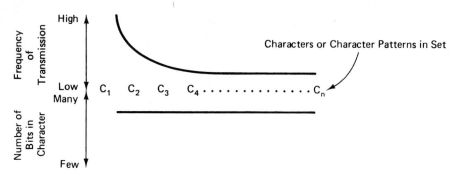

(a) Fixed Code with Variable Transmission Patterns

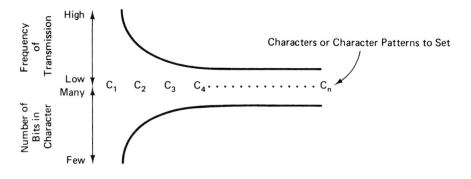

(b) Variable Codes with Variable Transmission Patterns

Figure 4–27. Fixed-length format problems.

manently eliminate the irrelevant portions of the data. Obviously, what is relevant or irrelevant depends on the data. For example, the figure representing the national debt is described in billions of dollars and is often calculated at an aggregate level with the tens, hundreds, thousands, and so on, positions compacted out of the number. While data compactions might be appropriate for the national debt, one would be hesitant to do it with a customer's checking account balance. Typically, data items with leading blanks or trailing zeros are eliminated with data compaction.

Reversible techniques provide for temporary elimination of portions of the data. Reversible techniques using semantic dependent procedures depend on the content and context of the data for data reduction; semantic independent procedures do not depend on either the content or context of the data. Some common data compression techniques are described next.

Huffman code.   The Huffman code is a widely used compression method. With this code, the most commonly used characters contain the fewest bits, and the less commonly used characters contain the most bits. For example, assume the characters A, B,

C, and D comprise the complete character set. Analysis reveals that, on an average, A accounts for 50% of the total transmitted traffic, B accounts for 25%, C for 15%, and D for 10%. A code to take advantage of the skewed character distribution might appear as in Figure 4–28(a). The following transmitted message could then be interpreted by the decision chart [Figure 4–28(b)]. The data are examined and decoded by reading the bit stream left to right. Notice the 0 acts as a deliminator, signifying the last bit of the character, except for the character that is sorted last in the distribution set.

$$
\begin{array}{cccccc}
111 & 10 & 0 & 0 & 110 & 10 \\
\downarrow & \downarrow & \downarrow & \downarrow & \downarrow & \downarrow \\
D & B & A & A & C & B
\end{array}
$$

Huffman codes have been used to achieve compression rates of 50% or better. The rate depends on individual user data streams. However, as an illustration, typical text

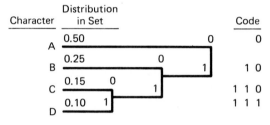

(a) Huffman Code

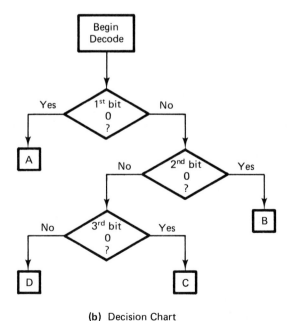

(b) Decision Chart

Figure 4–28. Huffman data compression.

transmissions using an 8-bit EBCDIC code can be reduced to an average character length of 4.8 bits. The overhead of computer resources to accomplish the compression at the transmitting site and decompression at the receiving site is offset by the increased throughput across the communications line.

Data compression also provides two other significant benefits. First, let us suppose an application requires a 9.6-kbit/s transfer rate, which entails expensive modems and a high-quality (more expensive) channel. If the data can be compressed by 50%, the application now only needs a 4.8-kbit/s link, which is less expensive and less subject to errors. Second, if the application is using a service (that is, a public packet network) that charges on traffic volume transmitted, the compression can reduce the volume of data and the vendor charges to the user.

Adaptive scanning.   This technique uses a dictionary to store frequently occurring strings of characters. The common character string is substituted by a shorter code. For example, program source code is often transmitted across a network. Thus, the character string PERFORM might appear often in a program written for a COBOL compiler. Adaptive scanning would examine the text and substitute a code (for example, @) in place of each PERFORM. The result is fewer bits transmitted.

Facsimile compression.   One of the most useful applications for data compression is the transmission of documents or graphics, commonly known as facsimile transmission (FAX). Documents lend themselves to compression because their contents have many recurring redundant patterns of space (white patterns) or print (black patterns). Facsimile compression treats each facsimile line as a series of white and black runs. The runs are coded based on their length, and the code is transmitted instead of the full "bit picture" of the document.

The compression is established through preestablished codes representing a picture element (PEL). The PEL defines the length of recurring white and black images. Each PEL is given a unique bit code. Figure 4–29(a) shows the codes for the modified Huffman code technique. Figure 4–29(a) contains codes for PELs with white or black run lengths up to 63; Figure 4–29(b) provides for encoding of PELs greater than 63. The two tables are used together to establish the exact code for longer PELs. (These tables conform to CCITT standards.)

To further understand facsimile compression, let us assume that the following PELs have resulted from a document line scan through a facsimile device. The PELs are decoded as:

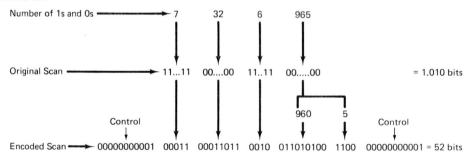

WHITE RUN LENGTH	CODE WORD	BASE 64 REP	BLACK RUN LENGTH	CODE WORD
0	00110101	0	0	0000110111
1	000111	1	1	010
2	0111	2	2	11
3	1000	3	3	10
4	1011	4	4	011
5	1100	5	5	0011
6	1110	6	6	0010
7	1111	7	7	00011
8	10011	8	8	000101
9	10100	9	9	000100
10	00111	a	10	0000100
11	01000	b	11	0000101
12	001000	c	12	0000111
13	000011	d	13	00000100
14	110100	e	14	00000111
15	110101	f	15	000011000
16	101010	g	16	0000010111
17	101011	h	17	0000011000
18	0100111	i	18	0000001000
19	0001100	j	19	00001100111
20	0001000	k	20	00001101000
21	0010111	l	21	00001101100
22	0000011	m	22	00000110111
23	0000100	n	23	00000101000
24	0101000	ø	24	00000010111
25	0101011	p	25	00000011000
26	0010011	q	26	000011001010
27	0100100	r	27	000011001011
28	0011000	s	28	000011001100
29	00000010	t	29	000011001101
30	00000011	u	30	000001101000
31	00011010	v	31	000001101001
32	00011011	w	32	000001101010
33	00010010	x	33	000001101011
34	00010011	y	34	000011010010
35	00010100	z	35	000011010011
36	00010101	A	36	000011010100
37	00010110	B	37	000011010101
38	00010111	C	38	000011010110
39	00101000	D	39	000011010111
40	00101001	E	40	000001101100
41	00101010	F	41	000001101101
42	00101011	G	42	000011011010
43	00101100	H	43	000011011011
44	00101101	I	44	000001010100
45	00000100	J	45	000001010101
46	00000101	K	46	000001010110
47	00001010	L	47	000001010111
48	00001011	M	48	000001100100
49	01010010	N	49	000001100101
50	01010011	Ø	50	000001010010
51	01010100	P	51	000001010011
52	01010101	Q	52	000000100100
53	00100100	R	53	000000110111
54	00100101	S	54	000000111000
55	01011000	T	55	000000100111
56	01011001	U	56	000000101000
57	01011010	V	57	000001011000
58	01011011	W	58	000001011001
59	01001010	X	59	000000101011
60	01001011	Y	60	000000101100
61	00110010	Z	61	000001011010
62	00110011	.	62	000001100110
63	00110100	≠	63	000001100111

(a)

WHITE RUN LENGTH	CODE WORD	BASE 64 REP	BLACK RUN LENGTH	CODE WORD
64	11011	1	64	0000001111
128	10010	2	128	000011001000
192	010111	3	192	000011001001
256	0110111	4	256	000001011011
320	00110110	5	320	000000110011
384	00110111	6	384	000000110100
448	01100100	7	448	000000110101
512	01100101	8	512	0000001101100
576	01101000	9	576	0000001101101
640	01100111	a	640	0000001001010
704	011001100	b	704	0000001001011
768	011001101	c	768	0000001001100
832	011010010	d	832	0000001001101
896	011010011	e	896	0000001110010
960	011010100	f	960	0000001110011
1024	011010101	g	1024	0000001110100
1088	011010110	h	1088	0000001110101
1152	011010111	i	1152	0000001110110
1216	011011000	j	1216	0000001110111
1280	011011001	k	1280	0000001010010
1344	011011010	l	1344	0000001010011
1408	011011011	m	1408	0000001010100
1472	010011000	n	1472	0000001010101
1536	010011001	ø	1536	0000001011010
1600	010011010	p	1600	0000001011011
1664	011000	q	1664	0000001100100
1728	010011011	r	1728	0000001100101
EOL	00000000001		EOL	0000000001

(b)

Figure 4–29. Modified Huffman code.

The control bits are used to delineate the beginning and ending of a line. Additional control bits may also be inserted for purposes of synchronization. The original scan established for overall run length of 1,010 bits, and the compression resulted in an encoded line of 52 bits. This results in a 19:1 compression ratio, which is a conservative achievement. Far better ratios are possible.

Just a few years ago, a standard $8\frac{1}{2}'' \times 11''$ document took over six minutes to be transmitted over a 48-kbit/s line. The modified Huffman technique cut this time significantly to approximately one minute. Recent improvements in compression techniques and modern speeds have further improved the process. Several years ago, the author shared a taxi at La Guardia airport with a representative from a facsimile vendor. He was carrying a portable FAX machine that his company was prototyping. The machine was purported to be able to transmit a standard $8\frac{1}{2}'' \times 11''$ document across a dial-up line in 20 seconds. Today's systems perform the tasks in about 10 seconds. It is now possible to compress a television transmission into a 56-kbit/s channel (although the fidelity and resolution are not very high in quality).

TERMINALS

The number and diversity of terminals are truly bewildering. Several hundred models are available from more than 200 vendors. The terminal market is one of the fastest-growing segments in the communications industry, and several million terminals have already been installed in the United States. Terminal selection is a difficult process, if for no other reason than the range of choices that exist. Moreover, the word *terminal* is open to many definitions, since some terminals today have the capabilities of computers.

Perhaps the best method to describe terminals is to begin with the simplest machines and move up to the more powerful and elaborate devices. In so doing, a classification scheme should prove useful for the initial discussions. Most terminals are broadly defined as teleprinters and/or cathode ray tube (CRT) devices. The teleprinter provides output through a printer device; the CRT uses a television-like tube. Some terminals have both facilities. These two type terminals are further classified as:

Dumb: Terminal has very limited functions and operates under complete control of other devices.

Smart: Terminal has hard-wired logic to give some capabilities such as selectable line speeds, special function keys, and screen cursor movement and scrolling.

Local storage: Terminal contains auxiliary storage such as disk or floppy disk.

Programmable: Software programs can be coded and executed in the terminal.

Teleprinters are usually serial printers in that they print one character at a time. Serial printers are further classified as impact printers (they mechanically hit or impact the page) and nonimpact (they use nonmechanical means to produce the image). The impact printers produce the character by using a solid character, like that of a typewriter, or by using a matrix of dots. Nonimpact teleprinters use the dot-matrix approach with either electrothermal or ink-jet mechanisms.

Dumb Teleprinters and CRTs

The basic dumb terminal or teleprinter consists of a keyboard for data entry and a display station, usually a printer. Some terminals of this type are read-only (RO) and do not contain a keyboard. These terminals are best exemplified by the ubiquitous Teletype 33 and Teletype 35. The Teletype Corporation has shipped over 700,000 model 33 and 35 terminals since 1962. These units are rather slow, using impact solid character printing at 10 characters per second (cps). Although they require frequent maintenance due to the large number of electromechanical parts, they have served the industry well. The IBM 2740 is another well-known terminal of this type.

In 1974, Digital Equipment Corporation (DEC) introduced a formidable competitor to the Teletype and IBM machines with the DECWRITER II. This terminal prints (dot matrix) at 30 cps and operates in half- or full-duplex on 110/150/300 bit/s lines. DEC's success with this terminal was extraordinary and it soon became an industry standard. The DECWRITER II (and its later improvement DECWRITER II LA36) is very reliable [meantime between failure (MTBF) is 2,000 hours] and comes with a variety of options. Teletype has marketed the model 42 and 43 to counter the DEC machines.

The dumb CRT, also called an alphanumeric display terminal, provides basic output display functions such as screen cursors, line insertions/deletions, screen paging, and screen erasing. The keyboards are typewriter style. These terminals usually operate at half- or full-duplex using ASCII code. Typical line speed is 9.6 kbit/s, with some vendors offering 19.2 kbit/s.

Smart Teleprinters and CRTs

The smart terminals provide quality output and more features than the dumb devices. They can often be used as word processors as well as data communications terminals. Smart terminals may be controlled by a microprocessor. They operate with a wide variety of line speeds, typically from 1.2 to 2.4 kbit/s. Some of these devices also provide for graphics support with the controlling software resident in the host. The smart CRTs also have additional facilities. For example, some devices have limited graphics and terminal bypass printing. The following features are usually standard: scrolling, paging, cursor positioning, cursor blinking, protected screen (keying into a form on the screen), tabulation, transmitting a partial screen (what is keyed in), line delete, screen erase, and character repeat.

Local Storage Terminals

This type of terminal provides considerable overlap in the classification scheme because storage is frequently an add-on option. In fact, many of the dumb and smart terminals provide storage as a standard feature (usually in random-access memory, RAM). The local storage feature is an important consideration for certain applications and should be examined as part of the terminal package. Some vendors provide the capability with little extra cost to the customer. The following storage options are available: (a) memory (RAM), (b) paper tape, (c) tape, (d) cartridges, (e) floppy disks, (f) voice-data unit (VDU), and (g) disk.

The Personal Computer

Personal computers (PCs) have had a major impact on the industry due to their effect on distributed processing. They are quite powerful and often include a computer, multiple workstations, and disk and software packages (compilers and utilities). The term *personal computer* describes a "small machine" that can be put to personal use, although the machines today are powerful enough for rather extensive business applications. Prior to the advent of the name, these machines were called microcomputers to connote their smallness, not particularly in size (although that as well), but as to their limited computing and input/output (I/O) capacity.

What was classified as a large-scale computer only 10 years ago is now called personal computer. Some of us carry the PC around as if it were a portable briefcase. Ten years ago, a large room was required to house the same computer capacity now contained in the briefcase.

Nonetheless, the personal computer is still considered to be a machine of limited capacity, especially when compared to the maxi computers of today. For instance, the large IBM 3090 (model 400) computers at 52.7 mips (millions of instructions per second) has 128 Mbytes of memory. Overall computing power is still a primary consideration in the purchase or acquisition of the PC. Because of these "limitations," some of the networking and communications capabilities of the PC are also limited.

COMMUNICATIONS FRONT ENDS

During the 1960s and early 1970s, data communications tasks were processed in the mainframe computer, and terminals were controlled by software residing in the host. In many instances, the software was written as part of the application code. This environment presented two rather serious problems.

First, as communications systems grew in size and complexity, the mainframe computer used more of its resources to manage the network. In turn, fewer resources were available for processing the user applications programs. Second, the applications programmers/analysts spent an increasing amount of their time and effort developing code to interface their system with the components in the network. Yet many of the communications tasks were common to all applications. For example, even though common code would allow the polling of a terminal to send messages for payroll, sales orders, and other applications, the code was written for each application and embedded within each unique system. These problems dictated a solution—the communications front-end processor.

This communications component is used to off-load the many communication tasks from the host. It is actually a computer with software, a logic unit, registers, and memory. In contrast to a generalized mainframe, the machine is designed to perform specialized tasks.

With the front end, the host is relieved of many communications-oriented functions, thereby allowing itself more resources for running the application's programs (see Figure 4–30). The front end also provides a very valuable service to the application programmer. It has powerful software for network and line management. As stated previously, earlier applications contained this code in each application. Today's application code need only contain a relatively simple I/O instruction to the communications interface in the host. The host passes the instruction to the front-end software for interpretation and execution.

Figure 4–31 shows a front end in more detail. The control unit is quite similar to the CPU in the host computer. It is capable of accessing memory and executing program instructions. These instructions come from the host communications software and the operating system within the front end. Next, memory is available for buffer areas to store messages coming into and out of the front end. The memory also stores the operating system. Moving up in Figure 4–31, we see a channel interface. This component provides an interface between the front end and the host computer. At the bottom of the figure, notice the line interface devices. These components provide the interfaces to the network.

Figure 4–31 also depicts the communications scanner. The maximum data rate of a line is determined by the frequency at which the specific line interface port is scanned

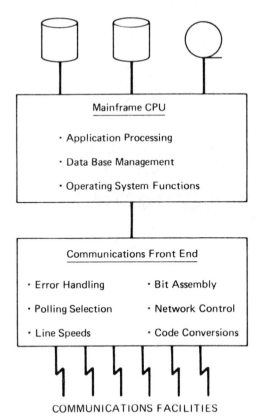

COMMUNICATIONS FACILITIES   **Figure 4–30.**   The front end.

Data to/from Host

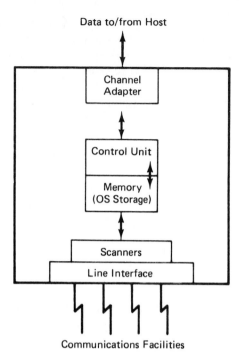

Communications Facilities

Figure 4–31.   Front-end components.

(that is, sampled) by the communications scanner. The front end can service different line speeds by increasing or decreasing the scanning frequency.

The communications scanner provides an example of the value of off loading functions from the host. Obviously, each attached line must be examined at periodic intervals for the bit streams of messages flowing into and out of the user applications. Assuming a front end has five lines attached at 1,200 bit/s speed, the scanner must examine each port every 8.3 μs (1 sec/1,200 = 0.00083 sec.). The five lines require bit-sensing operations to occur 6,000 times a second (1,200 bit/s $\times$ 5 lines = 6,000). Moreover, the data bits must be moved through the port and into a temporary buffer register to allow for the next arrival of a bit. Eventually, the received bits are assembled into bytes and then into messages for transfer to the host.

All these activities require some kind of control and the use of machine instruction cycles. Also required are interrupts to notify the system that the registers are full or empty. In our example, the five active lines feed 750 bytes into the node every second (1,200 bit/s $\times$ 5 lines $\div$ 8 bits per byte = 750 bytes). Assuming an interrupt is required to transfer a byte out of the temporary register, 750 interrupts per second must occur for the system to operate correctly. If we assume further that an interrupt requires an average of 30 μs, then 22.5 ms of every second is expended to service these lines (750 $\times$ 0.00003 = 0.0225). While this example represents only $2\frac{1}{4}\%$ of a processor's capacity, a typical network with many lines—some of much higher speeds—would consume substantial resources to do only one communications function: service the lines for bit/byte assembly/disassembly.

The front end performs the scanning and the byte assembly/disassembly process without borrowing valuable machine cycles from the host. Periodically, the host is interrupted to transfer blocks of data to it. In this manner, the front end relieves the host for other processing.

Line servicing and bit/byte assembly/disassembly are only one function provided by front-end processors. The following are other services typically found in the front end:

Buffering: The front end obtains and releases buffers as it receives and transmits data.

Error handling: Line errors and device errors are noted and recorded by the front end.

Control characters: The processor inserts and deletes transmission control characters.

Code translation: Front end provides code translation between dissimilar devices.

Message flow control: Governs the pacing and flow of messages across the attached lines.

Switched services: Provides services to switched dial-up lines.

Data link control interface: Processor provides data link control (DLC) interfaces to devices using different DLCs.

Polling and selection: Front end schedules all polling and selection messages to the attached devices.

SUMMARY

The components that make up a distributed data communications network are many and varied. However, several basic components are essential in any system. Obviously, a communications link is mandatory. Additionally, a DCE is needed at each end of the link to terminate the end-user devices. These DCEs are typically modems for analog lines and a digital/channel service unit for digital lines. Wide area networks normally employ packet switching in order to route the traffic properly through a network. WANs also widely employ the use of satellite systems because of their large footprint. Multiplexers are also common elements in data communications systems because of their attractive features in reducing the number of lines required in the network.

5

Software and Data Bases

INTRODUCTION

This chapter introduces software and data bases as they are used in communications systems. The intent of this chapter is to provide the reader with sufficient information to understand design issues that are addressed in later chapters. Therefore, be aware that this chapter is a general review of these technologies.

COMMUNICATIONS PROGRAMMING

Communications programming (software) performs the logic tasks that are not performed by a host operating system, the applications programs, and the data-base management systems. The communications programs reside in the host, front end, terminal controllers, terminals, and other components such as switches. The major portion of the communications software logic is located in the host and the front end. CSW will be used in this chapter as an abbreviation for communications software.

The applications programs perform the specific tasks required by the end user. Their requests for communications services are established by a program statement such as a READ, WRITE, GET, PUT, or a call for the execution of a software routine that provides the request to the communications control programs. This results in the applications programmer being able to structure programs much like any other program that accesses disks, printers, or tape files. The applications programmer is relatively free from concern about the communications environment. Consequently, network changes should not require changing the applications programs—only the communications software.

The communications programs interface with the user applications primarily through tables. As an applications system is implemented, parameters are placed into these tables describing the communications requirements of the application program or a group of applications. For example, the following requirements for line handling could be established by the parameters in the tables:

- Do not open line is for outgoing messages until there is a break in the incoming traffic.
- Conversely, hold up input traffic to periodically allow output traffic to be transmitted.
- Send and receive data from/to the user application one batch at a time. Stated another way, manage traffic as if it is a tape file and not an individual message.
- Accept one message and do not permit the use of the line until the user application program sends back a response (held-line discipline).

For installations that utilize front-end processors, a considerable amount of the communications software resides in these machines. For example, IBM in its front-end architecture uses the network control program (NCP) as the major controlling element for its communictions functions. In a sense, NCP is the operating system of the front-end processor. It is responsible for receiving commands from the host and translating these commands into communications functions. The major functions provided by a program such as NCP follows:

- Managing the dialing and answering of switched lines.
- Responding to a host-resident application program's READ/WRITE or GET/PUT to send/receive traffic on the attached communications lines.
- Assembling the user bits into an outgoing message and adding communications control characters to the user message.
- Disassembling the incoming message into bits and deleting the control characters.
- Controlling the scanners and LIBs in accordance with the line speeds in bits per second (bit/s) of an attached terminal and other components.
- Translating the codes of dissimilar devices. For example, translating EDCDIC code to ASCII code, and vice versa.
- Managing storage buffers; assigning and releasing the storage as messages move into and out of the front end. (Buffer storage is quite important due to a finite amount of memory storage available. Additionally, the manner in which buffer storage is managed can influence performance.)
- Analyzing problems on the communications lines by recording errors, storing statistics, performing diagnostics, and testing lines and attached components.
- Providing alternate paths for failed private point-to-point lines by providing a dial-up backup facility.

Many vendors today provide software tools to aid an enterprise in installing and maintaining communications software. For example, IBM provides communications languages for the use on its front-end processors as well as host software. This software is actually designed around macros that permit the communications programmer to define the parameters for the various network sources through the software. This approach allows each enterprise to install the software and then tailor the installation based on the parameters stored through the macro language.

Communications between Host and Front End

The communications software in many systems is located in the front-end processor (front end). This is an architecture favored by IBM, and most large IBM systems have specialized front-end processors that perform data communications functions for the host computers. Typically, the host computer is focused on supporting the applications programs. The host software in turn services these applications' programs and then passes transactions to the front-end software, which one hopes will provide additional and complimentary functions.

On a general level, the relationship of the host, its operating system, the user application software, the communications software in the host, and the front-end software is depicted in Figure 5–1 with the following operations:

Event 1: The user application program issues an output instruction. The operating system receives and analyzes the request and passes the request to the host communications software.

Event 2: The host resident communications software examines the user headers and validates and logs the request. Predefined tables provide information to the host CSW, such as routing, editing, and error checking. The software also establishes buffers for the application message, inserts any required control characters, and appends communication control headers. Control is passed back to the operating system.

Event 3: A channel program is invoked by the operating system. The channel accepts the message and transmits it across the channel line to the front end.

Event 4: The channel adapter receives and notifies the front-end operating system of the message.

Event 5: The front-end operating system examines the communications headers, performs table lookups on the application message, and activates the communications scanner and the appropriate line interface device.

Event 6: The scanner provides the timing to effect the message transfer. The line interface device buffers the data and provides the necessary signals to activate the attached modem's circuits.

Event 7: After modem synchronization, the data are transmitted to the remote device. The remote device accepts the data and relays them to the user.

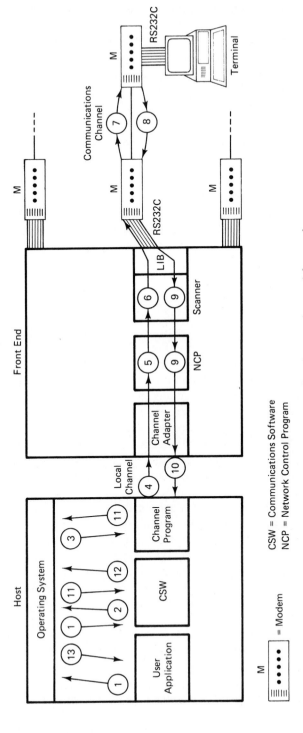

Figure 5-1. Data flow between host and front end.

CSW = Communications Software
NCP = Network Control Program

M = Modem

117

Event 8: The remote device sends back a reply; the two modems synchronize themselves and data are moved back into the line interfacing through the timing of the scanner.

Event 9: The front-end operating system is notified of the arrival of the data; it processes the data as appropriate. (For example, it determines that the message is destined for the host and not another communications line.)

Event 10: The channel interface is activated and the message is transferred to the host channel program.

Event 11: The host is notified of the message and it directs the host CSW to assume responsibility for processing the incoming data.

Event 12: The host CSW examines the headers to determine necessary action and passes the data to the user's application's work area buffers. It also logs the traffic, stores statistics, and, if appropriate, eventually terminates the session.

Event 13: The user program is activated by the host operating system. It accesses the data from its work area and continues to execute.

Applications Software

Another major set of software residing in a computer is the end users' applications code. In the majority of instances, this software is not concerned with the details of communications operations but focuses itself on solving user problems, supporting user needs (such as inquiry response, applications data-base access, etc.). Nonetheless, a well-designed distributed network must consider the support and placement of applications software in the various computers operating in the network.

Realistically, the network manager may have no control over (a) the nature of the applications software, (b) its efficiency (or inefficiency), or (c) in which host the applications reside. Indeed, in many installations today, the network manager has little control over end-user applications. In many instances, end-user applications are thought of as a separate process to that of the network. This approach works well in many cases because the impact of the user applications on a network may be minimal. But, in other cases, the nature of the user application and the traffic it generates (both sending and receiving) has profound impact on network operations. Moreover, in certain instances, the design of a user application can affect network performance.

The problem of many network operations today rests on the false assumption that networks support end-user applications and end-user data in a transparent manner. This cliche is bandied about throughout the industry, in many instances by network vendors and consultants designing networks and contractors vying for developing networks for end-user organizations.

It many not be possible for some network administrators to have a say in what happens with end-user application software. Ideally, a network should be able to accept any type of network applications and its data and transport them safely through the network to the end recipient. In the real world, consideration must be made to many other aspects of the nature of the application and the data. As examples:

- The amount of traffic generated into and out of the application
- Whether the application needs secure communications (encrypted)
- The throughput requirements of the application
- Any response time/delay requirements.

Later chapters address this issue in more detail.

DATA BASES

One might question why the subject of data bases is included in a book about communications and networks. The simplest explanation is that networks exist for the purpose of transporting data between computers, terminals, and data bases. Thus, data bases are an integral part of data communications systems and networks. We must understand at least the rudiments of data-base technology in order to grasp the issues related to network architectures, communications line configurations, topology layouts, and distributed processing.

The discussion of network data bases is divided into three parts. The basic terms and concepts are covered in this section.

Data Storage

Data bases usually reside on disk storage devices. A disk consists of several circular platters (disks), much like a stack of records on a turntable. The disks are separated by a small space and each side of the disk allows for the recording and reading of magnetic bit patterns. READ/WRITE heads are placed between each disk surface in order to process the data stored on the platter. The data are stored on concentric ring tracks around the disk.

The platters or disks on a disk unit rotate around a central spindle, passing across the READ/WRITE (R/W) heads. The disks are divided into tracks and cylinders. The *cylinder* consists of reading surfaces on the same area of each platter. Each recording surface is called a *track*. The cylinder concept is used to improve access efficiency. If data are stored across tracks, the R/W heads must mechanically move across the disk after each track is accessed. On the other hand, storage at the cylinder level necessitates accessing data only by electrically switching on/off the proper set of R/W heads. A full cylinder can be accessed before the R/W heads are moved.

Data are stored on the disk tracks. The user data are stored as physical records, preceded by control and key address areas. The physical record in this example consists of three user records (logical records). The three user records are stored or blocked together for two reasons:

1. The blocking reduces overhead space, since the control and key address areas are needed only for each physical record.

2. Access overhead is reduced. A READ request from an application program causes the transfer of the entire physical record with one input operation. Subsequent READs then access the resident block within a memory buffer.

Substantial storage and timing savings can be achieved by blocking. However, if contiguous logical records are not used by the application program, then the data transfer is wasted. For example, if the user wants logical record 1 only, the other two records are transferred into memory but are not used by this program. Consequently, data-base design requires a careful assessment of end-user access needs in order to cluster and block the data correctly.

This simple data-base structure illustrates a critical point in network data bases (wherein many users are accessing the same logical and physical records): The physical structure format and storage of the data must match the users' access needs.

Floppy disks used on personal computers have similar characteristics to that of hard disks. They are so named because of their flexible nature. The floppy disk contains tracks as well as sectors, which are portions of a track, typically an area of 512 bytes. The floppy architecture controls input/output by reading and writing a number of sectors (called *clusters*). Some floppy disks can store over 1.2 megabytes of data per disk, but a user has fewer options on blocking when using a floppy.

Organization

Modern data bases are organized with a complex set of software called a *data-base management system* (DBMS). These systems off-load many of the data-related tasks from the application programmer. (The off-loading concept is similar to the rationale for front ends and communications software.) An application can issue a READ, WRITE, GET, or PUT to the DBMS, which in turn will locate, format, and access the requested data. The DBMS makes use of an access method to handle the details of the physical access to the data bases (see Figure 5–2). The DBMS provides the user interface to the access method through logical user views called *schemas* and *subschemas*. The logical views are translated into the physical structure and internal view by the access method. These terms and concepts will be described in the following section.

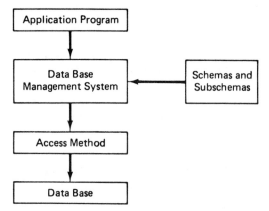

Figure 5–2. Data-base management system organization.

Physical access.   Data are stored on disk in one of three ways: sequential, indexed, or random (direct). *Sequential storage* simply means that records are stored one after the other on the disk track. A record in the middle of the data track cannot be obtained without first going past the preceding records.

The *indexed method* provides a unique identifier or key for each record. For example, an employee number could be a key for a personnel record. The key is used by the access method to compute a disk address and location through the index. This concept is illustrated in Figure 5–3. The application program executes an instruction that requests an employee record with the key (employee number) of 04420. The request is passed to the DBMS, which interprets the request (more on DBMS functions shortly) and passes the task to an indexed access method.

The access method has several indexes available to assist it in locating the record. First, it compares the employee key (EMPNO = 04420) to its high-level index and determines that the record is on one of the cylinders in the 40–79 group. (The key in the index represents the highest possible value of a key within the group.) Next the access method scans the cylinder index and determines that cylinder 43 contains the record. The track index for cylinder 43 is searched and the record is found to be located on track 10. Finally, track 10 is sequentially accessed through the disk READ/WRITE mechanisms and the control and address areas on the disk. The employee record is found, read into the computer, and placed into the application's work space.

The efficiency of the indexes in an indexed system is quite important. If possible, they should be memory-resistant in order to reduce lengthy input/output (I/O) processing to obtain their values. Moreover, indexed systems often use additional facilities to locate records that are added to a data base. For example, employee record 04420 might contain a pointer (address) to another area of disk that contained a recent addition of the record with EMPNO = 04421. This approach allows a sequential structuring of the files but can create considerable overhead and complexity.

The third major access structure, *random* or *direct*, relies on the record key to provide the disk address. Typically, a key is "hashed" or subjected to a calculation to obtain the address. For example, an employee record with a key of 02576 could be translated to cylinder and track address by the calculation. The hashing method is attractive because it usually requires only one seek to the disk to obtain a record. Also, it is less complex than the indexed technique.

The users usually have no choice of the access method to support their application. However, network designers and network data-base administrators must be knowledgeable about the details of vendors' access methods because their performance affects the ability of the network to support the user requirements. Many vendors' DBMSs offer all three access methods and even several variations on them. Detailed discussion of access methods is beyond the scope of this book, but the reader is encouraged to pursue the topic further if data access, response time, and retrieval/update costs are of interest or concern.

DBMS architectures (models).   Above the access method is the DBMS itself. It is structured and presented to the end user in such a manner that the user can view the data in a logical sense. This means that the user need not be concerned about track

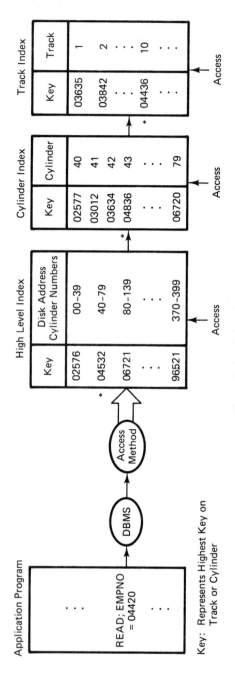

Figure 5-3. Indexed storage.

storage, cylinder access, index maintenance, or many other laborious tasks. Rather, the users view the data in the context of their requirements. DBMS architecture is also called a DBMS model, form, or structure. The most commonly used data-base models are the following:

- Hierarchical
- Plex or network
- Relational

Hierarchical model. The hierarchical (sometimes called a tree) model is shown in Figure 5–4. The user sees a tree with hierarchical members of the root, the top of the hierarchy. The members can be thought of as records or segments containing user data.

The lower levels are designated as children to the upper level, which logically enough is a parent level or node. All the second-level elements in Figure 5–4 are called twins to each other, since they are in the same hierarchical position in the data base. The lower levels are usually considered to contain multiple occurrences of segments.

Hierarchical data bases are useful for some applications and offer a convenient schema and subschema for the partitioning of the data base to distributed sites. For example, a data base of a large organization could be modeled hierarchically with the root segment containing data on the parent company (perhaps a holding company), the second-level segments containing data on the subsidiaries, and the third level representing branches and departments of the subsidiaries. Obviously, some user data do not logically appear as a hierarchical organization and other approaches are then used.

Plex or network model. This model is distinguished by a child having more than one parent and presents a more involved structure. A common example is a personnel data base where multiple retirement options exist for multiple employees [see Figure 5–5(a)]. The plex model can be depicted with the use of arrows [see Figure 5–5(b)].

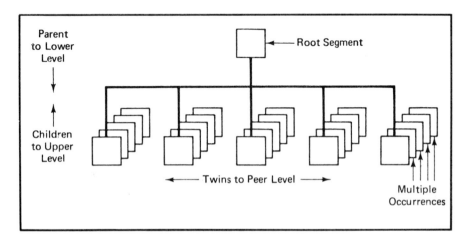

Figure 5–4. Hierarchical model.

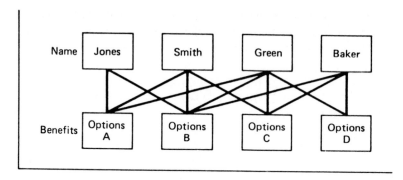

(a) Multiple Relationships

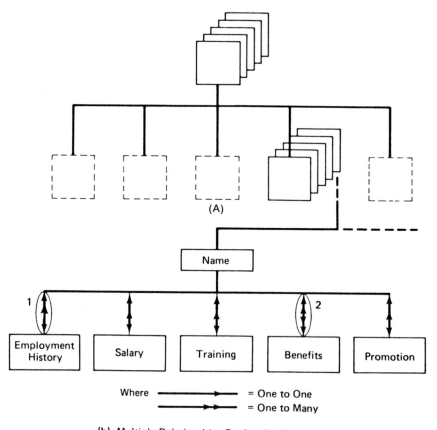

Where ———————▶ = One to One

———————▶ = One to Many

(b) Multiple Relationships Depicted with Arrows

Figure 5–5. Plex or network model.

The single arrow in circle 1 indicates that an Employment History segment has one parent, Name. The double arrow indicates that the Name segment has many Employment History segments. The double arrows in circle 2 indicate a many-to-many relationship in which employees choose multiple Benefit plan options.

The many-to-many relationships occur frequently in applications and can present very complex user views (not to mention the resulting complex physical storage and access). Recently, automated teller machines (ATMs) have become quite popular. The ATMs allow bank customers to make deposits and withdraw money after banking hours. Many banks have formed consortiums to share the physical ATM facility. Thus, ATMs have several owners and the owners have several ATMs, a typical many-to-many relationship.

Relational model.   The relational model has gained considerable popularity and use due to the simplicity of its user views. In its simplest form, the relational data base is presented as an organized number of two-dimensional tables (also called *flat files*). The display form is familiar and understandable to practically everyone. Figure 5–6 shows a typical relational model. The organization consists of an inventory data base.

Relational data-base technology uses several unique terms. The following is a list of these terms in the context of Figure 5–6.

Relation: The relation is the table itself (Inventory Relation).

Tuple: This describes the row in a relation. The first tuple in the Inventory Relation contains part #634.

Attribute: The attribute is the name of the type of column (also called *role name*).

Key: A column or a set of columns whose value(s) *uniquely* identify a row. The Inventory Relation's tuples (rows) can be uniquely identified by Component Part # and Location. A key consists of one column and a candidate key consists of more than one column.

Prime attributes: Attributes that are members of at least one candidate key.

Element: This describes the field in the tuple.

INVENTORY RELATION

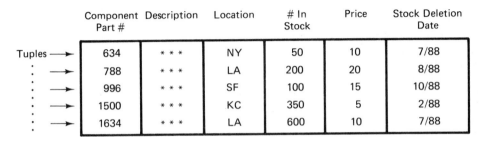

	Component Part #	Description	Location	# In Stock	Price	Stock Deletion Date
Tuples →	634	* * *	NY	50	10	7/88
→	788	* * *	LA	200	20	8/88
→	996	* * *	SF	100	15	10/88
→	1500	* * *	KC	350	5	2/88
→	1634	* * *	LA	600	10	7/88

Figure 5–6.   Relational model.

Degree: The number of columns in the relation. The Inventory Relation contains six columns.

Cardinality: The number of rows in the relation. The Inventory Relation contains five rows.

N-ary relations: A table with N columns.

Relational data bases adhere to certain rules and conventions:

- The rows (tuples) of a relation are never duplicated.
- Each relation represents a single concept. Any repeating occurrences and resulting many-to-many relationships are placed in smaller relations.
- The columns contain like data elements.
- The ordering of the rows in a relation is not significant, but column ordering is significant.
- Each row has a fixed number of fields, all explicitly named.
- Repeating occurrences may cause redundancy across the relations.
- An attribute in the key cannot be discarded without destroying the key's unique identification of the tuple.

We will see that the relational model can be a very useful concept for network and distributed data bases. Stable data structures are important to data bases in a network, and the relational model can provide for more stable structures than the hierarchical and plex models. However, we need some additional information before relating the ideas to networks.

The attractiveness of the relational architecture comes from the theory of normalization; it provides a rigorous discipline for structuring the data in the relations. The primary objective of normalization is to simplify or eliminate update, deletion, and insertion problems in a data base. The major goal of a relational model is to achieve the third normal form:

> An attribute of a relation (attribute y) is functionally dependent on another attribute in the relation (attribute x), such that each value in x has no more than one value in y associated with it. Therefore, x determines y; x is the determinate. A third normal form exists when every determinant is a key. Stated another way, all items in a record are completely dependent on the key of that record and nothing else.

These terms, concepts, and theories probably sound a bit farfetched so let us provide a pragmatic example to bring things into perspective. Keep in mind that the goal is to provide simplicity to the user. Figure 5–7(a) shows the Inventory Relation again. However, it does *not* exhibit the third normal form and can present some serious problems when updates and deletions are applied to the data base.

To illustrate, let us assume the price of Component Part #634 is to be changed from $10 to $12. In Figure 5–7(a), this update affects more than one row (tuple). The

INVENTORY	Component Part #	Description	Location	# In Stock	Price	Stock Deletion Date
	634	• • •	NY	50	10	7/88
	788	• • •	LA	200	20	8/88
	996	• • •	SF	100	15	10/88
	1500	• • •	KC	350	5	2/88
	634	• • •	LA	600	10	7/88

(a) Initial Form

PRICE	Component Part #	Description	Price
	634	• • •	10
	788	• • •	20
	996	• • •	15
	1500	• • •	5

INVENTORY	Component Part #	Location	# In Stock	Stock Deletion Date
	634	NY	50	7/88
	788	LA	200	8/88
	996	SF	100	10/88
	1500	KC	350	2/88
	634	LA	600	7/88

(b) Two Relations

PRICE	Component Part #	Description	Price
	634	• • •	10
	788	• • •	20
	996	• • •	15
	1500	• • •	5

INVENTORY LOCATION	Component Part #	Location	# In Stock
	634	NY	50
	788	LA	200
	996	SF	100
	1500	KC	350
	634	LA	600

STOCK DELETION DATE	Component Part #	Stock Deletion Date
	634	7/88
	788	8/88
	996	10/88
	1500	2/88

(c) Three Relations

Figure 5–7. Normalizing the network data bases.

third normal form principle is violated because the x value (Component Part #) is associated with *more than one* y value (Price). This makes updating difficult because all tuples in the relation must be accessed and searched to ensure all values are correctly changed.

The solution to the update problem is to "normalize" the one relation to a Price Relation and an Inventory Relation, as in Figure 5–7(b). It can be seen that changing the price of a part will not affect any other value in *either* relation. (We are progressing toward a simpler organization.)

The two-relation data base still presents a violation of the third normal form principle. For example, Component Part #634 is to be removed from the active data-base inventory on July 31, 1988 (7/88). With the present two-relation data base, the deletion of the first tuple of the Inventory Relation removes *all* information on where the component is located. This may not be a desirable feature of the data base, since the stock still has financial value. To correct the deletion problem, the data model is normalized to create three relations [Figure 5–7(c)]. The Inventory Location Relation maintains the location of *all* parts, even after they are removed from the active inventory.

The reader may be puzzled about the duplicate Component Part # in the Location Relation of Figure 5–7(c): Part Number Component Part #634 is located in New York and Los Angeles. Does this situation create ambiguity and violate the rules of relational models? The answer is no *if* the Location Relation uses the two attributes Component Part # and Location to form the relation's *candidate* key.

Schemas and Subschemas

The structures in Figure 5–7(c) represent the schema of the Inventory data base. The schema provides a map or chart of the data, shows the names of the attributes, and establishes the relationships of data elements. It provides the overall view of the data base. It says nothing about the physical structure on disk or the physical access method. The term *subschema* refers to a user's or programmer's map of the data base. A subschema is usually a subset of the schema.

For example, inventory control personnel would be interested in the shelf dates of components at various locations in order to answer the questions. "What components are to be removed from the active inventory this month, where are they located, and how many components will be removed?" This user's view can be satisfied by joining the Location and Stock Deletion Date relations; the Price Relation is not needed.

Typically, organizations have hundreds of subschemas and individual users often have multiple subschemas to satisfy different kinds of retrieval and update requirements. This presents a challenging problem for the data-base and network designers: They must provide for a *physical* design that satisfies all user subschemas at all nodes in the network. The problem manifests itself in (a) the physical location of the data on the disk and (b) the physical location of the data within the network. In essence, the problem is translating logical views to efficient physical data structures.

Subschemas and physical data structures in the network. The first problem of the location of the data on the disk is illustrated in Figure 5–8. User A, the inventory control analyst, wants efficient, fast, and inexpensive access to his or her view.

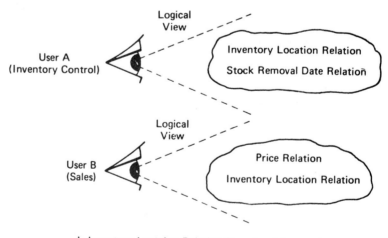

Figure 5–8. Subschemas and physical storage of data on disk.

Conversely, user B, in the sales office, wishes the same service to some of the same data found in user A's subschema. Naturally, both users want minimum access overhead to obtain the data. Placing the data in one *physical* block is the most efficient method. However, what is efficient for one user is not necessarily efficient for another. The database designer must examine both subschemas, the relative priority between the users, their frequency of use, and time of use in order to implement the best physical layout on the disk. In many cases, the common data will be placed in separate physical blocks as a compromise solution.

This kind of situation should be kept transparent to the user community if at all possible. The DBMS systems of today can provide for considerable transparency. However, an organization must be careful not to penalize its users from the standpoint of disk storage costs, DBMS overhead, and extra I/O charges. In fact, the shared data bases should be given discounts (I/O, higher priorities, etc.) to encourage their use. While a DBMS may provide powerful capabilities to the users, if they appear to be expensive to use, the users will access the shared data base only to spin off specialized and redundant files for their exclusive use. Uncontrolled data redundancy presents very serious problems to organizations. Consequently, the translation of the user's subschema to the physical structure is an important task.

The translation of the subschemas to physical locations in the network is of even greater importance. As shown in Figure 5–9, our two users are located in different cities. Where should the commonly used data be stored, in San Francisco or San Diego? Can they be stored in both places? If so, how are the redundant data elements kept in synchronization between the two sites? How are hundreds of subschemas analyzed to determine the proper location of the network data bases? One might question if this type of problem exists when the data are not stored at remote locations, but within a *network* environment, perhaps within a building. The problem is certainly not as serious, but the access of data across multiple data bases can create unacceptable response time to the end user. The overhead and delay of accessing multiple files is a key design issue and a major factor in the networking of multiuser data bases with personal computers.

These questions and others are of paramount importance. Their answers determine,

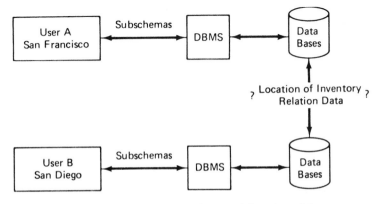

Figure 5–9. Subschemas and network location of data.

to a great extent, the quality and expense of the network and its ability to provide service to the end users.

The value of understanding the concepts of data-base technology should now be evident. We will continue this subject in sections of Chapters 13 and 14. Those readers interested in pursuing the subject immediately can skip to these sections. The intervening material is not required to grasp the subject matter.

SUMMARY

The principal purpose of a data communications system is to promote the sharing of user data and software. The decision of where to locate data bases is a critical factor in the design of a data communications network. In addition, certain software packages do not lend themselves to downline loading to low capacity machines. Consequently, it may be necessary to access software at a central computer from the distributed sites. This requirement should be weighed against the communications overhead involved in the process.

6

Transmission Impairments

INTRODUCTION

The data contained in a message, packet, or frame do not always arrive correctly at the receiving site. For numerous reasons, a bit or several bits can become distorted or garbled during transmission. In this chapter, we explore the major transmission impairments that cause errors in the data, as well as preventive measures to decrease the probability of the errors occurring. In this chapter, we will learn how to deal with those error conditions that cannot be completely eliminated.

FACTORS CONTRIBUTING TO ERRORS

A typical voice-grade, low-speed line experiences a rate of one error bit in every 100,000 bits transmitted (or $1:10^5$). Some user applications find this error rate acceptable and might choose to ignore an infrequent error. For example, a 120-Hz telegraph line could transmit for several hours and experience only one error during this period. This error rate would most likely be inconsequential for applications that transmit text. However, certain applications cannot tolerate any errors. For example, the loss of 1 bit in a transmission of financial data could have severe consequences for an accounting system. For these applications, the transmission must be made as error free as possible.

Treating errors in a data communications system is a more difficult task than one might imagine. Four factors contribute to this situation.

1. Distance between components
2. Transmission over hostile environments
3. Number of components involved in transmission
4. Lack of control over the process

Distance between Components

Computers and terminals connected by communications links may be located hundreds of miles from each other. The transmission speed of the signals between the sites can be very fast, as in a radio transmission (186 miles per 1 ms), or considerably slower, as in certain wire pairs (10 miles per 1 ms). Whatever the propagation speed may be, the distance introduces a delay.

To illustrate the point, consider a one-way satellite transmission. The up-link and down-link signals require a minimum of 240-ms propagation time (22,300 miles/186,000 miles/s = 0.120 × 2 = 0.240), which is more often around 270 ms, depending on the location of the earth stations. A two-way transmission on a half-duplex link to effect a dialogue between the two sites then requires 540 ms of transmission time. Effective interactive systems should not have a response time of greater than an average of 2 sec. Given this satellite path, designers have one-quarter of their window taken away solely from transmission propagation delay.

A shorter transmission delay of 20 to 30 ms on land links between the East and West coasts of the United States can affect performance and error control measures in many systems. For example, updating replicated data bases in a network requires that multiple update transactions be transmitted to all affected sites. The transactions arrive at the sites at different times and, relative to the speed of the computers and channel I/O operations, the arrival delays can be significant. To obtain consistency among the multiple copies, updates must be delayed at those sites receiving the transaction first. If a transaction is garbled during transmission, further delay is introduced while the error is analyzed and corrective action taken. Error analysis is made difficult due to the distance involved and the inherent delays. It is not unusual for an error condition on a transmission path to disappear after a few fractions of a second. Such an error would usually be identified in a centralized mainframe environment. Simply stated, the longer the delay in error analysis, the more difficult it is to identify and resolve the error.

Transmission over Hostile Environments

When we consider the differences between the data communications and centralized mainframe environments, it becomes clear that data communications systems are more subject to error because of the operations in a hostile environment. A microwave signal is illustrative. During transmission it may encounter varying temperatures, fog, rain, snow, as well as other microwave signals that tend to distort the signal.

On the other hand, the flow of data inside a computer room is subject to strict temperature, humidity, and electromagnetic radiation controls. It is not surprising that the error rate on a channel inside a computer room is several orders of magnitude better than that of a voice-grade communications line.

Number of Components Involved in Transmission

A transmission through a communications system travels through several components, and each component introduces the added probability of errors. For example, as a signal moves through the network, it must pass through switches, modems, multiplexers, and other instruments. If the interfaces among these components are not established properly, an error is likely to occur. The components themselves often introduce errors; for instance, some of the carrier's older circuit switches can create considerable interference on the line. Moreover, line segments connected in tandem (to form an end-to-end channel) are more prone to error than one stand-alone link. Networks tend to have tandem links.

Lack of Control over the Process

The classical centralized mainframe operating system (OS) exercises considerable control over its resources. Very little happens without the permission of the OS. In the event an error occurs, the operating system interrupts the work in progress, suspends the problem program, stores its registers and buffers, and executes the requisite analysis to uncover the problem. In a sense, the error and problem are frozen to simplify the analysis. A data communications network may not allow for this type of control. First, it is often impractical to suspend and freeze resources because they may be used by other components. Second, their condition may have changed by the time network control receives the error indication. Third, networks do not always operate under the tight centralized manner found in the centralized mainframe. For example, one computer in a network may not be allowed to control and analyze errors affecting it because they occur in other parts of the system.

UNITS OF MEASUREMENT AND OTHER TERMINOLOGY

The Decibel

The term *decibel* (dB) is used in communications to express the ratio of two values. The values can represent power, voltage, current, or sound levels. It should be emphasized that the decibel (a) is a ratio and not an absolute value, (b) expresses a logarithmic relationship and not a linear one, and (c) can be used to indicate either a gain or a loss. A decibel is 10 times the logarithm (in base 10) of the ratio:[1]

$$dB = 10 \log_{10} P_1/P_2$$

where dB = number of decibels
P_1 = one value of the power
P_2 = comparison value of the power

---

[1] A *logarithm* is really an exponent. For example, $2^3 = 8$ and $3 = \log_2 8$ are identical. The log of a number is the power to which some positive base must be raised to equal that number.

Decibels are often used to measure the gain or loss of a signal. These measurements are quite valuable for testing the quality of lines and determining noise and signal losses, all of which must be known in order to design the network. For example, suppose a communications line is tested at the sending end and receiving end. The P_1/P_2 ratio yields a reduction of the signal power from the sending to receiving end by a ratio of $200:1$. The signal experiences a 23-dB loss ($23 = 10 \log_{10} 200$). The log calculations are readily available from tables published in math books.

The decibel is often used to describe the level of noise on a circuit in a signal-to-noise ratio. As the following table shows, 0 dB is equivalent to a $1:1$ ratio of the signal to noise.

Decibels (dB)	Signal-to-Noise Ratios
0	1:1
+3	2:1
+6	4:1
+9	8:1
+10	10:1
+13	20:1
+16	40:1
+19	80:1
+20	100:1
+23	200:1
+26	400:1
+29	800:1
+30	1,000:1
+33	2,000:1
+36	4,000:1
+39	8,000:1
+40	10,000:1

Transmission measurements may also need an absolute unit. The dBm is used for this purpose. It is a relative power measurement in which the reference power is 1 milliwatt (0.001 watt):

$$\text{dBm} = 10 \log_{10} P/0.001$$

where P = signal power in milliwatts (mW)

This approach allows measurements to be taken in relation to a standard. A signal of a known power level is inserted at one end and measured at the other. A 0 dBm reading means 1 mW.

Common carriers use a 1004-Hz tone (referred to as a 1-kHz test tone) to test a line. The 1-kHz tone is used as a reference to other test tones of a different level. The test tone is used to establish a zero transmission level point (TLP). The TLP establishes a point at which the 1-kHz tone is expected. A +6 TLP is a point where the 1-kHz tone would be +7 dBm.

Resistance

The current running through a wire and an electromagnetic transmission in the atmosphere both encounter resistance. Particles in the wire and the atmosphere provide opposition to the signal. The reader may have felt a conducting wire and noticed it was hot, an indication that significant resistance existed. The resistance creates a loss of signal strength, described as *decay* or *attenuation*.

Inductance

A conductor need not be connected directly to another conductor to transfer a signal. For example, an increased current on a wire produces an expanded magnetic field outward from the conductor. This magnetic field can affect other wires and circuits, and in many instances, it can create an induced voltage in another component. Induction coils are used extensively to transfer signals and to step up or step down their voltages.

Capacitance

Materials tend to collect and hold an electric charge even after the voltage source is disconnected. For example, wire cable tends to store charges between the wires in the cable.

Transmission impairments can occur due to "stray" capacitance and inductance. The components in data communications systems all have capacitive and inductive effects on each other. While the effects can be small, they can also cause data errors.

MAJOR IMPAIRMENTS

Transmission impairments can be broadly defined as random or nonrandom events. The random events cannot be predicted. Nonrandom impairments are predictable and, therefore, are subject to preventive maintenance efforts. The following list contains the major kinds of transmission impairments found on voice-grade circuits:

    Random
       White noise
       Electrical noise
       Transients
       Cross talk
       Echoes
       Intermodulation noise
       Phase jitter
       Radio signal fading
    Nonrandom
       Attenuation
       Delay
       Harmonic distortion
       Spacing and marking distortion

Random Distortions

White noise.   Chapter 3 discussed how the *nonrandom* movement of electrons creates an electric current that is used for the transmission signal. Along with these signals, all electrical components also experience the vibrations of the *random* movement of electrons. These vibrations cause the emission of electromagnetic waves of all frequencies. The phenomenon is called *white noise* because it contains an average of all the spectral frequencies equally, just as white light does. Other kinds of noise exist that can affect transmission quality. For example, space noise results from the sun and other stars radiating energy over a broad frequency spectrum. Atmospheric noise comes from electrical disturbances in the earth's atmosphere.

White noise is identified by other names (Gaussian, background, thermal, hiss). It forms a constant signal on the communications line against which the data signal must be sent. The power of white noise is proportional to temperature. This has important consequences for satellite transmissions because the transmitters can operate at reduced power if shielded from the sun.

Shannon's law demonstrates that noise is one determinant of the information capacity of a communications line. The signal-to-noise ratio must remain at a level to keep the signal separated from the noise. Figure 6–1(a) illustrates the process. The initial signal is amplified and transmitted across the line. As will be explained shortly, its strength decreases as it traverses the communications path. Notice, however, that the noise never drops below a certain level (at point 1). The signal is amplified at point 2 and brought back to its original strength. The white noise is also amplified. In this illustration, some of the frequencies of the signal mix with the noise. (Once this happens, the two cannot be separated.) Obviously, the spacing of the amplifiers is an important consideration, since improper spacing will allow the mixing of the noise and the data signal.

One solution to the noise problem for voice communications is the use of a compandor [Figure 6–1(b)]. This device prevents strong (high-amplitude) signals from overloading an amplifier. It reduces the volume range by compressing these signals before they are transmitted. The low-amplitude or weak signals are also raised above the probable noise level for transmission across the line. Since the noise is not yet at the transmitter, the noise level is not amplified by the compandor. The process is reversed at the receiver. The compandor restores the signal to its original range, and the noise is lowered to a level below the level that existed on the channel.

Unfortunately, compandors can present problems for data transmission. A data stream using amplitude modulation (AM) or quadrature amplitude modulation (QAM) may be distorted by the compandors. Frequency modulation (FM) signals operate better but may have problems, since the compandors sometimes introduce unwanted frequencies into the transmission.

Electrical noise.   This impairment includes aspects of background noise but warrants further discussion. Electrical noise stems from high-voltage, high-frequency interference on an alternating current (ac) line, typically a power line. Two basic types

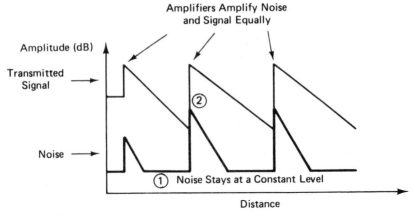

(a) Signal and Noise Relationship

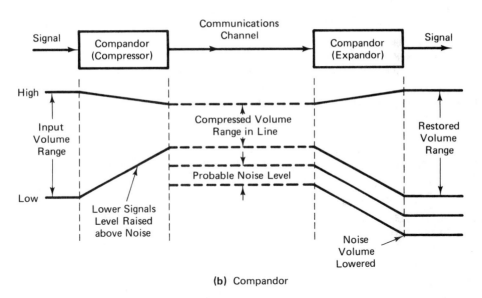

(b) Compandor

Figure 6–1. Channel noise.

of electrical noise exist: *common mode* (electrical interference between line and ground) and *transverse mode* (interference across lines).

Electrical noise stems primarily from two sources. First, *radio frequency interference* (RFI) comes from television, radio, microwave, and radar transmissions. Distant lightning can create electrical noise, and machinery such as arc welders are a source as well. Second, *electromagnetic interference* (EMI) comes from such equipment as motor drive devices and heating and cooling units. Even seemingly innocuous devices such as electric pencil sharpeners and electric typewriters are a source of EMI.

Transients.   This impairment is a major cause of errors in a data transmission. The sources of transients are many. All unwanted electronic effects, such as voltage changes, dialing noise, dirty electrical contacts, and movement of poorly connected electrical joints are contributing factors to impulse noise. The telephone system's older step-by-step switches and the electrical power companies' power supplies are also a major source of transients.

The effect of a transient can be seen in Figure 6–2. The original digital pulse binary bit stream represents the base 10 number 281. In Figure 6–2(a), the data are received as sent. If a transient is introduced, as in Figure 6–2(b), the bits are altered and the number 281 is changed to represent the number 347, as in Figure 6–2(c).

The problem is actually more complex than this illustration shows. A 1-bit error can usually be detected and corrected at the receiving site. A transient may last 10 ms. Consequently, a 4,800-b/s transmission would have about 50 bits affected by the 10-ms impairment; a 9,600 bit/s line would lose about 100 bits. In either case, parity checking would not work and error correction would be more difficult. The message would usually be retransmitted.

Transients can be classified as follows:

- Impulse noise
- Gain hits

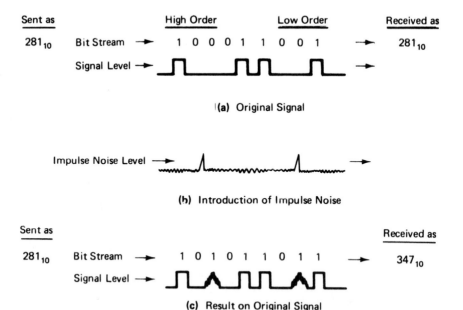

Note: Be Aware that Impulse Noise May Affect Groups of Bits.

Figure 6–2.   Effect of impulse noise.

- Dropouts
- Phase hits

Impulse noise is mostly "people-made" [see Figure 6–3(b)]. It stems from sources such as switches, call terminations, and repair and installation activities of maintenance personnel. The noise creates a spike in the signal and can result in data errors, especially in systems with high data rates; a lower data rate device can usually distinguish between the spike and the signal. Studies show that impulse noise spikes last less than 1 ms and most effects disappear within 4 ms.

Gain hits [Figure 6–3(c)] resemble impulse noise but they are defined to last at least 4 ms and not exceed 12 dB from the received signal. A gain hit is perceived as data by AM and QAM modems. An AT&T/Bell Standard is to limit gain hits to no more than eight (more than 3 dB from signal) within a 15-minute period. Gain hits are also called line *surges*.

Dropouts [Figure 6–3(d)] are gain hits greater than 12 dB lasting longer than 4 ms. Since such a severe and prolonged transient creates serious problems, AT&T/Bell stipulate that a dropout should occur no more than once every 30 minutes. However, the telephone or data carrier companies may not have control of dropouts if they occur in the electrical power company's facilities. These types of dropouts are called (a) sags

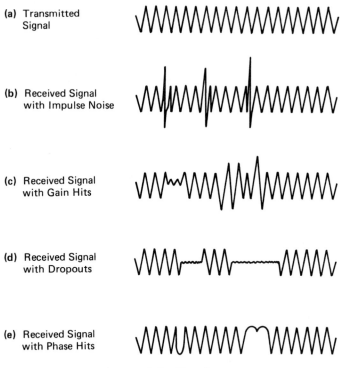

(a) Transmitted Signal

(b) Received Signal with Impulse Noise

(c) Received Signal with Gain Hits

(d) Received Signal with Dropouts

(e) Received Signal with Phase Hits

Figure 6–3. Transients.

(short voltage transients), (b) brownouts (slightly longer periods of voltage reduction), and (c) blackouts (total power outages).

Phase hits [Figure 6–3(e)] affect the phase or frequency of a carrier signal and can create data errors in FM and PM modem transmissions. The common standard is to hold phase hits to no more than eight in 15 seconds for those that change the signal phase by more than 20°.

Cross talk.   Most of us who use the public telephone network have experienced the interference of another party's faint voice on our line. This is cross talk, the interference of signals from another channel. One source of cross talk is in physical circuits that run parallel to each other in building ducts and telephone facilities. The electromagnetic radiation of the signals on the circuits creates an inductance effect on the nearby circuits. Cross talk can also occur with the coupling of a transmitter and receiver at the same location, which is called *near-end* cross talk, or NEXT. The coupling of a transmitter to an incorrect remote receiver is called *far-end* cross talk, or FEXT.

Frequency-division multiplexers (FDMs) are often a source of cross talk. The adjacent subchannels may interfere with others if the filters do not cut off the extraneous and overlapping frequencies of the channels.

Echoes.   Almost everyone using a telephone has also experienced echoes during a conversation. The effect sounds like one is in an echo chamber; the talker's voice is actually echoed back to the telephone handset. Echoes are caused by the changes in impedances in a communications circuit. (*Impedance* is the combined effect of inductance, resistance, and capacitance on a signal at a particular frequency.) For example, connecting two wires of different gauges could create an impedance mismatch. Echoes are also caused by circuit junctions that erroneously allow a portion of the signal to find its way into the return side of a four-wire circuit.

Figure 6–4 shows one way in which echoes occur on a voice-grade line. At the top of the figure (point 1), the signal comes into a circuit for transfer to a two-wire path (point 2). The signal enters a junction called a *hybrid coil*. This device prevents excessive feedback across the junction of the returning lines (point 3). In addition, the junction contains a balancing network that balances the impedance matches of the lines and the hybrid coils. However, some of the signal, through inductance, may find its way into the return circuit. It is then strengthened by the amplifier at 3, thus creating an echo on the line.

An echo is often not noticed. The feedback on a short-distance circuit happens so quickly that it is imperceptible. Generally, an echo with a delay of greater than 45 ms (0.045 second) presents problems. For this reason, long-distance lines and satellite links employ devices to reduce the strength of the return signal. These devices, called *echo suppressors* or *cancellers*, are discussed later.

Intermodulation noise.   Earlier chapters describe the common carriers' frequency multiplexed systems wherein many voice-grade circuits are modulated onto a high-capacity link, such as coaxial cable and microwave. These channels can interfere

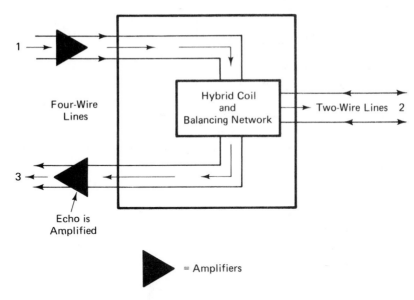

Figure 6–4. Echoes.

with each other if the equipment is slightly unlinear. Typically, two signals from two separate circuits combine (intermodulate) to form a frequency band reserved for another circuit. The reader has likely heard intermodulation noise during a telephone call; it sounds like a jumble of low-speaking voices, none clearly perceptible.

Intermodulation noise can occur in the transmission of data when a modem uses a *single* frequency to keep the line synchronized when data are not being sent. The single frequency may actually modulate a signal on another channel. This problem can be avoided by transmitting either a variable-frequency signal or a signal of low amplitude. Intermodulation noise can also stem from the data within the message transmission. A repetitive code in the transmission could create the problem.

Phase jitter. Occasionally, a signal's phase will jitter, causing an ill-defined crossing of the signal through the receiver. The signal appears to be frequency or phase modulated. Noise-laden signals resemble jitter but are caused by different impairments. Jitter is usually created by a multiplexed carrier system that creates a forward and backward movement of the individual frequency, and a ringing current (of 20 Hz) can cause phase jitter on an adjacent channel. Most phase jitter measurements are made below 300 Hz.

Radio signal fading. Microwave transmissions are particularly subject to fading. This impairment occurs in two ways. The first, *selective fading*, occurs when the atmospheric conditions bend a transmission to an extent that signals reach the receiver in slightly different paths (Figure 6–5). The merging paths can cause interference and create data errors. Other channels in the microwave transmission are not affected by a

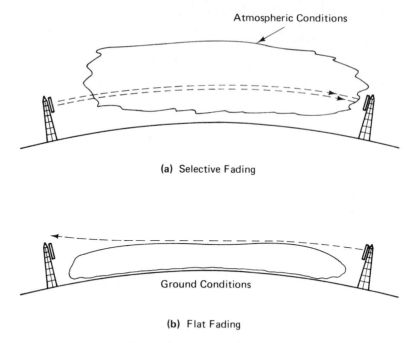

Figure 6–5. Microwave fading.

selective fade. Therefore, backup channels are usually provided to allow for protection against this problem.

Flat fading is a more serious problem because it can last several hours and alternate channels will not provide relief. Flat fading occurs during fog and when the surrounding ground is very moist. These conditions change the electrical characteristics of the atmosphere. A portion of the transmitted signal is refracted and does not reach the receiving antenna.

Nonrandom Distortions

Attenuation.   The strength of a signal attenuates (decays) as it travels through a transmission path. The amount of attenuation depends on the frequency of the signal, the transmission medium, and the length of the circuit. Unfortunately, signal attenuation is not the same for all frequencies. The nonuniform loss across the bandwidth (Figure 6–6) can create amplitude distortion (which is also referred to as attenuation distortion) on a standard voice channel. It can be seen that signal loss increases at the higher frequencies. Consequently, those media that use high-frequency bands (coaxial cable, microwave) require the signal to be strengthened (with analog amplifiers or digital repeaters) more often than a low-frequency open-wire pair. Generally, it is desirable to amplify a signal after it has been attenuated by 20 dB. Given this requirement, an 8-kHz coaxial cable with an attenuation of 10 dB per mile would require signal amplification every 2 miles.

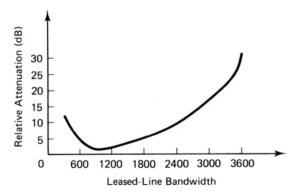

Figure 6–6.   Attenuation.

Attenuation distortion is measured by comparing the loss at any frequency to the loss of a 1,004-Hz reference signal. For instance, a 2,800-Hz signal with 6 dB more loss than the reference signal would have an attenuation distortion of 6 dB.

Delay.   A signal is comprised of many frequencies. These frequencies do not travel at the same speed and, therefore, arrive at the receiver at different times [see Figure 6–7(a)]. Excessive delays create errors known as *delay distortion* or *envelope delay*. The problem is not serious for voice transmissions because a human ear is not very sensitive to phase. However, delay distortion creates problems for data transmissions.

The variation of propagation is equivalent to a phase shift and is also called *phase distortion*. The problem is depicted in Figure 6–7(b), which shows the effect of the delay of a wave from the 1- and 3-kHz frequency components.[2] The higher frequency expe-

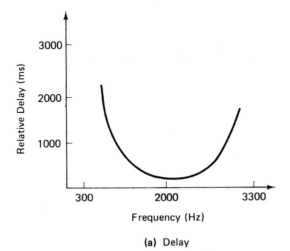

(a) Delay

Figure 6–7.   Delay distortion.

[2]*Data Communications Testing*, Hewlett-Packard training manual #5952-4973, Colorado Telecommunications Division, Colorado Springs, CO 80933.

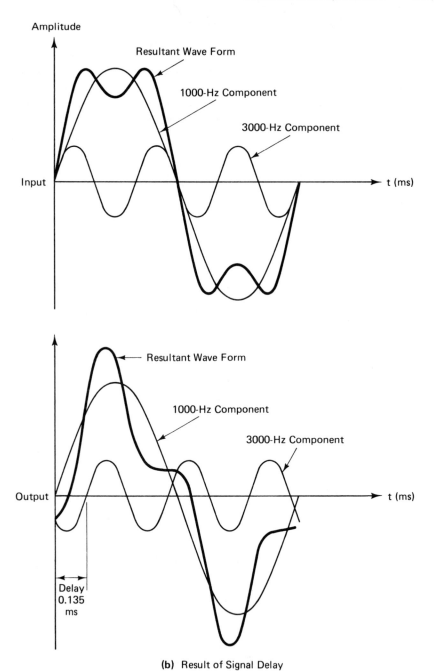

(b) Result of Signal Delay

Figure 6–7.   (cont.).

riences 0.135 ms more delay, which significantly changes the resultant shape of the wave at the receiver.

Harmonic distortion.   Certain electronic components generate signal components that are not present in the original transmitted signal. Amplifiers, modulators, and demodulators may produce these added signals. They are called harmonics because they are integer multiples of the original signal. The effect is also called *nonlinear distortion*. The amplitude of the output of the device is nonlinearly proportional to the input.

Spacing and marking distortion.   This error occurs when the receiving component samples the incoming signal at the wrong interval or threshold, and/or the signal takes too long to build up and decay on the channel. This problem can occur in interfaces

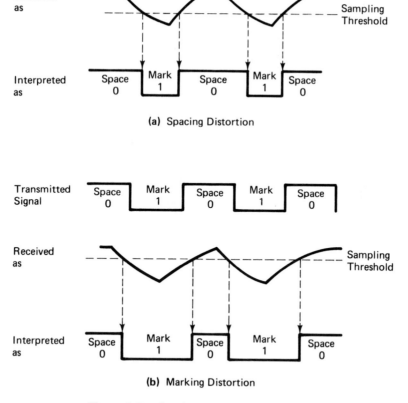

Figure 6–8.   Spacing and marking distortion.

such as EIA-232-D when the EIA standard is not followed. EIA specifies that the capacitance of the cable and the terminator shall be less than 2,500 pF (picofarads, a measure of capacitance). If this specification is violated, the transition from a one (mark) to a zero (space), and vice versa, may exceed the EIA-232-D standard stated as "time required to pass through the -3 V to $+3$ V or $+3$ V to -3 V transition region shall not exceed 1 millisecond or 4% of a bit time, whichever is smaller."

Figure 6–8 shows the consequences of violating the specification. The signal takes too long to complete the transitions from or to marks and spaces. Spacing distortion results when the receiver produces space bits longer than the mark bits. Marking distortion occurs when the mark bits are elongated. These problems may cause data errors, especially if the sampling clock is inaccurate and noise exists on the line.

ERROR CONTROL METHODS

Given that transmission impairments exist, what can be done to mitigate their effect? In this section we examine several options and choices that can reduce substantially the data errors that result from the transmission distortions.

An individual component in a communications system may be quite reliable and relatively error free. For example, AT&T sets a goal of channel outage on a long-distance microwave link at 0.0002 annually—less than 2 hours. Yet this impressive performance means little if all components in the system are not equally error free. Like the links in a chain, the communications network is only as strong as its weakest component. Figure 6–9 shows a typical, rather simple data communications configuration. Twenty-two components complete the full setup. Let us assume that each component is reliable enough to give 99.9% availability. (Let us also exclude point 22, the human operator, since we can never expect that kind of availability.) A 99.9% availability might be considered adequate for certain systems, but this figure is for each individual component. Since the components are in tandem, the overall availability of the systems must be computed by multiplying each availability number together, yielding 0.979. Obviously, 97.9% availability is substantially different from 99.9%. If one component is down, it makes little difference, from the standpoint of availability, if the others are up and running.

Murphy's law states that if anything can go wrong, it will. In developing error control methods for a data communications system, some of Murphy's corollaries should all be kept in mind:

- Nothing is as easy as it looks.
- Everything takes longer than you think.
- If there is a possibility of several things going wrong, the one that will cause the most damage will be the one to go wrong.
- The probability of anything happening is in inverse ratio to its desirability.
- Murphy was an optimist.

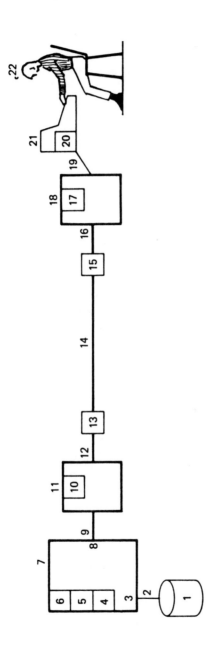

1. Disk Data Set
2. Channel
3. Channel Software
4. Data Base Management System
5. Applications Program
6. Operating System
7. Computer Hardware
8. Channel Software
9. Channel
10. Front End Software
11. Front End Hardware

12. Port Interface
13. Modem
14. Communications Line
15. Modem
16. Port Interface
17. Terminal Controller Software or Microcode
18. Terminal Controller Hardware
19. Cable
20. Terminal Software (possibly)
21. Terminal Hardware
22. Human Operator

Figure 6–9. Possible error points.

Perceived Availability

Murphy's law notwithstanding, the primary objective in devising error control methods is to provide perceived availability to the user. This means that an error or malfunction in the network remains invisible; the user perceives that the system is fully operational. From the user's point of view, perceived availability is achieved by the network providing optimum performance in

> Mean time between failure (MTBF)
> Mean time to recover (MTTREC)
> Mean time to repair (MTTREP)

MTBF should be increased to the greatest extent possible. This is accomplished in two ways. First, failures are reduced to the maximum extent possible and, second, the scope of effect of the failures is kept as isolated as possible.

MTTREC is kept as low as possible. In the event of a failure, the recovery should be fast. For example, redundant components should assume network functions without perceptible delay. In the event a component fails, MTTREP requires rapid diagnosis of the problem and facilities that provide rapid corrective action.

The MTBF, MTTREC, and MTTREP performance factors should be continuously monitored. The installation should establish performance thresholds against which the system is measured. The statistics should provide for both trend analysis and identification of potential trouble areas for preventive maintenance.

Mitigating the Effects of Distortions

Combating noise.   The first task in dealing with a noise problem is to determine the type and extent of the noise. Noise power should be measured. Since noise usually manifests itself within a predominant frequency component, weighting filters are often used to identify the noise source. Several techniques are used to measure noise. One of the most common is the use of the *C-message filter* and the *notch filter*.

The C-message filter [Figure 6–10(a)] measures typical noise levels that exist in a telephone voice transmission. It is not really relevant to data transmissions, but it is widely used for noise measurements. The notch filter is used with the C-message filter because noise is generated by the data communications device. The notch filter [Figure 6–10(b)] removes the signal (tone) before the noise is measured. Typically, a 1,004-Hz test tone is transmitted and notched out so the resultant noise can be measured [Figure 6–10(c)].

The *signal-to-noise ratio* (S/N) can be computed by comparing the level of the test tone with the noise. An acceptable channel limits the S/N ratio to 28 dB minimum. This check is a quick and easy method to determine the quality of a channel, but, unlike the notched filter, it does not isolate the source of the noise.

The telephone company can run other tests to check for noise. The *peak-to-average ratio* (P/AR) is very useful for a quick measurement of the circuit. The measurement is

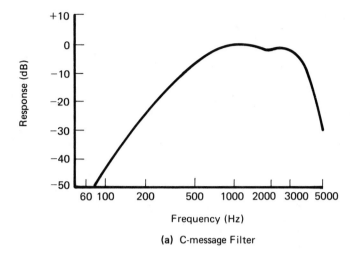

(a) C-message Filter

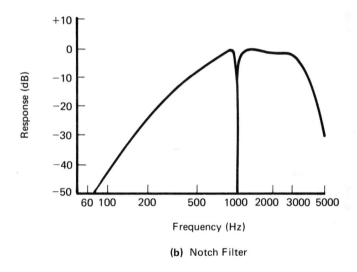

(b) Notch Filter

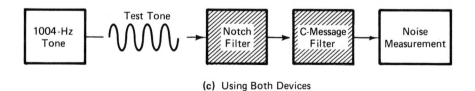

(c) Using Both Devices

Figure 6–10. Noise with tone.

most sensitive to noise, delay, and attenuation distortion. P/AR is determined by transmitting a complex signal of multiple frequencies and measuring the peak-to-average amplitudes at the receiver. A P/AR of 100 indicates a signal with no degradation.

Noise can never be completely eliminated. However, the use of shielded cable can reduce the effect of many forms of noise. Coaxial cable is shielded and is widely used because of its relative immunity to noise. Of course, optical fibers are noise free and are widely used in areas where noise is a problem.

Power line noise can also be diminished by the installation of power protection devices. Some of the more commonly used are the following:

Passive filter: attenuates noise in a specific band of frequencies.

Surge suppressor: clips high-voltage transients.

Ultraisolation transformer: suppresses common-mode noise.

Constant voltage transformer: limits current to protect against overloads and short circuits.

Uninterrupted power supply (UPS): provides power in case of brownouts or blackouts.

Several of these functions can be acquired in one device.

Combating cross talk and intermodulation noise.   Shielding can diminish the effect of cross talk on cable pairs, and filters are often employed on frequency-division multiplexing systems to avoid channel overlap. Most carrier systems also place guard bands between channels to reduce channel interference (see Figure 6–11). Nonetheless, a large noise spike on the channel is still often detected on adjacent channels.

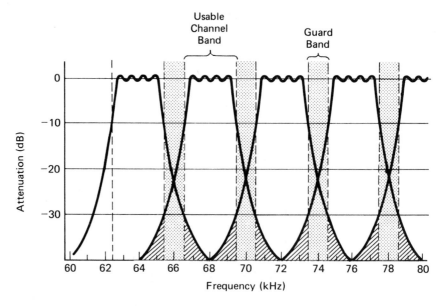

Figure 6-11.   Guard bands and filters.

Dealing with echoes. *Echo suppressors* are used by the telephone company to filter out the unwanted signals that are sent back to the transmitter. For example, in Figure 6–4, a suppressor can be placed on the return circuit to block the echoes.

Echo suppressors cannot be used for data transmission over a voice line. The speech detector is designed to detect speech signals. Moreover, the delay in reversing the activation of the suppressors at each end often causes the clipping of the first part of a signal. The clipping effect is probably familiar to the reader. It does not usually present serious problems in a voice transmission but can cause bit distortions in a data transmission.

Since the telephone network is a primary facility in a data communications network, the echo suppressors must be disabled for data transmissions. This is accomplished by the transmission of a 2,000- to 2,250-Hz signal for approximately 400 ms. The suppressor is deactivated until no signal is on the line for about 50 ms. In the event the transmission of messages is not continuous, a signal must be placed on the line to keep the suppressors disabled. Carrier signals can accomplish this purpose. The reader may have had an occasion to dial up a computer. Upon completing the dial, a high-pitched tone can be heard. This tone indicates that the caller has a connection to the computer, and it also disables any echo suppressors that may be on the line.

Echo cancellation is another technique for handling echoes. As Figure 6–12 illustrates, a canceller is placed near the origin of the echo. A reference signal (Y) is sent to the canceler. The echo (R) is returned to point A along with the near-end talker signal (X). The canceller then uses the Y reference signal to produce a replica (R1) of the R echo, and this replica is subtracted from the signal. Thus, the echo is canceled.

Echo cancellation is used in both voice and data transmission. The Y reference signal for a data echo canceler is the sequence of transmitted data signals. Half-duplex data channels have no echo problem, since there is no receiver on the transmitting end to be affected by the echo.

Phase jitter solutions. Phase jitter presents few problems for voice transmission, since the ear is insensitive to phase, but phase modulation modems are particularly sensitive to phase jitter.

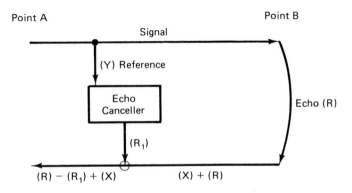

Figure 6–12. Echo cancellation.

Phase jitter can be measured by sending a test tone (usually 1,004 Hz) to a receiver that establishes a reference phase to measure the jitter (based on the phase reference). Most carrier standards permit no more than 10° or 15° jitter on their systems.

Diminishing the effects of attenuation and delay distortion.   A user has two options in reducing the effects of attenuation and delay distortion. *Line conditioning* can be purchased from the telephone company for leased lines. The carrier adds special equipment to the circuit, such as amplifiers, attenuation equalizers, and delay equalizers.

Conditioning provides measures to diminish the problems of attenuation and delay, but it does not remove the impairments. Rather, it provides for more consistency across the bandwidth. For attenuation, the common carrier introduces equipment that attenuates those signals in the bandwidth that tend to remain at a higher level than others. Thus, attenuation still occurs but is more evenly distributed across the channel. The same idea is used in delay. The faster frequencies are slowed so that the signal is more consistent across the band.

An attenuation equalizer adds a loss to the lower frequencies of the signal, since these frequencies delay less than the higher frequencies in the band (see Figure 6-6). The result is that the signal loss is consistent throughout the transmitted band. After equalization is applied, amplifiers restore the signal to its original level.

A delay equalizer compensates for envelope delay. As Figure 6-6 shows, the higher frequencies reach the receiver ahead of the lower frequencies. Consequently, the equalizer introduces more delay to these frequencies to make the entire signal propagate the receiver at the same time.

The second option is to use modems that are equipped with equalizers. Conditioning is not available over the switched telephone network, so these modems may be required, especially for high data rates of transmission.

Most modems that operate with speeds up to 4.8 Kbit/s use fixed equalizers. These devices are designed to compensate for the average conditions on a circuit. However, the fixed equalizers are being replaced with dynamic (or automatic) equalization. The modem analyzes the line conditions and adjusts its equalization accordingly. The adjustments take place without interrupting the flow of traffic. The adjustments occur very rapidly, on the order of 2,400 times a second for a 9.6-Kbit/s modem.

Testing and Monitoring

The majority of communications networks have a network management center (NMC). The NMC is responsible for the reliable and efficient operation of the network. It monitors and tests the communications systems and repairs or replaces failed components. The NMC is also responsible for day-to-day preventive maintenance operations in the network. It uses a wide variety of tools and techniques to keep the network running smoothly and to provide perceived availability to the user. The NMC may use the following equipment; all described here have overlapping functions.

Typical Diagnostic Equipment

Testing and monitoring communications channels and networks are very important in achieving perceived availability to the user. Without question, a high positive correlation exists between problem resolution/system availability and the use of diagnostics and monitoring. The use of test equipment allows a facility to isolate and identify the majority of problems and to furnish the carrier with credible data. If the carrier has test results from which to begin the troubleshooting analysis, hours of downtime are often saved.

A typical testing and monitoring facility is illustrated in Figure 6–13. Notice that it provides for the testing of both sides of the data circuit-terminating equipment (DCE). It also allows the testing of analog or digital circuits. A facility such as this uses several types of diagnostic equipment.

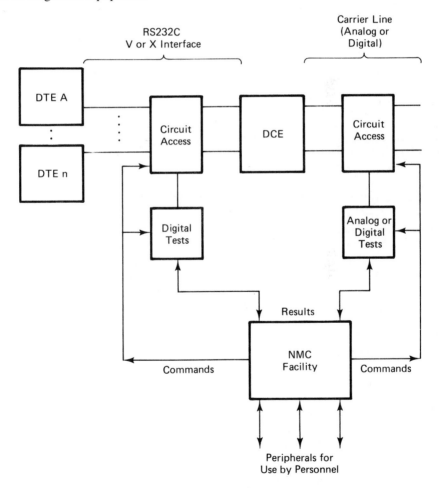

Figure 6–13.   Testing and monitoring facility.

Pattern generators and *analyzers* introduce a signal into the channel. A typical product transmits specific bit patterns and analyzes the return signal in order to detect errors at specific points in the channel. These devices pinpoint error locations and measure bit error rates.

Pattern generators need not interrupt main channel data flow. A technique known as *side-channel testing* provides simultaneous data and test signal transmission. To implement side-channel diagnosis, a modem divides the channel into two subchannels, one for data and one for testing. The testing channel can be used for network diagnosis when connected to diagnostic equipment through the secondary channels (that is, pins 12, 13, 14, 16, and 19) of an EIA-232-D interface.

A *breakout box* plugs into the two cables connecting two devices by using an interface such as an EIA-232-D. The breakout box acts like a tap and enables the testing of signal timing, voltage levels, and data quality. Breakout boxes are also used to test the data terminal equipment (DTE) circuitry (that is, logic) for the EIA-232-D or V and X series interface.

Many terminals, especially intelligent devices and personal computers, allow the user to check the logic, screen, and keyboard functionality. Testers that perform these tasks are also available. The testing procedure involves CRT screen pattern display or scrolling so the operator can monitor the device's performance. The operator checks the screen output for pattern inconsistencies.

A *protocol tester* simulates the system host and terminal ends to verify that the line protocol, usually stored in the DTEs, is functioning properly. Most of the numerous protocol testers available test the following commonly used protocols:

- IBM binary synchronous communications (BSC)
- IBM synchronous data link control (SDLC)
- ISO high-level data link control (HDLC)
- CCITT X.25
- Various asynchronous protocols

Protocol testers verify such functions as polling, device select, the proper sending and receiving of status messages (for example, from a device coming on line for the first time), correct user data transmission, and the DTE message error-checking capability. Most protocol testers operate under three test modes: monitor, simulate, and data analysis.

With *monitor mode*, the tester is connected to the EIA-232-D/V.24 interface. The mode is passive; the tester monitors the data flow and displays it to an operator for analysis. The operator determines if the protocol is deviating from the norm.

A protocol tester also can *simulate* components on a circuit. Typically, it duplicates the function of the host computer, a modem, or even the communications channel.

The last mode, *data analysis*, is used to display data for interpretation and analysis. This mode allows the operator to examine the data to determine if they are the source of an error or if they have been distorted because of another problem.

A *transmission monitor* passively monitors a circuit to analyze the quality of a signal. A typical monitor performs the following tests:

- Marking and spacing distortion
- Gain hits
- Background noise
- Delay
- Carrier signal dropouts
- Harmonic distortion
- Clock slip (loss of synchronization)
- Jitter
- Skew (percentage of errors mistaken as 1s or 0s)

Bit and Block Error Rates

Channel quality is often measured by the number of erroneous bits received during a given period. This bit error rate (BER) is derived by dividing the number of bits received in error by the number of bits transmitted. A typical error rate on a high-quality telephone channel is as low as $1 : 10^5$. In most cases, the errors occur in bursts and cannot be predicted precisely. The BER is a useful measure for determining the quality of the channel, calibrating it, and pinpointing its problems.

BER should be measured over a finite time interval, and the time measurement should be included in the description of the error rate. The following equation calculates BER:

$$BER = B_e/RT_m$$

where R = channel speed in bits per second
        B_e = number of bits in error
        T_m = measurement period in seconds

The actual bit sequences are important to BER. Pseudorandom bit sequences have all the appearance of random digital data. These sequences, generated in repeating lengths of $2^n - 1$ bits, will generate all but one possible word combination of bit length n. The most common sequences are 511 and 2,047 bits long, representing n = 9 and n = 11, respectively.

The block error rate (BLER) is a ratio of the number of blocks received that contain at least one erroneous bit to the total blocks received. BLER is thus calculated by dividing the number of blocks received in error by the number of blocks transmitted.[3] The

[3]The block size of a frame is an important design consideration, since the larger block sizes are more likely to contain an error bit. Smaller-sized blocks are less likely to encounter an error but decrease overall throughput of user data bits due to the additional overhead of control headers and trailers in each block. Thus, the designer must determine the optimum block size from the standpoint of BLER rate and overhead/throughput, as well as delay/response time.

BLER is an effective calculation for determining overall throughput on the channel and is often used by network designers to perform line loading and network topology configuration.

Another useful calculation is to determine the percentage of seconds during a stated period in which no errors occur. Error-free seconds (EFS) are calculated by

$$\% \text{ EFS} = [(S - S_e)/S] \times 100\%$$

where S = measurement period in seconds
  S_e = number of 1-second intervals during which 1 bit error occurred

The parameter S is important, since, like T_m in BER, it is necessary to specify a measuring interval. The period tested may be hours or even days.

EFS is a valuable measure of performance on channels where data are transmitted in blocks (for example, an HDLC/SDLC channel). BER is not a very good measure of performance of throughput, but it is widely used to evaluate the performance of modems and other DCEs.

Loopbacks

A failed communications link is tested by placing the modems in a loopback mode. Practically all modems can be put into loopback tests with a switch on the modem (see Figure 6–14). The loopback signals are analyzed to determine their quality and the bit error rate resulting from the tests. The loopbacks can be sent through the local modem to test its analog and digital circuits; this test is called a *local loopback*. If the bit error rate is not beyond a specified level, the next step is likely to be a *remote line loopback* that tests the carrier signal and the analog circuitry of the remote modem. The remote modem must be placed in the loopback mode in order for this test to be completed. Care should be taken in drawing conclusions from the remote analog loopback tests, since the looped signal may be tested at twice its specification. Due to this problem, it is often

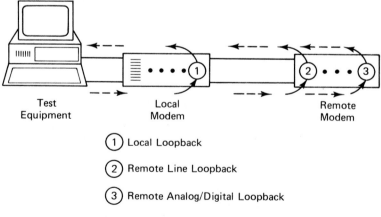

① Local Loopback

② Remote Line Loopback

③ Remote Analog/Digital Loopback

Figure 6–14. Loopback tests.

advisable to send the signal through the remote modem digital circuitry in order to boost the signal power. This test is called a *remote digital loopback.*

Troubleshooting Flow Charts

Figures 6–15 and 6–16 provide logic flow charts to aid in the analysis of a communication channel. Figure 6–15 illustrates a general logic chart to analyze the channel. Figure 6–16 shows a typical approach in using loopback testing.

Correcting Errors

In Chapter 7 we discuss methods that detect errors and request a retransmission of the errored data. Retransmission is a time-honored compromise to the error-laden channel and it has served the industry well. Nonetheless, other techniques have emerged that not only detect an error but, in many cases, correct the error without requesting a retransmission. One of these techniques, trellis-coded modulation (TCM), is highlighted here to give the reader an idea of the value of forward error correction (FEC) techniques.

One can reasonably pose the following scenario. Granted, the many elements involved in a data transmission will often create errors. Yet the transmission/signal always starts at a known value and the value is confined within certain limits. Suppose a method is devised whereby the signal (derived and coded from the user data bit stream) is allowed to assume only certain characteristics (*states*) on the line. Furthermore, suppose the user bits are interpreted such that only certain of the states are allowed to exist from prior states.

This means that the transmitting device would accept a series of user bits and develop additional yet restricted bit patterns from the user bits. Moreover, the previous user bit pattern (called a state) would be allowed to assume only certain other bit patterns (states).

The transmitter and receiver are programmed to understand the allowable states and the permissible state transitions. If the receiver receives states and state transitions (because of channel impairments) that differ from predefined algorithms, it is assumed an error has occurred on the circuit.

But FEC goes further. Since, by convention, the transmitter and the receiver know the transmission states and the permissible state transitions, the receiver can analyze the received signal and make a "best guess" as to what state the signal should assume. It analyzes current states, compares them to previous states, and makes decisions as to the most relevant state.

The process is illustrated in Figure 6–17. (The reader might wish to refer back to Figure 4–10 for a refresher on constellation patterns.) The original signal in Figure 6–17(a) is transmitted to allow the four states depicted in the four circles. Remember from discussions in Chapter 4 that the points in the figure represent states or various combinations of phase and amplitude modulation.

Due to transmission impairments, the signal is interpreted as depicted in Figure 6–17(b). A conventional receiver would interpret the signal in an entirely different constellation pattern and misconstrue 1s for 0s, and vice versa.

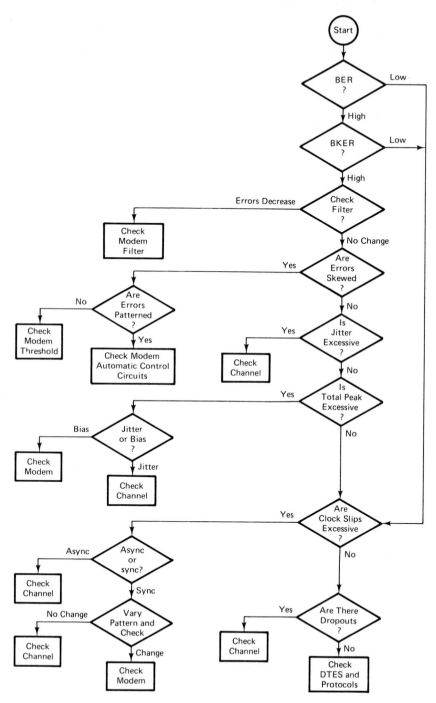

Figure 6-15. General logic chart for troubleshooting.

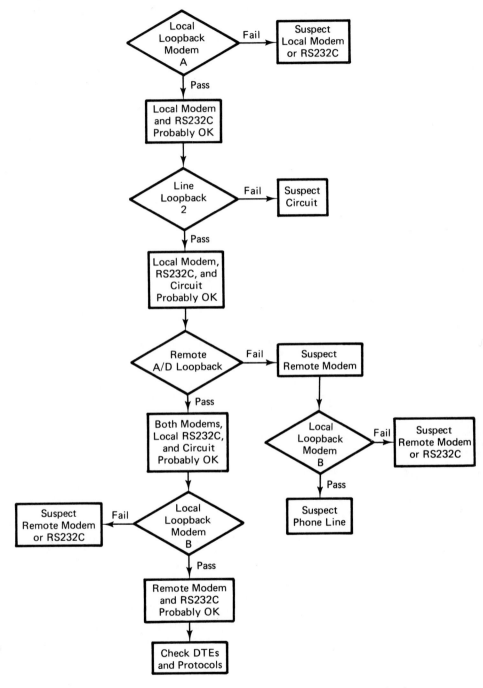

Figure 6–16.   Logic chart for troubleshooting a full-duplex circuit.

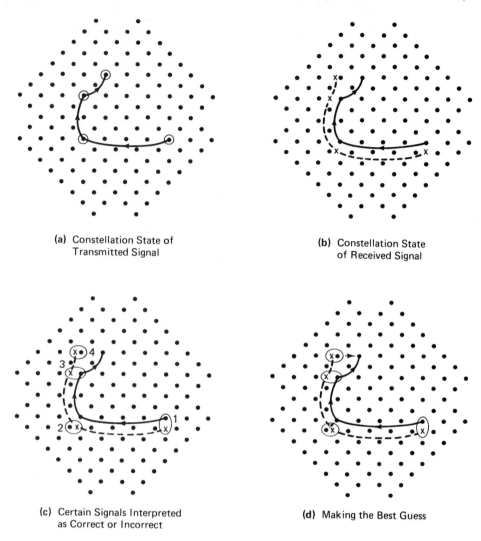

(a) Constellation State of
    Transmitted Signal

(b) Constellation State
    of Received Signal

(c) Certain Signals Interpreted
    as Correct or Incorrect

(d) Making the Best Guess

Figure 6–17. Trellis-coded modulation for forward error correction.

Figure 6–17(c) shows that the received signal, while certainly erroneous, is not entirely invalid. Received signals 1 and 3 are close enough approximations of the original signal such that the predefined state transition rules based on prior states can be used to make a best guess on the signal and essentially forward error correct the errors in Figure 6–17(d).

What does FEC hold for data communications systems and networks? It has the potential to redo much of our software and hardware that concerns itself with the transmission and reception of data in our currently existing systems. But until FEC becomes more pervasive, data link controls (line protocols) will remain our major tool for handling transmission impairments.

SUMMARY

Due to the frequency of errors that occur on communications links, the network administrator must undertake many actions to ensure that data are received correctly at the end-user device. Problems that are common and only slightly bothersome in the telephone networks can create havoc in data networks. A structured and organized preventive maintenance plan is essential for the health of any network. Diagnostic testing and the emphasis of perceived availability to the user are essential to any successful operation. Increasingly, with the use of optical fiber links the job of maintaining clean lines is being made easier. In addition, forward error correction techniques have become a valuable tool for decreasing errors on the communications network.

7

Data Link Controls/Line Protocols

INTRODUCTION

This chapter examines data link controls (also called line protocols). The discussion in the chapter focuses on the operations of several types of protocols with emphasis on asynchronous, synchronous byte-oriented, and synchronous bit-oriented systems. Later discussions focus on how data link controls handle errors and how flow control operations are obtained at the link layer. We finish the chapter with a discussion on several line protocols that are used in the industry.

DATA ACCOUNTABILITY AND LINE CONTROL

Since certain errors are inevitable in the system, a method must be provided to deal with the periodic data distortions that occur within a transmission. The data communications system must provide each site with the capability to send data to another site. The sending site must be assured that the data arrive error free at the receiving site. The sending and receiving sites must maintain complete accountability for all messages. In the event the data are distorted, the receiving site must have the capability of notifying the originator to resend the erroneous message or otherwise correct the errors.

The movement of traffic to and from the many points within the network must flow in a controlled and orderly manner. This means that the sending and receiving sites must know the identification and sequencing of the messages being transmitted among all users. The connection path between sites is usually shared by more than one user (as in

162

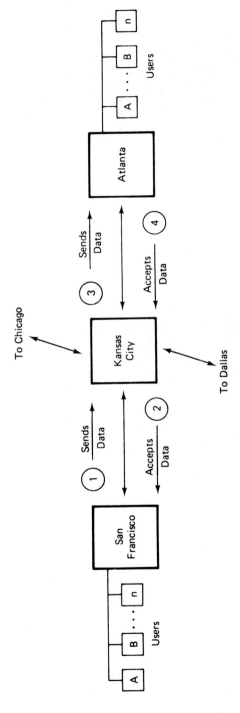

Figure 7-1. Message flow in a network.

a multidrop configuration); consequently, procedures must provide for the allocation and sharing of the path among the many users.

Data link controls (DLCs), or line protocols, provide for these needs. They manage the flow of data messages across the communications path or link. The link control is responsible *only* for the traffic between adjacent nodes/stations on a line. Once the data are transmitted to the adjacent node and an acknowledgment of the transmission is returned to the transmission site, the link control task is complete for that particular transmission.

DLCs consist of a combination of software and hardware and are located at each site in the network. The DLC is concerned with providing the following functions to the network:

- Synchronizing the sender and receiver
- Controlling the sending and receiving of data
- Detecting and recovering transmission errors between two points
- Maintaining awareness of link conditions

A multinode network that has intermediate points between a session of two users would operate as depicted in Figure 7–1. User terminal A in San Francisco sends data across the network to user terminal B in Atlanta as part of user A/B session. The data could, for example, be passed to an intermediate node at Kansas City (event 1). The DLC in Kansas City receives the data, checks for errors, and sends a receipt acknowledgment (ACK) of the data to San Francisco (event 2). Kansas City then assumes responsibility for the data. In event 3, Kansas City sends the data to Atlanta, which checks the data and sends an acceptance response to Kansas City (event 4). Thus, the DLC relays the message through the network, much like the passing of a baton in a relay race.

The DLC does not provide the user with end-to-end accountability. User A did not receive any indication of receipt of data in Atlanta, the final end point. Since data link controls do not provide for end-to-end access and flow control, a higher level of control is required to provide for session-to-session accountability and control.

THE HDLC SPECIFICATION

Before we describe how link protocols work, the HDLC (high-level data link control) standard should be discussed. Many users and vendors are adapting HDLC or HDLC subsets as their principal line control system. Such a move is good news for users because it simplifies the interfacing of different vendor products.

HDLC is supported by many standards groups (for example, CCITT, ECMA, ISO, ANSI) and used by most vendors. It has many features and options that make up the HDLC "superset." If a vendor implements certain parts of the standard, then the implementation is considered an HDLC subset. Later in the chapter, we discuss a "subset" of HDLC called SDLC (Synchronous Data Link Control), which will provide us an opportunity to explain further this important link protocol.

CLASSIFICATION OF DATA LINK CONTROLS

Data link controls can be described and classified by (a) message format, (b) line control method, (c) error-handling method, and (d) flow control procedure.

Message Format

Asynchronous. The message format of a DLC is either asynchronous or synchronous. Asynchronous formats originated with older equipment with limited capabilities, but are still widely used due to their simplicity. Their main disadvantage is the overhead of the control bits; for example, a ratio of two control bits (start/stop bits) to 8 user character bits is not unusual.

Notwithstanding, many variations and improvements have been made to asynchronous protocols and, in spite of the overhead, DLCs with asynchronous formats still remain one of the dominant data link controls. Asynchronous techniques are found in practically all systems that use teleprinter and teletype terminals, and constitute the format for the vast majority of personal computers.

Synchronous byte oriented. The DLCs with synchronous formats are further distinguished as byte- or bit-oriented formats. The synchronous byte-oriented DLC was developed in the 1960s but is still widely available. It uses the same string of bits and bytes to represent data characters and control characters. For example, the control field EOT (end of transmission) might occur in a user data stream, in which case the DLC logic could mistakenly interpret the data as control information. Most versions of synchronous byte techniques have logic provisions to handle this problem.

Byte protocols also use a format in which the control fields occur in variable locations within the frame. For example, the control field STX (start of text) might occur in a nonfixed location, depending on whether the frame has a header.

Synchronous bit oriented. The more advanced synchronous DLCs use the bit-oriented approach. In this method, line control bits are always unique and cannot occur in the user data stream. The logic of the DLC examines the data stream before it is transmitted and alters the user data if it contains a bit configuration that could be interpreted as a control indicator. Of course, with this approach, the receiving DLC has the capability to change the data stream to its original contents. The bit-oriented DLC achieves code transparency. Furthermore, bit protocols use the individual bits for line control, not the full character itself. This means the logic is not dependent on a particular code such as ASCII or EBCDIC. Finally, the control fields/bits usually reside in fixed locations within the frame.

Line Control Method

At the broadest level, data link control methods are classified as (a) primary/secondary, (b) peer to peer, or (c) a combination of these. Primary/secondary (or master/slave) protocols provide for one station (such as a computer) to manage all traffic on the channel. The other stations (typically terminals and other computers) must obtain permission from the primary station before they can transmit data. Peer-to-peer protocols have no master station. In this situation, all stations are equal and use the channel under some form of contention or negotiation.

Polling/selection. The most common method of line primary/secondary control is through the use of polling/selection techniques. This process is illustrated in Figure 7–2. A site in the network is designated as the master or primary station. This site is responsible for the sending and receiving of messages between all secondary or slave sites on the line. In fact, the secondary sites cannot send any messages until the master station gives approval.

Let us suppose site B wishes to send data to site A on the San Francisco master station line. The master station begins this process by sending a polling message to B (event 1). In effect, the poll message says, "Site B, have you a message to send?" Site B responds by sending a message to the master site (event 2). The master site checks the message for errors and responds back to B with a positive acknowledgment (ACK) as event 3.

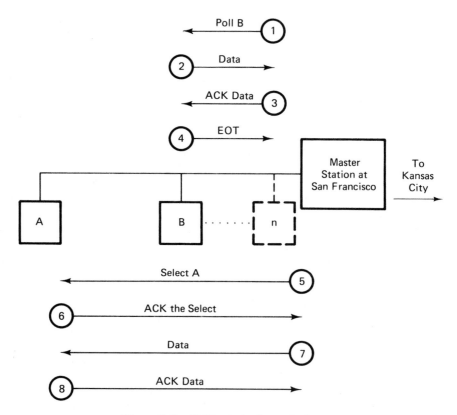

Figure 7–2. Polling/selection techniques.

There are many variations of the polling/selection technique. For example, some vendors' implementations allow B to continue sending messages, eventually terminating the process with an end-of-transmission (EOT) message (event 4). Others provide an EOT indicator within the final message itself, which eliminates event 4 and an overhead message.

The selection process begins in event 5. Now, the master site informs A that it has data destined for A by sending a selection message. This message means, "Site A, I have data for you; can you receive?" Site A must respond with a positive acknowledgment (ACK) or negative acknowledgment (NAK) as in event 6. The receiving station may not be able to accept a message. For example, it may be busy or its storage buffers may be full. If A can receive the message, the master site transmits it (event 7). The message is checked for errors at A and an acknowledgment is relayed to the master station (event 8). User A could then respond to user B by going through the master station and executing the process again.

It is useful to compare Figure 7–1 with Figure 7–2. In Figure 7–2, the master site in San Francisco controls the user terminals within its local environment. In Figure 7–1, the intermediate node in Kansas City controls the San Francisco and Atlanta points. This means that the polling/selection approach allows a site to be a master to one part of the network and a slave to another part.

The polling/selection protocol is very widely used for several reasons:

- The centralized approach allows for hierarchical control. Traffic flow is directed from one point, which provides for simpler control than a noncentralized approach.
- Priorities can be established among the users. Certain computers and terminals can be polled or selected more frequently than others, thus giving precedence to certain users and their applications.
- Sites (terminals, software applications, or computers) can be readily added by changing polling/selection tables within the DLC logic.

There is a price to pay for all these features. The polling/selection DLC incurs a substantial amount of overhead due to the requirement for polling, selection, ACK, NAK, and EOT control messages. On some networks, the negative responses to polls (in which a terminal or user application is solicited for data but has nothing to send) can consume a significant portion of the network capacity. We shall see that the more recent implementations of the polling/selection DLC (in SDLC) use some clever methods to reduce the number of overhead messages.

Timeouts.   Timeouts allow the link control station to check for errors or questionable conditions on the line. A timeout occurs when a polled station does not respond within a certain time. The nonresponse condition evokes recovery action on the part of the controlling station.

The timeout threshold is dependent on three factors: (a) signal propagation delay to and from the polled station, (b) processing time at the polled station, and (c) turnaround delay at the polled station (raising the clear-to-send circuit) on a half-duplex line.

These factors are highly variable and depend on the line type, line length, modem performance, and processing speed at the polled terminals' site. A timeout threshold for a network using leased full-duplex lines operating within a distance of 150 miles between the polling and polled site might range between 30 to 60 ms. The threshold for the same arrangement, using satellite links, could be as great as 900 ms due to the longer propagation time and additional delays at intermediate points (earth stations). Local networks operating within small confines might use a timeout threshold of a very few milliseconds or microseconds. It is evident that the personnel tasked with the software or chip design of the link control method must work closely with the communications engineers, or have an understanding of the characteristics of electronic signaling, in order to design the appropriate timeout logic.

Hub Polling.   A variation of polling/selection is known as hub polling. This approach is used on a multipoint line to avoid the delay inherent in the polled terminals turning around a half-duplex line to return a negative response to the poll. In this operation, the master station sends a poll to a terminal on the line. This terminal turns the line around with a message to the master station if it has data to send or, under another version, it ''piggybacks'' the data onto the poll and forwards both to the next station on the line. If it has no data, it sends the polling message to the next terminal on the line. If this terminal is busy, idle, or has nothing to send, it relays the polling message to the next appropriate station. The transmission of this poll continues in one direction without additional turnarounds. Eventually, a terminal will be found that has data for the master station. Thus, hub polling eliminates the line turnaround time that occurs if each terminal receives a poll from the host.

Contention.   Contention is a widely used peer-to-peer link control method. It differs significantly from polling/selection, since there is no master station. With contention, each site has equal status on the line, and the use of this path is determined by the station that first gains access during an idle line period. Contention DLCs must provide for a station to relinquish the use of the path at an appropriate interval of time in order to prevent line domination from one site.

An example of contention controls is provided in Figure 7–3. The path is multi-dropped with sites A, B, C, and D on the line. Each site, using a line signal sensing device, determines if a message is traveling on the path (through sensing the signal). If there is a message, the sites defer to it. Since the messages are being transmitted at very high speeds, the waiting periods are usually quite short.

Figure 7–3 shows that site D has transmitted a message destined for A. Sites B and C monitor the line, determine if it is occupied, and wait a brief period before sensing again. If both B and C have a message to transmit, each will attempt to gain access to the path after the message from D is received at A. Assuming site C gains access first, site B must wait until C has completed the transmission of its data. Like the polling/selection method, user A could check for errors and send an ACK or NAK message to D when the path becomes available. Remember that site A recognizes its message by address detection.

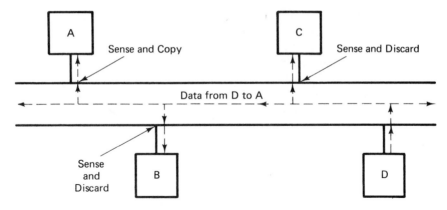

Figure 7–3. Contention data link control.

The contention control method experiences occasional collisions of messages. This occurs when more than one site senses an idle line and transmits messages at approximately the same time. The messages' signals intermix and become distorted. In these situations, the sensing devices must be capable of detecting the collision and must so indicate to the DLC logic. The logic must then direct the stations to resend the messages that have been distorted.

Contention control is widely used today, primarily because of its relative simplicity and the absence of a master station. The polling/selection approach suffers from the vulnerability of the primary site to failure, which could bring down all sites on the link. Since the contention method does not rely on a controlling site, a failed site does not prevent the other sites from communicating with each other. Moreover, the many overhead messages (polls, selections, etc.) found in polling/selection methods do not exist in the contention DLCs.

One major disadvantage of a contention DLC is the inability to provide priorities for the use of the transmission path. Since all stations are equal, none has priority over others, even though some user stations and applications may require greater use of the facilities. Since many of the contention DLCs are used on local networks with very high speed paths, the equal allocation may not be discernible to the station with more frequent access needs. Moreover, priorities could be established within a user's system.

Another potential disadvantage of the contention network is the distance limitation placed on it. For example, if two sites are located at a remote distance from each other, it is possible for both stations to transmit, turn themselves ''off'' (that is, go on to other activities), and never detect the signal or the collision due to the propagation delay of the signals traveling on the line. The contention logic must be designed to handle this situation.

Time slots. Time slot control avoids the collision problem found in the contention DLC by reserving times of access to the communications path. For example, in Figure 7–4 each site or station is given a slot of time on the link. During the period that the station has access to the path, it typically can send one or a predetermined multiple

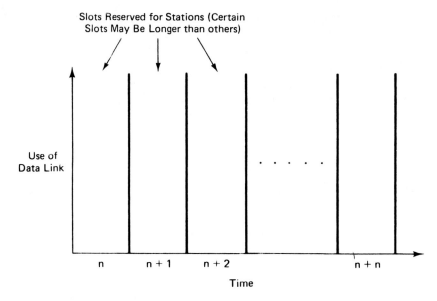

Figure 7–4. Time slot controls.

number of messages. The next station then gains access and transmits its messages across the communications link.

Time slot link controls are simple and are found in many applications and networks today. Their principal disadvantage is the wasted line capacity that occurs when a station's time slot is not used because it has nothing to transmit. Most time slot DLCs now avoid this problem with additional capabilities. The discussions in this book on multiplexers, local networks, and satellite transmission techniques (time-division multiple access, TDMA) provide more information on time slot control methods.

Error-Handling Method

The method of detecting and correcting errors in a message is a key selection criterion for a data link control. Some vendors have more efficient techniques than others. The majority of offerings provide for one of the methods discussed here.

Certainly, one option is to simply ignore errors. For instance, the transmission of textual data may not require that every bit of the text arrive error free. Assuming a bit error rate of $1:10^5$ (that is, one error bit in every 100,000 bits), a 400-page book could be transmitted with but 35 Baudot code characters in error. A $1:10^5$ error rate is not pushing the state of the art by any means, so ignoring errors is a viable option.

However, many applications cannot afford errors. Financial data systems, such as an electronic transfer of funds between customers' bank accounts, must have completely accurate data messages arrive at the end point. In these applications, the data link controls must detect and handle any errors that occur on the path.

It is sometimes difficult for individuals to understand that the reliability and speed of a communications path through a network are appreciably different from the flow of data in a conventional mainframe environment where all components are located in one room or one building.[1] A computer-to-disk channel can operate at data transfer speeds of 10^7 to 10^9 b/s with an error rate of 1 in 10^{12} or 10^{13} bits sent—very fast and very reliable. In contrast, a dial-up telephone line transmits data at a rate of 10^3 to 10^4 b/s, at an error rate of 1 in 10^4 bits. The combined bit transfer times error rates for the in-house environment is 10 orders of magnitude better than a dial-up line in a network. Consequently, error-handling techniques in a data communications system necessarily require considerable attention.

Bit-checking techniques.   Most methods used to provide for data error detection entail the insertion of redundant bits in the message. The actual bit configuration of the redundant bits is derived from the data bit stream.

Vertical Redundancy Check.   The vertical redundancy check (VRC) is a simple technique. It consists of adding a single bit (a parity bit) to each string of bits that comprise a character. The bit is set to 1 or 0 to give the character bits an odd or even number of bits that are 1s. This parity bit is inserted at the transmitting station, sent with each character in the message, and checked at the receiver to determine if each character is the correct parity. If a transmission impairment caused a "bit flip" of 1 to 0 or 0 to 1, the parity check would so indicate. However, a 2-bit flip would not be detected by the VRC technique, which creates a high incidence of errors in some transmissions. For example, multilevel modulation (where 2 or 3 bits are represented in a signal cycle) requires a more sophisticated technique. The single-bit VRC is also unsuited to most analog voice-grade lines because of the groupings of errors that usually occur on this type of link.

Longitudinal Redundancy Check.   The longitudinal redundancy check (LRC) is a refinement of the VRC approach. Instead of a parity bit on each character, LRC places a parity (odd or even) on a block of characters. The block check provides a better method to detect for errors across characters. It is usually implemented with VRC and is then called a two-dimensional parity check code (see Figure 7–5). The VRC–LRC combination provides a substantial improvement over a single method. A typical telephone line with an error rate of $1:10^5$ can be improved to a range of $1:10^7$ and $1:10^9$ with the two-dimensional check.[2]

Echoplex.   This technique is used in many asynchronous devices, notably personal computers. Each character is transmitted to the receiver, where it is sent back or echoed to the original station. The echoed character is compared with a copy of the transmitted character. If they are the same, a high probability exists that the transmission is correct.

[1] Andrew S. Tanenbaum, *Computer Networks* (Englewood Cliffs, NJ: Prentice Hall, 1981) p. 56.

[2] Anthony Ralston (ed.), *Encyclopedia of Computer Science* (New York: Van Nostrand Reinhold, 1976) p. 385.

Characters

Bits in Characters	1	2	3	...	n	LRC ↓
1	0	1	0			0
2	1	0	0			0
3	1	0	1			1
4	0	0	1			0
5	0	1	0			0
6	1	0	1			1
7	0	0	1			0
VRC →	0	1	1			1

Figure 7–5.   VRC–LRC and two-dimensional parity check.

Echoplex requires the use of full-duplex facilities. In the event a full-duplex configuration is not available, a device is usually switched to *local echo*, which sends the echo through the local modem back to the user device. Local echo permits the system to operate as if it were echoplex, but be aware that local echo does not check for errors across the link.

Hamming Code.   The Hamming code is a more sophisticated variation of the VRC. It uses more than 1 parity bit per byte or character. The parity bit values are based on various combinations of the user character, and the parities are inserted in between the bits of the character. For example, in one Hamming approach, a byte of bits b_1 b_2 b_3 b_4 b_5 b_6 b_7 carries a 10-bit code as p_1 b_1 p_2 b_2 b_3 p_3 b_4 b_5 b_6 b_7. The parity bit p_1 is set odd or even based on the values of b_1, b_3, b_5, and b_7; p_2 is based on b_2, b_3, b_6, b_7; and p_3 is based on b_4, b_5, b_6, and b_7. The Hamming code achieves better results than a VRC or an LRC; however, it does carry more overhead.

Cyclic Redundancy Check.   Several other techniques are in use today. One that is quite widely used is the cyclic redundancy check (CRC). Figure 7–6 shows an example of CRC use. The CRC approach entails the division of the user data stream by a predetermined binary number. The remainder of the number is appended to the message as an FCS (frame check sequence) field. The data stream at the receiving site has another calculation performed and compared to the FCS field. If the remainder is zero, the message is accepted as correct.

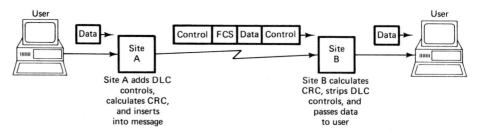

Figure 7–6.   Cyclic redundancy checking.

The divisor polynomial $X^{16} + X^{12} + X^5 + X^0$ is often used (1000100000100001) in data communications. It can detect, ''all possible single-error bursts not exceeding 16 bits, 99.9969% of all possible single bursts 17 bits long, and 99.9984% of all possible longer bursts.'' This provides for 1 bit error per every 10^{14} bits transmitted and is much better than the other methods.

Flow Control

It should be recognized that a DLC must manage the transmission and receipt of perhaps thousands of messages in a short period of time. The DLC must move that data traffic efficiently. Communications lines should be evenly used, and no station should be unnecessarily idle or saturated with excessive traffic. Thus, flow control is a critical part of the network.

Stop-and-wait. Figure 7–7 depicts the stop-and-wait DLC. This DLC allows one message to be transmitted (event 1), checked for errors with techniques such as VRC or LRC (event 2), and an appropriate ACK or NAK returned to the sending station (event 3). No other data messages can be transmitted until the receiving station sends back a reply. Thus, the name *stop-and-wait* is derived from the originating station sending a message, stopping further transmission, and waiting for a reply.

The stop-and-wait approach is well suited to half-duplex transmission arrangements, since it provides for data transmission in both directions, but only in one direction at a time. Moreover, it is a simple approach requiring no elaborate sequencing of messages or extensive message buffers in the terminals.

Its major drawback is the idle line time that results when the stations are in the wait period. Most stop-and-wait data link controls now provide for more than one terminal on the line. The terminals are still operating under the simple arrangement. They are fairly inexpensive with limited intelligence. The host or primary station is responsible for interleaving the messages among the terminals (usually through a terminal controller that is in front of the terminals) and controlling access to the communications link.

The simple arrangement depicted in Figure 7–7 also creates serious problems when the ACK or NAK is lost in the network or on the line. If the ACK in event 3 is lost, the master station times out and retransmits the same message to the secondary site. The redundant transmission could possibly create a duplicate record in the secondary site user data files. Consequently, data link controls must provide a means to identify and sequence the transmitted messages with the appropriate ACKs or NAKs. The logic must have a method to check for duplicate messages.

A typical approach to solve this problem is the provision for a sequence number in the header of the message. The receiver can then check for the sequence number to determine if the message is a duplicate. The stop-and-wait DLC requires a very small sequence number, since only one message is outstanding at any time. The sending and receiving station need only use a 1-bit alternating sequence of 0 or 1 to maintain the relationship of the transmitted message and its ACK/NAK.

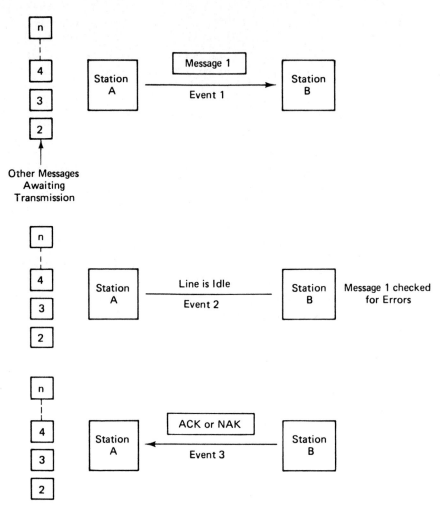

Figure 7–7. Stop-and-wait data link control.

Figure 7–8 shows how this arrangement works. In event 1, the sending station transmits a message with the sequence number 0 in the header. The receiving station responds with an ACK and a sequence number of 0 (event 2). The sender receives the ACK, examines the 0 in the header, flips the sequence number to a 1, and transmits the next message (event 3). The receiving station receives and acknowledges the message with an ACK 1 in event 4. However, this message is received garbled or is lost on the line. The sending station recognizes that the message in event 3 has not been acknowledged. It performs a timeout and retransmits this message (event 5). The receiving station is looking for a message with a sequence number of 0. It discards the message, since it is a duplicate of the message transmitted in event 3. To complete the accountability, the receiving station retransmits the ACK of 1 (event 6).

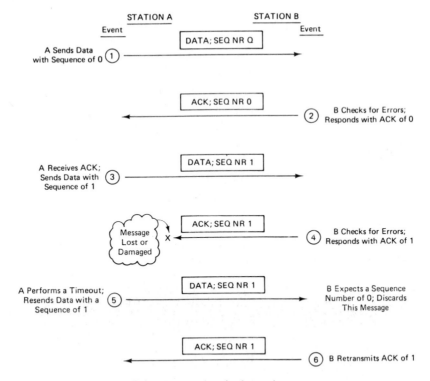

Figure 7–8. Stop-and-wait alternating sequence.

Sliding-window control.   The inherent inefficiency of the stop-and-wait DLC resulted in the development of techniques to provide for the overlapping of data messages and their corresponding control messages. The newer data link controls employ this method. The data and control signals flow from sender to receiver in a more continuous manner, and several messages can be outstanding (on the line or in the receiver's buffers) at any one time.

These DLCs are often called *sliding windows* because of the method used to synchronize the sending sequence numbers in the headers with the appropriate acknowledgments. The transmitting station maintains a sending window that delineates the number of messages (and their sequence numbers) it is permitted to send. The receiving station maintains a receiving window that performs complementary functions. The two sites use the windows to coordinate the flow of messages between each other. In essence, the window states how many messages can be outstanding on the line or at the receiver before the sender stops sending and awaits a reply. For example, in Figure 7–9(a) the receiving of the ACK of message 1 allows the San Francisco site to slide its window by one sequence number. If a total of 10 messages could be within the window, San Francisco could still transmit messages 5, 6, 7, 8, 9, 0, and 1. (Keep in mind that messages 2, 3, and 4 are in transit.) It could not transmit a message using sequence 2 until it had received an ACK for 2. The window wraps around to reuse the same set of numbers.

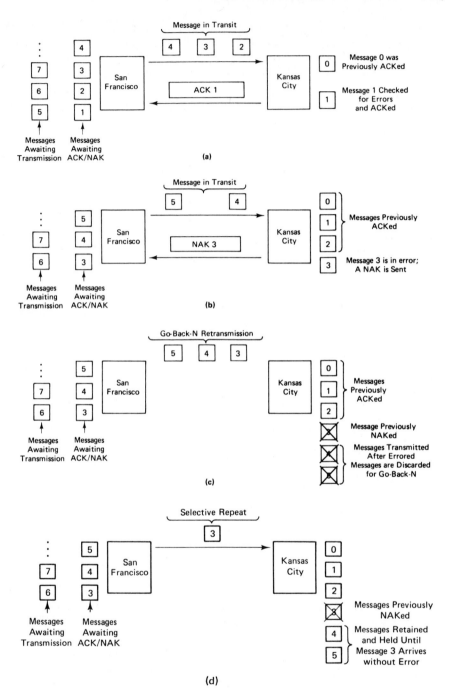

Figure 7-9. Sliding window data link control.

Go-Back-N.   The Go-Back-N method is a sliding window technique. It allows data and control messages to be transmitted continuously. In the event an error is detected at the receiving site, the erroneous message is retransmitted, as well as all other messages that were transmitted after the errored message.

Figure 7–9 shows the message flow of the Go-Back-N method. In Figure 7–9(a), messages 2, 3, and 4 are transmitted on the line to Kansas City and an ACK of previously received message 1 is sent back to San Francisco. Notice the full-duplex transmission scheme. In Figure 7–9(b), messages 4 and 5 are on the path; Kansas City has now received messages 2 and 3. It determines that message 3 is in error and transmits a NAK to the originating station. San Francisco responds to the NAK in Figure 7–9(c) by retransmitting message 3, as well as messages 4 and 5.

One might question why messages 4 and 5 are retransmitted, since it could mean a duplication of effort and result in wasted resources. These concerns are valid but the approach also provides a simple means to keep the messages in the proper sequence between the two points, which in turn simplifies the software or chip logic and decreases the length of certain control fields in the message. An error-causing condition on the line (such as a rainstorm on a microwave path) might affect not just one message, but the subsequent messages that are traveling down the path as well. For example, a 20-ms distortion on a 50-kb/s line will distort 1,000 bits, possibly in more than one message. Consequently, these messages may be retransmitted anyway, because they are in error.

Selective Repeat.   The Selective Repeat method provides for a more refined approach. In contrast to the Go-Back-N, the only messages retransmitted are those that are NAKed. In Figure 7–9(d), message 3 only is resent from the originator in San Francisco.

Studies reveal that the Selective Repeat DLC obtains greater throughput than the Go-Back-N. However, the differences are not great if the comparison is made on a reliable transmission path. The Selective Repeat DLC requires additional logic to maintain the sequence of the resent message and merge it into the proper place on the queue at the receiving site, since all traffic should be delivered in the same order it is transmitted. Consequently, the Go-Back-N is found in more data link controls than is the Selective Repeat DLC.

The window size of these data link controls is an important element in the determination of message accountability and efficient line utilization. Due to delay in the propagation of a signal, a message requires a certain amount of time before all bits of the message arrive at the receiver and the acknowledgment is returned to the sender. The window size should allow for a continuous flow of data. The returned ACKs should arrive before the sender has transmitted all messages within its window. This timing allows the sliding of the sending window and prevents the sender from waiting for the ACK. In other words, the window size should keep the line busy. It can be seen that the window size is an important design decision.

Many varieties of data link controls are found in the industry today. Generally, each vendor has chosen to develop its own version of a DLC. The result is incompatibility between vendor products. However, due to the influence of the larger vendors and international standards, many companies have now developed compatible DLCs (principally around HDLC) in order to market products that will interface into the other companies' components. This has helped foster standard data link controls but, as we will see in later discussions, multiple standards, methods, and procedures continue to present significant problems to the users of these products.

EXAMPLES OF DATA LINK CONTROLS

The previous discussion focused on the types of DLCs in existence today. We will now examine six systems that use various combinations of the formats, line control, error handling, and flow control methods.

The six data link controls are as follows.

1. 2740 asynchronous control
2. XMODEM protocol
3. Kermit
4. Binary synchronous communications (BSC) control
5. Synchronous data link control (SDLC)
6. Satellite protocols
7. Frame relay

2740 Asynchronous Control

It is unlikely you have this device in your office today. It was very widely used several years ago and is discussed here to provide background information. The IBM 2740 terminal uses the asynchronous half-duplex transmission technique. It has options for buffers, but the 2740 logic still provides start and stop bits around each character in the transmission. The model 1 operates at 134.5 bit/s; the model 2 has options for speeds of 75 to 600 bit/s. The 2740 is a rather old machine and is used here to illustrate an early DLC. It uses an older IBM code called extended binary coded decimal (EBCD). It is a 6-bit code with a seventh bit inserted for parity checking. In addition, the code provides for functions to control the 2740 printer, for example, new line, backspace, and uppercase.

The code set is the same for data and control characters. This problem is approached by using special characters to inform the terminal logic that the transmission is either user data or control characters. The EOT character places the link and all terminals in the control mode, and the EOA (end-of-addressing) character places the system in the text (or user data) mode.

The 2740 uses vertical redundancy checking for error detection. The parity bit is turned on to create odd parity of the character. The receiving logic checks each character for an odd number of 1 bits and signals the transmitter if it detects an error condition. The system also uses the longitudinal redundancy check.

Figure 7–10 shows an exchange of transmissions between a host and a 2740 terminal. The picture shows data moving directly into and out of the terminal. A 2740

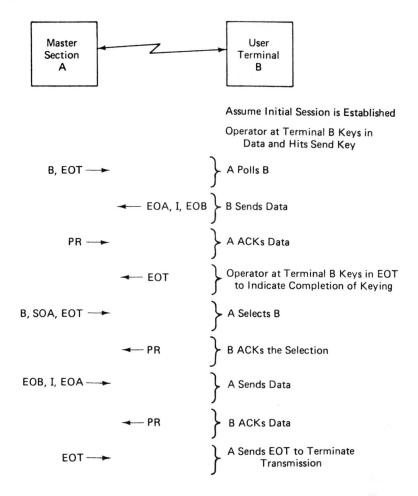

Figure 7–10. 2740 asynchronous transmissions.

control unit is actually involved in this process. The following legend is used to trace the transmission flow; four formats are allowed:

1. A, C   → or ← C, A
2. C, I, C → or ← C, I, C
3. C   → or ← C
4. C, A, C → or ← C, A, C

where C = control character(s)
    A = address of terminal
    I = user information field

A control character precedes the address and user data. The legend does not show the start/stop bits; remember that each character has these bits around them. Figure 7-10 shows an arrow to indicate the direction of the transmission.

For purposes of understanding Figure 7-10, an explanation of the control character is provided.

EOT (end of transmission): Puts system into control mode. EOT also indicates a poll when transmitted from the master station.

EOA (end of addressing): Puts system into text mode. EOA is also a positive ACK to a poll.

EOB (end of block): Signals the end of a block of user data (text). Always followed by the LRC check.

PR (positive response): Positive ACK of transmission. PR is also a positive acknowledgment to a master station's selection transmission.

SOA (start of addressing): Signals the beginning of an addressing (that is, selection) operation.

Figure 7-10 illustrates the overhead of the asynchronous method. Each character (not shown) may contain the start/stop bits. Moreover, nine separate transmissions are required to transmit two user data messages, and no other transmissions take place during this process. On the other hand, it is a simple arrangement and well suited to low-speed teleprinter applications.

COMMUNICATIONS PROTOCOLS

The XMODEM Protocol

One of the most widely used asynchronous protocols in the world is named the XMODEM protocol. It was developed by Ward Christensen in the late 1970s. Christensen not only has supplied XMODEM to the public but other communications programs as well. The XMODEM protocol is also referred to as the Christensen protocol. The XMODEM protocol has several offshoots. For example, MODEM2 and MODEM7 are both derived from the original XMODEM protocol.

XMODEM is found in practically all vendor products today. It typically comes as a standard package when one purchases a communications product from a PC store. It is rare today to see any communications packages for asynchronous devices that do not include an XMODEM offering or one of the XMODEM "derivatives."

XMODEM is a stop-and-wait, automatic request for repeat (ARQ) protocol. As shown in Figure 7-11, it uses a fixed-length data field of 128 bytes. Its other fields are all 1 byte each. The XMODEM Protocol Data Unit (PDU) is often referred to as a packet, this discussion will use the term *frame* because it correctly defines the link layer PDU. The SOH is a 1-byte start of header indicator that signifies the beginning of the frame. The next field contains the sequence number. After initialization, sequencing

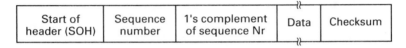

Figure 7–11. The XMODEM protocol data unit.

begins with the first frame with a value of one. The next field contains the 1s complement of the sequence number. This field is used to check for the integrity of the sequence number. The approach at the receiver for handling this operation is to complement one of these fields and XOR it at the other. If the result is zero, it signifies that neither field is in error. If the fields are not identical, XMODEM will send a negative acknowledgment to request retransmission.

The data field is a fixed length field of 128 bytes. It may contain any type of syntax (binary, ASCII, Boolean, text, etc.). The last field is the 1-byte checksum field. This field is used to determine if an error exists in the data field. It does not check for errors in other parts of the protocol data unit.

The XMODEM sending process is quite simple (see Figure 7–12). Interestingly, the operations begin on the receiver side (often referred to as a receiver-driven protocol). The receiver must begin the data transfer by sending a NAK to the transmitter. Upon receipt of the NAK, the transmitter understands that it must send its first frame. The data transfer operation begins by the transmitter forming a 128-block frame, sending the traffic, and waiting for an acknowledgment. If the last frame has been sent, the transmitter sends an EOT, receives an acknowledgment, and ends the communications process. If it is not the last transmission, it waits for an acknowledgment or a NAK. Additionally, the transmitter may also receive a cancel signal (CAN). This rather simple protocol has no method of recovering from a sequence error. Consequently, the receiver will send a CAN to indicate a sequencing problem. This requires that the transmission process be aborted.

This process proceeds with the software looping through the various if statements and the various conditional statements, until an EOT or a CAN is received.

With variations, these examples are derived from Joe Campbell's, *C Programmer's Guide to Serial Communications* published by Howard W. Sams & Company. This book is highly recommended for the reader who wishes to know the detailed operations of asynchronous protocols.

The receiver's job is not much more complex than that of the sender's. See Figure 7–13. Upon sending a NAK to inform the sender that it is ready to receive data, the receiver waits for incoming traffic. XMODEM uses a timer at the receiver to control when to inform the transmitter that it is not receiving traffic. If a frame does not arrive within a specific period of time (earlier implementations were 10 seconds), the receiver sends a NAK to the sender.

Upon receiving a valid frame with an SOH byte, the receiver checks for a valid packet sequence number using the second and third fields of the protocol data unit. It then edits the sequence number to determine if it is the correct sequence number. If not, it sends back a CAN to the transmitter. It then checks for the integrity of the data field

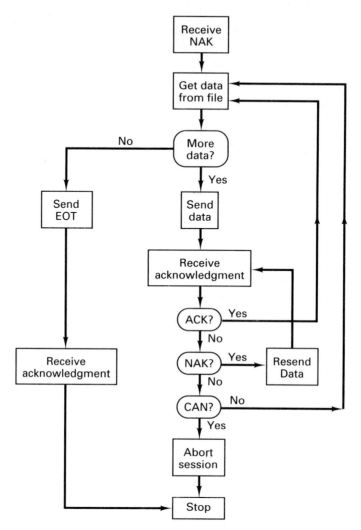

Certain retries and timeouts are not shown

Figure 7–12. XMODEM sender logic.

by using the checksum. If all goes well, it accepts the traffic by sending an ACK. Finally, if it receives an EOT, it sends an acknowledgment of the EOT and ends the transfer operation.

The XMODEM protocol is implemented in some versions with a 2-byte cyclic redundancy check instead of the original single-byte checksum. The CRC algorithm for this version of XMODEM uses the CCITT polynomial $X^{16} + X^{12} + X^5 + 1$.

No one knows who brought this version of XMODEM into the public domain. It has been told that Ward Christensen gives credit to John Mahr, although other implementations cite the designer for this enhancement to be Paul Hansknecht.

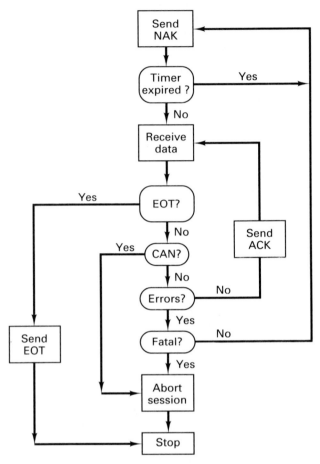

Figure 7–13. XMODEM receiver logic.

Certain timeouts are not shown

The only difference in using a checksum and the CRC sum is that the receiver and transmitter must exchange an initial signal to indicate if they are using the CRC implementation of XMODEM. Instead of sending the NAK signal to the sender, the receiving modem sends the character C.

The reader should be aware that some packages that use MODEM7 may employ both CRC and checksum operations in their protocol. Certain timing operations are implemented during startup to determine if the sender will respond to the C character within a certain period. It is a good idea to check with your vendor to see how the specific implementation of your protocol uses the checksum/CRC operation.

The Kermit Protocol

The Kermit protocol is an asynchronous protocol designed for transferring files. It was developed at Columbia University by Frank Da Cruz and Bill Catchings. The protocol is a very robust system providing for many options in transferring of files between two computers. In so far as possible, Kermit remains transparent to the specific operating systems and mainframes. Indeed, Kermit was designed to support file transfer between IBM and DEC computers.

Information on Kermit may be obtained from: Kermit Distribution, Columbia University Center for Computing Activities, 7th Floor, Watson Laboratory, 612 West 115th Street, New York, NY 10025.

The transfer procedures for Kermit are somewhat similar to XMODEM (see Figure 7–14). The file transfer process begins after the sender receives a NAK packet. It then sends a *send initiate* packet, which is used to begin the negotiation for the file transfer. After this process, the sender sends a file header packet, which contains the name of the file and the characteristics of the file. The successful reception of the file header enables the sender to begin sending data. Each data unit is acknowledged by the receiver. After the file transfer process is over, the sender sends an *end-of-file* (EOF) packet, determines if it has more files to send, and, if not, stops the process.

During the transfer operation, Kermit ensures that the characters transmitted are kept transparent to any network software or operating system by ensuring that control fields are properly identified and that control-like fields are recoded in the data field until presented to the end-user file.

One of the most attractive features of Kermit is the logic devoted to the support of transferring any type of data, including ASCII, binary files, Boolean fields, decimal fields, and so on.

Before transmitting the user data, Kermit makes certain that the ASCII control characters inserted by the user are recoded during the transmission process to prevent any system from mistakenly acting upon them or absorbing them.

It performs this support operation by the CHAR function in which a control character has the value of 20 HEX added to it. The effect of this operation is to "move" the character into the printable string column of the ASCII table. The UNCHAR function reverses the process.

It is possible (likely) that control-like values could be placed in the user data field (after all, we have no control over what the user places in these fields). If actions are not taken on these values, a system could mistakenly assume these are legitimate control characters. Kermit handles this process by appending these fields with a # sign and XORing with 40 HEX. The XORing is used instead of just adding 40H because it keeps the high-order bit intact.

In addition, Kermit supports several operations to ensure that 7-bit and 8-bit files operate properly.

These operations consume considerable overhead in the creation of additional control characters. Consequently, Kermit provides a simple compression scheme to reduce the amount of traffic on the communications channel.

The Kermit packet consists of six major fields (see Figure 7–15). The *mark* field is coded as an ASCII SOH (value 1). This signifies the beginning of the packet.

The *LEN* field is a length field that defines the number of bytes in the packet following the LEN field. The maximum total packet length is restricted to no greater than 96 bytes.

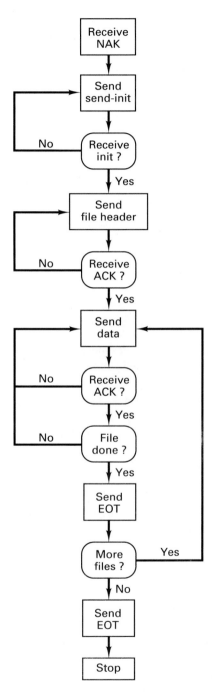

Figure 7–14. The Kermit file transfer procedure.

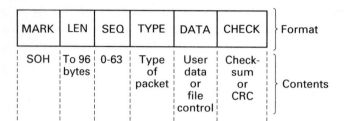

Figure 7-15.   The Kermit packet.

The *SEQ* field is used to sequence each packet. It is a wraparound counter in that once it reaches the maximum value of 63, it returns to 0 and continues to count.

The *type* field defines the type of packet. It could contain a number of characters to define such packets types as data, ACKs, NAKs, EOTs, EOFs, and so on.

The *data* field contains user data, control information regarding the file transfer, or nothing.

The *check* field is used to determine if the packet was damaged on the transmission. Kermit permits several options for the use of the check field. One option uses a simple checksum, another uses a cyclic redundancy check.

The type field in the Kermit packet is coded to provide information about end data or control fields (see Figure 7-16). If coded with a *D*, this packet contains traffic from a file being transmitted. The *Y* code is used to acknowledge the successful transmission of a packet. The *Y* packet is also sent in response to a send initiate packet. The *NAK* packet is used to reject a packet that would require a retransmission from the sender. The *send initiate* packet is used to inform the receiver of this packet about the parameters to be used during the file transfer operation. The *file header* packet must contain the name of the file to be transmitted. The *error* packet is sent when an unrecoverable error (a fatal error) has been encountered. The *EOT* packet is sent when all files have been

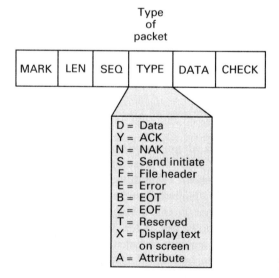

Figure 7-16.   The type field.

transmitted, and the *EOF* is sent when one file has been completely transmitted. The *display text* on the screen is used to signify that the transmitted information is to be displayed. The *attribute* packet is used to send additional information about the file, such as administrative data (date, time, password information, security information, etc.).

The S(SEND-INT) packet as shown in Figure 7–17, is the most complex packet because it is used for the sender and receiver to define their operating parameters during the file transfer. The *MAXL* field defines the maximum permissible packet size that can be received.

The *TIME* field specifies a timeout value that the receiver waits before taking a timeout and taking remedial action.

The *NPAD* parameter defines the number of padding characters to be sent in front of each packet. This technique is widely used in half-duplex protocols to allow devices to switch from transmitter to receiver modes. Upon detecting the PAD the receiver can change its mode of operation. The *PADC* identifies the padding character to be used for the process. The *EOL* is used to terminate the packet field itself. The *QCTL* is used for the control character escape. Its value defaults to # sign. The *OPT* represents other optional fields. The *CAPS* field is one of several options that have been added to Kermit in the past few years. This field can be coded to define that sliding window protocols are to be used, provide other information about file attributes, as well as to permit an extended length for a Kermit packet. The extended length field permits Kermit packet to range up to 9,024 bytes.

Binary Synchronous Control

In the 1980's, Binary synchronous communications was one of the most widely used data link control methods in the world. Until the advent of SDLC (discussed next), BSC was IBM's major DLC offering. Many vendors offer a BSC-like product; many others offer BSC emulation packages. The product is also called *bisync*, a short term for its full

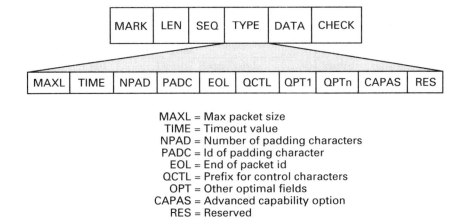

MARK | LEN | SEQ | TYPE | DATA | CHECK

MAXL | TIME | NPAD | PADC | EOL | QCTL | OPT1 | OPTn | CAPAS | RES

MAXL = Max packet size
TIME = Timeout value
NPAD = Number of padding characters
PADC = Id of padding character
EOL = End of packet id
QCTL = Prefix for control characters
OPT = Other optimal fields
CAPAS = Advanced capability option
RES = Reserved

Figure 7–17. Example of the S packet.

title. The method is intended for half-duplex, point-to-point, or multipoint lines. A complete description of BSC can be found in IBM's "Binary Synchronous Communications—General Information" (GA 27-3004).

BSC operates with EBCDIC, ASCII, or Transcode. All stations on a line must use the same code. If ASCII code is used, older versions use a vertical redundancy check and a longitudinal redundancy check. If EBCDIC or Transcode is used, error checking is accomplished by cyclic redundancy checking.

BSC is a half-duplex protocol. Transmissions are provided two ways, alternately. The protocol supports point-to-point and multipoint connections, as well as switched and nonswitched channels. BSC is a code-sensitive protocol, and every character transmitted across a BSC channel must be decoded at the receiver to see if it is either a control character or end-user data. As stated previously, code-sensitive protocols, also called byte or character protocols, are code dependent in that the specific code (EBCDIC, IA5/ASCII) dictates the interpretation of the control fields. The bit protocols are more code transparent because the control fields are not code dependent and do not rely on a specific code for the interpretation of the protocol. We will see several examples of these points in this chapter.

BSC uses the alternating sequence acknowledgment discussed earlier. The receiving station replies with an ACK0 to the successful reception of even-numbered messages and an ACK1 to odd-numbered messages. A reception of two consecutive identical ACK characters alerts the transmitting station to an exceptional situation.

The bisync message format is shown in Figure 7–18. The figure does not show all the possibilities for the format of a BSC message but only a sampling of some of the major implementations of the BSC message format. The SYN characters are used as described in Chapter 3. Other control character functions are as follows:

> *EOT (end of transmission):* Signifies end of transmission, and also can place system in control mode (similar to 2740 method).
>
> *SOH (start of header):* This field is not defined in BSC logic but is user or application dependent. The header is optional.
>
> *STX (start of text):* Places system in user data (or text) mode. (Note the similarity to the 2740 method.) Also used for polling and selection indicators.
>
> *ETX (end of text):* Signifies end of user data (text).
>
> *ETB (end of block):* If user data are divided into multiple blocks, the ETB signal is sent at the end of each block except the last one.
>
> *ACK0 (positive acknowledgment):* This field positively acknowledges (ACKs) even-numbered text blocks.

Error check field	ETX or ETB	User data	STX	Header	SOH	SYN	SYN

Figure 7–18. Bisync (BSC) format (several other format options are available).

ACK1 (positive acknowledgment): This field positively acknowledges (ACKs) odd-numbered text blocks.

NAK (negative acknowledgment): This is used to negatively acknowledge polls/ selects and other control messages.

ENQ (enquiry): On a point-to-point line, this asks if the station can accept a transmission. On a multipoint line, ENQ is used to initiate polling and selection.

DLE (data link escape): Provides a method to use different codes.

Control codes must be excluded from the text and header fields. BSC addresses the problem with the DLE control code. This code is placed in front of the control codes STX, ETX, ETB, and SOH to identify these characters as valid line control characters. The simplest means to achieve code transparency is the use of DLE.STX or DLE.SOH to signify the beginning of noncontrol data (user data) and DLE.ETX, DLE.ETB, or DLE.ITB to signify the end of user data. The DLE is not placed in front of user-generated data. Consequently, if bit patterns resembling any of these control characters are created in the user text and encountered by the receiving station, the receiving station assumes they are valid user data.

The DLE places the line into a *transparent text mode*, which allows the transmission of any bit pattern. This capability is also important when BSC is used on different types of applications. For example, engineering or statistical departments in a firm often use floating-point notation due to the need for large magnitudes in numbers of very precise fractions. Conversely, accounting departments use fixed-point notation to provide for accurate fractions (two decimal places for cents). BSC accepts these kinds of numeric representations by the use of DLE.

The DLE presents a special problem if it is generated by the end-user application process, since it could be recognized as a control code. BSC handles this situation by inserting a DLE next to a data DLE character. The receiver discards the first DLE of two successive DLEs and accepts the second DLE as valid user data.

Line modes.   The BSC channel or link operates in one of two modes. The *control* mode is used by a master station to control the operations on the link, such as the transmission of polling and selection messages. The *message* or text mode is used for the transmittal of an information block or blocks to and from the stations. Upon receiving an invitation to send data (a poll), the slave station transmits user data with either an STX or SOH in front of data or a heading. These two control characters place the channel in the message or text mode. Thereafter, data are exchanged under the message mode until an EOT is received. The EOT changes the mode back to control. During the time the channel is in message mode, the channel is dedicated to the exchange of data between two stations only. All other stations must remain passive. The two-station message mode is also called the *select-hold* mode.

BSC also provides for contention operation on a point-to-point circuit. In this situation, one of the stations can become the master by "bidding" to the other station. The station accepting the bid becomes the slave. A point-to-point line enters the contention mode following the transmission of reception of the EOT.

The ENQ code plays an important role in BSC control modes. Its functions are:

Poll: Control station sends with an address prefix.

Select: Control station sends with a different type of address prefix.

Bid: Point-to-point stations send to contend for control station status.

Figure 7–19 shows an exchange of transmissions in a BSC environment. The following legend is used to trace the transmission flow and formats (for simplicity, the SYNs are not shown):

1.   C, A, C $\longrightarrow$ or $\longleftarrow$ C, A, C
2.   C, I, C $\longrightarrow$ or $\longleftarrow$ C, I, C
3.   C $\longrightarrow$ or $\longleftarrow$ C

where C = control characters
     A = address of station
     I = user information field

In actual transmission, SYN characters precede the message, and the control characters, address, and I field (if appropriate) follow.

Control fields follow the message as well. Figure 7–19 shows arrows to indicate the direction of the transmission. It also shows upper- and lowercase letters in the A field: uppercase depicts a poll; lowercase depicts a select.

BSC provides other features. The following additional control fields show these facilities.

WACK (wait before transmitting): This field provides a positive ACK of the message and also requests holding up any transmissions until the sending station sends an ENQ and receives an ACK.

RVI (reverse interrupt): This provides the capability to stop the current transmission sequence to service higher-priority work.

TTD (temporary text delay): This allows the transmitting station to delay its sending of a message and still retain control of the line.

BSC was designed in the 1960s and has served the industry well. The early applications usually had a human operator at the remote station and the half-duplex approach was sufficient. As applications and data communications became more sophisticated, more powerful data link control techniques were needed. These requirements gave rise to the bit-oriented, full-duplex, sliding window protocols, such as HDLC and SDLC.

Synchronous Data Link Control

Synchronous data link control is IBM's major DLC offering today. The product was introduced in 1973 to support communications lines among teller terminals in banks. The offering is discussed in this book for two reasons: (a) it is widely used in the United States and (b) it is quite similar to the international standard HDLC. The product is in

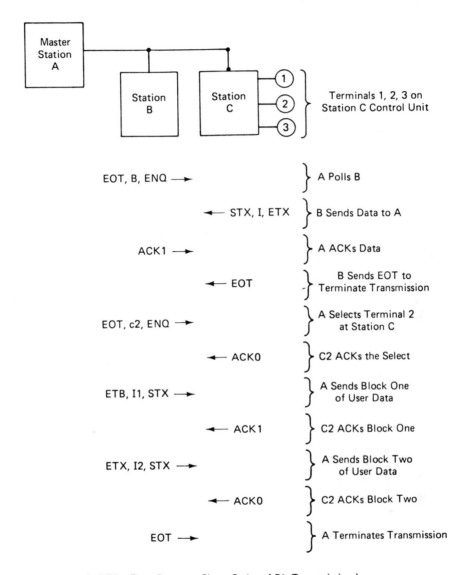

(NOTE: Flow Does not Show Order of Bit Transmission.)

Figure 7–19. Multipoint bisync transmissions.

many of IBM's communications components and will eventually replace the BSC offering.

SDLC uses the synchronous, bit-oriented, Go-Back-N methods. It controls a single line configured as point to point, multipoint, or loop. It operates on half-duplex, duplex, switched, or private lines. It also provides for duplex, multipoint operation in which a station can transmit to one station while receiving from another.

SDLC uses variations of the polling/selection technique. The primary station is responsible for the control of the line. It initiates all transmissions (such as a poll) from the secondary stations with a command. The stations reply with a response. The primary station can also be a secondary station to another primary station.

SDLC frame. SDLC messages are transmitted across the line in a specific format called a *frame* (see Figure 7–20). The beginning and ending flags each consist of an 8-bit byte pattern of 01111110. These fields serve as references for the beginning and ending of the frame, like a SYN field. The ending flag may serve as a beginning flag for the next frame. Multiple flags may be repeated between frames to keep the line in an active state.

SDLC is code transparent and the only unique bit stream is the flag field. The logic will not allow the 01111110 pattern to be transmitted in other parts of the frame. At the transmitting end, SDLC examines the frame contents (flag fields excluded) and inserts a 0 after any succession of five consecutive 1s within the frame. The receiving site receives the frame, recognizes the first flag, and then removes any 0 that follows five consecutive 1s. Consequently, SDLC is not dependent on any specific code such as ASCII or EBCDIC. It does require that all fields in the frame be in multiples of 8 bits after the stuffed 0s have been removed.

The address field follows the beginning flag. The address identifies the secondary station. SDLC also allows addressing a number of stations on the line (group address), as well as all stations (broadcast address). A poll frame identifies the polled secondary station. A response also contains the address of the secondary station.

The control field defines the function of the frame and, therefore, invokes the SDLC logic at the receiving and sending stations. The field is an 8-bit byte and can be in one of three formats.

1. *Unnumbered format* (U) frames are used for control purposes such as initializing secondary stations, disconnecting stations, testing stations, and controlling modes of responses from stations.

2. *Supervisory format* (S) frames are used to positively acknowledge and negatively acknowledge user data (information frames). Supervisory frames do not carry user data. They are used to confirm received data, report busy or ready conditions, and report frame numbering errors.

3. *Information transfer* (I) frames contain the user data.

The next field of the frame is the frame check sequence field. This field contains a 16-bit sequence that is computed from the contents of the address, control, and infor-

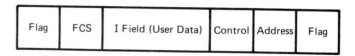

Figure 7–20.   SDLC frame.

mation fields at the transmitting stations. The receiver performs a similar computation to determine if errors have been introduced during the transmission process. The receiver will not accept a frame that is in error.

SDLC control field. The control field is further described in Table 7–1. The low-order bits (rightmost) identify the frame format (11 for unnumbered, 10 for supervisory, 0 for information). The remainder of the bits define the specific type and function of the frame:

UI (unnumbered information): This command allows for transmission of user data in an unnumbered (that is, unsequenced) frame.

RIM (request initialization mode): The RIM frame is a request from a secondary station to a primary station for an SIM command.

SIM (set initialization mode): This command is used to initialize the primary-secondary session. UA is the expected response.

SNRM (set normal response mode): This places the secondary station in an NRM (normal response mode). The NRM precludes the secondary station from sending any unsolicited frames. This means the primary station controls all message flow on the link.

TABLE 7-1 SDLC CONTROL FIELD

Command Response	Format	Control Field	Low Order →		Command	Response	I-Field Prohibited	Resets Nr and Ns
UI	U	000	P/F	0011	X	X		
RIM	U	000	F	0111		X	X	
SIM	U	000	P	0111	X		X	X
SNRM	U	100	P	0011	X		X	X
DM	U	000	F	1111		X	X	
DISC	U	010	P	0011	X		X	
UA	U	011	F	0011		X	X	
FRMR	U	100	F	0111		X		
BCN	U	111	F	1111		X	X	
CFGR	U	110	P/F	0111	X	X		
RD	U	010	F	0011		X	X	
XID	U	101	P/F	1111	X	X		
UP	U	001	P	0011	X		X	
TEST	U	111	P/F	0011	X	X		
RR	S	Nr	P/F	0001	X	X	X	
RNR	S	Nr	P/F	0101	X	X	X	
REJ	S	Nr	P/F	1001	X	X	X	
I	I	Nr	P/F	Ns 0	X	X		

DM (disconnect mode): This frame is transmitted from a secondary station to indicate it is in the disconnected mode.

DISC (disconnect): This command from the primary station places the secondary station in the normal disconnected mode. This command is valuable for switched lines; the command provides a function similar to hanging up a telephone.

Note: The initialization, normal response, and normal disconnected modes are the three allowable modes in SDLC.

UA (unnumbered acknowledgment): This is an ACK to the SNRM, DISC, or SIM command.

FRMR (frame reject): The secondary station sends this frame when it encounters an invalid frame. This is not used for a bit error indicated in the frame check sequence field but for more unusual conditions, such as a frame that is too long for a secondary station's buffers or an erroneous control field.

BCN (beacon): Explained later during discussions on loop configurations.

CFGR (configure): Explained later during discussions on loop configurations.

RD (request disconnect): Request from a secondary station to be disconnected.

XID (exchange station identification): This command asks for the identification of a secondary station. It is used on switched facilities to identify the calling station.

UP (unnumbered polls): Explained later during discussions on loop configurations.

Test: This frame is used to solicit testing responses from the secondary station.

RR (receive ready): Indicates secondary or primary station is ready to receive. It is also used to ACK or NAK information frames.

RNR (receive not ready): Indicates secondary or primary station is temporarily busy. It is also used to ACK or NAK information frames.

REJ (reject): This frame can be used to explicitly request the transmission or retransmission of information frames. This command or response is very useful when the frame sequencing becomes out of order.

I (information): This frame contains the user data. It can also ACK and NAK received frames.

Frame flow control.   SDLC uses the sliding-window technique to manage the flow of frames between the sender and receiver. Each station maintains a send (Ns) and receive (Nr) count. A sending station counts each outgoing frame and transmits the count in the Ns portion of the control field. The receiving station receives and checks the frame. If the frame is error free and properly sequenced, it advances its Nr count by one and sends an ACK with the appropriate Nr count to the transmitter.

The station's Nr and Ns fields are set to 0 at session initialization. The flow of frames and the incremental counting at each end of the Nr and Ns fields provide the capability for the receiving station's Nr count to be the same as the transmitting station's Ns field of the *next* frame to be transmitted.

The Nr and Ns counts in the control field are each 3 bits, thus allowing a counting capacity of 8 using the binary numbers of 0 through 7. As in most sliding-window techniques, the window wraps around to 0 after the count reaches 7. Up to seven unconfirmed frames can be outstanding at one time between the two stations.

SDLC provides for inclusive acknowledgment. For example, an ACK of a frame with an Ns count of 5 essentially says, "I have received and accepted all frames up to and including the frame with Ns = 4. The next frame I receive from you should have an Ns = 5."

The P/F (poll/final) is the fifth bit in the control field and provides the following functions: (a) the primary station turns the P bit on to indicate a poll or a checkpoint to the secondary station and (b) the secondary station turns the F bit on to indicate the last frame of transmission.

The SDLC link can only have one outstanding P bit at a time. It requires a response from a secondary station in the form of an F bit set to 1. By convention, this bit is called a P bit when the frame is transmitted from a primary station and an F bit when the frame is from a secondary station. The one-to-one relationship of the P/F bit function helps to implement the flow of frames on the link. This will become more evident when we view some actual examples.

Figures 7–21 and 7–22 provide examples of SDLC exchanges of data and control frames. The following legend is used to trace the transmission flow and formats:

1.   F, FCS, [C], A, F $\longrightarrow$ or $\longleftarrow$ F, A, [C], FCS, F
2.   F, FCS, I, [C], A, F $\longrightarrow$ or $\longleftarrow$ F, A, [C], I, FCS, F

The control field is further divided into the following formats (C/R means command/response) and is surrounded by brackets ([   ]) to aid in its identification.

1.   Nr, P/F, Ns $\longrightarrow$ or $\longleftarrow$ Ns, P/F, Nr
2.   Nr, P/F, C/R $\longrightarrow$ or $\longleftarrow$ C/R, P/F, Nr
3.   P/F, C/R $\longrightarrow$ or $\longleftarrow$ C/R, P/F

where F = flags
     A = address of secondary station
     C = control field
     Ns = count of sending sentence field
   P/F = P: poll bit on
         $\overline{P}$: poll bit off
         F: final bit on
         $\overline{F}$: final bit off
     Nr = count of receiving sequence field
   FCS = frame check sequence field
     I = information (user) field

Loop transmission.   SDLC also has the hub-polling capability. The arrangement, called *loop transmission*, provides for the primary station (loop controller) to send command frames to any or all the stations of the loop. Each secondary station decodes

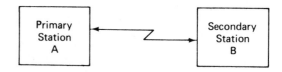

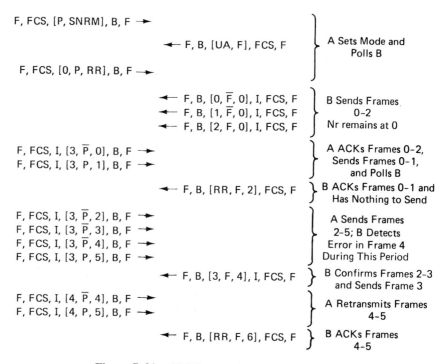

Figure 7–21. SDLC transmission with one station.

the address field of each frame and accepts the frame, if appropriate. The frame is also passed to the next station (down-loop station.)

After the loop controller has completed the transmission of the command frames, it sends eight consecutive 0s to signal the secondary stations of the completion of the frames. It then transmits continuous 1s to indicate it is in a receive mode and awaits the receiving of the 1s to ascertain that the loop is complete.

The following additional formats are used for loop transmission:

UP (unnumbered polls): This frame is useful for loop operations because it gives the secondary station the option of responding to the poll. The poll can then be transmitted around the loop and used by all stations without regard to any previous sequence (Nr or Ns) binding.

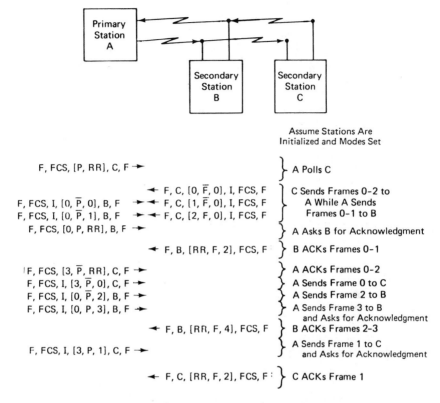

Figure 7–22. SDLC multipoint transmission.

CFGR (configure): This command provides for several testing and configuration features (clearing functions, placing a station in receive-only mode, placing stations off line).

BCN (beacon): This frame is used to trace down problems with the carrier signal—to determine what part of the path is causing the problem. It causes the secondary station to suppress transmission of the carrier or to begin transmitting the carrier again after suppressing it.

The unnumbered polls serve to evoke frames from the secondary stations on the line and can be sent from the primary station after the continuous 1s have completed the loop. Figure 7–23 shows an SDLC loop operation. The legend shown earlier still pertains. In addition, the CA means a common address is intended for all stations.

HDLC and SDLC differences.   IBM considers SDLC to be a subset of the HDLC specification in that it uses an option of HDLC called the *unbalanced mode.* This means the link is controlled by one primary station; all other stations are secondary sites

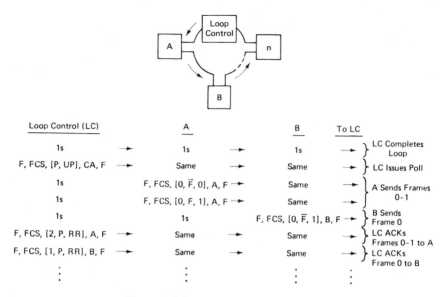

Figure 7–23. SDLC loop transmission.

and can only transmit upon receiving a P bit from the primary. HDLC provides another option called the *balanced mode* wherein both stations are combined. That is, they are both a primary and secondary station and control the traffic on the link by one site's primary frames controlling the other site's secondary frames, and vice versa. Balanced mode is suited for point-to-point links. The unbalanced mode is designed for multipoint configurations.

SDLC does not use other options of HDLC, yet it is not a true subset because it provides the hub-polling configuration, which is not in the HDLC command/response repertoire.

Communications Satellites and Data Link Controls

From Chapter 4, the reader may recall that geosynchronous satellites incur an end-to-end signal propagation of several hundred milliseconds and, under certain conditions, as long as 900 ms. Certain DLCs do not execute efficiently on satellite links. In some instances, the propagation delay can cause the DLC software to wrap around itself, continuously executing its timeout code waiting for the incoming message. Additionally, a stop-and-wait technique (such as bisync) would spend a good deal of valuable channel time awaiting the next block of data. On the other hand, the sliding-window techniques such as SDLC are better suited to satellite transmission due to the continuous sending and receiving of messages between the two sites. Notwithstanding, the TDMA approach has become the preferred channel-control mechanism for satellites because it does not rely on the high overhead of polling/selection protocols.

Satellite vendors now offer components that allow a user site to maintain the older data link controls. The components, called *delay compensation units* (DCU), terminate the user's DLC locally and build another data block into a delay-insensitive satellite DLC. The DCU responds locally to the terminal or computer as if it were the remote site.

Frame Relay

A technology that has gained increased attention in the past few years is frame relay. Its popularity and rapid use stem from the fact that transmission systems today are experiencing far fewer errors and problems than they did in the 1970s and 1980s. During that period, line protocols were developed and implemented to cope with error-prone transmission circuits. However, with the increased use of optical fibers and conditioned lines, protocols that expend resources dealing with errors become less important.

The second factor that has contributed to the increased use of frame relay is the need for higher-capacity network interfaces (in bits/s). The technology of the 1980s focused on kilobit rates, which are inadequate to serve as applications that need large transmissions of data, such as bit-mapped graphics, telemetry systems, and large database transfers.

The technology developed with wide area networks in the 1980s and 1990s was designed to cope with noisy lines and relatively slow speed interfaces. Today, the WAN is acting as a bottleneck as the transit between local area networks. LANs operate in the megabit range and, with some exceptions, WANs are restricted to the kilobit range.

In addition, many of the protocols that are in existence today were designed to support relatively "unintelligent" devices, such as nonprogrammable terminals. Today, these devices operate with powerful microprocessors and have many capabilities. They are able to handle many tasks that were heretofore delegated to network components.

Frame relay is designed to eliminate and/or combine certain operations residing in the data link protocol as well as most of the operations that a conventional network layer performs. It implements the operational aspects of statistical multiplexing found in the X.25 protocol and the efficiency of circuit switching found in TDM protocols.

The end effect of this approach is increased throughput and decreased delay and the saving of "CPU cycles" within the network because some services are eliminated.

The frame relay link operations are much simpler than the conventional data link control. Essentially, it performs two operations: (a) it uses flags to check for the presence of the frame on the link and (b) it performs an FCS check. If the FCS check reveals an error, the frame is discarded and the link layer takes no remdial action. Figure 7–24 shows the operations on a frame relay link.

The reader may be wondering about the sense of discarding traffic and not taking any remedial action. After all, most users do not like to lose data. The idea of frame relay is to place the responsibility for data integrity in another layer. Under most circumstances, the transport layer assumes this responsibility. But let there be no confusion: If one cares for one's data, error checking must be performed somewhere because errors do occur.

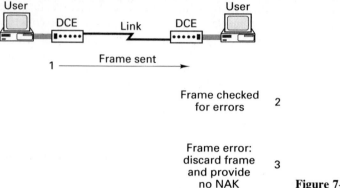

Figure 7-24. Frame relay operations.

If the essence of frame relay was the simple elimination of ACKing and NAKing, the technology would not have made much of an impact in the industry. However, frame relay is used as a supporting technology for public network offerings that provide customers ''bandwidth on demand''—a technology that is quite attractive for bursty data communications systems.

Frame relay is discussed in more detail in *Data Link Protocols*, published by Prentice Hall and written by this author. Naturally, it is highly recommended.

SUMMARY

The progress in developing and using improved link control techniques has been slow due to the investments in the machines and software that support the older approaches. Nonetheless, standards such as HDLC and products such as SDLC are in wide use today; they offer significant improvements over a 2740 or BSC product. In spite of the increased complexity of the new DLC techniques and the requirement for more sophisticated machines to support them, the new DLCs provide opportunities to reduce overall costs due to more efficient line utilization, increased reliability, and better error control.

8

Digital Transmission

INTRODUCTION

This chapter examines data communications systems that use digital technology. The techniques for encoding analog voice signals to digital streams are also covered. Prevalent digitization schemes are examined and compared as well as encoding schemes. T1 hierarchy is examined in this chapter as well as ISDN and broadband ISDN.

The data communications industry is evolving toward the use of all-digital networks. These networks carry digital bit images instead of the conventional voice-oriented analog signal. In the near future, networks will be integrated to transmit digital images of data, voice, facsimile, graphics, television, and any other image.

ADVANTAGES OF DIGITAL TRANSMISSION

If it had to be done over again, it is probable that analog technologies would never have been used. Digital transmission schemes are more attractive for several reasons. First, long-haul digital signals are more error free than analog signals. As depicted in Figure 6–3, the line noise and other distortions are periodically amplified with the analog signal. Digital transmission entails the use of regenerative repeaters wherein only the absence of a pulse (binary 0) or the presence of a pulse (binary 1) need be detected. Thereafter, the signal is completely reconstructed. The repeaters create a signal as good as the orig-

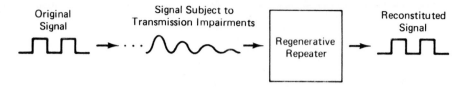

Figure 8-1. Digital signals and signal regeneration.

inal transmission (see Figure 8-1). Consequently, digital signals can experience more distortion and cross talk and a higher noise-to-signal ratio than analog signals.

Second, the rapidly declining costs of circuitry and processors make digital schemes increasingly attractive. The ideas and theories of digital transmission have been around for many years; the introduction of inexpensive large-scale-integration (LSI) circuitry now makes the concepts cost-effective.

Third, many transmission types can be accommodated with a digital facility. Television, data, voice, telegraphy, facsimile, and even music can be multiplexed together. The digital network treats all signals as binary values in the form of digital pulses of a positive zero, or negative voltage. This capability is quite valuable because organizations will be able to implement one network for *all* transmissions. Digital transmissions use a data transmission unit to send the binary bits directly onto the network. Analog transmissions (such as voice and television) use an analog-to-digital converter (A/D) to translate the signal to binary images at the transmitter. At the receiver, a digital-to-analog device (D/A) converts the signal back to an analog form (see Figure 8-2).

Fourth, digital transmission is inherently more secure than analog transmission. Encryption is relatively easy. The older analog scramblers are not very effective against the decoding ability of the computer. Moreover, scrambled speech can often be deciphered by a trained listener. Digital encryption costs less than analog scrambling.

Fifth, the newer satellite transmission schemes use digital transmission to increase reliability and signal throughput. The schemes are based on time-division multiplexing (TDM) using digital bit streams. The approach will see increasing use as satellites use higher bands in the electromagnetic spectrum.

Sixth, newer transmission technologies such as optical fibers benefit from digital transmission. For example, lasers are used to transmit pulses of light to represent binary bits.

Seventh, recent advances in voice digitization point to reduced bandwidth requirements for sending voice-generated signals. Speech can be digitized at 2,400 bits, which permits four simultaneous conversations on a voice-grade circuit. Digitizing speech at this bit rate is expensive, but the decreasing costs of LSI circuitry point toward more cost-effective digitization arrangements.

Last, switching and control signaling can be accomplished more effectively with digital facilities. The two components can be more fully integrated because equipment can be made common for both. Switching and signaling are more reliable and efficient using digital techniques.

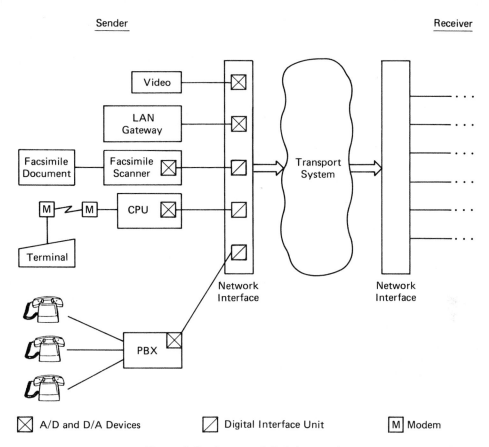

Figure 8–2. Integrated digital networks.

HOW DIGITAL TRANSMISSION WORKS

It was established in 1937 that the periodic sampling of a signal at a rate twice the highest frequency in the sample would provide all the intelligence required to capture the signal and reconstruct it at a later time. A voice-grade line would, therefore, require a minimum sampling rate of 6,600 times a second, since the voice-grade band is about 300 to 3,300 Hz. Channels actually occupy a 4-kHz bandwidth, so the Bell T1 carrier system uses a rate of 8,000 samples per second.

Digitizing an analog signal consists of three steps: sampling, quantizing, and encoding. The technique is shown in Figure 8–3. Each analog signal is sampled every 125 μs (1 sec/8,000 samples = 0.000125). The sample is assigned a level based on the signal amplitude at the time of the sample. The assignment of a level is based on a scale of 256 values and is called a *quantizing scale*. The number 256 permits 8 binary bits to be used to represent any one of the possible sample levels. The quantized levels are coded

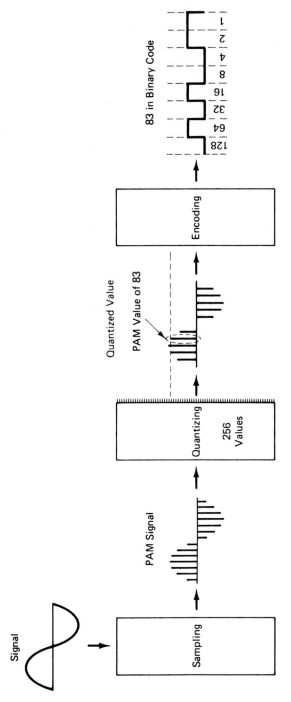

Figure 8–3. Sampling, quantizing, and encoding.

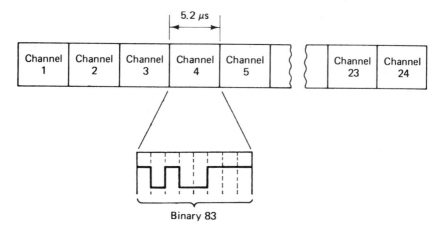

Figure 8–4. The multiplexed frame.

with the 8 bits and then converted to a digital pulse stream for transmission. The eighth bit is periodically used for supervisory and signalling purposes. This complete process is termed *pulse code modulation* (PCM) and is the most common digitizing technique in use today.

Common carriers transmit 24 voice channels together with time-division multiplexing techniques. The T1 carrier system provides the multiplexing by sampling the 24 channels at a combined rate of 192,000 times per second (8,000 times per second per channel × 24 channels = 192,000). Figure 8–4 shows how the 24 channels are multiplexed into a frame. The frame contains one sample from each channel, plus an additional bit for frame synchronization. Thus, the complete frame is 193 bits (8 bits per channel × 24 channels + 1 sync bit = 193 bits). Since a frame represents only 1 of the required 8,000 samples per second, a T1 system operates at 1,544,000 to accommodate all 8,000 frames (193 bits per frame × 8,000 frames = 1,544,000). Each sample in the frame has a TDM slot of 5.2 μs (1 sec/192,000 = 0.0000052). In addition, each of the 24 channels requires a 64-kbit/s rate: 8,000 samples per second × 8 bits per sample = 64,000.

The 193rd bit performs a function similar to the start bit in an asynchronous transmission and a sync byte in a synchronous transmission. It is used to establish and maintain synchronization between the sending and receiving sites. The bit alternates as 1 or 0 in each succeeding frame. Since this alternating pattern seldom occurs very long in the data/voice frames, the receiver can ''sync'' on these framing pulses. The timing mechanisms at the sender and receiver are synchronized to permit the connection of the correct channel of the frame to both ends at exactly the same times.

DIGITIZATION SCHEMES AND VOICE DIGITIZATION RATE

Voice digitization rate (VDR) describes the number of bits required to represent the voice signal. From the preceding description of digital techniques, we know that a voice channel is sampled at 8,000 times per second, with 8 bits representing each sample. A

64-kbit/s VDR is required to carry the coded signal. Actually, a higher VDR rate is required to assure high voice quality and signal control. The 64-kbit/s VDR is high and entails a large bandwidth with associated high transmission costs. Yet a lower VDR requires more expensive translation devices and usually results in a poorer quality of voice reproduction. Current technology encompasses schemes to reduce the VDR, but they must be weighed against the cost of signal conversions and the quality of the signal. Most of these schemes use PCM-based techniques.

Companded PCM

A lower VDR can be achieved by taking advantge of two common characteristics of the human ear and speech. First, the ear is more sensitive to low sound levels. Second, speech occurs more frequently at the lower levels. Ear sensitivity is actually logarithmic, experiencing incremental insensitivity at higher levels of sound.

Companded PCM uses a device called a *compander* (compressor–expander) to boost the smaller-level signals and attenuate (or hold constant) the larger amplitudes. The process uses nonuniform quantizing levels to give more steps to the smaller amplitude signals (see Figure 8–5); the compressed levels give more gain to these signals. The compander gives more steps to the lower signals to reduce the effect of quantizing noise: A voice signal can never be reproduced exactly because the quantizing steps

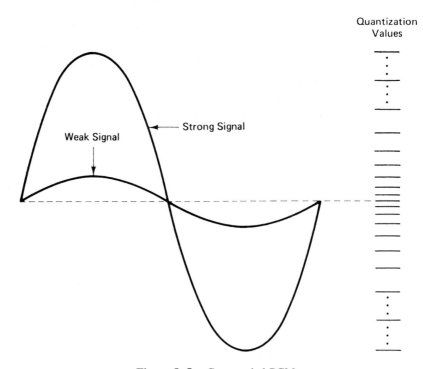

Figure 8–5.   Companded PCM.

introduce a discrete, nonanalog function to an analog process. The resulting inaccuracy is called *quantizing noise*. Lower-level signals are particularly susceptible to quantizing error, so a compander is used to provide more steps to those signals.

Companded PCM, also called log PCM, yields VDRs of 32 to 64 kbit/s. AT&T's D2 system uses this technique to achieve a VDR of 64 kbit/s using 256 (2^8) quantizing levels; the D2 channel bank provides excellent quality in voice reproduction.

Differential PCM

This scheme is a variation of PCM. An analog voice signal yields consecutive samples that are close to each other on a quantizing scale. Consequently, differential PCM (DPCM) transmits binary pulse streams to represent the difference between consecutive samples and not the sample itself. DPCM yields VDRs ranging between 32 and 48 kbit/s.

A DPCM codec (coder–decoder) samples an input and uses the signal to apply a predictive weight to the next sample. The value actually transmitted is the difference between the value of the current input and its predicted value. A more sophisticated version, the adaptive DPCM (ADPCM), dynamically alters the quantizing levels based on the input signal's amplitude. The ADPCM yields an effective VDR of 24 kbit/s.

Delta Modulation

This technique is a variation of DPCM. It encodes the transmitted binary bit stream from the changes of the input samples, but the differences between the samples are transmitted as one of two levels represented by a 1 or 0, or one of the four levels with 00, 01, 10 or 11. The delta modulation sampling device detects changes in successive samples by providing a feedback mechanism of a previous sample to the current sampling gate. Delta modulation is a simple and inexpensive process and achieves a VDR rate of 16 to 32 kbit/s. Moreover, by adding a compander, the quality of the signal can be improved by providing more quantizing levels to the smaller signals; this technique is called *adaptive delta modulation* (ADM) or *companded delta modulation* (CDM).

Analysis–Synthesis Techniques

These techniques are attractive from the VDR standpoint, generally 2.4 to 9.6 kbit/s. Analysis–synthesis does not preserve the analog speech wave form as in the other methods. Rather, certain characteristics of the human voice are encoded and transmitted. The codes contain information on resonance frequencies of the vocal tract for particular positions of the tongue, lips, and other speech-related organs. Analysis–synthesis will likely see increasing use as the cost of its speech digitizers (vocoders) decrease.

DIGITAL PULSE CODES

The codes commonly used in data communications are listed next. Other codes are available, but these digital schemes are found in most systems today.

- Nonreturn to zero (NRZ)
- Return to zero (RZ)
- Biphase

Nonreturn to Zero

Figure 8–6(a) shows the NRZ pulse code. The signal level throughout a bit cell (or bit duration) remains stable. In this example, the signal level remains high for a bit 1 and goes low for bit 0. The code could also use a high signal for a 0. The choice depends on the probability of the occurrence of 1s or 0s in the transmission. The alternative chosen should provide the code that yields the greater number of signal transitions in order to improve synchronization.

NRZ is widely used in data communications systems. The asynchronous process described in earlier chapters uses the NRZ coding scheme. The universal asynchronous receiver transmitter chip (UART) uses NRZ code. The UART has become an informal industry standard.

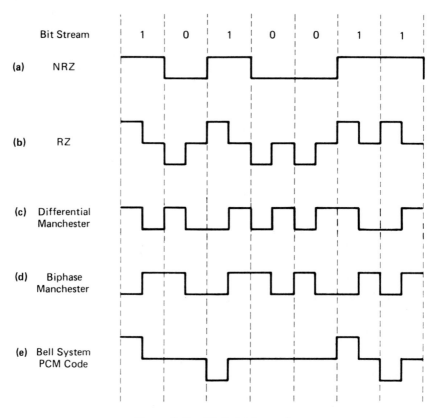

Figure 8–6. Digital pulse codes.

While NRZ makes efficient use of bandwidth (a bit is represented for every signal change, or baud), it does suffer from the lack of self-clocking capabilities. Self-clocking is best achieved when each successive bit cell undergoes a signal-level transition. A continuous stream of 1s or 0s would not create a level transition until the bit stream changed to the opposite binary number. Consequently, the receiver may not know where to begin bit sampling or what group of bits constitutes a character (byte). The NRZ scheme requires an independent clocking mechanism, often a separate transmission. This approach solves the non-self-clocking deficiency of NRZ but incurs additional synchronization problems if the data signal and clocking signal ''drift'' from each other as they traverse down the communications path. The clocking and synchronization problems with NRZ codes can be diminished through the randomized NRZ code. The NRZ signal is passed through a component that randomizes the bit stream to increase the number of signal-level transitions.

Return to Zero

In return to zero code, the cell stays high for a part of the bit duration and returns to a low level for the remaining time. The standard RZ code, RZ-L, represents a 1 with a high level at the beginning of the cell and goes low during the second half. A 0 is represented with first a low signal, than a high signal. Figure 8–6(b) illustrates the RZ code. A second form of RZ is ratio encoding, which uses two-thirds of the bit cell to represent a high signal level and the remaining one-third to represent a low signal level. The most common forms of RZ use equal periods to represent both levels.

RZ codes provide a transition in every bit cell. Consequently, they have good synchronization characteristics. RZ is a self-clocking code because of its bit cell transition properties. However, since RZ experiences two signal transitions within each cell, its information-carrying capacity is not as great as the NRZ code. To achieve synchronization capabilities, RZ requires a baud that is twice the bit-per-second rate.

Biphase

Biphase codes have several variations and as many names: phase encoding, frequency encoding, and frequency shift encoding. All biphase codes have at least one level transition per bit cell, which is similar to RZ codes. However, most of the biphase codes have the 1s or 0s defined by the direction of the signal-level transition.

A biphase code is shown in Figure 8–6(c). This is known as differential Manchester coding. The polarities of the signal are dependent on the last half of the previously transmitted bit cell. For a binary 0, the preceding signal element is the opposite polarity of the first half of the 0 bit cell. The situation is reversed for a binary 1; the polarity of the previous signal element is the same as the first half of the 1 bit cell.

Biphase codes are found extensively in magnetic recording and in data communications systems utilizing optical fiber links. The codes are used in applications requiring a high degree of accuracy; the code is self-clocking.

One of the variations of biphase is the Manchester code. It is used in several data communications systems, notably the local area network Ethernet. The Manchester code is illustrated in Figure 8–6(d). It provides a low to high level in each bit cell to represent a 1, and a high to low level to represent a 0. The Ethernet data rate is 10 Mbit/s, so each bit cell is 100 nanoseconds (ns) long (1 sec/10,000,000 b/s = 0.0000001). The double-level transition requires a baud that is twice the data rate. However, with the wide bandwidth of coaxial cable (and optical fibers), this does not present a serious problem, but it does require more expensive interfaces.

COMMON-CARRIER PULSE CODES

Communications carriers use a variation of the return to zero coding scheme [see Figure 8–6(e)]. A high-level signal represents 1 bit, *but* the next 1 bit is a low negative signal. In other words, successive 1 bits have opposite polarity. The 0 bits are represented as a low nonnegative level or an absence of a pulse signal. In addition, the 1 pulses have a level transition at midcell. This scheme is called *bipolar transmission;* the use of alternate polarities to represent the pulse train is known as *alternate mark inversion* (AMI).

The AMI scheme provides a convenient way to detect an error. For example, if a bit is distorted and interpreted as an opposite polarity, the AMI convention is violated and an error detected.

Newer systems replace AMI and use a technique called binary eight zero substitution (B8ZS), which allows users to transmit any combination of 0s and 1s. A code replaces eight consecutive 0s at the transmitter and removes the code for the eight 0s at the receiver.

The earlier T systems used some other conventions that have created problems. First, the original T-1 system (also called D1) used a 7-bit quantizer with an 8-bit sample field, which gave the carrier a bit in each byte for control and signaling (off-hook, ring signal, etc). When the 8-bit 256-level quantizer was implemented, the carrier "robbed" a user bit in the sixth and twelfth frames for signaling and control. Essentially, the user had $7\frac{5}{6}$ effective bits per sample, which was adequate for voice. However, data transmissions cannot afford the luxury of bit robbing, since the practice renders the data inaccurate and probably useless. The change also made the D1 devices incompatible with the new devices (D2, D3, and D4), which required the carrier to retrofit with conversion devices.

Second, for timing purposes the earlier systems (and many modern systems as well) required that any 24-bit interval must have at least 3 1 bits and no more than 15 consecutive 0 bits. If the transmission violates this convention, the AMI code is altered to provide the needed polarity changes. Again, such a procedure is unacceptable for data transmissions. Shortly, we will examine newer and more advanced systems that overcome some of these limitations.

REGENERATIVE REPEATERS

Earlier discussions in this chapter explained that digital regenerative repeaters provided for more error-free transmission than analog signals. The equipment also permits higher data rates. The bandwidth of a communications channel places a restriction on the data rate. If bit pulses are transmitted over a line at too high a rate, the signal becomes distorted, and the faster the data rate, the more the signal is impaired. However, if repeaters are placed close enough together on the line, a high bit rate can be transmitted. All that is needed is to recognize the absence or presence of a binary pulse. Regenerative repeaters permit the data rate to be high and the distortion to be severe. If repeaters were placed every few hundred feet, a very high bit rate could be achieved.

The earlier repeaters on the T1 system were spaced 6,000 feet apart. They replaced loading coils, which are analog components on the line. The loading coils are used to keep impedance and attenuation constant over the length of the line. They are designed for voice-frequency signals and are not found in present digital carrier systems.

THE DIGITAL HIERARCHY

The North American digital hierarchy is shown in Figure 8–7. It has five levels of digital data rates that are combined to form the hierarchy by channel banks and multiplexers. The levels are designated T carriers or as digital signal numbers (DS):

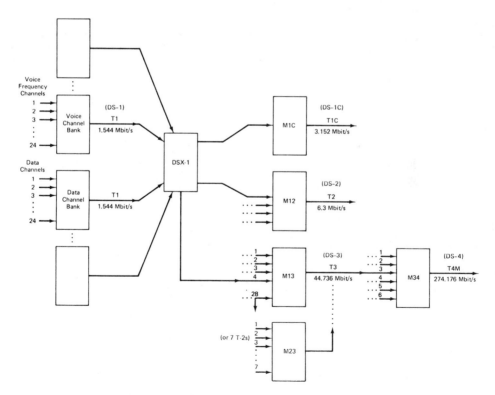

Figure 8–7. The North American digital hierarchy.

	SPEED	PCM VOICE CHANNELS
DSO	64 kbit/s	—
DS-1	1.544 Mbit/s	24
DS-1c	3.152 Mbit/s	48
DS-2	6.312 Mbit/s	96
DS-3	44.736 Mbit/s	672
DS-4	139.264 Mbit/s	2,016

The T1 (DS-1) carrier was developed in the 1960s by Bell Labs to operate over twisted pair cables on interoffice and toll trunks. Regenerative repeaters are placed every 6,000 feet using No. 22 gauge cable pairs. The T1 system carries 24 voice channels. The T1 carrier uses a D1 channel bank (now becoming obsolete). The device uses 128 quantizing steps for the pulse code modulation. The T1C was later developed as an upgrade to T1 lines. It is similar to T1.

The DS-2 carrier system was implemented in 1972 for use on the intertoll trunks. It carries 96 voice channels or one video channel. The DS-3 system serves as a bridge between the other carriers. Utilizing the M13 multiplexer, it provides a 44.736 Mbit/s data rate.

The DS-4 system transmits 139.264 Mbit/s over coaxial cable and provides for 2,016 voice channels. A typical coaxial cable conduit contains 18 cables, so the DS-4 system can handle a considerable amount of traffic.

As with so many other data communications sytems, other countries and the CCITT have developed systems that are different from those of the United States. The CCITT recommendation is somewhat similar to the AT&T system, but the basic carrier speed is 2.048 Mbit/s. However, the synchronization bit alignment in the frames differs and the functions are also different. Moreover, the CCITT standard provides for either 64- or 62.6-kbit/s data rates. Also, the frame lengths vary significantly. Obviously, integrating international digital networks will require interface and conversion facilities. Consequently, the ISDN-recommended standard has been developed.

INTEGRATED SERVICES DIGITAL NETWORKS

The ISDN consists of a series of recommended standards, published by CCITT, that defines an end-to-end digital network, offering a wide range of user services with a limited set of user–network interfaces. The PTTs in Europe have already implemented ISDN prototypes with the intent of moving to nationwide ISDNs within 5 to 7 years. The United States and Canada have also begun ISDN developments, and vendors are now building ISDN interfaces and functions for the emerging technology.

One might reasonably ask, ''Why should I have one network for everything?'' The answer is simple: to reduce duplication, complexities of interfaces, and (eventually) costs. Many organizations use 6 to 10 separate networks to handle their data communications requirements (telephone switched, telephone nonswitched, telex, teletex, telegraph, public packet systems, private packet systems, etc.). The intent of ISDN is to use one technology to service all these heretofore disparate systems.

The basic structure of the ISDN is illustrated in Figure 8–8, which shows three important aspects of the standard: *functional groups*, *reference points*, and *access points*. Functional groups are functions that may be needed to support a user access arrangement. Reference points are the conceptual points dividing functional groups and usually consist of physical interfaces and connectors. Access points establish which of the seven ISO layer entities is used at the functional groups or reference points.

NT1 (network termination 1) includes functions associated with the physical termination of the network (for example, power transfer, timing, testing, maintenance). NT2 (network termination 2) includes functions commonly found in PBXs, local area networks, and cluster/terminal controllers. TE1 (terminal equipment, type 1) is an end-user device that complies with the ISDN recommendations. TE2 (terminal equipment, type 2) is an end-user device, but uses current technology like EIA-232-D and the existing V and X series of interfaces. The TA (terminal adapter) allows the current technology to be used in the new ISDN; in effect, the TA is a protocol converter.

The S and T interfaces are used with ISDN configurations. The R interface serves current configurations, again like EIA-232-D or X.21.

Access points 1 and 2 describe the *bearer* services invoked from ISO layers 1 to 3. Currently, 10 bearer services are fully or partially defined in the ISDN. Three examples follow:

1. A 64-kbit/s circuit-mode service to support digitized speech
2. A 64-kbit/s circuit-mode service to support data
3. A packet-mode service to support an X.25 virtual call

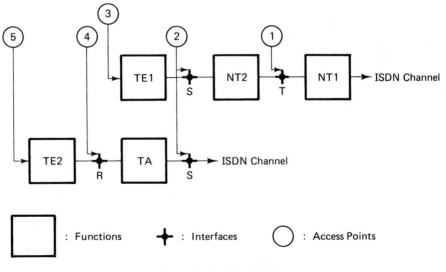

Figure 8–8. The ISDN.

Access points 3 and 5 describe the *teleservices* invoked from ISO layers 4 to 7. These services include support functions in other CCITT standards, such as terminal equipment, telematic services, and graphics.

Access point 4 uses the services of other CCITT standardized services, such as the X and V series of recommendations.

The ISDN is also built on the concept of clear channel signaling: A separate channel (the D or E channel) carries signaling information for circuit switching, while other channels (for example, B channels) carry user information streams. The D channel can also carry packet-switched data. The ISDN permits several A and D channel interface structures. The most important are the following:

- *Basic interface* of two user B channels at 64 kbit/s each and 1 D channel at 16 kbit/s (2B + D)
- *Primary rate B interface* of:
    1.544 mbit/s for 23 B + D or
    2.048 mbit/s for 30 B + D

DIGITAL PBXs

Digital technology is playing a key role in the booming PBX industry. The PBX, in existence for many years, was developed to switch telephone calls in office buildings. Earlier PBXs used crossbar or step-by-step methods to switch analog calls. Today, modern PBXs use computer-based control to perform a multitude of functions, including voice digitization and digital switching. The digital PBX has replaced its analog counterpart because it is cheaper and easier to maintain and switches native digital devices (terminals, processors) more efficiently.

In the 1970s and early 1980s, the PBX provided a few data communications capabilities, but the machines were limited for a number of reasons:

- The architecture was designed for voice traffic (long holding times of resources through the PBX switch).
- Bursty traffic (with short holding times) from user terminals made inefficient use of the voice-dedicated path in the PBX.
- A user workstation needed separate wires and input ports to the PBX for voice and data.
- Likewise, if the PBX switched traffic to a central host computer, *each* user terminal required an output port from the PBX to the computer.

Today's PBX or CBX (computer branch exchange) has been changed significantly to support voice as well as data traffic. Line cards at the PBX now handle voice and data at the same port. A user workstation can utilize the same pair of wires for voice and data transmissions.

The PBX switch is now digitized. It switches voice and data in digital frames through the PBX memory, which allows the PBX architecture to be shared in a much more flexible and dynamic manner than the older channel-dedicated machines. Moreover, the modern PBX provides one or a number of ports to a host computer. In this manner, multiple user sessions are concentrated onto the PBX-to-computer port.

Equally important, the newer PBXs have adapted many data communications features such as data link controls, X.25 packet interfaces, and local area network support (Chapter 9). Figure 8–9 provides an example of these systems with AT&T's System 75/85 PBX family. The following options (labeled 1 to 17 in the figure) are available with the PBX:

1. One-pair wire to support conventional EIA-232-D, EIA-449, V.35 devices up to 64 kbit/s using AT&Ts DCP (digital communications protocol).

2. One-pair wire to support digital phones and EIA-232-D asynchronous terminals, operating at a total speed of 136 kbit/s (64 kbit/s PCM voice; 64 kbit/s data; 8 kbit/s for control/signaling).

3. Interface unit for IBM 327X terminal family. Converts 2.358-Mbit/s coaxial transmission to 64 kbit/s one-pair wire.

4. Interface unit for IBM 327X cluster controller family; provides same conversion as in option 3.

5. Two-pair wire to AT&T's Dataphone digital service (DDS) at 56 kbit/s.

6. Two-pair wire to a 1.544-Mbit/s T-1 carrier interfaced to a host computer.

7. Two-pair wire to other PBXs via T-1.

8. Conventional asynchronous EIA-232-D ports.

9. Interface of PBX to AT&T's local area network ISN, with additional interfaces to the following:

10. Connection into either bisync (BSC) or SNA (systems network architecture)/SDLC devices.

11. Conventional interfaces into EIA-232-D asynchronous devices.

12. Optical fiber connection to a remote ISN interface/concentrator, supporting IBM 327X cluster controllers with their connections to IBM hosts.

13. The same configuration as option 12, except individual 327X terminals are supported with a coax/wire-pair converter (balun).

14. Wire-pair connections into the Starlan local area network.

15. A coaxial cable interface into an Ethernet local area network.

16. Optical fiber connection into another ISN or AT&T 3B20 computer or a VAX computer.

17. Wire-pair connections to a telephone company DDS or a DS-1 with transmission speeds up to 2.048 Mbit/s.

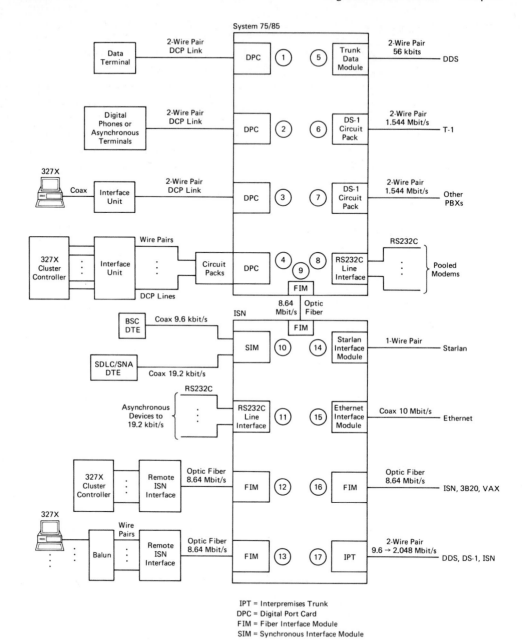

Figure 8–9.   AT&T PBX options.

DIGITAL SWITCHING

Increasingly, digital technology is being used to perform the routing and switching functions of PBXs and telephone company network switches. Figure 8–10 shows a simple digital time-division switch. The switch controls the gates to a common bus, which are opened and closed at various time periods to allow the digital bits to be transmitted between the devices attached to the switch. If DTE A is communicating with DTE F, the switch closes a gate to DTE A and to DTE F during the same slot period, which permits a segment of speech or data to be transferred across the bus to the receiving device. The bus could also be computer memory, which is used as input store and output store between the two devices.

Since a PCM sampling speed is 8,000 samples per second, a digital switch must be able to provide 8,000 slots for *each* connection. Therefore, for n sessions, the PBX must be switching at a speed of n $\times$ 8,000.

The PBX switch separates the individual PCM signals and switches them through a *time slot interchange facility* (TSI). The TSI can be a nonblocking switch in that there are the same number of input slots available as there are output slots. However, with more complex systems, the TSIs are usually connected to another to form a digital switch called the *time multiplexed switch* (TMS). A TMS is essentially an n by n switch (n = the number of connections). The TMS provides for another dimension, time. Unlike other switching systems and older PBXs, which leave the path up for duration of a call, a TMS is changed for each of the n time slots in the digital frames. The concept is

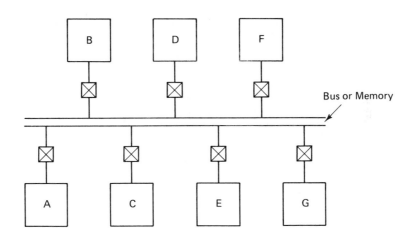

Figure 8–10.   Digital switching.

similar to the virtual connection concept of packet switching and X.25. A physical path (or bandwidth) is shared by multiple users.

EMERGING DIGITAL TECHNOLOGY

In the past few years, linear predictive coding (LPC) has been used for voice digitization. Like DPCM, it uses predictive techniques on samples but also periodically updates the predictor parameters. Speech is synthesized into frames corresponding to the samples; the frames contain data on the amplitude, pitch, or frequency of the sample.

LPC is used in a technique called *constructive synthesis* to produce digitized voice. This technique does not preserve the shape of the original voice wave form. Instead, the speech signal is broken down into subcomponents called *phonemes*, which are the basic units of a language. All utterances can be represented by phonemes (for example, two labial phonemes, p and b, are found in *pit* and *bit*). The U.S. style of the English language has 42 phonemes.

Constructive synthesis systems accept nonhuman input (such as CRT text), break the words into phonemes, and store them in LSI ROM memory. Later, the phonemes are strung together according to a set of rules to form the speech output. The signal is stored on an LPC speech chip. The phonemes are usually further divided into *allophones* to enhance the quality of the voice.

A more sophisticated version of constructive analysis is *analysis–synthesis*. This technique analyzes a human voice, encodes the signal, and then uses a prestored vocabulary with LPC analysis to produce the stored digitized voice signal. The primary difference between the two is that analysis–synthesis uses actual speech as input and constructive synthesis uses stringed phonemes. Analysis–synthesis yields better-quality speech, but it is more expensive and time-consuming. For example, a 1-second utterance using analysis–synthesis techniques requires over 100 times as many bit storage cells.

The LPC and synthesis techniques have paved the way for many exciting and useful digital applications. Automobile instrumentation, children's learning tools, automatic answering devices, error messages, and "talking" factory assembly lines are some examples.

BROADBAND NETWORKS

Broadband networks are becoming the subject of increasing interest, not only to network vendors but to network users as well. Their high throughput features provide an organization with many opportunities for developing high-capacity and integrated systems.

The purpose of a broadband network is to provide a transport service for any type of application (see Figure 8–11). Telephone service, video service, data service, teleshopping, CAD/CAM, FAX, and so on, are all supported by a broadband network.

The broadband network supplies sufficient bandwidth to transmit all images between customer devices. Broadband networks are designed to support low-frequency

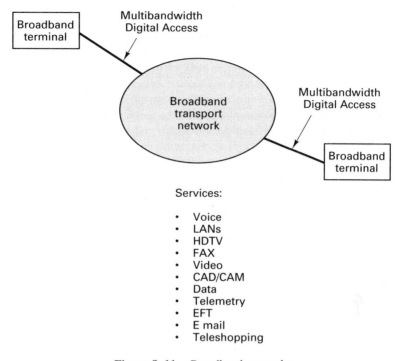

Figure 8–11. Broadband networks.

voice channels up to a digital H4 channel. Typically, broadband systems are designed to support the following types of channels:

CHANNEL	TYPE	BIT RATE
A	Voice Frequency	3.2 kHz analog
B	Digital	64 kbit/s
D	Digital	16 or 64 kbit/s
E	Digital	64 kbit/s
H0	Digital Broadband	384 kbit/s
H11	Digital Broadband	1536 kbit/s
H12	Digital Broadband	1920 kbit/s
H4	Digital Broadband	150 Mbit/s

The principal focus of attention today on broadband networks is on the synchronous optical network (SONET). The metropolitan area network (an 802.6 MAN) serves as the backbone network for lower-speed LANs and host computers. It also serves as the entrance and exit protocol into the broadband WANs, such as SONET. Interfaces are also provided by rate adapters (RAs), terminal adapters (TAs), and broadband network termination points (BNTs).

The fundamental architecture to support this topology is the SONET, shown in Figure 8–12. Its basic transfer rate is 155.52 Mbit/s. Traffic is managed through the asynchronous transfer mode (ATM) switch.

The ATM forms the basis for broadband networks. This technology provides for demand excess to a network by multiplexing user information into fixed-length slots called cells. The traffic is identified and managed through virtual connection identifiers.

ATM is a new technology that has yet to be tested in the marketplace. Considerable research is being conducted in the industry based on the CCITT I and G Recommendations.

Signaling Hierarchies for the Emerging Technologies

During the past 30 years, three different digital signaling hierarchies have evolved. These hierarchies were developed in Europe, Japan, and North America. Fortunately, all are based on the same pulse code modulation signaling rate of .000125 sample slots. Therefore, the basic architectures interwork reasonably well. However, the multiplexing hierarchies differ considerably (see Figure 8–13).

Japan and North America base their multiplexing hierarchies on the DS-1 rate of 1.544 Mbit/s. Europe uses a 2.048 Mbit/s multiplexing scheme. Thereafter, the three approaches multiplex these schemes in multiple integers.

The signaling digital hierarchy (SDH) uses the schemes that have been in existence for all these years but specifies a different multiplexing hierarchy. The basic SDH rate is 155.52 Mbit/s and then uses a n × 155.52 multiplexing scheme. Smaller rates than 155.52 Mbit/s are available. This smaller rate is called the synchronous transport signal-level 1 (STS-1) and its rate is 51.840 Mbit/s. The optical counterpart of STS-1 is called the optical carrier-level 1 signal (OC-1).

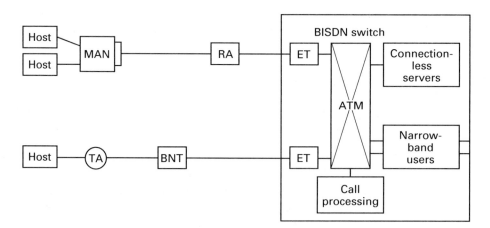

Figure 8–12.   BISDN topology.

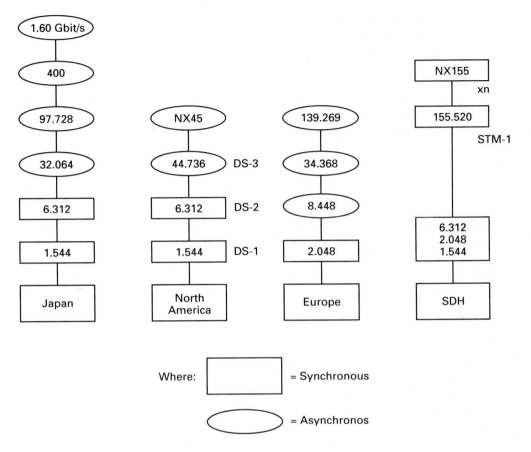

Figure 8–13. SDH hierarchies.

SONET

SONET is a signaling standard that was developed by the Exchange Carriers Standards Association (ECSA) for ANSI. The SONET standard has been incorporated into a signaling digital hierarchy standard published by the CCITT in its G.707, G.708, and G.709 Recommendations. In addition, Bellcore supports this standard on behalf of the U.S. Regional Bell Operating Companies (RBOCs).

Bellcore intends SONET to meet the following goals: (a) transparent interoperability between multivendor equipment, (b) enhanced positioning of network services, (c) asynchronous network for transfer of multimedia traffic, and (d) enhanced operations, administration, maintenance, and provisioning (OAM&P) services.

The standard provides specifications for optical signals and multiplexing hierarchies. It supports any type of service ranging from DS0 to 2488.32 Mbit/s.

Figure 8–14 shows a simplified diagram of a SONET configuration. Three types of equipment are employed in a SONET system: (a) path-terminating equipment, (b) line-terminating equipment, and (c) section-terminating equipment. The path-terminating equipment consists of a SONET terminal or switch. The line-terminating equipment is a SONET hub. And the section-terminating equipment is a SONET regenerator.

Each of these components utilizes substantial OAM&P information (overhead). Path-level overhead is inserted at the SONET terminal and carried end to end. The overhead is added to DS1 signals when they are mapped into virtual tributaries (VT, explained shortly) and for end-to-end STS-1 payloads.

Line overhead is used for STS-N signals. This information is created by line-terminating equipment such as STS-N multiplexers. The section overhead is used between adjacent network elements such as SONET regenerators.

Figure 8–15 shows an example of SONET multiplexing schemes. SONET service adapters can accept any signal ranging from DS1 to BISDN. Additionally, sub-DS1 rates (such as DS0) are supported. The purpose of the service adapter is to map these signals into STS-1 envelopes or multiples thereof. Notwithstanding, all traffic is initially converted to a synchronous STS-1 signal (51.84 Mbit/s or higher).

Lower-speed signals (such as DS1) are first multiplexed into VTs, which are sub-STS-1 payloads. Eventually, several STS-1s are multiplexed together to form an STS-N signal. These signals are sent to an electrical/optical (E/O) converter where a conversion is made to an OC-N optical signal.

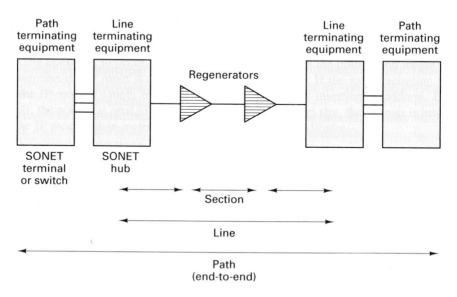

Source: Bell Northern Research

Figure 8–14.   SONET configuration.

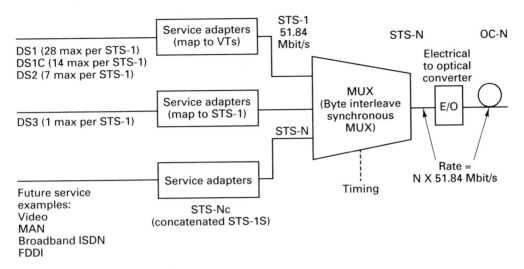

VT: Virtual tributary
STS: Synchronous transport signal
OC: Optical carrier

Source: Bell Northern Research

Figure 8–15.   SONET multiplexing.

SONET is designed to support a wide variety of payloads. Figure 8–16 summarizes typical payloads of existing technologies.

The SONET multiplexer accepts these payloads as sub-STS-1 signals (or VTs). The VT of these subrates is designated as a VT-type in the following manner:

- DS1 = VT1.5
- CEPT1 = VT2
- DS1C = VT3
- DS2 = VT6

The synchronous transport signal-level 1 forms a basis for the optical carrier-level 1 signal. OC-1 is the foundation for the complete synchronous optical signal hierarchy.

Type	Digital Bit Rate	Voice Circuits	T-1	DS3
DS1	1.544 Mbit/s	24	1	—
CEPT1	2.048 Mbit/s	30	—	—
DS1C	3.154 Mbit/s	48	2	—
DS2	6.312 Mbit/s	96	4	—
DS3	44.736 Mbit/s	672	28	1

Figure 8–16.   Typical payloads.

Level	Rate (Mbit/s)
OC-1	51.84
OC-3	155.52
OC-9	466.56
OC-12	622.08
OC-18	933.12
OC-24	1,244.16
OC-36	1,866.24
OC-48	2,488.32

Figure 8–17. SONET signal hierarchy.

The higher-level signals are derived by the multiplexing of the lower level signals. The high-level signals are designated as STS-N and OC-N, where N is an integer number. As illustrated in Figure 8–17, OC transmission systems are multiplexed by the N values of 1, 3, 9, 12, 18, 24, 36, and 48. In the future, multiplexing integrals greater than 48 will be incorporated into the standard. Presently, signal levels OC-3, OC-12, and OC-48 are most widely supported multiples of OC-1.

The basic transmission unit for SONET is the STS-1 frame. The frame consists of 90 columns and 9 rows of 8-bit bytes (octets). Therefore, the frame carriers 810 bytes or 6,480 bits. SONET transmits at 8,000 frames/second; therefore, the frame length is 125 microseconds. This approach translates into a transfer rate of 51.840 Mbit/s (6,480 × 8,000 = 51,840,000). As Figure 8–18 shows, the first three columns of the frame contain transport overhead, which is divided into 27 bytes with 9 bytes allocated for

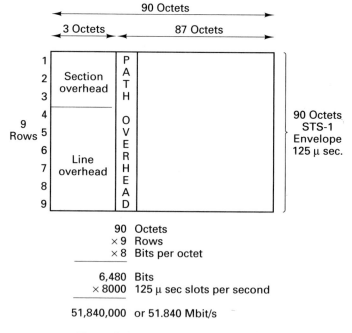

Figure 8–18. STS-1 signal (SONET).

section overhead and 18 bytes allocated for line overhead. The other 87 columns comprise the STS-1 envelope capacity (although the first column of the envelope capacity is reserved for STS path overhead).

The 87 columns are also called the synchronous payload envelope (SPE). Although, the reader should be aware that the actual user payload consists of 86 columns or 774 bytes. Therefore, user payload operates at 49.536 Mbit/s (774 × 8,000 = 49,536,000). Obviously, the user payload can support VTs up to the DS3 rate (44.736 Mbit/s).

The STS-1 frame is transmitted row by row from left to right. Each byte is transmitted with the most significant bit first.

SUMMARY

The use of long-distance analog lines is diminishing rapidly throughout the industrialized world. Digital techniques offer clear advantages over analog transmission schemes, principally in cost and efficiency. Notwithstanding, for the foreseeable future analog technology will remain the prevalent form of communications of user access lines (local loop). ISDN and SONET are slowly but surely finding their way into the industry, and recent advances point to their use with higher-capacity broadband ISDN operations.

9

Distributed Network Architectures

INTRODUCTION

This chapter highlights two network architectures. The Open Systems Interconnection (OSI) standard is included because of its potential impact and use in the industry. The second example is the Internet suite of protocols, more commonly known as TCP/IP (Transmission Control Protocol/Internet Protocol). The last part of this chapter discusses migration issues (TCP/IP to OSI) and the U.S. Government Open System Interconnection Profile (GOSIP).

ARCHITECTURES AND PROTOCOLS

The term *architecture* is commonly used today to describe networks. Paraphrasing the dictionary definition, an architecture is a formation of a structure. Stated another way, it is a system of structure. A network architecture describes what things exist, how they operate, and what form they take. An architecture encompasses hardware, software, data link controls (DLCs), standards, topologies, and protocols. With the exception of protocols, all these terms have been described in previous chapters.

Like architecture, the term *protocol* is borrowed from other disciplines and professions. In basic terms, a protocol defines how network components establish communications, exchange data, and terminate communications, just as a diplomatic protocol defines the rules for social parlance.

Data link controls certainly qualify as one form of protocol—at the line (or link) level. Other protocols are also needed in the network to provide proper communications "parlance" beyond the individual line DLC. As we shall see, these higher-level protocols are an integral part of the network architecture.

LAYERED PROTOCOLS

Modern networks are implemented using the concept of layered protocols. The early networks providing communications service were relatively simple and did not use layers. Terminals were connected to a computer in which several software programs controlled the terminal transmission and placed the data onto a telephone line. The line was usually attached to an interface unit within or connected to the computer.

As organizations became larger, more complex, and more geographically dispersed, the supporting communications software and hardware assumed more tasks and grew in size and function. Unfortunately, many of these components grew haphazardly. The system often became unwieldy and difficult to maintain. In some instances, telecommunications programs became complex monoliths. When these systems were changed, the resulting output sometimes had unpredictable results.

The older networks often had several different protocols that had been added in a somewhat evolutionary and unplanned manner. The protocols in the networks had poorly defined interfaces. It was not uncommon for a change in the network architecture at one site to adversely affect a seemingly unrelated component at another site. Often, the components in a network were simply incompatible. The concept of layered protocols developed largely as a result of this situation.

The basic purpose of layered protocols is to reduce complexity, provide for peer-to-peer layer interaction across nodes, and allow changes to be made in one layer without affecting others. For example, a change to a routing algorithm in a network control program should not affect the functions of message sequencing, which is located in another layer in the protocol. Layered protocols also permit the partitioning of the design and development of the many network components. Since each layer is relatively self-contained, different teams (perhaps dispersed at various distributed sites) can work on different layers.

Layered functions also owe their origin to several concepts generally called *structured techniques*. These ideas provide an impetus to design hardware or software systems that have clearly defined interfaces. The systems contain modules that perform one function or closely related functions (sometimes called *cohesiveness* or *binding*). In addition, these techniques can produce a system in which a change to a module should not affect any component in a system that the changed module does not control. This approach is called either *loose coupling* or *atomic action*.

Layered network protocols also allow interaction between functionally paired layers in different locations. This concept aids in permitting the distribution of functions to remote sites. In the majority of layered protocols, the data unit passed from one layer to another is usually not altered. The data unit contents may be examined and used to append additional data (trailers/headers) to the existing unit.

For example, layer B might examine a field in a message that was inserted by layer A. The field might contain a logical address of the recipient of the message; layer B would translate this logical address to a node address. Then, perhaps layer C would interpret the node address into an actual physical communications line address. If the line became inoperable, layer C would make the necessary changes to a line address without affecting layers A or B. This is one advantage of layered network protocols: The network can be reconfigured without affecting those components that work with logical or virtual addresses. At the receiving end, layer C would pass the message to layer B (from the communications line); layer B would examine the logical address and institute the actions for the message to go to the proper logical recipient.

The relationship of the layers is shown in Figure 9–1. Each layer contains entities that exchange data and provide functions in a *logical* sense with peer entities at other sites in the network. Entities in adjacent layers interact through the common upper and lower boundaries in a *physical* sense by passing parameters such as headers, trailers, and data parameters. For brevity, the term *header* will be used hereafter. An entity in a higher layer is referred to as N + 1 and an entity in a lower layer is N − 1. The services provided by higher layers are the result of the services provided by all lower levels. The primitives are standard names used to communicate among the layers.

Typically, each layer (except the lowest) adds header information to data. The headers are used to establish peer-to-peer sessions across nodes, and some layer implementations use headers to invoke functions and services at the N + 1 or N − 1 adjacent layers (see Figure 9–2). At the transmitting site, an end user invokes the system by

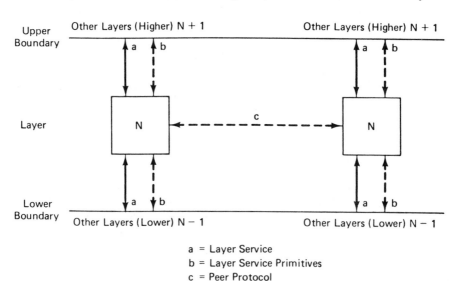

a = Layer Service
b = Layer Service Primitives
c = Peer Protocol
N = Peer Entities

Figure 9–1. OSI layers.

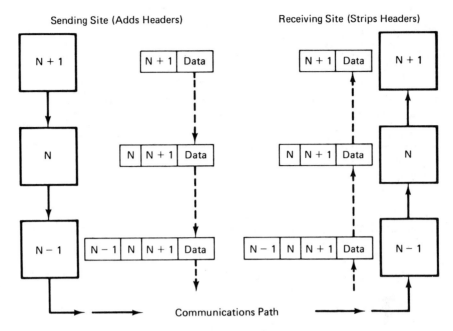

Figure 9-2. Layer interaction.

passing data, primitive names, and control messages to the highest layer of the protocol. The system passes the data physically through the layers, adding headers and invoking functions in accordance with the rules of the protocol. At the receiving site, a reverse process occurs. The header and control message invoke services and a *peer-to-peer* logical interaction of entities across the nodes. Generally, layers in the same node communicate with parameters passed through primitives, and peer layers across nodes communicate with the use of the headers. It is important to emphasize once again that layer (N) behavior should be atomic, exhibiting strong functional binding within itself and loose coupling to layers N + 1 and N − 1.

OPEN SYSTEMS INTERCONNECTION

The ideas just discussed are found in the OSI Model. The purpose of OSI is to provide protocols for different vendors'/manufacturers' products to connect with each other, thus allowing an open systems interconnection of user applications. The work has proceeded and several layers of the model have now been defined. Figure 9-3 shows the seven layers of the OSI model. The following discussion of the functions in each layer reflects the level of standards and agreements reached thus far. Several layers are fairly well defined. Others are in process of definition within the ISO working groups.

The ISO layered concept uses the principles explained in the previous section. As illustrated in Figure 9-4, peer entities and functions communicate logically across nodes.

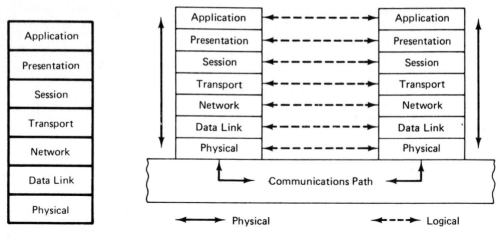

Figure 9-3. OSI layers.   **Figure 9-4.** OSI layer interaction.

The physical flow of the data, headers, and parameters moves through each layer at each node. Each layer's services are defined concisely with specifications of its functions to the peer layer and to the N + 1 and N − 1 layers.

Physical Layer

The physical layer provides for the transparent bit transmission between the data link entities. Its purpose is to activate, maintain, and deactivate physical connections between the data terminal equipment (DTE) and the data circuit-terminating equipment (DCE). Physical level standards have been widely used for years. CCITT has established X.21, which specifies the functions at this level for leased circuits. (X.21 also specifies circuit-switching functions at the network layer.) EIA-232-D and RS449 are other examples of physical level standards. Since the dominant American standard, EIA-232-D, has been used to explain how this level works, we will address, in a general manner, the OSI standards in this section.

V.24 is another widely used standard in many parts of the world. Many of the products in your office are described as V.24 compatible. V.24 contains the definitions of the channels (pins) between DTEs and DCEs. EIA-232-D uses different channel (or pin) identifiers, but the channels perform quite similar functions. V.24 defines more channels than does EIA-232-D because other interface standards utilize V.24 as well. In a sense, EIA-232-D can be considered a subset of V.24. Practically all layered networks use X.24/EIA-232-D at the physical level. Some vendors state they use X.21*bis*. Do not be confused with this statement; X.21 *bis* is functionally equivalent to EIA-232-D and *not* X.21.

Several other standards are widely used throughout the world. The majority of the standards use the basic pin arrangements of V.24 or EIA-232-D. The V series stipulates recommended standards for data transmission in telephone networks:

X.20*bis*	Asynchronous for V series
X.21*bis*	Synchronous for V series
V.21	300 b/s switched lines
V.22	1,200 b/s leased lines
V.22*bis*	2,400 b/s switched lines
V.23	300/1,200 b/s switched lines
V.26	2,400 b/s leased lines
V.26*bis*	2,400/1,200 b/s switched lines
V.26*ter*	2,400 b/s switched or leased lines
V.27	4,800 b/s manual equalizer, leased lines
V.27*bis*	4,800/2,400 b/s automatic, equalizer leased lines
V.27*ter*	4,800/2,400 b/s switched lines
V.29	9,600 b/s leased lines
V.32	9,600 b/s switched lines
V.35	48 kbits/s using 60- 108-kHz bands
V.25	Automatic call unit

X.21 uses the functional and electrical specifications of X.24 (Table 9–1), X.26, and X.27 (see Figure 9–5). In a leased line operation, the physical level X.21 standard specifies changing the C and I circuits from off to on to initiate data flow between DTEs. The DTEs must be using the same data link (N + 1) protocol. The T and R circuits are used to transmit data between the DTE and DCE. The C circuit is used to control data flow and call requests (for switched service). The C remains on for leased circuits. The

TABLE 9–1 X.24 FUNCTIONAL CHARACTERISTICS

Circuit Designation	Circuit Name	Data		Control		Timing	
		From DCE	To DCE	From DCE	To DCE	From DCE	To DCE
G	Signal ground or common return						
Ga	DTE common return				X		
Gb	DCE common return			X			
T	Transmit		X				
R	Receive	X					
C	Control				X		
I	Indication			X			
S	Signal timing					X	
B	Byte timing (optional)					X	

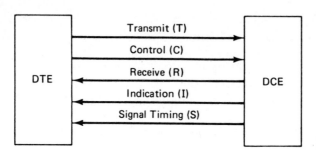

Figure 9–5. X.21 interface.

S circuit provides timing to the DTE and the I circuit serves as an alternate indicator to the DTE.

Data Link Layer

Chapter 7 describes the functions of the data link layer. In that chapter, IBM's synchronous data link control was explained. SDLC (synchronous data link control) is very closely related to ISO's standard, HDLC (high-level data link control). IBM contends that SDLC conforms to a defined operational subset of HDLC, the unbalanced normal class of procedure. This simply means that IBM's approach provides for a primary or master station. HDLC's balanced mode allows for combined stations in which all stations can send *and* receive commands and responses.

The differences between SDLC and HDLC are as follows:

- SDLC supports a subset of HDLC modes; that is, the unbalanced normal class.
- HDLC permits any number of bits in the I field. SDLC permits any number of 8-bit bytes.
- HDLC does not provide a TEST command and response for link testing.
- SDLC provides for loop operations with the CFGR (configure) command and the CFGR and BCN (beacon) responses. HDLC does not include loop configurations.
- Certain other commands/responses vary. For example, IBM does not use the request disconnect (RD) response.

The reader can refer to Chapter 7 for a detailed discussion of the data link functions. Be aware that HDLC and SDLC are similar, but specific implementation planning requires further analysis.

Network Layer for Wide Area Networks

The network layer for wide area networks is implemented by the X.25 packet interface standard. This specification describes how packet-type data are transferred across the data terminal equipment/data circuit-terminating equipment interface. In X.25, a DCE is considered to be a node into a packet network. X.25 establishes the packet format, packet control identifiers, call setup, data flow management, packet windows, call termination, and many other useful features. The X.25 standard has gained acceptance in the industry and is used in many networks and vendor products.

X.25 was developed to provide a standard method for a user gaining access to the services of a packet-switched network. Its need became evident as *public* packet networks came into existence in the 1970s in Europe, Canada, and the United States. The CCITT recognized that each vendor or country would develop its own user-to-network interface protocol if efforts were not undertaken to establish a standard for all systems, and, indeed, X.25 has proved to be effective from this standpoint, since most vendors now use it as the DTE/network DCE protocol.

X.25 actually consists of three layers: layer 1 (physical layer) uses X.21, X.21 *bis* (EIA-232-D) or other accepted V or X series interfaces. Layer 2 (data link layer) uses Link Access Procedure, Balanced (LAPB), a subset of HDLC. Layer 3 contains the DTE/DCE interface specification.

The principal EIA-232-D and V.24 circuits required for X.25 are as follows:

	EIA-232-D	V.24
Send data	BA	103
Receive data	BB	104
Request to send	CA	105
Clear to send	CB	106
Data set ready	CC	107
Data terminal ready	CD	108.2
Carrier detect	CF	109

Figure 9–6 illustrates four options on establishing an end-user session under X.25. Figure 9–6(a) shows a switched virtual call (VC). The source site transmits a control packet to request a session or connection. The call request packet is transmitted to the destination site where it is either accepted or rejected. X.25 defines limits to the number of end-user sessions allowed at one time. Assuming the request is accepted, a call accepted packet is returned to the requester. Both of these control packets contain identifiers to provide for a session or call binding. After call establishment, the packets containing user data are exchanged, with X.25 defining the packet flow control and window rules. After all data have been transmitted, a clear request control packet is sent to the receiving site, and the session can be terminated by a clear confirmation packet.

A connection can also be obtained through a *permanent virtual circuit* [Figure 9–6(b)]. This option is analogous to a leased line in a telephone network: the transmitting DTE is assured of obtaining a connection to the receiving DTE through the packet network. X.25 requires that a permanent virtual circuit be reserved before the session begins. Consequently, an agreement must be reached by the two DTEs and the packet network carrier before a permanent virtual connection (PVC) will be allocated. Thereafter, when a transmitting DTE sends a packet into the packet network, the identifying information in the packet shows the requesting DTE has a permanent virtual circuit connection to the receiving DTE. Consequently, a connection will be made by the net-

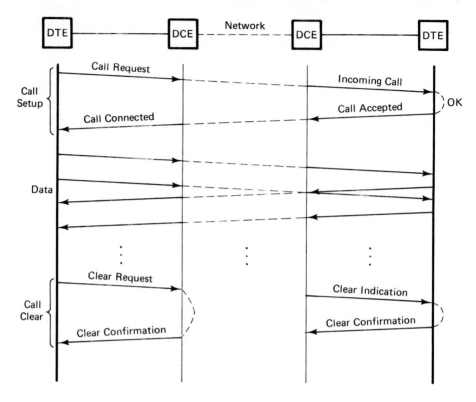

(a) X.25 Switched Virtual Call (VC)

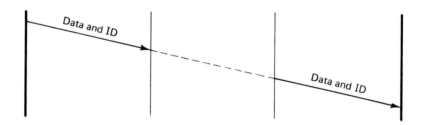

(b) X.25 Permanent Virtual Circuit (PVC)

Figure 9–6. X.25 interface options.

work and the receiving DTE without further arbitration and session negotiation. PVC requires no call setup or clearing procedures, and the logical channel is continually in a data transfer state.

Another technique, the fast select facility, was incorporated into the standard. The 1984 release of X.25 provides the fast select as an essential facility, which means that

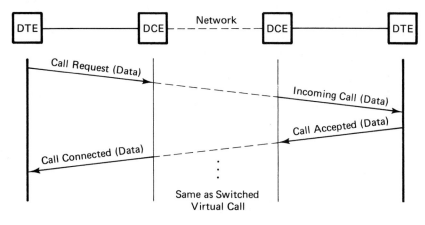

(c) X.25 Fast Select Call

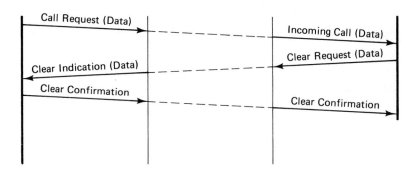

(d) X.25 Fast Select with Immediate Clear

Figure 9–6 (cont.).

vendors or manufacturers implementing X.25 should implement fast select in order to be a certified X.25 network supplier.

Fast select provides for two options. The first option is the *fast select* call [Figure 9–6(c)]. A DTE can request this facility on a per call basis to the network node (DCE) by means of an appropriate request in the header of a packet. The fast select facility allows the call request packet to contain user data of up to 128 bytes (octets). The called DTE is allowed to respond with a call-accepted packet, which can also contain user data. The call request/incoming call packet indicates if the remote DTE is to respond with clear request or call accepted. If a call accepted is transmitted, the X.25 session continues with the normal data-transferring and clearing procedures of a switched virtual call.

Fast select also provides for a fourth call connection feature of the X.25 DTE to DTE interface, the *fast select with immediate clear* [Figure 9–6(d)]. As with the other fast select option, a call request contains user data. This packet is transmitted through the network to the receiving DTE, which, upon acceptance, transmits a clear request (which also contains user data). The clear request is received at the origination site as a clear indication packet. This site must return a clear confirmation. The clear confirmation packet cannot contain user data. Thus, the forward packet sets up the network connection and the reverse packet brings the connection down.

The idea of the fast selects is to provide support for user applications that have only one or two transactions, such as inquiry/response applications (point of scale, credit checks, fund transfers). These applications cannot effectively use a switched virtual call because of the overhead and delay required in session establishment and disestablishment. Moreover, these types of applications cannot benefit from the use of a permanent virtual circuit because their occasional use would not warrant the permanent assignment of resources at the sites. Consequently, the fast selects have been incorporated into X.25 to meet the requirement for specialized uses of a network and to provide for more connection-oriented support than the datagram offered. Both DTEs must subscribe to fast select or the network will block the call.

The packets and sessions between the users at the DTE are identified by logical channel numbers. Each packet contains fields to identify a channel group (0–15) and an individual (channel) number (0–255) within the group. X.25 defines 0–4,095 logical channels at each packet node; each logical channel operates independently of others. A "free" logical channel must exist in order to complete a session establishment (that is, a virtual call). The actual range of logical channels used for virtual calls can be established by the specific network implementation.

The logical channel number serves to identify a specific user session with the packet network node (that is, the DCE); it also identifies the specific packets from multiple user sessions that are transported across one data link. For example, three users could be sharing a line to the network DCE node. The user packets are placed into the I field of the data link level frames. The receiving DCE uses the logical channel numbers to specifically identify each user packet, since data link control does not provide addressing beyond the identification of the user DTE address and the network DCE address.

Figure 9–7 illustrates the logical channel assignments for virtual calls and permanent virtual circuits. Actual assignment is determined by the implementing network. The channels are assigned as follows (refer to Figure 9–7 for explanation of the acronyms). The term *one-way* does not mean the transmission is in one direction only, but describes if the call originates locally (outgoing) or remotely (incoming).

LCI to LIC: Range of logical channels assigned to permanent virtual circuits.

LIC to HIC: Range of logical channels assigned to one-way incoming virtual calls.

LTC to HTC: Range of logical channels assigned to two-way virtual calls.

The packet formats are concisely defined by X.25. The formats depend on the type of packet (call request, data, etc.). Figure 9–8 shows the format for a call request/ incoming call packet. The general format identifier field indicates the format of the

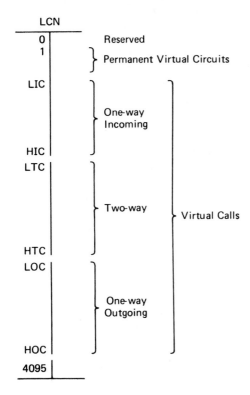

LCN = Logical Channel Number
LIC = Lowest Incoming Channel
HIC = Highest Incoming Channel
LTC = Lowest Two-way Channel
HTC = Highest Two-way Channel
LOC = Lowest Outgoing Channel
HOC = Highest Outgoing Channel

Note: Brackets may be expanded or contracted
to permit flexibility in numbering.

Figure 9–7. X.25 logical channels.

packet. The logical channel group number and the logical channel number fields identify the channel assignment of the call. The third byte or octet contains the identifier of the packet type.

The packet-type identifiers for call setups, clearings, and data flows are as follows:[1]

[1] The list does not contain all the packet identifiers. Other packets that deal with interrupts, flow control, restart, reset, and diagnostics are beyond the scope of this overview. For a detailed explanation of X.25, refer to Uyless Black, *Computer Networks: Protocols, Standards and Interfaces*. (Englewood Cliffs, NJ: Prentice Hall, 1993).

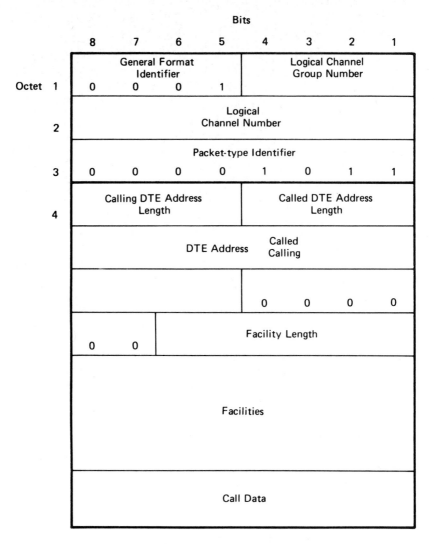

Figure 9-8. Packet format for a call request packet.

DTE to DCE	DCE to DTE	Bits of Third Octet							
		8	7	6	5	4	3	2	1
Call request	Incoming call	O	O	O	O	1	O	1	1
Call accepted	Call connected	O	O	O	O	1	1	1	1
Clear request	Clear indication	O	O	O	1	O	O	1	1
Clear confirmation	Clear confirmation	O	O	O	1	O	1	1	1

The address length and address fields contain information on the calling and called DTEs. The facility fields are present when the user site requests facilities (discussed shortly). Figure 9–8 is an example of a control packet. An actual data packet also contains fields to maintain sequencing of the packets between the two sites. The fields are the packet receive sequence number P(r) and the packet send sequence number P(s). These fields are placed in the third octet of the header for data packets.

The flow-control principles of X.25 are similar to the ideas discussed on DLC windows and flow control in Chapter 7. The control is established at the DTE/DCE interface for each logical channel in each direction. The control is established by the receiver. The P(s) and P(r) fields are used to regulate the windows. Notice that both layers 2 and 3 (X.25) use windows for flow control. X.25 permits windows (w) of 2 for each direction or other windows established by a facility. When the P(s) of the next packet to be transmitted by the DCE is within the window, the DCE can transmit. Likewise, the receiving DCE can receive, assuming the packet is in sequence. The transmission of P(r) back to the originator serves to reopen or widen w; when transmitted, it becomes the lower window edge. The value of P(r) must be within the range from the last P(r) received by the DCE and up to and including the P(s) of the next data packet to be transmitted by the DCE.

One might reasonably ask, "Why have sequencing and flow control at both the data link and network (packet) layers?" The answer to this question is that *each* logical channel session on the data link needs to be managed and controlled. The data link layer treats all packets (and logical sessions) alike; they are simply placed in the I field of the frame, relayed to the next adjacent node on the link, and delivered to the network layer. The DTE and network node (DCE) use the logical channel numbers and sequence numbers to manage the individual user sessions that are connected into the packet network.

Interestingly, the OSI Model does not define a network layer for a local area network. The reason for this seeming anomaly is because the OSI Model uses the IEEE 802 LAN standards for their LAN layers. The IEEE 802 model contains only a physical and data link layer. Notwithstanding, an additional network protocol is used and placed on top of LAN, and this protocol is known as a connectionless network layer. This term means that no virtual circuits are set up (as in X.25) and little accountability is maintained on the traffic. Due to the prevalence of connectionless network protocols in the Internet suite, we will defer our discussion of this aspect of the network layer to the material later in the chapter on TCP/IP.

X.75

X.25 is designed for users to communicate with each other through one network. However, an additional need exists to allow two independent users operating on two separate networks to establish communications to share resources and exchange data. X.75 is designed to meet this need. The standard has been in development for almost 10 years; it was published as a provisional recommendation in 1978 and amended in 1980 and again in 1984.

The object of X.75 is to allow internetworking; it provides a *gateway* for a user to communicate through multiple networks with another user. The standard assumes the networks use X.25 procedures.

X.75 is quite similar to X.25. It has many of the features described earlier with X.25, such as permanent virtual circuits, virtual call circuits, logical channel groups, logical channels, and the control packets depicted. The architecture is divided into physical, link, and packet levels, with X.75 interfacing two X.25 network layers.

X.25/X.75 facilities.   X.25/X.75 specifies user facilities. A description of several of these features should give the reader a better idea of X.25/X.75 functions.

- Extended packet sequence numbering changes the P(s) and P(r) parameters from 8 to 128.
- Throughput classes assignment provides for a definition of the bit per second rate from the calling DTE. Rates vary from 75 bit/s to 48 kbit/s.
- Packet retransmitting sets rules for retransmission using P(s) and P(r) as well as reject packets.
- Incoming calls barred prevents incoming virtual calls from being presented to the DTE.
- Outgoing calls barred prevents the DCE from accepting outgoing virtual calls.
- One-way logical channels restrict the logical channel to either outgoing or incoming calls.
- Closed user group permits preestablished DTEs to communicate with each other but precludes communication with all other DTEs.
- Several other user group facilities provide for group incoming access, outgoing access, incoming calls barred, and outgoing calls barred.
- Reverse charging charges the receiving DTE for the virtual call.
- Nonstandard packet sizes allow use of packets other than 128 bytes (octets).
- Fast select (discussed earlier) provides service to transaction-type applications.

Transport Layer

The transport layer was approved in October 1984. It is considered to be a critical part of the OSI network because it is the first layer in which the end user has complete control, since the X.25 network layer is generally considered to reside at the network vendor's node, and X.25 does not provide end-to-end integrity. The transport layer provides the following:

- Mapping transport addresses onto network addresses
- Multiplexing transport connections onto network layer connections to increase user throughput across the layer
- Error detection and monitoring of service quality

- Error recovery
- Segmentation and blocking
- Flow control of individual connections of transport layer to network and session layers
- Expedited data transfer

The transport layer establishes a transport connection between two users by obtaining a network connection that best matches the user requirements for costs, quality of service, multiplexing needs, data unit size, and address mapping. During the data transfer, the layer provides for sequencing, blocking, segmenting, multiplexing, flow control, identification, error control, and error recovery. Error detection and recovery are important considerations, since the transport layer is the first layer at the end-user site. Although the lower layers may be physically located in an end-user location, they are considered part of the network and are not in the user's domain.

The ISO has adopted a five-class approach for the transport layer. The classes are established to accommodate different lower-layer entity functions and are based primarily on the amount of error checking and recovery furnished by the lower layers. The classes are summarized as follows:

Class 0: Provides very little error recovery. Oriented toward text transmission.

Class 1: Provides for some error recovery. Oriented toward the use of X.25 at the network layer.

Class 2: Provides for more error recovery. Oriented toward a reliable network that provides error recovery but not much error notification to higher levels. This class also provides for the multiplexing capability.

Class 3: Combines the provisions of classes 1 and 2.

Class 4: Provides for extensive error detection and recovery. Checks for damaged data and lost and out-of-sequence packets. It is supportive of the self-contained datagrams.

Session Layer

The session layer serves as a user interface into the transport layer and is responsible for managing an end-user application program's exchange of data with another end-user application (for example, two COBOL programs).

The layer provides for an organized means to exchange data between user applications, such as simultaneous transmission, alternate transmission, checkpoint procedures, and resynchronization of user data flow between user applications. The users can select the type of synchronization and control needed from the layer.

Until the past few years, this layer was not standardized and each vendor used proprietary approaches to achieve these functions. For example, SNA's data flow control layer contains session layer functions. The OSI now includes this layer in its architecture.

Presentation Layer

The presentation layer provides services dealing with the syntax of data; [that is, the representation of data. It is not concerned with the meaning of semantics of the data]. Its principal role is to accept data types (character, integer) from the application layer and then negotiate with its peer layer as to the syntax representation (such as ASCII). The layer consists of many tables of syntax (teletype, ASCII, Videotex, etc.).

This layer also contains a language called Abstract Syntax Negotiation One (ASN.1), which is used to describe the structure and syntax of data. It is similar to a COBOL file description.

The presentation layer also contains protocols that are used to describe the basic encoding rules (BERs) for the transfer of data between computers.

This layer has not been used very much, but is gaining support from vendors and users. Most implementations now use the CCITT defined standards, X.208, X.209, X.216, and X.226, which are in conformance with the OSI Model.

Application Layer

The application layer is concerned with the support of the end-user application process. It serves as the end-user interface into the OSI Model.

The layer contains service elements to support application processes such as file transfer, job management, financial data exchange, programming languages, electronic mail, directory services, and data-base management.

This layer is changing as new standards are added to it by the CCITT and the ISO.

The X.400 Message Handling Services resides in this layer, as well as the File Transfer and Access Management (FTAM). The X.500 Directory Services also reside here.

Among the most widely used standards in this layer are the non-OSI Internet protocols: the File Transfer Protocol, the Simple Mail Transfer Protocol (SMTP), and TELNET, a terminal protocol.

OTHER OSI STANDARDS

The OSI layered model holds great promise and, as the top layers are published, many vendors will develop their products in accordance with the specifications. For example, IBM and DEC have announced support for the upper layers. The lower three levels have already seen wide use, and X.25 has become prevalent in many networks. Yet one is still left with the problem of interfacing existing techniques and protocols to the new methods. For example, the asynchronous, stop-and-wait terminals are widespread and not likely to go away in the near future. The CCITT has published a recommended standard for nonpacket mode interface into the X.25 layers. Figure 9–9 shows the packet assembly/disassembly (PAD) function, also known as X.3. Its basic functions are as follows:

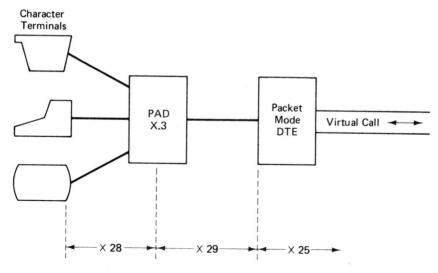

Figure 9-9.   Packet assembly/disassembly function.

- Provides for a start/stop, asynchronous DTE (terminal) access into the X.25 DTE (computer)
- Assembles characters into packets destined for packet-mode DTE
- Disassembles packets destined for start/stop DTE
- Handles virtual call setup and clearing procedures
- Provides a protocol conversion for the start/stop DTE into the X.25 layer

The specifications actually encompass three protocols. X.3 defines the PAD, X.28 defines the protocol between the terminal and the PAD, and X.29 defines the protocol between the PAD and the packet-mode DTE. X.25 then provides the interface between the packet-mode DTE and the DCE.

The PAD facility keeps a profile of up to 22 parameters of each terminal it services. The terminal user selects certain functions that the PAD is to perform. Some possible functions include the terminal's ability to escape from a data transfer state and a character echo back to terminal. The terminal also has the ability to signal (data forwarding) that all data have been transferred by sending the PAD a carriage return, a delete, a timeout, or some other ASCII control character. In addition, an idle-time delay service gives the PAD permission to send data if no data forwarding signal has been transmitted. The PAD also provides the terminal with an option to discard all traffic sent to it. The terminal has carriage return and line-folding options, as well as the ability to select input/ output speeds ranging from 50 bit/s to 64 kbit/s. Table 9-2 summarizes PAD parameters. The start/stop mode DTE gains access to the PAD through a switched or leased telephone circuit using several physical level interfaces.

X.28 provides procedures for the terminal and PAD interface. The terminal sends signals to the PAD requesting certain functions, such as setting up a virtual call. In turn,

TABLE 9-2 X.3 PAD PARAMETERS

X.3 Parameter Reference Number	Description
1. PAD recall	Escape from data transfers mode to command mode
2. Echo	Controls the echo of characters sent by the terminal
3. Data forwarding	Defines the characters to be interpreted by the PAD as a signal to forward data
4. Idle timer delay	Selects a time interval of terminal activity as a signal to forward data
5. Ancillary device control	Allows the PAD to control the flow of terminal data using X-ON/X-OFF characters
6. Control of PAD service signals	Allows the terminal to receive PAD messages
7. Operation of the PAD on receipt of breaking signal from DTE	Defines PAD action when a break signal is received from the terminal
8. Discard output	Controls the discarding of data pending output to a terminal
9. Padding after carriage return	Controls PAD insertion of padding characters after a carriage return is sent to the terminal
10. Line folding	Specifies whether the PAD should fold the output line to the terminal
11. Binary speed of DTE	Indicates the speed of the terminal
12. Flow control of the PAD	Allows the terminal to control the flow of data being transmitted by the PAD to the terminal
13. Line-feed insertion	Controls PAD insertion of line feed after a carrier return is sent to the terminal
14. Line-feed padding	Controls PAD insertion of padding characters after a line feed is sent to the terminal
15. Editing	Controls whether editing by PAD is available during data-transfer mode
16. Character delete	Selects character used to signal character delete
17. Line delete	Selects character used to signal line delete
18. Line display	Selects character used to signal line display

TABLE 9–2 *(cont.)*

X.3 Parameter Reference Number	Description
19. Editing PAD service signals	Controls the format of the editing PAD service signals
20. Echo mask	Selects the characters that are not echoed to the terminal when echo (parameter 2) is enabled
21. Parity treatment	Controls the checking and generation of parity on characters from/to the terminal
22. Page wait	Specifies the number of lines to be displayed at one time

the PAD notifies the terminal of its activity in fulfilling the terminal commands and its servicing of the preestablished profile.

X.29 specifies the protocol between the PAD and the packet-mode DTE. The X.25 packet (see Figure 9–9) contains a field to identify the call request from a start/stop DTE. The first octet (bits 1 to 4) contains codes to determine the use of the PAD message. Subsequent octets contain parameters values, status flags, and error codes.

POTENTIAL PROBLEMS OF MERGING TWO TECHNOLOGIES

Many communications systems were designed using the polling/selection concept, which uses overhead messages to poll and select the remote sites and to ACK or NAK the receipt of data. On the other hand, packet-switching technology entails data exchange only on demand (with a call request, a datagram, or a fast select). In addition to the PAD-like facilities of X.3, X.28, and X.29, a public network vendor often supports a protocol-conversion function of polling/selection to packet switching for its customers. The user should examine carefully the function from the standpoint of (a) end-to-end integrity and (b) costs to transmit data.

Figures 9–10, 9–11, and 9–12 depict three options in implementing the interface. In the first option, *all* messages are transported from end to end, including polls, ACKs (acknowledgments), NAKs (negative acknowledgments), selects, and negative responses to polls. This option is quite attractive from the standpoint of simplicity and end-to-end accountability (two features that should be given high priority). However, the network uses much of its capacity carrying packets containing the overhead messages of the polling/selection protocol.

Option 2 terminates the polling/selection protocol locally at both ends of the network. The host and front end establish their own polling/selection routine, as do the terminals and the terminal controller. Polls, selects, and other commands are issued to buffers at the local sites. The transfer of data across the packet network occurs when

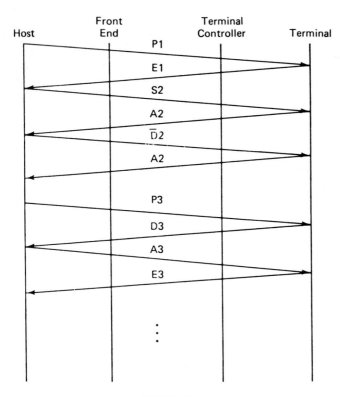

SYMBOLS

Pn = Poll for Terminal n
Sn = Select for Terminal n
En = EOT for Terminal n
An = ACK
Nn = NAK
Dn = Data from Terminal n to Host
$\overline{D}$n = Data from Host to Terminal n

Figure 9-10. Option 1 of polling/se-
lection packet-switching interface.

either the front end or terminal controller ACK a block of data sent from the host or a terminal. Due to this approach, the buffers at the sites might overflow. Consequently, the interface logic must provide for closing the receive windows of the front end or controller when their buffers fill. Figure 9-11 shows the window closing at point 1 after the D2 packet is received. The window is open at point 2 upon a buffer being released later in the process.

Option 2 certainly cuts down on much of the overhead found in option 1. Only user data are packetized for transfer through the network. However, the end user loses end-to-end accountability with this option. The user must assume that everything is working correctly and that all data sent are received and forwarded to the user application or terminal. Another disadvantage is the software complexity to manage the local protocols and control the flow of messages into and out of the buffers.

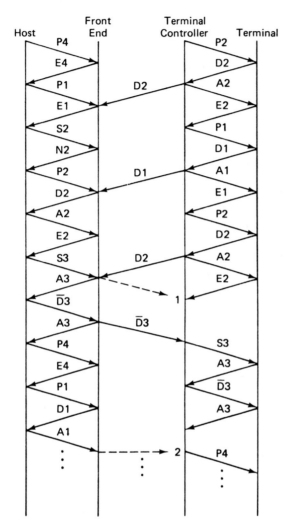

SYMBOLS

Pn = Poll for Terminal n
Sn = Select for Terminal n
En = EOT for Terminal n
An = ACK
Nn = NAK
<u>Dn</u> = Data from Terminal n to Host
D̄n = Data from Host to Terminal n

Figure 9–11. Option 2 of polling/selection packet-switching interface.

The third option represents a compromise between the first two choices. This approach continues with a local protocol terminal but transmits end-to-end ACKs/NAKs and selects through the network. Option 3 must provide for the potential cross flow

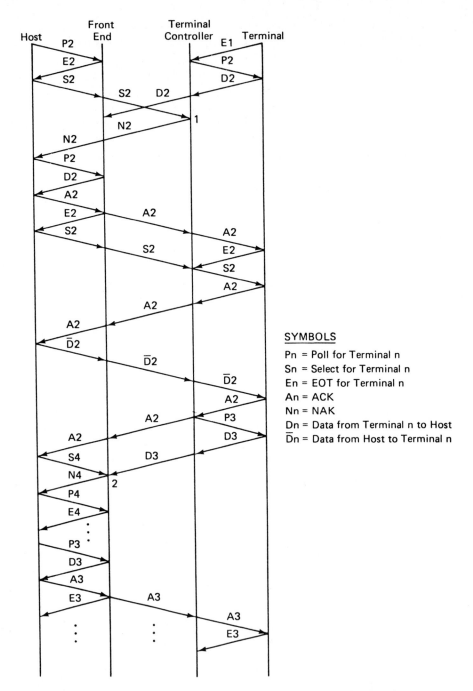

Figure 9-12. Option 3 of polling/selection packet-switching interface.

through the networks of conflicting packets. For example, at point 1 in Figure 9–12 the host has issued a select to terminal 2. However, at the same time, data from terminal 2 have been transmitted to the front-end buffer. A typical polling/selection protocol requires an ACK to terminal 2 in this situation. However, the terminal controller must transmit a NAK that forces the host to poll the data from terminal 2; after the poll, a select is then issued and data are finally transmitted to the host.

Point 2 in Figure 9–12 illustrates other software complexities. The front end responds negatively to the select 4 because data from terminal 3 are awaiting service. Although two different terminals are involved, the terminal controller expects an ACK for *any* outstanding data block before accepting any other commands.

The advantages of option 3 are end-to-end accountability and the absence of polls across the packet network. The software complexity is the main disadvantage of option 3.

Public networks should provide for a variation of these options. Since users ordinarily pay for usage based on packet volume, the vendor-specific approach is well worth a close examination. Moreover, the vendor's method of providing data integrity and end-to-end accountability is often of paramount importance for certain user applications. The transport layer of the OSI Model is tasked with the provision of end-to-end integrity. Since this layer is a relatively new addition to distributed networks, the reader is encouraged to consult with the vendor in determining how the network handles user data.

THE TCP/IP SUITE OF PROTOCOLS

In the early 1970s, several groups around the world began to address the problem of network and application compatibility. At that time the term *internetworking*, which means the interconnecting of computers and/or networks, was coined. The concepts of internetworking were pioneered by the CCITT, the ISO, and especially the original designers of the ARPANET. (The term *ARPA* refers to the Advanced Research Projects Agency, which is part of the U.S. Department of Defense.)

The procurement for ARPANET took place in 1968. The machines selected for this procurement were Honeywell 316 interface message processors (IMPs). The initial effort was contracted through Bolt Bernak & Newman (BBN), and the ARPANET nodes were initially installed at UCLA, University of California at San Bernardino, the Stanford Research Institute (SRI), and the University of Utah. The well-known Request for Comments (RFCs) came about from this early work.

These initial efforts led to the development of an earlier protocol, the network control program, and later the Transmission Control Protocol/Internet Protocol.

Two years later, the first significant parts of the Internet were placed into operation. At about this time, DARPA started converting some of its computers to the TCP/IP suite of protocols. By 1983 DARPA stated that all computers connected to ARPANET were required to use TCP/IP.

TCP/IP and the OSI

Before we move into some tutorial discussions of TCP/IP, it should be stated that the use of TCP/IP and related protocols continues to grow in the industry. This situation has raised some interesting points *vis-à-vis* the OSI Model. A substantial number of people believe that TCP/IP is a more viable approach for a number of reasons. First of all, TCP/IP is here; it works. Second, a wealth of products are available that use the TCP/IP protocol suites. Third, it has a well-founded, functioning administrative structure through the Internet Activity Board (IAB). Fourth, it provides easy access to documentation. Fifth, it is used in many UNIX products.

Notwithstanding the above comments, it is the intent of the original Internet sponsor, the Department of Defense, to move away from the TCP/IP protocol suites. (We will discuss these issues in the last chapter of this book.) However, it should also be stated that the Internet approach is to stay with the existing standards and protocols and to write new specifications, if necessary. The stated approach is also to include the international standards if they are available. Lastly, the Internet approach is to remain vendor independent as far as possible. Again, we will have more to say about the OSI, TCP/IP issue in the concluding section of this chapter.

The Internet Layers

The software and hardware operating on TCP/IP networks typically consist of a wide range of functions to support the communications activities. The network designer is faced with an enormous task in dealing with the number and complexity of these functions. To address these problems, an Internet is structured by "layering" the functions.

Even though modern networks are now described by dividing them into seven conceptual layers, the Internet architecture is based on four layers. Figure 9–13 depicts the Internet layer architecture. The bottom layer of Internet contains the subnetworks and the subnetwork interfaces. They provide the capability of delivering data within each network. Examples of subnetworks are Tymnet, Transpac, ARPANET, an Ethernet LAN, and so on. Even though this layer includes a "subnetwork," in actual implementations the data link and physical layers are required in all machines that are communi-

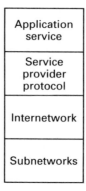

Figure 9–13.   The Internet layers.

cating with a subnet or a gateway. Therefore, be aware that Figure 9–13 is quite abstract because this layer must also include the data link and physical layers. Later figures will show this lower layer in more detail.

The next layer is the internetwork. This layer provides the functions necessary for connecting networks and gateways into a coherent system. This layer is responsible for delivering data from the source to the final destination. This layer contains the Internet Protocol (IP) and the Internet Control Message Protocol (ICMP). As discussed later, other supporting protocols for route discovery and address mapping also reside with IP at this layer.

The third layer is known as the service provider protocol layer. This layer is responsible for end-to-end communications. If connection oriented, it provides reliability measures and has mechanisms that account for all traffic flowing through an Internet. This layer contains the TCP and the User Datagram Protocol (UDP).

Finally, the upper layer is called the applications service layer. This layer supports the direct interfaces to an end-user application. The Internet applications are responsible for functions such as file transfer, remote terminal access, remote job execution, electronic mail, and so on. This layer contains several widely used protocols, such as the File Transfer Protocol (FTP).

Example of the Layer Operations

Figure 9–14 shows the relationship of subnetworks and gateways to layered protocols. The layers depicted earlier in Figure 9–13 have been changed to show the lower data link and physical layers, and the upper layers have been renamed with terms that are now more widely used in the industry.

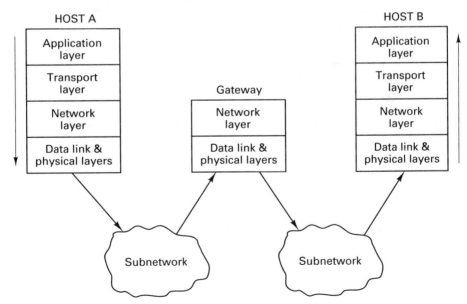

Figure 9–14. Example of Internet layer operations.

In this figure it is assumed that the user application in host A sends an application PDU to an application layer protocol in host B, such as a file transfer system. The file transfer software performs a variety of functions and appends a file transfer header to the user data. In many systems, the operations at host B are known as *server* operations and the operations at host A are known as *client* operations.

As indicated with the arrows going down in the protocol stack at host A, this unit is passed to the transport layer protocol. This layer performs a variety of operations (discussed in later chapters) and adds a header to the PDU passed to it. The unit of data is now called a *segment*. The PDU from the upper layers is considered to be data to the transport layer.

Next, the transport layer passes the segment to the network layer, also called the IP layer, which again performs specific services and appends a header. This unit (now called a datagram in Internet terms) is passed down to the lower layers. Here, the data link layer adds its header as well as a trailer, and the data unit (now called a *frame*) is launched into the network by the physical layer. Of course, if host B sends data to host A, the process is reversed and the direction of the arrows is changed.

The Internet protocols are unaware of what goes on inside the network. The network manager is free to manipulate and manage the PDU in any manner necessary. However, in most instances the Internet PDU (data and headers) remains unchanged as it is transmitted through the subnet. In Figure 9–14, we see its emergence at the gateway where it is processed through the lower layers and passed to the IP (network) layer. Here, routing decisions are made based on the addresses provided by the host computer.

After these routing decisions have been made, the PDU is passed to the communications link that is connected to the appropriate subnetwork (consisting of the lower layers). The PDU is reencapsulated into the data link layer PDU (usually called a frame) and passed to the next subnetwork. As before, this unit is passed through the subnetwork transparently (usually), where it finally arrives at the destination host.

The destination (host B) receives the traffic through its lower layers and reverses the process that transpired at host A. That is, it decapsulates the headers by stripping them off in the appropriate layer. The header is used by the layer to determine the actions it is to take; the header governs the layer's operations.

The PDU created by the file transfer application is passed to the file transfer application residing at host B. If host A and B are large mainframe computers, this application is likely an exact duplicate of the software at the transmitting host. However, the application may perform a variety of functions, depending on the header it receives. It is conceivable that the data could be passed to another end-user application at host B, but in many instances, the user at host A merely wants to obtain the services of a server protocol, such as a file transfer or electronic mail server. If this is the case, it is not necessary for an end-user application process to be invoked at host B.

In order to return the retrieved data from the server at host B to the client at host A, the process is reversed by the data being transferred down through the layers in the host B machine, through the network, through the gateway, to the next gateway, and up the layers of host A to the end user.

The Internet Protocol

IP is an internetworking protocol developed by the Department of Defense. The system was implemented as part of the DARPA internetwork protocol project and is widely used throughout the world. IP is quite similar to the ISO 8473 (the Connectionless Network Protocol or CLNP) specification. Many of the ISO 8473 concepts were derived from IP.

IP provides a connectionless service. It permits the exchange of traffic between two host computers without any prior call setup, and it is possible that traffic can be lost between the two end user's stations. For example, the IP gateway enforces a maximum queue length size, and if this queue length is violated, the buffers will overflow. In this situation, the additional datagrams are discarded in the network. For this reason, a higher-level transport layer protocol (such as TCP) is essential to recover from these problems.

IP hides the underlying subnetwork from the end user. In this context, it creates a virtual network to that end user. This aspect of IP is quite attractive because it allows different types of networks to attach to an IP gateway. As a result, IP is reasonably simple to install and because of its connectionless design, it is quite robust.

IP Services

When a gateway receives a datagram, it checks the header to determine the type of traffic it is processing. If the traffic is an Internet datagram, it passes the datagram to the Internet header check routine. This module performs a number of editing and validity tests on the IP datagram header. If checks are performed and not passed, the datagram is discarded. If the checks are performed and passed, the Internet destination address is examined to determine (1) if the datagram is addressed to this gateway or (2) if the datagram is destined for another gateway. If it is not destined for this gateway, the datagram is passed to the IP forwarding routine for further routing.

Routing operations. The IP gateway makes routing decisions based on the routing list. If the destination host resides in another network, the IP gateway must decide how to route to the other network. Indeed, if multiple hops are involved in the communications process, then each gateway must be traversed and the gateway must make decisions about the routing.

Each gateway maintains a routing table that contains the next gateway on the way to the final destination network. In effect, the table contains an entry for each reachable network. These tables could be static or dynamic, although dynamic tables are more common. The IP module makes a routing decision on all datagrams it receives.

IP source routing. IP uses a mechanism called source routing in which an upper layer protocol (ULP) determines how the IP gateways route the datagrams. The ULP has the option of passing a list of network addresses to the IP module. The list contains the intermediate IP nodes that are to be transited during the routing of the datagrams to the final destination. The last address on the list is the final destination of an intermediate node.

When a gateway receives a datagram, it uses the addresses in the source routing field to determine the next intermediate hop. IP uses a pointer field to learn about the next IP address. If a check of the pointer and length fields indicates the list has been completed, the destination IP address field is used for routing. If the list is not exhausted, the IP module uses the IP address indicated by the pointer.

The IP module then replaces the value in the source routing list with its own address. Of course, it must then increment the pointer by one address (4 bytes) in order for the next hop to retrieve the next IP address in the route. With this approach, the datagram follows the source route dictated by the ULP and also records the route along the way.

Loose and strict routing.   IP provides two options in routing the datagram to the final destination. The first, called *loose source routing*, gives the IP modules the option of using intermediate hops to reach the addresses obtained in the source list as long as the datagram traverses the nodes listed. Conversely, *strict source routing* requires that the datagram travel only through the networks whose addresses are indicated in the source list. If the strict source route cannot be followed, the originating host IP is notified with an error message. Both loose and strict routing require that the route recording feature be implemented.

Route recording option.   The route recording option operates in the same manner as source routing with the route recording feature just discussed. Any IP module that receives a datagram must add its address to a route recording list. In order for the route recording operation to occur, the receiving IP module uses the pointer and length fields to determine if any room is available to record the route. If the route recording list is full, the IP module simply forwards the datagram without inserting its address. If it is not full, the pointer is used to locate the first empty full octet slot, the address is inserted, and the IP module then increments the pointer to the next IP slot.

The timestamp option.   Another very useful option in IP is the provision for timestamping the datagram as it traverses each IP module through the internet. This feature allows a network manager to not only determine the route of the datagram through the internet but also the time at which each IP module processed the datagram. This can be quite useful in determining the efficiency of gateways and routing algorithms.

Length and pointer fields are used to identify the proper slot to place an IP address *and* the timestamp related to this address. Therefore, the pointer increments itself across an IP address and the timestamp for the address.

The time used with the timestamp is based on milliseconds (ms) using universal time. Obviously, the use of the universal time does not guarantee completely accurate timestamps between machines, because machines' clocks may vary slightly. Nonetheless, in most networks the universal time in milliseconds provides a reasonable degree of accuracy.

Fragmentation and reassembly.   An IP datagram may traverse a number of different networks that use different PDU sizes, and all networks have a maximum PDU size, called the maximum transmission unit (MTU). Therefore, IP contains procedures for dividing (fragmenting) a large datagram into smaller datagrams. It also allows the ULP to stipulate that fragmentation may or may not occur. A reassembly mechanism is invoked at the final destination, which places the fragments back into the order originally transmitted.

When an IP gateway module receives a datagram that is too big to be transmitted by the transit subnetwork, it uses its fragmentation operations. It divides the datagram into two or more pieces (with alignment on 8-octet boundaries). Each of the fragmented pieces has a header attached containing identification, addressing, and, as another option, all options pertaining to the original datagram. The fragmented packets also have information attached to them that defines the position of the fragment within the original datagram, as well as indicates if this fragment is the last fragment.

IP handles each fragment operation independently. That is, the fragments may traverse different gateways to the intended destination, and they may be subject to further fragmentation if they pass through networks that use smaller data units. The next gateway uses an offset value in the incoming fragment to determine the offset values of fragmented datagrams. If further fragmentation is done at another gateway, the fragment offset value is set to the location that this fragment fits relative to the original datagram and not the preceding fragmented packet.

The Transmission Control Protocol

Many distributed networks use TCP. TCP was developed for use in ARPANET, but it is now used throughout the world. It has several similarities to the OSI transport protocol, and many of its features were incorporated into OSI's Transport Protocol Class 4 (TP4).

This section also examines the User Datagram Protocol, which is used in place of TCP in a number of applications.

Earlier discussions stated that IP is not designed to recover from certain problems, nor does it guarantee the delivery of traffic. IP is designed to discard datagrams that are outdated or have exceeded the number of permissible transit hops in an Internet.

Certain user applications require assurance that all datagrams have been delivered safely to the destination. Furthermore, the transmitting user may need to know that the traffic has been delivered at the receiving host. The mechanisms to achieve these important services reside in TCP (UDP is connectionless and does not provide these services).

The job of TCP can be quite complex. It must be able to satisfy a wide range of applications requirements, and equally important, it must be able to accommodate to a dynamic, distributed network. It must establish and manage sessions (logical associations) between its local users and these users' remote communicating partners. This means that TCP must maintain an awareness of the users' activities in order to support the users' data transfer through an Internet.

Operations of TCP.   As depicted in Figure 9–15, TCP resides in the transport layer of layered model. It is situated above IP and below the upper layers. The figure also illustrates that TCP is not loaded into a gateway. It is designed to reside in the host computer or in a machine that is tasked with end-to-end integrity of the transfer of user data.

This figure also shows that TCP is designed to run over the IP. Since IP is a connectionless network, the tasks of reliability, flow control, sequencing, opens, and closes are given to TCP. TCP and IP are tied together so closely that they are used in the same context TCP/IP.

Many of the TCP functions (such as flow control, reliability, sequencing, etc.) could be handled within an application program. But it makes little sense to code these functions into each application. Moreover, applications programmers are usually not versed in error-detection and flow control operations. The preferred approach is to develop generalized software that provides community functions applicable to a wide range of applications and then invoke these programs from the application software. This allows the application programmer to concentrate on solving the application problem, and it relieves the programmer from the details and problems of networks.

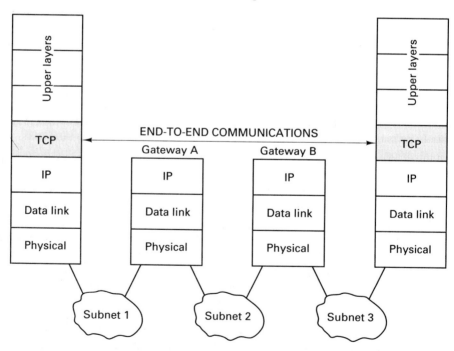

Figure 9–15.   TCP.

TCP provides the following services to the upper layers. This section reviews each of the services.

- Connection-oriented data management
- Reliable data transfer
- Stream-oriented data transfer
- Push functions
- Resequencing
- Flow control (sliding windows)
- Multiplexing
- Full-duplex transmission
- Precedence and security
- Graceful close

TCP is a *connection-oriented protocol*. This term refers to the fact that TCP maintains status and state information about each user data stream flowing into and out of the TCP module. The term used in this context also means TCP is responsible for the end-to-end transfer of data across one network or multiple networks to a receiving user application (or the next upper layer protocol). Referring to Figure 9–15, TCP must ensure that the data are transmitted and received between the two hosts across three networks (Subnet 1, Subnet 2, and Subnet 3).

TCP is responsible for the *reliable transfer* of each of the data passed to it from an upper layer. Consequently, it uses sequence numbers and acknowledgments to account for user traffic. A sequence number is associated with each octet transmitted. The receiving TCP module uses a checksum routine to check the data for damage that may have occurred during the transmission process. If the data are acceptable, TCP returns an ACK to the sending TCP module. If the data are damaged, the receiving TCP discards the data and uses a sequence number to inform the sending TCP about the problem. Like many other connection-oriented protocols, TCP uses timers to ensure that the lapse of time is not excessive before remedial measures are taken for either the transmission of acknowledgments from the receiving site and/or the retransmission of data at the transmitting site.

TCP receives the data from an upper layer protocol in a *stream-oriented* fashion. This operation is in contrast to many protocols in the industry. Stream-oriented protocols are designed to send individual characters and *not* blocks, frames, datagrams, and so on. The bytes are sent from an ULP on a stream basis, byte by byte. When they arrive at the TCP layer, the bytes are grouped into TCP *segments*. These segments are then passed to the IP (or another lower-layer protocol) for transmission to the next destination. The length of the segments is determined by TCP, although a system implementor can also determine how TCP makes this decision.

Implementors of TCP who have worked with block-oriented systems, such as IBM operating systems, may have to make some adjustments in their thinking regarding TCP performance. TCP allows the use of variable-length segments because of its stream-oriented nature. Therefore, applications that normally work with fixed blocks of data (such as a personnel application that sends fixed employee blocks or a payroll application that transmits fixed payroll blocks) cannot rely on TCP to present this fixed block at the receiver. Actions must be taken at the application level to delineate the blocks within the TCP streams.

TCP also checks for duplicate data. In the event the sending TCP retransmits the data, the receiving TCP discards the redundant data. Redundant data might be introduced into an Internet when the receiving TCP entity does not acknowledge traffic in a timely manner, in which case the sending TCP entity retransmits the data.

In consonance with the stream transfer capability, TCP also supports the concept of a *push* function. This operation is used when an application wants to make certain that all the data that it has passed to the lower layer TCP have been transmitted. In so doing, it governs TCP's buffer management. To obtain this function, the ULP issues a send command to TCP with a push parameter flag set to 1. The operation requires TCP to forward all the buffered traffic in the form of a segment or segments to the destination. The TCP user can use a close connection operation to provide the push function as well.

In addition to using the sequence numbers for acknowledgment, TCP uses them to *resequence* the segments if they arrive at the final destination out of order. Because TCP rests upon a connectionless system, it is quite possible that duplicate datagrams could be created in an Internet. TCP also eliminates duplicate segments.

TCP uses an inclusive acknowledgment scheme. The acknowledgment number acknowledges all octets up to and including the acknowledgment number less one. This approach provides an easy and efficient method of acknowledging traffic, but it does have a disadvantage. For example, suppose that 10 segments have been transmitted, yet due to routing operations, these segments arrive out of order. TCP is obligated to acknowledge only the highest contiguous byte number that has been received without error. It is not allowed to acknowledge the highest arrived byte number until all intermediate bytes have arrived. Therefore, like any other connection-oriented protocol, the transmitting TCP entity could eventually timeout and retransmit the traffic not yet acknowledged. These retransmissions can introduce a considerable about of overhead in a network.

The receiver's TCP module is also able to *flow control* the sender's data, which is a very useful tool to prevent buffer overrun and a possible saturation of the receiving machine. The concept used with TCP is somewhat unusual among communications protocols. It is based on issuing a ''window'' value to the transmitter. The transmitter is allowed to transmit a specified number of bytes within this window, after which the window is closed and the transmitter must stop sending data.

TCP also has a very useful facility for *multiplexing* multiple user sessions within a single host computer onto the ULPs. As we shall see, this is accomplished through some rather simple naming conventions for ports and sockets in the TCP and IP modules.

TCP provides *full-duplex transmission* between two TCP entities. This permits simultaneous two-way transmission without having to wait for a turnaround signal, which is required in a half-duplex situation.

TCP also provides the user with the capability to specify levels of *security* and *precedence* (priority level) for the connection. Even though these features are not implemented on all TCP products, they are defined in the TCP standard.

TCP provides a *graceful close* to the logical connection between the two users. A graceful close ensures that all traffic has been acknowledged before the virtual circuit is removed.

TCP ports and sockets.   A TCP upper layer user in a host machine is identified by a *port* address. The port address is concatenated with the IP Internet address to form a *socket*. This address must be unique throughout an Internet, and a pair of sockets uniquely identifies each end point connection. As examples:

Sending socket = source IP address + source port number

Receiving socket = destination IP address + destination port number

Although the mapping of ports to higher layer processes can be handled as an internal matter in a host, the Internet publishes numbers for frequently used higher-level processes. Table 9–3 lists the commonly used port numbers along with their names and descriptions.

Even though TCP establishes numbers for frequently used ports, the numbers and values above 255 are available for private use. The remainder of the values for the assigned port numbers have the low-order 8-bits set to zero. The remainder of these bits are available to any organization to use as they choose. Be aware that the numbers 0 through 255 are reserved and they should be avoided.

Retransmission procedures.   TCP does not have an explicit *negative acknowledgment* (NAK). Rather, it relies on the transmitting entity to issue a timeout and retransmit data for which it has not received a *positive acknowledgment* (ACK).

Choosing a value for the retransmission timer is deceptively complex. The reason for this complexity (see Figure 9–16) stems from the fact that (a) the delay of receiving acknowledgments from the receiving host varies in an Internet; (b) segments sent from the transmitter may be lost in the Internet, which obviously invalidates any round trip delay estimate for a nonoccurring acknowledgment; (c) (and in consonance with (b)) acknowledgments from the receiver may also be lost, which also invalidates the round trip delay estimate.

Because of these problems, TCP does not use a fixed retransmission timer. Rather, it utilizes an adaptive retransmission timer that is derived from an analysis of the delay encountered in receiving acknowledgments from remote hosts.

Returning to Figure 9–16, the round trip time (RTT) is derived from adding the send delay (SD), the processing time (PT) at the remote host, and the receive delay (RD). If delay were not variable, this simple calculation would suffice for determining

TABLE 9–3   INTERNET PORT NUMBERS (NOT EXHAUSTIVE)

Number	Name	Description
5	RJE	Remote Job Entry
7	ECHO	Echo
11	USERS	Active Users
13	DAYTIME	Daytime
20	FTP-DATA	File Transfer (Data)
21	FTP	File Transfer (Control)
23	TELNET	TELNET
25	SMTP	Simple Mail Transfer
37	TIME	Time
42	NAMESERV	Host Name Server
43	NICKNAME	Who Is
53	DOMAIN	Domain Name Server
67	BOOTPS	Bootstrap Protocol Server
68	BOOTPC	Bootstrap Protocol Client
69	TFTP	Trivial File Transfer
79	FINGER	Finger
101	HOSTNAME	NIC Host Name Server
102	ISO-TSAP	ISO TSAP
103	X400	X.400
104	X400SND	X.400 SND
105	CSNET-NS	CSNET Mailbox Name Server
109	POP2	Post Office Protocol 2
111	RPC	SUN RPC Portmap
137	NETBIOS-NS	NETBIOS Name Service
138	NETBIOS-DG	NETBIOS Datagram Service
139	NETBIOS-SS	NETBIOS Session Service

a retransmission timer. However, as stated earlier, since delay in the Internet is often highly variable, other factors must be considered.

RFC 1122 concedes that the original TCP approach to time out and retransmission is inadequate. With new systems, the *Van Jacobsen's* slow start approach is used: Upon a timeout, TCP shuts its window to one. Upon receiving an ACK, it opens its window to one-half of the size the window was before the timeout occurred.

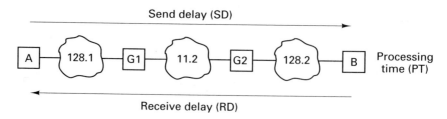

Figure 9–16.   Round trip delay.

OSI AND TCP/IP

Since the Internet protocols (TCP/IP and related protocols) dominate the marketplace today, the transition to the OSI protocols is not a trivial task. The coexistence of OSI and TCP/IP in one network requires extensive and complex protocol conversion packages. None of the Internet protocols is compatible with its counterparts in the OSI Model. TCP is dramatically different from TP4; and, while IP and CLNP are quite similar in functions, the manner in which they perform these functions differ. Therefore, an enterprise is faced with a significant outlay of resources if TCP/IP and its related protocols are to coexist with the protocols found in the OSI Model.

The one protocol that would not require extensive mapping is the route discovery protocol, published as open shortest path first (OSPF) in the Internet suite and published as IS-IS in OSI.

A typical approach for interworking the OSI and TCP/IP software is the provision for a gateway. A gateway's principal job is to convert the PDUs coming from one network to a form compatible with the PDUs going into the receiving network.

Gateways can be structured to perform strictly communications functions such as IP routing, OSPF/IS-IS route discovery, address mapping with ARP-type protocols, and ICMP operations.

However, considerable focus is being placed on building gateways that perform conversion functions at the upper layers as well, where gateways provide mail service between the Internet mail protocols and the OSI mail protocols.

In an actual operating environment, it is not likely that most enterprises would implement a pure OSI stack for the foreseeable future (see Figure 9–17). As a transition to OSI, a mixed-stack approach is more likely. This entails the use of the more widely accepted and widely used OSI protocols being placed on top of TCP/UDP and IP. The widely used X.400 message handling system protocol is the key player as is the ISO FTAM system.

An application layer gateway may be the simplest and least expensive solution to enable GOSIP hosts in a network to communicate with non-GOSIP hosts (see Figure 9–18).

Pure TCP stack	Pure OSI stack	Mixed stack
FTP	FTAM	X.400
	ACSE	
TCP	Presentation	TCP
	Session	
IP	Transport	IP
	CLNP	
Network service	Network service	Network service

Figure 9–17.   Pure and mixed stacks.

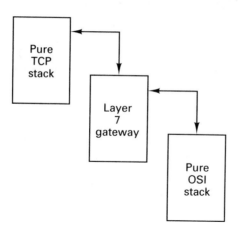

Figure 9–18. A Single interoperation procedure.

In this configuration, the application layer gateway can operate in a dual-protocol host with special software residing "above" the application process in each protocol stack. This software automatically transforms requests from one protocol into the corresponding commands for the other protocol.

For example, a user on a TCP/IP host could use the File Transfer Protocol to request the application layer gateway to access a file from a GOSIP host. The application layer would use the OSI FTAM protocol to get the remote file and pass it to the requester via FTP.

In this respect, the Internet Engineering Task Force (IETF) codified an application layer gateway mapping facility for Simple Mail File Transfer (SMTP, which runs over TCP/IP) to X.400 in Request for Comment 987. This software provides a mapping from SMTP message fields to the X.400 message structure. It also translates the SMTP recipient address into an X.400 recipient address, and vice versa.

The Defense Information Systems Agency (DISA) has adopted this approach as its central strategy for the transition from Milnet to GOSIP.

Another viable approach for coexistence between the Internet protocols and the OSI protocols is the use of gateways between a TCP/IP network and "local" OSI networks (see Figure 9–19). The simplest approach is to keep the gateways operating at layers 1, 2, and 3, and to isolate them from the application protocol layer conversions. This would allow the end systems to assume responsibility for the ULP mappings.

Additionally, the end systems could run either a pure or mixed stack. This approach would not affect configurations at the gateways, if the gateway's traffic is restricted to the lower-layer operations.

Figure 9–20 shows in more detail how a translation gateway would operate. The IP network would continue to run the IP stack of protocols (the Internet protocol, OSPF, ICMP, ARP, etc.) and a translation module would exist to interpret the CLNP datagrams coming into the gateway. Based on the values of the fields in the CLNP header, the translator would take actions at the gateway and, in most instances, convert the fields to an appropriate IP header for launching the traffic through the IP network.

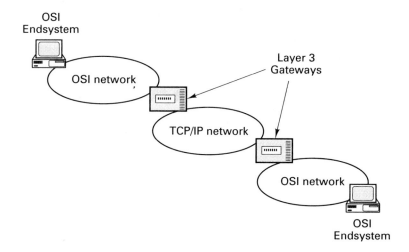

Figure 9–19. Internet gateways.

This mapping function is actually fairly "clean" in that CLNP and IP have many functions that are quite similar. The support features of time-to-live, segmentation, and so on, are common across both protocols. One of the major translation functions would be the mapping of ICMP PDUs to the CLNP error control field.

A gateway that does conversions of the upper layers would typically be required to map between two major protocol types: (a) message handling for electronic mail and (b) file transfer.

Figure 9–21 shows a gateway that is also called a mail server. Its function is to provide translation between CCITT's X.400 message handling system and Internet's

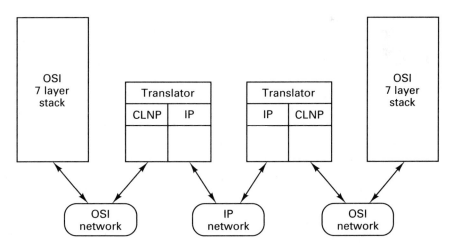

Figure 9–20. IP/CLNP gateways.

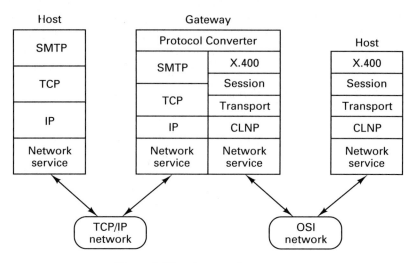

Figure 9-21. A messaging gateway.

SMTP. X.400 supports electronic mail through its Interpersonal Messaging Protocol (IMP).

The conversion is not very clean, in that X.400 has considerably more features than SMTP. Notwithstanding, the Internet publishes RFCs to provide guidance on how the protocol converter would execute the translation functions between the two protocols.

The gateway can also translate the lower-layer protocols as well. In this example, translation can be made between TCP and TP 4, and IP and CLNP.

As shown in Figure 9-22, a TELNET user on a TCP/IP end system in a TCP/IP network wishes to log in to an OSI end system on a GOSIP/OSI network. This request is passed to a dual-host end system that serves as a gateway between the TCP/IP and OSI networks. The dual-host system has application software above the application layers to convert the TELNET request to a virtual terminal formatted request that is then passed on to the OSI end system. The exchange of data between the disparate end systems takes place via the translation application software.

Since one protocol profile in virtual terminal is nearly identical to the TELNET protocol, this conversion can be accomplished in that instance with relatively little investment in software.

Another approach for coexistence between Internet and OSI protocols is the use of end systems to provide mapping and conversion functions. The stacks are not really much different from having a separate gateway server to perform the function. It simply means that the overhead for providing the translation functions must be provided by the host machine. In this example, conversion is made between FTP and FTAM as well as the lower-layer protocols. The Internet authorities also publish RFCs to provide guidance for mapping between FTP and FTAM (see Figure 9-23).

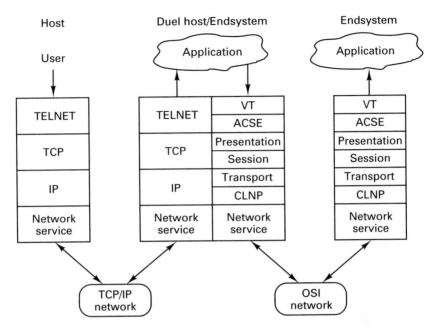

Figure 9–22. Remote log-in services.

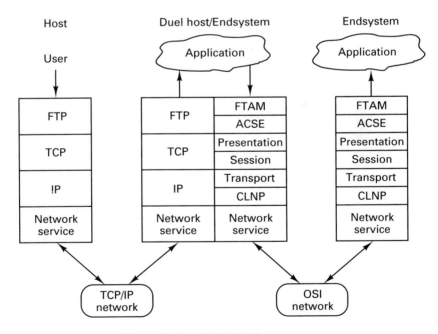

Figure 9–23. FTP/FTAM support.

Figure 9–24 shows a TCP/IP end system with an OSI end system via a dual-protocol host/end system is shown. The dual-protocol host has complete GOSIP and TCP/IP protocol suites available as part of its networking capabilities.

A user on such a host has the option of invoking either TCP/IP protocols such as TELNET for remote log in, FTP for file transfer, or SMTP for electronic mail or the analogous OSI application layer protocols including Virtual Terminal Protocol (VTP) for remote log in, FTAM for file transfer, and X.400 for electronic mail.

This approach has the advantage of allowing both TCP/IP and OSI hosts to exist on the same subnetwork. Thus, a dual-protocol host/end system can be used to communicate to any GOSIP or TCP/IP destination. This approach will permit the preservation of ''legacy'' systems until the next round of upgrades and procurements while also permitting the installation of mandated GOSIP systems.

The National Institute of Standards and Technology (NIST) has developed and tested prototype gateways connecting the Department of Defense SMTP and X.400 protocols and its FTP and FTAM protocols. This effort demonstrated the viability of dual-host/end system gateways. In addition, DISA has committed to providing quality gateways for early GOSIP users on the Defense Data Network (DDN).

Application programming interfaces (APIs) provide the ''software glue'' between applications and the communications software provided by OSI. Figure 9–25 indicates five locations in the OSI stack where APIs might be implemented.

The most common interfaces are at the transport and applications layers. In the case of transport, APIs can be used to interface ''legacy'' applications such as SMTP, FTP, and TELNET to the OSI transport system. This approach would support the strategy of running current applications over OSI.

In the case of applications layer interfaces, APIs can enable gateway connections such as those that allow ''legacy'' electronic-mail systems to interconnect via X.400. This approach enables LAN-electronic-mail users to preserve their user interface and other capabilities while achieving global connectivity. APIs can also be used to provide

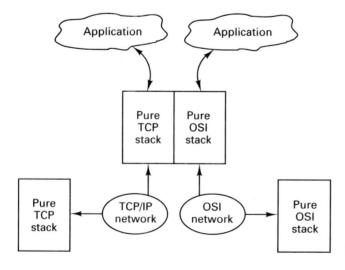

Figure 9–24. Dual-host/end system.

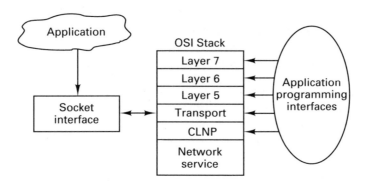

Figure 9–25. Programmable interfaces.

electronic mail-enabling applications such as electronic data interchange (EDI) and electronic funds transfer (EFT).

While the design of OSI assumed "exposed" interfaces at several layers, it has
not yet described or standardized APIs. Currently, vendors provide proprietary APIs. A
number of X.400 vendors joined together under the aegis of the XAPI Association to
develop a standard X.400 API for gateways, and other alliances have formed with the
same intent. There is also an effort under way to standardize APIs within the ISO.

GOSIP

The U.S. government sponsors a program designed to foster the use of the OSI standards. Its title is The Government Open Systems Interconnection Profile or GOSIP.

NIST sponsors the GOSIP workshops. These workshops meet quarterly in Gai-
thersburg, Maryland, to review ongoing work that has occurred during the prior three
months.

Each year a new version of the workshop agreements is published and (with each
publication) the standards become more complete and more defined.

GOSIP is published by the U.S. government as Federal Information Processing
Standards Publication no. 146, or simply FIPS 146. For the seminar attendee who wishes
to obtain more information, you should ask NIST for the *Stable Implementation Agreements for Open Systems Interconnection Protocols*.

In addition, anyone is welcome to attend the OSI workshop. Its registration fee is
small and it is a very valuable learning experience. Of course, the workshop members
encourage active participation. This makes good sense because it adds intellectual force
as more people participate in the standards development.

One might ask, "Why is another body needed to define standards that, in effect,
are already written?" The answer is that many of the OSI protocols are written in a
somewhat generic sense. For example, many fields defined in the PDUs of the OSI
standards are fairly general (in the description of the contents). One of the purposes of
a program such as GOSIP is to further define and refine the OSI standards and the fields

in the OSI PDUs. In addition, GOSIP provides guidance on testing for conformance and interoperability.

GOSIP establishes that OSI systems are to be used in Request for Proposals (RFPs) for new networking systems. When possible, OSI is to be used when existing networking systems are upgraded and enhanced.

GOSIP is to be used as the one standard reference for government agencies when developing, acquiring, or purchasing information technology systems. In no uncertain terms, GOSIP states that OSI must be used by all federal government agencies.

Conditions may exist in a federal agency or department where it is not feasible to use some of the OSI standards. Therefore, GOSIP permits under certain conditions the heads of federal agencies and departments to approve waivers to the FIPS. Moreover, the agency head may delegate this authority to an official within the department or agency.

Waivers can be granted only when potential compliance with the OSI standard would negatively affect the agency or department mission. Waivers can be granted if compliance would create a severe financial impact on an operator (which could not be offset by the savings from the agency).

Requests for waivers are sent to NIST to the attention of FIPS Waiver Decisions. It must also be sent to the House of Representatives and the Senate for publication in the *Federal Register*. The waiver is also published in the *Commerce Business Daily*.

The waiver request should contain detailed and adequate back up for the request. Obviously, NIST is going to judge the merit of the request on the validity of the waiver request. Consequently, reasons should be given as to why the waiver should be granted. It should include a detailed description of the systems involved. It should also include the total period that the waiver is requested and a plan for when GOSIP will be implemented.

The principle importance of any of these waiver requests is a full description of the negative impact on the agency's mission and of course any negative financial impact.

GOSIP Version 1

GOSIP Version 1 was published in June 1988. It still serves as the basis for many of the federal agency and department strategic plans. Figure 9–26 shows the GOSIP Version 1 profile.

The Upper Layer Protocol implementations are quite simple. The major aspects of the upper layers deal with FTAM and X.400. In addition, ACSE is required at the applications layer as well as the basic services for the presentation and session layers.

The transport layer is defined only with transport layer class 4. The network layer provides for either an X.25 network interface protocol or the connectionless network protocol (CLNP, published as ISO 8473).

The lower two layers of GOSIP Version 1 support protocols and interfaces for a wide area network or for a local area network. The left side of Figure 9–26 shows the lower two layer protocol stack for a WAN with the use of LAPB, V.35, and EIA-232. The right side of the figure shows a protocol stack for LANs with emphasis on the use of carrier sense multiple access/collision defect (CSMA/CD), token bus, and token ring.

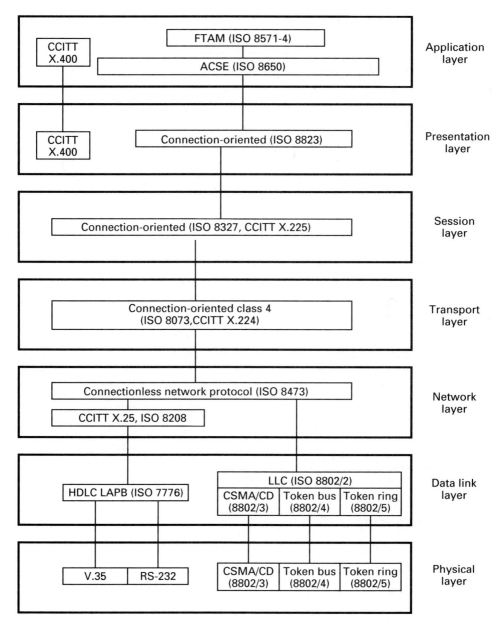

Figure 9–26. GOSIP version 1.

Resting above all of the LAN protocols, of course, is logical link control (LLC), which must exist on any type of ISO 8802 or IEEE 802 network.

The reader may be somewhat confused by the numbering for the data link and physical layer LAN protocols. The ISO publishes its standards with four digits. The

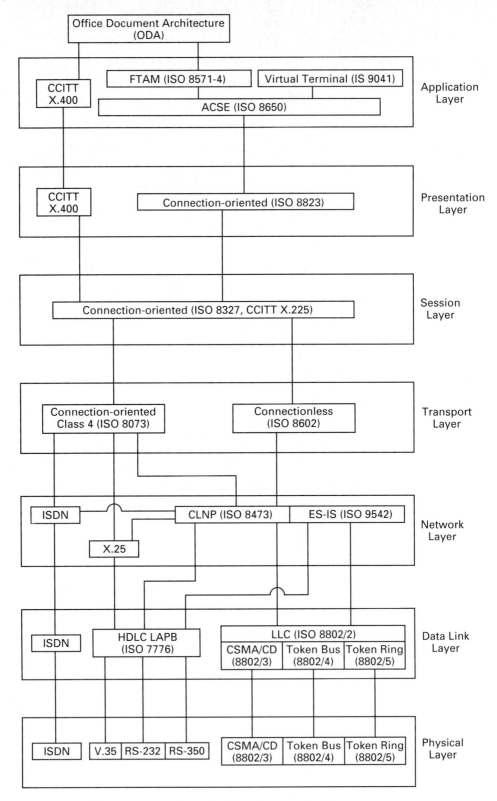

Figure 9-27. GOSIP version 2.

8802 is functionally equivalent to the IEEE 802. Indeed, the IEEE is the authoritative body for these LAN standards. The ISO publishes them unaltered with changed numbers.

GOSIP Version 2

GOSIP Version 2 in Figure 9–27 represents a considerable enhancement in functionality over GOSIP Version 1. The major changes that have occurred in the application layer are the additions of the virtual terminal service published under IS 9041 as well as the office document architecture (ODA) specifications. Version 2 continues to use the CCITT Red Book X.400 version. Therefore, X.400 still operates at the application and presentation layers. The X.400 Blue Book version moves X.400 into the application layer.

Another major change is the addition of connectionless transport layer protocol services with ISO 8602.

The network layer has also undergone considerable enhancements. For example, the end system-intermediate system (ES-IS) protocol has been added and is published as ISO 9542. The other addition at the network layer is the ISDN network layer service published as Q.931.

The reader should note the variety of interface and connection options that are offered through GOSIP Version 2 at the network layer with other entities in the network layer as well as the transport and data link entities.

The changes at the lower layers mainly reflect the addition of ISDN at the data link layer (with the use of LAPD) as well as at the physical layer, principally with the basic and primary access rates. GOSIP Version 2 has also added RS-350 at the physical layer to provide for higher speed interfaces than that offered by RS-232.

The GOSIP Version 2 remains the same for LAN protocols.

SUMMARY

The modern data communications network is usually built with layered protocols. The OSI Model and the Internet model serve as the foundation for these networks. Some organizations are planning a migration to OSI, using GOSIP as a guide. Other organizations intend to remain with the Internet suite.

10

Servers, Remote Procedure Calls, and Transfer Syntaxes

INTRODUCTION

This chapter is an extension of the first part of the previous chapter. In that chapter, the reader was introduced to distributed networks, and the lower-layer protocols. The full discussion is not complete however. After all, assuming these protocols deliver the data to the end-user device—what then? Additional software is needed to deliver the data to the applications programs that use the lower layers. This chapter provides an overview of this software, and an examination of the OSI Remote Operations Service Element (ROSE).

THE CLIENT–SERVER MODEL

Many communications processes today are organized around a client–server model. This model is based on the idea that personal computers and workstations operate as clients. These clients communicate over a network to a server. The client's responsibility is to formulate a simple request for a service for the server to perform. In turn, the server performs the operation and sends back a reply to the client. This request–reply concept is imbedded into most client–server networks that provide services such as file services, data-base services, electronic mail services, terminal services, and so on.

The client–server approach is widely used in local area networks in which diskless workstations access servers to obtain application software, files, and electronic mail. This approach always uses a request–reply dialogue, and the request is always initiated by the client.

REMOTE PROCEDURE CALLS

The OSI Model and the TCP/IP suite support a process for remote operations and remote procedure calls (RPCs). The remote procedure operation is based on a client–server model that is an asymmetric type of communication. This means that a requester, such as a client, sends a request message a process, identified as a server. It waits for an action to occur and receives a reply about the success or failure of the request. The client is not aware of the server's location (the server could be on a different machine in the network). This approach is in contrast to most of the OSI protocols and entities in which transfer is symmetric, in which traffic flows in both directions at the same time. Figure 10–1 shows the operations of asymmetric and symmetric protocols.

The Stub

Many remote procedure operations are implemented in the client–server operation through a technique called *stub* (see Figure 10–2). The stub is actually a procedure such as read or write and can be defined for each server's clients. The procedure, such as read, becomes a library procedure (for example, in UNIX) and the client can obtain the services through a simple read statement (again, a UNIX call). The read would identify the file that is to be read, the number of bytes to be read, and a buffer to contain the result of the read. This then becomes a simple message transfer to the server, after which the client waits for a reply from the server. Upon the reply arriving, the client caller is once again given control.

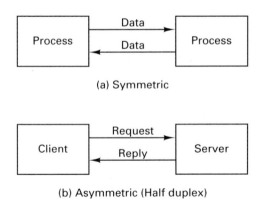

(a) Symmetric

(b) Asymmetric (Half duplex)

- Client sending a message to server = program callng a procedure for a result

- Client initiates action and waits for its completion and a reply

- Client unaware that server is a different machine

Figure 10–1.   Remote operations.

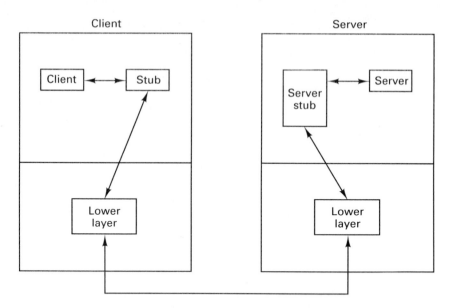

Figure 10–2. Remote operations with the Stub.

These procedure calls obviate costly I/O commands such as those incurred with OSI request primitives—or even worse, interrupts, which must be implemented with indication primitives.

Implementations differ. A stub may actually be involved in transferring the data, or a stub may be a client's to server's agent (which actually passes traffic back and forth between servers).

Problems with Remote Calls

While remote procedure calls seem to be quite simple, problems can occur if a server fails. Consider the case where the request is executed successfully, but the request is not sent back to the client before the server fails. Assume the client repeats the operation and resends the traffic (once the server comes up). Then the reply is successfully executed and sent back. If no harm is done with this type of operation, it is called *idempotent*. However, not all operations are idempotent. For example, what happens if this client were sending money to another account and ends up sending the money twice?

A convenient method for approaching the problem can be categorized in one of four methods: only once, at most once, at least once, or last of many.

In the ideal world, a call is carried out only one time. This ideal world is really not achievable, because it is not possible to prevent servers from crashing, software from failing, and so on. The second form of handling the problem is called at most once. With this operation, if an error has occurred with the server, a stub will return an error call to the client. In this case, retransmission is not attempted. The client knows that the operation has either not been performed or has been performed one time. In either case, it keeps matters simple and recovery is then the client's responsibility.

The third type of approach to this problem is called at least once. With this approach, the client uses a timeout and retry values to attempt the operation. When it eventually receives replies, it knows the operation has been performed at least once, and perhaps many times. For idempotent, this operation works fine. If the operation is not idempotent it is a good idea for the client (or its stub) to uniquely identify each transaction so that it may discern which transaction is appropriate and to make certain that others are either backed out or filtered out. This approach is called the last of many, perhaps a better term would be one of many.

It is quite possible that in remote procedure operations a client can fail after issuing an RPC. This process, in which a server has no waiting client (where the client is the parent) is called the *orphan*. There are a number of ways to handle this problem. With the process called extermination, the server or its machine recovers from the crash by determining which RPCs were in process when the problem occurred. It then takes actions to exterminate these processes. How the clients are informed would be a matter of local choice. Another term to describe the problem is the *grand-orphan*. This occurs when the orphan issues an RPC that creates a grand-orphan. The grand-orphan could in turn create another grand-orphan, which is a great-grand-orphan. The process of handling this operation is to keep bookkeeping accounts of the running processes once the system is up and to exterminate all chains.

Another approach for killing orphans is a process called *expiration*. It requires no bookkeeping tables; it simply is a rule that a server is given a discrete amount of time to complete the process. If the process is not completed within this time, remedial action may be taken. The client may be asked for a new time, the RPC may be canceled, and so on.

Yet another approach for handling the orphan problem is called *reincarnation*. This approach may be needed in the event that extermination does not eliminate all orphans. For example, in a highly distributed network, it is possible that the grand-orphans may have been partitioned into other machines that are not reachable. In this case, the recovering client will broadcast a message out to all machines and they are requested to kill off all server operations.

A gentle reincarnation would selectively kill off server operations.

OSI REMOTE PROCEDURE OPERATIONS

The OSI remote procedure call is the Remote Operations Service Element. It is based on two basic concepts: sending a request for an operation to a server and conveying the results of that operation to the client. The results of the operation can report on various combinations of success or failure.

ROSE also uses class numbers to describe the result of the operation, either for synchronous or asynchronous communications processes. Figure 10–3 summarizes the ROSE processes.

Result of Operation	Expected Reporting from Performer
Success or Failure	If successful, return result.
	If a failure, return an error reply.
Failure Only	If successful, no reply.
	If a failure, return an error reply.
Success Only	If successful, return a result.
	If a failure, no reply.
Success or Failure	In either case, no reply.

Class Number	Definition
1	Synchronous: Report success (result) or failure (error)
2	Asynchronous: Report success (result) or failure (error)
3	Asynchronous: Report failure (error) only
4	Asynchronous: Report success (result) only
5	Asynchronous: Report nothing

Figure 10–3. ROSE terminology.

The ROSE operations are considered connectionless in that timers and retrys are not invoked for this service. Thus, primitives from the invoker consist of the RO-IN-VOKE req which is mapped to a PDU and sent to the remote application entity (AE) in the form of an RO-INVOKE ind. The reader should notice in Figure 10–4 that no response or confirm primitives are involved in this service. After the operation has been performed, the server returns the RO-RESULT req, which is eventually presented to the client as the RO-RESULT ind. The values in the Protocol data units (PDUs) must provide the invoke ID to correlate a request with a reply as well as an operation value that identifies a particular operation that is to be performed. The operation class defines synchronous or asynchronous operations and the type of reply that is to accompany them.

Figure 10–5 shows how a ROSE requestor can obtain the services of a remote operations protocol machine (ROPM) through the RO-INVOKE request. The RO-IN-VOKE request is passed to the requesting ROSE entity, which can only accept this if it is in a particular state as indicated by a. In the protocol state machine, this is classified as STA02. Event 1 depicts that the ROSE entity creates a remote operation service request PDU from the parameters in the RO request primitive. It then sends either a RT-TRANSFER request to the RTSE or a P-DATA request to the presentation layer as indicated in b, remains in STA02 after transferring this primitive. At the remote machine, a P-DATA indication or RT-TRANSFER indication primitive is sent to the accepting ROSE entity. As indicated by c, this can only be accepted if this entity is in STA02. In event 2, the application data unit is received through the primitive. Then, event 3 shows that, if this PDU is acceptable, an RO-INVOKE indication is sent to the performer of the service.

Assuming the requester (typically a server) is able to perform the action, it returns an RO-RESULT request to the requesting ROSE entity. As indicated by a, this is only accepted if in STA02. The requesting ROPM machine forms a result reply PDU and sends this through the RT-TRANSFER request to a sending Reliable Transfer Service

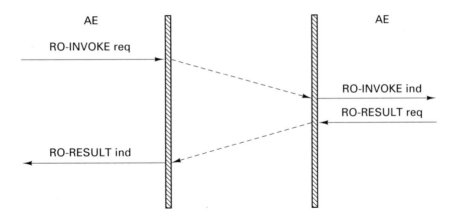

Parameters in the Operations

- Invoke-ID   Identifies the RO-INVOKE service and correlates the request
                     with corresponding replies.

- Linked-ID   Identifies a child operation and specifies the invocation of a
                     linked parent operation.

- Operation-value   Identifies the operation to be performed. The value is supplied by
                     the requestor and must be agreed upon by the acceptor.

- Operation-class   Defines a synchronous or asynchronous operation and the type of
                     expected reply.

- Argument   The argument of the invoked operation.

- Result   The result of an invoked and successful operation.

- Error-value   Identifies the error that occurred during the operation.

- Error-parameter   Provides additional information about the error.

- Priority   Defines the priority of the corresponding APDU.

- Reject-reason   Identifies the reason for a rejection.

- Returned-   Contains the parameters of the primitive if a corresponding APDU
  parameters   cannot by transferred by the ROSE provider.

Figure 10–4.   ROSE invocation and a result.

Element (RTSE). (The presentation layer is not shown in this operation.) At the requesting site, the receiving RTSE transfers the PDU through the RT-TRANSFER indication. c indicates that this can only be accepted if in STA02. Accepting at the remote operations protocol machine accepts this traffic and examines the PDU and creates an appropriate RO-RESULT as event 3.

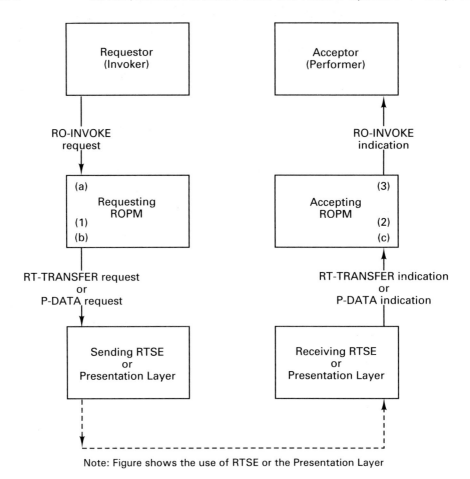

Note: Figure shows the use of RTSE or the Presentation Layer

Figure 10–5. ROSE operations: Invocation of an operation.

Figure 10–6 shows the result of the operations in Figure 10–5. The remote server returns the RO-RESULT request to (in this example) RTSE. In turn, RTSE relays the data unit to its peer RTSE entity at the local client. The traffic is passed through the RT-TRANSFER indication to the ROPM and then to the end-user with the RO-RESULT indication primitive.

SUN'S REMOTE PROCEDURE CALL

The Sun Microsystems RPC is widely used throughout the industry and now exists as a Request for Comment (RFC) document within the Internet framework. For the reader who wishes more information about the Sun RPC, RFC 1057 contains a succinct and well written tutorial. We summarize some of the major aspects of the Sun RPC in this section.

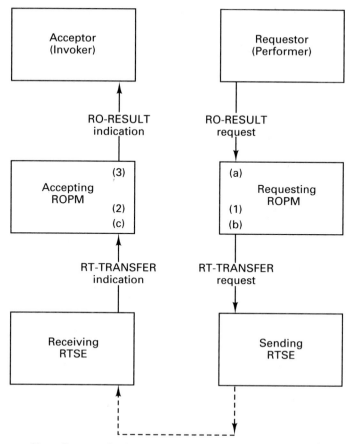

Note: Presentation layer did not participate in this operation

Figure 10–6. ROSE operations: Returning the result.

Sun's RPC is quite similar to the general operations discussed earlier in this chapter regarding remote procedure calls. It uses the concept of a client which sends a request and a server which sends back a reply. The caller initiates the action by sending a call message to a server and then waits for the reply to return. The call contains the version number of the protocol, the specification of the procedure that is to be invoked, authentication fields, reply fields, as well as an identifier to correlate replies and responses.

The server, as with most RPC systems, waits passively for the arrival of the call message. When the call message is received, the server examines the fields in the message and if the authentication is proper, the version correct, and the procedure can be identified, the server will then perform the requested operations and return a reply message.

Sun's RPC also supports a concept called batching, which allows the client to send more than one call message to a server. The client need not wait for a reply for each request, but sends a "batch" of messages to the server. In turn, the server operates on these messages and then provides a reply for the messages.

In addition, the Sun RPC supports a broadcast feature. As the term implies, this operation allows the client to transmit a broadcast to numerous parties. It then waits for replies from these parties. With this technique, servers only respond when a call has been executed properly. Errors are not reported upon with the broadcast approach.

The Sun RPC will reject a call if the version in the request differs from the version supported by the server or if authentication problems occur.

SUPPORTING PROTOCOLS FOR AN RPC

RPCs are mainly connectionless in how they operate. That is to say, they have no timers recovery from a non-response of a server. Generally, some means must exist to provide for the reliability for the RPC operation. If a user operation requires reliability, a common approach is to implement a transport layer underneath the remote procedure call. For example, OSI's transport protocol class 4 (TP4) or the Transmission Control Protocol (TCP) are sound solutions to this problem.

It is also feasible to run RPC over a connectionless transport layer, such as the User Datagram Protocol (UDP). If this option is implemented, the end user is tasked with sequencing, timeouts, duplicate detection operations, etc. In essence, the user must implement many of the features of TP4 or TCP.

On the other hand, certain applications may not require any type of connection-oriented services. If this is the case, then the protocol stack can be quite "lean" with connectionless operations occurring throughout the layers.

OBTAINING THE SERVICES OF A REMOTE SERVER

One of the more interesting problems with a remote procedure environment is determining where the remote process is located. That is to say, finding the needed server and the host on which the server is operating. A common approach to handle this situation is to predefine the identity and the location of the server, and make this known to all systems that wish to use the remote processes. Afterwards, the client is required only to identify what service is to be performed by which serving process at which location. One widely-used approach is found in the UNIX operating system through the implementation of sockets between the local and remote processes.

This section provides several examples of the UNIX operating system and its remote socket operations. We cite the 4.3 BSD UNIX interfaces because of their prevalence in the industry. Additionally, the creation of sockets through the TCP/IP protocols is illustrated.

The concept of a *socket*, is part of the BSD UNIX I/O concept, and is really nothing more than an end point in the communications process. Unlike some socket concepts with I/O files, the TCP/IP BSD UNIX concept allows a socket to be created without providing a destination address. A destination address in a later system call will be used to create a final binding between the sending and receiving addresses.

The bold coding below shows the system call that creates a socket. It is identified as *socket* and consists of three arguments. The *domain* field describes the protocol family (a domain) associated with the socket. As examples, it could include the Internet family, PUP family, DEC family, Appletalk family, etc. The type argument stipulates the *type* of communications desired with this connection. The programmer can establish values to specify a datagram service, reliable delivery service or a raw socket. The third argument allows the programmer to code the type of service that each of the *protocols* within the protocol family provides. This argument is required because protocol families usually consist of more than one protocol. It is the task of the programmer to supply the specific protocol in this argument. If it is left at 0, the system will select the appropriate protocol within the domain.

The domain values are available in the <sys/socket.h> file. The UNIX domain is AF_UNIX; the Internet domain is AF_INET. The socket types are also found in file <sys/socket.h> and are coded in the systems call as: SOCK_STREAM = a reliable, stream service; SOCK_DGRAM = a datagram service; SOCK_RAW = a raw socket (to provide access to underlying protocols [for communications programmers]).

s = socket (domain, type, protocol)

We learned earlier that UNIX allows a socket to be created without furnishing addresses (in UNIX V, called a name) for the socket. Communications cannot occur until local and foreign internet address are declared for the association between the communicating entities. In the UNIX domain, local and foreign path names are used. The bold coding below shows the system call to establish the local address with the socket. The *bind* call sets up one half of an association. The first argument in the list is called *s* and contains the integer number value of the socket. The local *name* argument can vary but usually consists of three values, the protocol family, the port number and an internet address. The *namelen* argument contains the length of the second argument.

bind(s, name, namelen)

The bold coding shown below shows the next step in mapping the TCP/IP connection between two machines. The *connect* system call allows the programmer to connect a socket to a destination address. As the coding illustrates, the *s* (socket number), the *name* (destination id), and *namelen* (name length) are included as arguments. The name parameter identifies the remote socket for the binding.

The asymmetric nature of port bindings allows an easy implementation of a client-server relationship. The server issues a bind to establish a socket for a well-known services, such as FTP. It then listens passively for a client to send a connect request to the server's passive socket.

If a connection is unsuccessful, an error is returned to the requestor. Over 20 error codes are available with the connect call. A couple of examples are: ECONNREFUSE

= the host refusal of the connection because the server process cannot be found given the name furnished; ETIME OUT = the connection attempt took too long.

connect(s, name, namelen)

After a server has set up a passive socket, it then listens for incoming connections that are requested (only supported on reliable stream delivery). This operation is performed with the *listen* system call. It takes form shown in the bold coding below.

The parameter *s* is the socket on which connections will occur; the *backlog* parameter establishes the maximum queue size for holding incoming connection requests. If the queue is full, an incoming connection request is refused with an indication of: ECONNREFUSED. Other error codes associated with listen are: EBADF = s is invalid; ENOISOCK = s is not a socket; EONOTSUPP = socket does not support a listen operation.

listen(s,backlog)

After the listen has been executed, the accepting entity (usually a server) must wait for connection requests. It uses the *accept* system call for this operation. The accept pulls the first entity in the queue to service. It takes the form, shown in the next bold coding.

The s parameter is the listening socket; the *addr* parameter contains the *sockaddr* of the connecting entity; *addrlen* is the length of the address. If the operation succeeds, a new file descriptor *ns* is allocated for the socket and the new descriptor is returned to the requestor.

newsock = accept(s,addr,addrlen)

After all these system calls have executed successfully, the application entities can exchange data. Data exchange is accomplished through the *write* system call which is depicted in the next example. The call is quite simple. It contains three arguments. The argument contains the socket identifier (*descriptor*), the buffer (*buf*) is a pointer in memory which contains the user data, the length field (*sizeofbuf*) determines the length of the buffer search for the user data.

write(descriptor,buf,sizeofbud)

To receive data, the *read* system call is invoked. Its format is illustrated next. The reader probably sees the repetitive aspects of the design of the system calls. This call contains the socket identifier (*descriptor*), the identification of the buffer (*buf*) in which the data will reside, and the length indicator (*sizeofbuf*) which describes the number of bytes that are to be read.

read (descriptor,buf,sizeofbuf)

A socket can be closed if it is no longer needed with the following system call.

close (s)

Data may continue to be sent and/or delivered—even after the close is issued (check with your vendor for this feature). After some period of time, the data will be discarded. If the user does not wish to send and/or receive any more data, it can issue:

shutdown (s, how)

Where parameters for *how* are: 0 = not interested in receiving data; 1 = no more data will be sent; 2 = no more data will be sent or received.

Most operating systems offer many other procedure calls for the programmer to not only obtain services from the remote server, but to receive diagnostic information about the success or problems of the call. For example, a call can be issued to determine how many messages are waiting in a queue for a server.

Remote Commands

Distributed systems also provide capabilities for a process to be invoked from a local host to a remote host. This most often occurs when services are required at the remote host and/or when data are to be passed to a remote program for execution. Most operating systems today support some type of remote command execution. For example, the Berkeley Unix software (4.3 BSD) provides the rsh to invoke a program on another host. This capability not only allows a remote program to be executed, it also allows UNIX and C programs to write data as input to the remote process and read from the local program what the remote process has output. rsh also supports error reporting which can be differentiated from the user stream.

TRANSFER SYNTAX BETWEEN DISTRIBUTED PROCESSES

Another problem in remote operations occurs when the client and server use different types of syntax in their data representation. This rarely occurs in local procedure calls in which data types are the same within one host architecture. The problem is not insignificant for remote operations in that protocols such as TCP/IP employee the *big indian byte order* for the fields in the headers. Whereas, the (trivial file transfer protocol (TFTP) uses big indian byte order only for its 16 bit fields such as error codes and its block numbers, and uses ASCII characters for the transfer of other types of information such as the file name and the mode of transfer. Then there is the BSD 4.3 which uses binary values only on individual fields (single byte fields) and uses ASCII fields for certain control names. Clearly, what is needed is for a remote procedure call is an agreed upon transfer syntax. One such convention is published under the OSI Model by the ISO and CCITT.

The ISO and CCITT have developed a presentation and transfer syntax to be used by application layer protocols, that solve the problem of different syntaxes that may be used by the client and server. One widely used specification is ISO 8824. It is titled Abstract Syntax Notation One (ASN.1). In addition, ISO 8825 (the Basic Encoding Rules [BER]) provides a set of rules to develop an unambiguous bit-level description of data that are transferred between the machines. That is to say, it specifies the representation of the data. In summary, ASN.1 describes an abstract syntax for data types and values and BER describes the actual representation of the data. ASN.1 is not an abstract syntax, but a language for describing abstract syntaxes. Some people use the term ASN.1 to include abstract syntax and basic encoding rules. However, the two are different from each other.

The CCITT specifies X.208 and X.209 for the presentation level. X.208 specifies the ASN.1 language and X.209 specifies the basic encoding rules for ASN.1. In the 1988 Blue Books, the X.208 specification was aligned with ISO 8824 plus ISO 8824, Addendum 1 (except 8824 does not define some conventions on describing encrypted structures). X.209 is aligned with ISO 8825 plus ISO 8825, Addendum 1.

The task of these protocols is to perform the services of data structure description and representation. They are not concerned with the meaning or semantics of the data, but are concerned with preserving the meaning and semantics of the data.

These protocols accept various data types and negotiate/convert the representation. They are concerned with (a) the syntax of the data of the sending application, (b) the syntax of the data of the receiving application, and (c) the data syntax used between the entities that support the sending and receiving applications.

The latter service is called a *transfer syntax*. It is negotiated between the presentation entities in the machines. Each entity chooses a syntax that is best for it to use between it and the user's syntax, and then attempts to negotiate the use of this syntax with the other presentation layer entity. Therefore, the two presentation entities must agree on a transfer syntax before data can be exchanged. Moreover, it may be necessary for the presentation layer to transform the data in order for the two users to communicate.

Each piece of information exchanged between the local and remote processes has a *type* and a *value*. The type is a class of information, such as integer, Boolean, octet, etc. A type can be used to describe a collection or group of values. For example, the type integer describes all values that are whole number (non-decimal) numbers. The term data type is a synonym for type.

The value is an instance of the type, such as a number or a piece of alphabetic text. For example, if we describe ''P of type integer,'' and ''P: = 9,'' it means this instance of P has a value of 9. In an X.25 packet header, for example, the fields can be defined as of the integer or bit string type. In order for machines to know how to interpret data, they must first know the type of the data (values) to be processed. Therefore, the concept of type is very important to the presentation layer services.

ASN.1 defines three kinds of types:

- *Built-in:* Commonly used types in which a standard notation is provided
- *Character string:* Types containing elements from a known character set
- *Useful:* Types for representing dates and time and some other miscellaneous types

Built-in Types.   Several built-in types are summarized in Table 10-1.

Another important feature of these standards is the use of *tags*. To distinguish the different types, a structure of values (for example, a data base record) or a simple ele-

TABLE 10–1 BUILT-IN TYPES

Type	Function
Boolean	Identifies logical data (true or false conditions).
Integer	Identifies signed whole numbers (cardinal numbers).
Bit String	Identifies binary data (ordered sequence of 1s and 0s).
Octet String	Identifies text or data that can be described as a sequence of octets (bytes).
Null	A simple type consisting of a single value. Could be valueless placeholder in which there are several alternatives but none of them apply. A null field with no value does not have to be transmitted.
Sequence	A structured type, defined by referencing an ordered list of various types.
Sequence of	A structured type, defined by referencing a single type. Each value in the type is an ordered list (if a list exists). It can be used as a method of building arrays of a single type.
Set	A structured type, similar to the Sequence type except that Set is defined by referencing an unordered list of types. Allows data to be sent in any order.
Set of	A structured type, similar to the Sequence type except that Set of is defined by referencing a single type. Each value in the type is an unordered list (if a list exits).
Choice	Models a data type chosen from a collection of alternative types. Allows a data structure to hold more that one type.
Selection	Models a variable whose type is that of some alternatives of a previously defined Choice.
Tagged	Models a new type from an existing type but with a different identifier.
Any	Models data whose type is unrestricted. It can be used with any valid type.
Object Identifier	A distinguishable value associated with an object, or a group of objects, like a library of rules, syntaxes, etc.
Character String	Models strings of characters for some defined character set.
Enumerated	A simple type; its values are given distinct identifiers as part of the type notation.
Real	Models real values (for example: $M \times B^e$, where $M =$ the mantissa, $B =$ the base, and $^e =$ the exponent).
Encrypted	A type whose value is a result of encrypting another type.

ment (for example, a field within the data base record) can have a tag attached that identifies the type. For example, a tag for a funds transfer record could be PRIVATE 22. This is used to identify the record and inform the receiver about the nature of its contents. As we shall see, tags can be put to very clever uses. ASN.1 provides a tag for every type.

ASN.1 defines four classes of *types:* Each tag is identified by its class and its number (as in our example PRIVATE 22). The type classes are defined as:

- *Universal.* Application-independent types.
- *Application-wide.* Types that are specific to an application and used in other standards (X.400 MHS, FTAM, etc.).
- *Context-specific.* Types that are specific to an application but are limited to a set within an application.
- *Private-use.* Reserved for private use and not defined in these standards. Used by other agencies.

Several tags are used for the universal assignment. Remember, the tag is used to identify a class. The tag has two parts, a class identifier and a number. Table 10–2 depicts the universal class tag assignments.

TABLE 10–2 UNIVERSAL CLASS TAG ASSIGNMENTS

UNIVERSAL 1	BOOLEAN
UNIVERSAL 2	INTEGER
UNIVERSAL 3	BITSTRING
UNIVERSAL 4	OCTETSTRING
UNIVERSAL 5	NULL
UNIVERSAL 6	OBJECT IDENTIFIER
UNIVERSAL 7	Object Descriptor
UNIVERSAL 8	EXTERNAL
UNIVERSAL 9	REAL
UNIVERSAL 10	ENUMERATED
UNIVERSAL 11	ENCRYPTED
UNIVERSAL 12–15	Reserved for future use
UNIVERSAL 16	SEQUENCE and SEQUENCE OF
UNIVERSAL 17	SET and SET OF
UNIVERSAL 18	NumericString
UNIVERSAL 19	PrintableString
UNIVERSAL 20	TeletexString
UNIVERSAL 21	VideotexString
UNIVERSAL 22	IA5String
UNIVERSAL 23	UTCTime
UNIVERSAL 24	GeneralizedTime
UNIVERSAL 25	GraphicString
UNIVERSAL 26	VisibleString
UNIVERSAL 27	GeneralString
UNIVERSAL 28	CharacterString
UNIVERSAL 29+	Reserved for additions

BASIC ENCODING RULES

X.209 and ISO 8825 describe the encoding rules for the values of types, in contrast to X.208 and ISO 8824, which are concerned with the abstract structure of the information. These basic encoding conventions provide the rules for the transfer syntax conventions.

The rules require that each type be described by a standard representation. This representation is called a *data element* (or just element). It consists of three components: type, length, and value (TLV), which appear in the following order:

Type   Length   Value

The type is also called the identifier. It distinguishes one type from another and specifies how the contents are interpreted. The length specifies the length of the value or contents. The value (contents) contains the actual information of the element. These components are explained shortly.

The transfer data element is illustrated in Figure 10–7. It can consist of a single TLV or a series of data elements, described as multiple TLVs. The element consists of an integral number *n* of octets, written with the most significant bit (MSB), 8, on the left and the least significant bit (LSB), 1, on the right:

XXXXXXXX

87654321

The single-octet identifier is coded as depicted in Figure 10–8(a). Bits 8 through 7 identify the four type classes by the following bit assignments:

Universal	00
Application-wide	01
Context-specific	10
Private-use	11

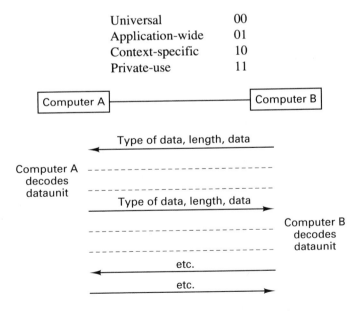

Figure 10–7. The type-length-value convention.

Class   P/C   Tag number

8	7	6	5	4	3	2	1

Note:
For tag numbers greater than 30,
identifier is coded with extension octets   **Figure 10–8.**   The type field.

Bit 6 identifies the forms of the data element. Two forms are possible. A *primitive* element (bit 6 = 0) has no further internal structure of data elements. A *constructor* element (bit 6 = 1) is recursively defined in that it contains a series of data elements. The remaining five bits (5 through 1) distinguish one data type from another of the same class. For example, the field may distinguish Boolean from integer information. If the system requires more than five bits, bits 5 through 1 of the first octet are coded as 11111_2 and bit 8 of the subsequent octets are coded with a 1 to indicate more octets follow and a 0 to indicate the last octet. Figure 10–8(b) illustrates the use of multi-octet identifiers.

The length (L) specifies the length of the contents. It may take one of three forms: short, long, or indefinite. The short form is one octet long and is used when L is less than 128. Bit 8 is always 0 and bits 7 through 1 indicate the length of the contents. For example, a contents field of 16 octets is described by the L field as 00010110_2.

The long form is used for a longer contents field: greater than or equal to 128 and less than 2^{1008} octets. The indefinite form can be used when the element is a constructor. It has the value of 1000000_2 or 80_{16}. For the indefinite form, a special end-of-contents (EOC) element terminates the contents. The representation of EOC is 00000000_{16}.

The contents (value) is the substance of the element, i.e., the actual information. It is described in multiples of eight bits and is of variable length. The contents are interpreted based on the coding of the identifier (type) field. Therefore, the contents are interpreted as bit strings, octet strings, etc.

The format for the type field for the transfer syntax is based on the use of an 8-bit octet or extensions if large tag numbers are needed.

The field consists of three "subfields." A two bit class value is used to identify if the class is universal, context specific, private, or application specific. The P/C bit stands for primitive/constructed. This bit is set to a zero if the object is a simple type, it is set to 1 if it is a structured or complex type (that is to say, consisting of more than one type).

The remaining five bits contain the value for the tag. This could be coded as a universal number, it could be coded to represent context specific, or application tags.

Be aware that the type field must precede *each* value. Consequently, a considerable amount of overhead can be incurred with the use of the transfer syntax.

The Presentation Context Identifier (PCI)

The machines that communicate with the transfer syntax must be able to relate the abstract syntax coded with ASN.1 to a specific transfer syntax. This is performed through what is called a presentation context identifier (PCI). The PCI can be used to identify the context needed for the transfer between the two machines. It is also used as a means

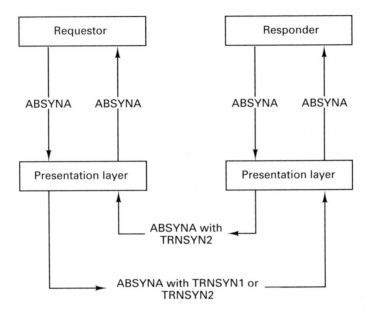

Figure 10–9. Negotiating syntaxes.

to negotiate syntax between the two entities. The sum of all these contexts are called the defined context set (DCS).

Figure 10–9 shows an example of how two entities could define and negotiate context sets as well as a transfer syntax. For example, an application layer entity (a requestor) can present a request to the presentation layer suggesting the use of a syntax named ABSYNA. The presentation layer decides that it can support ABSYNA with transfer syntax 1 (TRNSYN1). It codes this information in a message and sends it to the other entity.

The receiving presentation layer examines this traffic and decides that it can support either presentation syntax A. It sends this information to the application layer.

The application layer, in turn, returns a response. It informs its presentation layer that it supports ABSYNA. Consequently, the presentation layer relays this information back to the originating presentation layer in a response message confirming the use of transfer syntax 1.

The local presentation layer receives this traffic and then informs the application layer entity that ABSYNA will be used as the syntax for this connection.

THE DISTRIBUTED COMPUTING ENVIRONMENT (DCE)
AND THE DISTRIBUTED MANAGEMENT ENVIRONMENT (DME)

The DCE

The Distributed Computing Environment (DCE) is developed through the Open Software Foundation Inc. (OSF). It was released in 1990 and is intended to provide a transparent way to obtain distributed services from different types of architectures and applications. To achieve this goal, DCE isolates the user from concern about physical locations of network resources (for example, such as a file). A programmer writing an application program need only insert a few simple parameters to DCE. DCE accepts these parameters and locates the resources to meet the request of the application.

Figure 10–10 provides a functional view of the DCE. The user application is supported by the DCE cache manager. The cache manager makes use of a directory server through an RPC to determine the location of a security server. The security server authenticates the request, and returns a transaction to the DCE cache manager. Next, the cache manager sends another RPC to the file location server, which returns information about the location of the file. Then, in event 4, the cache manager uses yet another RPC to the security server to obtain a key to access the actual file server. If all goes well, the file server is accessed for the application's operation (event 5).

DCE is organized into two major components: (a) distributed services and (b) data sharing services. The distributed services functions are used to help programmers to use distributed resources through the use of threads, remote procedures, directory services, as well as security and time services. Data sharing services is considered to be a user of the distributed services. They provide for services such as accessing distributed files and distributed printing services.

The thread service is so named because it allows an application to issue multiple remote procedure calls (RPCs). In conventional RPC environments, the application issues one RPC and then waits for the reply. With threads, an application program can issue more than one RPC and thread takes care of the task of interleaving these calls and making certain that they are coordinated with the program. For example, a program could issue a call and instead of waiting for the results of that call to come about it could

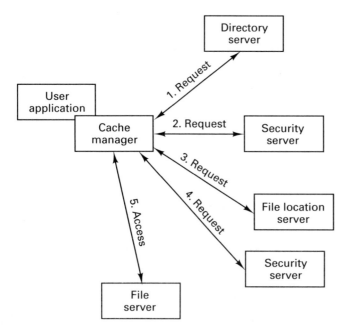

Figure 10–10. A functional view of the DCE.

immediately issue another call. This approach relieves significantly the tasks normally assigned to applications that are tasked with accessing multi servers and/or providing a variety of different calls to one server. Threads relieves the applications programmer of many nuances of RPC pitfalls.

As stated earlier, the DCE has a directory service which allows the application program to provide a "user-friendly" name to the system and directory services will identify the proper network elements with regard to the name. This part of DCE is organized into four components: (a) cell directory service (CDS), (b) the global directory agents (GDA), (c) the global directory service (DGS), and (d) the X/Open directory service (XDS).

The CDS is based on a cell concept (the term cell has no relationship to physical level cells in ATM and MAN technology). The idea here is for the CDS to examine the first part of a name in order to determine if the requested information resides in a local cell. If it does reside in a local cell, it is accessed and supplied. If not, it repasses the request to the GDA (which in some technologies would be called a name server). If the access is successful here, the information is provided to the client. The idea of this architecture is for the GDA to act as a gateway to other naming domains. The approach is quite similar to the Internet's domain name system (DNS) in which a GDA would roughly map to a foreign name server.

The DCE also provides for security services. This is implemented with what is called the distributed security service (DSS). The DSS is implemented through the Massachusetts Institute of Technology work under project Athena. This uses the Kerberos authentication system. Kerberos is a private key encryption system which provides three levels of security. The levels of security vary with the lowest requiring a relatively simple password authenticity with the upper levels requiring private encryption operations.

DCE also provides for a distributed file system service which allows an application to access a file across any node in the network (assuming that security and passwords have been properly authenticated). This service is called the distributed file system (DFS) and is based on the widely used Andrew file system (AFS). AFS is now sponsored by the Transarc Corporation.

The DME

The point has been made several times in this book about the difficulty of interfacing distributed heterogeneous computers operating systems and network protocols. To address this problem, the Open Software Foundation, Inc. (OSF) has published the Distributed Management Environment (DME). This specification establishes procedures for building application programming interfaces (API) that can enhance the development of application programs that operate in a distributed network.

DME is similar to the distributed computing environment (DCE) which is also sponsored by OSF. Both are used to build distributed systems. DME actually uses DCE as part of its architecture.

The basic idea of DME is to allow application programs that have been developed by separate enterprises or vendors to communicate with each other in local or remote machines. It supports management operations through the use of CMIP or SNMP. DME provides the foundation for distributed applications and does not require each developer (within a company or within a vendor shop) to recreate a distributed operating platform.

DME is based on object-oriented programming and design. This is the basic architecture for the system. In any object-oriented design, objects must be defined. With DME, an object is actually a software program which contains information that defines characteristics of a managed object (such as terminal server). The software contains any information that a network manager deems appropriate, such as fault, data, or configuration data.

The software programs also contain object methods. Methods in object-oriented design are simply routines that manipulate data from the managed devices (as in our example, a terminal server). The data can be received or sent from these software pieces. The data can also be displayed on screens.

DME is modular since each object is a stand alone entity. Consequently, DME can be expanded to meet individual enterprise requirements. As with any object-oriented design, DME is built to remain transparent to the user of DME.

As stated earlier, DME utilizes the services of DCE. Therefore, DME also has access to remote procedure calls, naming services, and security servers.

The software objects are created and stored on servers that are running DME. They are activated in a very simple manner by simply placing some type of software call into an application (for example, a C program) and using a DME application programming interface (API) call.

DME also allows the interworking of non-DME applications. In fact, servers can interact with each other using non-DME applications or DME applications. DME objects can be stacked on top of each other by allowing objects to make DME API calls.

DME is organized around object services, also called the framework. The framework consists of three major parts: (a) the management request broker (MRB), (b) the object server, and (c) event services. See Figure 10–11.

The MRB uses the DCE directory service to respond to an application's request for object operations (such as retrieving data from the terminal server or displaying information about terminal server operations). In so doing, DCE also provides security and authentication services for DME.

The selection of the MRB was somewhat controversial. OSF finally selected Hewlett Packard's OpenView and Tivoli System Inc.'s WizDom. There was considerable criticism over the ability of OSF to integrate these two technologies. HP's OpenView part of MRB supports either SNMP or CMIP for transferring the network management information to and from (in our example) the terminal server, which is the managed object. This is not revolutionary in that many vendors support this approach. However, the Tivoli part of the MRB makes use of what is known as an object server. For example, a user application can send a request to an object server through an API. This API is called objcall which can be invoked through a C program. The system then will locate an object server that is storing the target object. HP's portion of MRB includes consol-

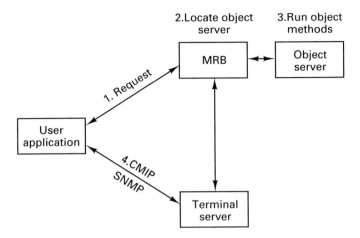

Chapter 10–11. Functional view of the DME.

idated management API (CM-API). This is also being used by the X/OPEN company LTD which will publish CM-API in its portability guide.

The object server actually contains the software objects. They receive a request from an application program and then activate the methods in the objects in accordance with the request-to-receive from the program. Presently, the object server supports calls from C++, ANSI-C, or IBM's object implementation language (OIL).

The third part of the object services is called event services. The function of event services is to provide a filtering feature (similar to a CMIP filter function) to actually generate CMIP traffic. Event services can be thought of as a CMIP M-event report (or an SNMP trap for that matter) in that they are unsolicited traffic created in a response to certain activities.

Another important aspect of DME is the user interface services. This service isolates the end user from all the intricacies of DME and will allow different enterprises to utilize a common interface. Hewlett Packard also provided this capability with its OpenView windows which is based on OSF's Motifs.

Using for example an X.500 directory service, the DME objects can be collected into powerful tools for the user community. With the use of DCE, authentication procedures and security methods can be invoked to insure the integrity of the directory. In addition, X.500 has considerable authentication features itself. Although, it should be recognized that X.500 *per se* is not a part of DME.

OSF also provides some additional auxiliary services. The software distribution utilities (again, developed at Hewlett Packard) supports downline loading of software to devices. The Massachusetts Institute of Technology's Palladium print system is also incorporated into DME. It provides for distributed printing and distributed printing services.

DME also has a software metering service which keeps account of the use of applications and how many copies of an application have been distributed. Obviously this is an important part of any distributed system to avoid legal problems.

SUMMARY

Remote procedure calls are used in many installations to support client-server operations. The process is simple on the surface, but must be given a great deal of thought, if implemented properly. ROSE is the international standard for remote procedure calls. DME and DCE are distributed applications that use the client-server and remote procedure call concepts.

Transfer syntax procedures are another key element in the distributed computing environment. They permit the negotiation of how the data are represented during the transfer process between the two machines.

11

Local Area Networks

INTRODUCTION

During the past few years, local area networks (LANs) have become one of the most publicized and controversial topics in the data communications industry. The publicity stems from *what* the LANs are purported to do for an organization; the controversy comes from *how* they are to do it. Due to the publicity, and in spite of the controversy, LANs are playing a prominent role in data communications, networks, and distributed processing.

LOCAL AREA NETWORKS: DEFINITIONS AND USAGE

The LAN is distinguished by the area it encompasses; it is geographically limited from a distance of several thousand feet to a few miles and is usually confined to a building or a plant housing a group of buildings. In addition to its local nature, the LAN has substantially higher transmission rates than networks covering large areas. Typical transmission speeds range from 1 to 30 Mbit/s. LANs do not ordinarily include the services of a common carrier. Most LANs are privately owned and operated, thus avoiding the regulations of the FCC or the state public utility commission. LANs are usually designed to transport data between computers, terminals, and other devices. Some LANs are capable of voice and video signaling as well. The LANs employ many of the techniques discussed in this book to manage data flow; for example, switching, digitizing schemes, data link controls, modulation, and multiplexing are often found in local area networks.

Local area networks have become popular for a number of reasons, the primary one is that most businesses transmit over 80% of their data and information locally; that is, within the local office or branch. This locality of data flow requires a transport system to move the data between the local machines. Moreover, many local applications (such as computer-to-computer traffic) require high transmission rates—certainly higher than the voice-grade technology (300 to 56,000 b/s) of the telephone carrier. LANs are seen by some organizations as a means to bypass local loops and all the problems inherent in the carrier's end-office connection.

Initially, LANs were developed as a means to tie together expensive resources for backup and sharing. For example, in the early 1960s vendors built channel adaptors to join CPUs and others developed interface boxes to allow smaller computers to act as "peripheral devices" to large mainframes. In the early 1970s, LANs were used to share memory and printers in order to expand the life of an organization's systems. Lately, LANs have been used to tie together components that have outgrown the centralized computer room.

LANs are also coming to the forefront as a means to implement distributed data processing (DDP) in an organization. As discussed in Chapter 10, DDP is a prevalent technology in the industry and local networks are one way to implement it.

Last but not least, LANs are seen as a path for increased office automation. LAN vendors are pushing their networks to sell their workstations such as word processors, printers, electronic files, and calendars. It is estimated that the vendor's revenue from office peripherals attached to the network will be 8 to 10 times that of the network itself. There is little debate that the white-collar office worker's environment can be made substantially more productive. The LAN-automated office is seen as one solution to the productivity problem.

MAJOR COMPONENTS OF A LOCAL AREA NETWORK

A LAN usually contains four major components (see Figure 11–1), which serve to transport data between end users.

1. A LAN's path may consist of coaxial TV cable or a coax baseband cable. Cable TV (CATV) coax is used on many networks because it has a high capacity, a very good signal-to-noise ratio, low signal radiation, and low error rates ($1 : 10^7$ to 10^{11}). Twisted

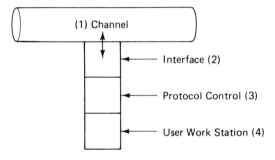

Figure 11–1. Major components in a local area network.

pair cable is also found in many LANs. Baseband coax is another widely used transmission path, giving high capacity as well as low error rates and low noise distortion. Optical fiber paths have increased in use, and their positive attributes virtually assure their place in the future. The immediate use of lightwave transmissions on local networks is point-to-point, high-speed connections of up to 10 miles. A transfer rate of over 300 Mbit/s can be achieved on this type of path. Infrared schemes using line of sight transmission are also used on the LAN path. Several vendors offer infrared equipment for modem and local loop replacement. Up to 100 kbit/s over 1-mile distances are possible with infrared schemes.

2. The interface between the path and the protocol logic can take several forms. It may be a single CATV tap, infrared diodes for infrared paths, or complex laser-emitting semiconductors for optical fibers. Some LANs provide regenerative repeaters at the interface; others use the interface as buffers for data flow and/or simple connections, like that of RS232-C.

3. The protocol control logic component controls the LAN and provides for the end user's access onto the network. Most LAN protocols employ methods and techniques discussed in Chapter 7. Other widely used LAN protocols are discussed later in this chapter.

4. Last of the four major components is the user workstation. It can be anything from a word processor to a mainframe computer. Several LAN vendors provide support for other vendor's products and certain layers of the OSI model.

LAN PROTOCOLS

Chapter 7 discussed data link controls (DLCs), which are used to manage the flow of data on a communications path (link). Local networks employ most of these concepts. For example, polling/selection, hub polling, contention, and time slots are all used in one form or another. Sliding windows and cyclic redundancy checks are also employed. Other approaches are also popular in the LAN industry. Consequently, they are discussed in detail here.

THE IEEE STANDARDS

The Institute of Electrical and Electronics Engineers (IEEE) publishes several widely accepted LAN recommended standards. These standards are very important because they encourage the use of common approaches for LAN protocols and interfaces. As a consequence, chip manufacturers are more willing to spend money to develop relatively inexpensive hardware to sell to (they hope) a large market. The IEEE LAN committees are organized as follows (also, see Figure 11–2):

IEEE 802.1   High level interface (and medium
              access control, MAC, bridges)

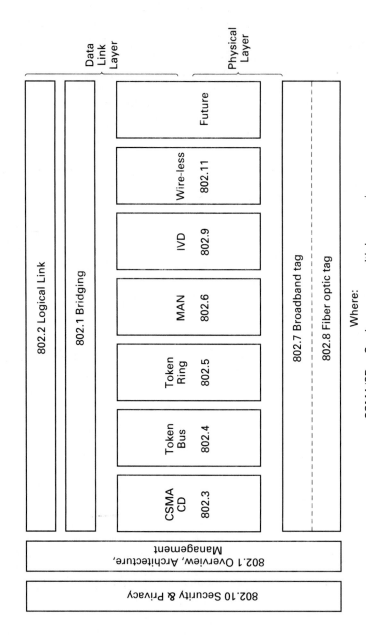

Figure 11–2. The IEEE 802 standards.

Where:

CSMA/CD = Carrier sense, multiple access/
collision detect
MAN = Metropolitan area network
IVD = Integrated voice data

The diagram shows the following blocks:

Data Link Layer includes: 802.2 Logical Link, 802.1 Bridging

Physical Layer includes: CSMA CD 802.3, Token Bus 802.4, Token Ring 802.5, MAN 802.6, IVD 802.9, Wire-less 802.11, Future

802.7 Broadband tag
802.8 Fiber optic tag

802.1 Overview, Architecture, Management

802.10 Security & Privacy

298

IEEE 802.2	Logical link control (LLC)
IEEE 802.3	Carrier sense multiple access/ collision detect (CSMA/CD)
IEEE 802.4	Token bus
IEEE 802.5	Token ring
IEEE 802.6	Metropolitan area networks
IEEE 802.7	Broadband LANs
IEEE 802.8	Fiber optic LANs
IEEE 802.9	Integrated data and voice networks
IEEE 802.10	Security
IEEE 802.11	Wireless networks

The IEEE standards are gaining wide acceptance. The European Computer Manufacturers Association (ECMA) voted to accept the 802.5 Token Ring as its standard. The NIST, the ISO, and ANSI have accepted these standards, and as we shall see, vendors and user groups are also using them.

In addition to the three basic standards of 802.3, 802.4, and 802.5 the IEEE also publishes the metropolitan area network (MAN) standard under the 802.6 number. An emerging standard, which is not yet complete, deals with integrated voice/data networks. It is identified with 802.9. The IEEE also sponsors standards dealing with broadband LANs under 802.7, optical fiber LANs under 802.8, and security aspects for LANs is 802.10. Wireless LANs, under 802.11, are also under development.

The 802.1 standard contains a number of standards. Network management is published in this standard as well as the 802.1 bridge.

Our discussions on LANs will revolve around the IEEE LAN 802 standards, which are widely used in the industry. Five of the 802 standards and one ANSI standard are germane to this chapter:

- 802.2: Logical link control
- 802.3: CSMA/CD
- 802.4: Token bus
- 802.5: Token ring
- 802.6: Metropolitan area networks
- Fiber-distributed data interface (FDDI)

Contention: CSMA/CD

A popular form of contention protocol is CSMA/CD. Its origin is the University of Hawaii's Aloha network. The Aloha network used a radio-based packet scheme in which the secondary stations independently transmitted to the master without regard to the other station's signals. The master station broadcasted at one band and all secondary stations at another. Since the secondary stations transmitted at random, frames often "collided" when transmitted from different stations at the same time. After such collisions, the stations waited a random time before retransmitting. The Aloha scheme yielded only 18.4% maximum channel utilization. The slotted Aloha scheme provided for more effective use of the channel. With this approach, each station was synchronized on a master clock and any transmitted packet began on a specific clock interval. Collisions still occurred, but slotted Aloha provided for 36.8% maximum channel utilization.

CSMA/CD uses some of the Aloha concepts. However, before transmitting a packet, a station "listens" for a signal on the path and does not transmit until the signal (that is, another station's packet) has passed through the cable. The sender then transmits its message. Collisions can still occur when two or more stations sense an idle channel and begin transmission. However, the CSMA/CD protocol monitors the channel for a collision during transmission. If a station's output does not match the signal on the channel, it knows a collision has occurred. The protocol then ensures that all other stations know of the collision. Some carrier sense protocols (like Aloha) provide for a central site to transmit a busy signal on a separate subchannel when it is receiving data. The CSMA/CD does not work this way, because it has no master station.

At each receiving station, the arrival of a frame is detected, which responds by synchronizing with the incoming signal. As the bits arrive, they are decoded and translated back into binary data.

The receiver checks the frame's destination address field to decide whether the frame should be received at its node. If so, it passes data to the user. It also checks for invalid frames by inspecting the frame check sequence to detect any damage to the frame enroute.

CSMA/CD networks work best on a bus, multipoint topology with bursty asynchronous transmission. All stations are attached to one path and monitor the signals on the channel through transceivers attached to the cable. Figure 11–3(a) shows a typical CSMA/CD bus structure.

Token Ring

Token-passing protocols can reside on a ring topology [see Figure 11–3(b)]. A *token* is a time slot or frame that is passed to the next station on the ring network. The frame contains the address of a station on the ring. The token is available to any station that has traffic to place in it. Upon using the token, the station sets a flag and places a destination address in the header to indicate the token is full. The token moves around the physical ring, is checked at each intermediate station for a relevant address, and is eventually passed to the destination node. The receiving station relays a receipt back to the originator by changing a bit flag in the token. The originating station must then make the token empty or free and pass it out onto the ring.

As with any protocol, some form of window control is needed with the token-passing scheme. For example, in IEEE 802.5, multiple tokens are not allowed, and a station is not allowed to use the same token twice. Duplicate tokens are not allowed due to the complexity of accounting for the tokens.

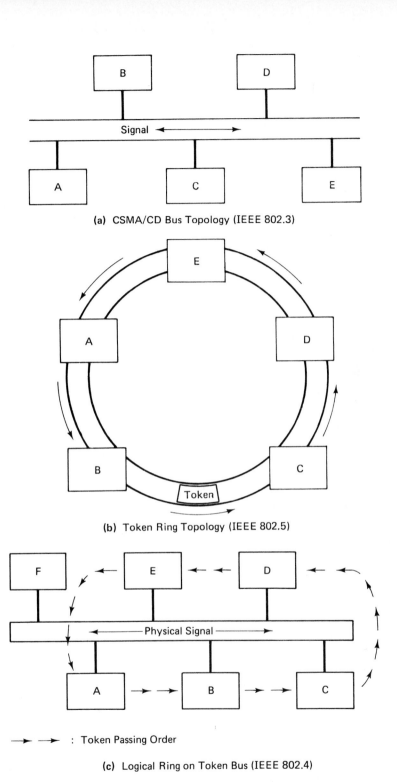

(a) CSMA/CD Bus Topology (IEEE 802.3)

(b) Token Ring Topology (IEEE 802.5)

⟶ ⟶ : Token Passing Order

(c) Logical Ring on Token Bus (IEEE 802.4)

Figure 11-3. Local area network topologies.

The 802.5 token ring uses priorities to establish which station is allowed to use the ring. The stations have priority established for access to the network. This is achieved by placing priority indicators within the token.

The process is illustrated in Figure 11–3(b), in which five stations are attached to a priority ring. Let us assume station A has a priority access of 1 (lowest priority), stations B and D have priorities of 2, and stations C and E have priorities of 3 (highest priority).

The token is passed around the ring from node to node. As the full (busy) token circles the ring, the stations vie for its use on the *next* pass around the ring by placing a request in a reservation field in the token. In this particular situation, if all the stations have data to transmit, the token is actually exchanged every other pass between stations C and E, since they have the highest priority on the ring. However, in most situations, the higher-priority stations will likely not be transmitting with every pass. Consequently, the priority ring configuration allows the lower-priority stations to seize the ring in the event the higher-priority stations are not active.

Token Bus

The token-bus topology is illustrated in Figure 11–3(c). Using a bus path, the stations pass the tokens by placing the address of the next logical recipient in the header of the packet. The signal passes along the bus and is physically monitored by all stations, but the token is made available to a receiving station based on the sending stations' placement of a station address in the destination header. In the event a token is passed to a failed node, the originator will time out, retransmit a given number of times, and eventually transmit to a successor station.

The token (right to transmit) is passed from stations in descending numerical order based on station address. When a station hears a token frame addressed to itself, it may transmit data frames. When a station has completed transmitting data frames, it passes the token to the next station in the logical ring. When a station has the token, it may temporarily delegate its right to transmit to another station by sending a request-with-response data frame.

After each station has completed transmitting any data frames it may have, the station passes the token to its successor by sending a token control frame.

After sending the token frame, the station listens for evidence that its successor has heard the token frame and is active. If the sender hears a valid frame following the token, it assumes that its successor has the token and is transmitting. If the token sender does not hear a valid frame following its token pass, it attempts to assess the station of the network and may implement measures to pass around the problem station by establishing a new successor. For more serious faults, attempts are made to reestablish the ring.

In Figure 11–3(c), note that the access to the system is always sequential. Under normal circumstances the access rights pass from station to station. Also, a station can receive data and respond to the token holder without being part of the logical ring. For example, station E can receive frames but cannot initiate traffic, since it is not part of the token-passing sequence.

Stations are added to an 802.4 bus by an approach called response windows:

- While holding the token, a node issues a solicit-successor frame. The address in the frame is between it and next successor station.
- Token holder waits one window time (slot time, equal to twice the end-to-end propagation delay).
- No response: Token transferred to successor node.
- Response: A requesting node sends a set successor frame and token holder changes its successor node address.
- Requester receives token, sets its addresses, and proceeds.

A node can drop out of the transmission sequence. Upon receiving a token, it sends a set successor frame to the predecessor, which orders it to give the token hereafter to its successor.

Metropolitan Area Network

The metropolitan area network standards are sponsored by the IEEE, ANSI, and the regional Bell Operating Companies. Although 802.6 was designed initially for a LAN to MAN support service, the telephone companies see it as a technology to provide for interconnecting LANs to its central office and even the interconnection of telephone switching facilities (see Figure 11–4).

802.6 also forms the basis for the switched multimegabit data service (SMDS), which is now being touted as the solution "WAN (wide area network) bottleneck." Therefore, the high-capacity LAN internetworking problem is solved with the use of 802.6 technology for the WAN connecting the LANs.

The MAN standard is organized around a topology and technique called *dual queue/dual bus* (DQDB). This term means that the topology uses two buses. Each of

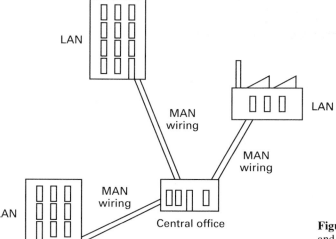

Figure 11–4. Relationship of LAN and MAN.

- Two unidirectional dual buses; capacity twice that of each bus
- Buses independent in the transfer of traffic
- Looped bus or open bus configurations
- DQDB independent of physical layer
  - ANSI D3: 77.736 Mbit/s over coax or fiber
  - ANSI SONET STS-3c: 155.520 Mbit/s over single-mode fiber
  - CCITT G-703: 34.368 Mbit/s or 139.264 Mbit/s over metallic medium
- Access control:
  - Prearbitrated (PA) for isochronous services
  - Queued arbitrated (QA)

Figure 11–5.   Dual queue dual/bus attributes.

these buses transmits traffic in one direction only. The implementation for MAN provides for transfer rates from 34 to 150 Mbit/s. The principal attributes of DQDB are summarized in Figure 11–5.

The DQDB provides for two types of access. One access is called *prearbitrated services*, which guarantees a certain amount of "bandwidth" that is useful for isochronous services such as voice and video. The second service is called *queued arbitrated service* and it is based on demand and is designed to accommodate bursted services such as data transmission.

A MAN is designed with two unidirectional busses. Each bus is independent of the other in the transfer of traffic. The topology can be designed as an open configuration or a closed configuration. Figure 11–6 shows the two alternatives.

Fiber-Distributed Data Interface

The fiber-distributed data interface was developed under the auspices of ANSI. ANSI subcommittee X3T9.5 coordinated the working groups that developed this standard. FDDI provides a standard for a high-capacity LAN using optical fibers.

The standard operates with a 100 Mbit/s rate. Dual rings are provided for the LAN so the full speed is 200 Mbit/s (see Figure 11–7). The protocol is a timed token procedure operating on the dual ring. The standard defines multimode optical fiber, although the ANSI is nearing completion of the description of transmission for single-mode optical fiber as well.

FDDI is quite resilient and provides for failure recovery by bypassing problem nodes. It also has station management capabilities. Logical link control operates above the MAC layer for additional optional features.

Due to the high capacity 100 Mbit/s technology, FDDI is a 10-fold increase over the Ethernet's 802.3. Obviously it has an even greater capacity than the 4 Mbit/s 802.5 LAN. Moreover, FDDI permits the LAN topology to extend up to 200 km (124 miles).

A typical FDDI network consists of a dual ring, which supports the transmission and reception of traffic through concentrators. Concentrators attach directly to the dual ring (both to the primary and secondary ring). The concentrator also connects to the user devices. These devices are defined as dual attachment stations (DASs) and single attachment stations (SASs). In either case, concentrators are used as the ring attachment.

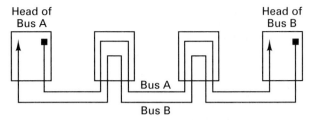

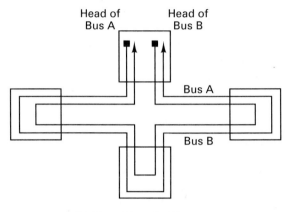

(b) Closed bus Architecture

Figure 11–6. The MAN bus architecture.

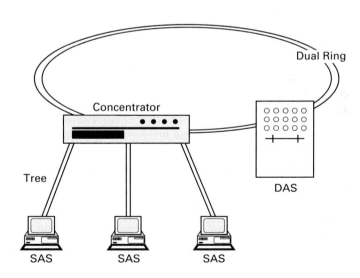

SAS = Single attachment stations
DAS = Dual attachment stations

Figure 11–7. FDDI network devices.

DASs connect to both rings or to the primary ring through the concentrator, whereas SASs attach only to the primary ring through a concentrator.

Logical Link Control

The IEEE efforts have emphasized the need to keep the OSI and 802 specifications as compatible as possible. The 802 committees split the data link layer into two sublayers: medium access control and logical link control. MAC encompasses 802.3, 802.4, 802.5, and others. The LLC includes 802.2. This sublayer was implemented to make the LLC sublayer independent of a specific LAN access method. The LLC sublayer is also used to provide an interface into or out of the specific MAC protocol.

The MAC/LLC split provides several attractive features. First, it controls access to the shared channel among the autonomous user devices. Second, it provides for a decentralized (peer-to-peer) scheme that reduces the LAN's susceptibility to errors. Third, it provides a more compatible interface with wide area networks, since LLC is a subset of the HDLC superset. Fourth, LLC is independent of a specific access method; MAC is protocol specific. This approach gives an 802 network a flexible interface with workstations and other networks.

LLC can be implemented in a number of ways on a LAN. At its most basic level, it is used to interface the LAN functions with the user applications. All IEEE 802 LANs require the use of LLC for this interface.

LLC can also be used for some rather elaborate connection management procedures and flow control operations. For example, one "type of LLC" allows the creation of connections between user stations as well as the use of positive and negative acknowledgments, sequencing number, and flow control operations with sliding windows.

If these functions seem excessive for certain user applications, LLC can be configured to perform minimal levels of service. In this configuration, LLC simply provides a minimal interface between the user application and MAC.

At the onset of the IEEE 802 work, it was recognized that a connection-oriented system would limit the scope and power of a LAN. Consequently, two connectionless models are now specified:

- Unacknowledged connectionless model
- Acknowledged connectionless model

Let us consider the reason for this approach. First, many local applications do not need the data integrity provided by a connection-oriented network. As examples: (a) Sensor equipment can afford to lose occasional data, since the sensor readings typically occur quite frequently, and the data loss does not adversely affect the information content. (b) Inquiry–response systems, such as point-of-sale, usually perform acknowledgment at the application level. These systems do not need connection-oriented services at the lower levels.

Second, high-speed application processes cannot tolerate the overhead in establishing and disestablishing the connections. The problem is particularly severe in the

LAN, with its high-speed channels and low error rates. Many LAN applications require fast setups with each other. Others require very fast communications between the DTEs.

An acknowledged connectionless service is useful for a number of reasons. Consider the operations of a LAN in a commercial bank. A data link protocol usually maintains state tables, sequence numbers, and windows for each station on the link. It would be impractical to provide this service for every station on the bank's local network. Yet, workstations like the bank's automated teller machines (ATMs) require they be polled for their transactions. The host computer must also be assured that all transactions are sent and received without errors. The data are too important to use a protocol that does not provide acknowledgments.

All 802 networks must provide unacknowledged connectionless service (type 1). Optionally, connection-oriented service can be provided (type 2). Type 1 networks provide no ACKs, flow control, or error recovery; type 2 networks provide connection management, ACKs, flow control, and error recovery. Type 3 networks provide no connection setup and disconnect, but they do provide for immediate acknowledgment of data units. Most type 1 networks use a higher-level protocol (that is, transport layer) to provide connection management functions. Figure 11–8 summarizes the LLC types.

Role of the Personal Computer

The personal computer has become a widely used device in local area networks. It serves a variety of support functions, such as workstations, file/print servers, and LAN controllers. Many LANs are designed solely to operate exclusively with personal computers.

The communications characteristics of personal computers bear many similarities to larger computers. However, differences exist that must be considered when using the PC for data communications. First, personal computers are usually asynchronous. Most PC vendors have not built their communications board (port) with the wires necessary for carrying the timing signals required for synchronous transmission. Some boards are available today that provide for synchronous systems.

It is possible for PCs to communicate with synchronous systems by placing an asynchronous-to-synchronous adapter unit between the PC and its modem. The adapter provides for signals to achieve clocking between the personal computer and the modem (pins 15 and 17 of RS232-C and pins 113 and 114 of V.24 interfaces).

Most PC modems use frequency modulation (FM) or phase modulation (PM) to

Types of Operations

1. Connectionless
2. Connection-oriented
3. Acknowledged connectionless

Classes of Operation

I. Connectionless
II. Connection-oriented and connectionless
III. Acknowledged connectionless and connection-oriented
IV. I, II, & III

Figure 11–8. LLC types and classes.

carry the signal across the telephone channel. The most common approach is known as *frequency shift keying* (FSK) used with split-stream modems. The concept is quite simple; two different frequency tones are used to represent either the 0 or 1 bit.

Almost all PCs use full-duplex modems as well. Utilizing the FSK concept, the full-duplex modems use four different tones, two tones for the transfer of 1s and 0s in one direction and two for transfer of 1s and 0s in the opposite direction.

The majority of PC modems operate at 1,200 and 2,400 bit/s. The 2,400-bit/s modem is a relative newcomer. These are full-duplex dial-up asynchronous modems and are V.22*bis* compatible.

Many PCs use "smart modems." These modems have built-in intelligence that allows the PC to control functions such as program-controlled dialing. Smart modems are controlled through the use of special characters transmitted from the PC. The characters command the modem to perform communications functions.

The PC is often used as a tool to tie into the company's larger-scale computer system (mainframe computers). Several reasons exist for linking PCs to mainframes. First, the PC provides a valuable tool for distributing the work load onto less expensive machines to perform simple tasks. Second, the PC often needs to use the processing power of the mainframe. For example, the PC cannot readily perform complex calculations. Third, the PC operator may wish to share the software and the data bases of the mainframe computer. Sharing is quite common in almost all offices today where users perform certain calculations with their own PC, but go to the mainframe to obtain support for interaction with other applications and data bases.

Some personal computer literature indicates that the versions of the vendors' various products for linking to other computers are compatible. Unfortunately, this is not always the case. The vendor often modifies data communications packages to enable the package to run efficiently on specific hardware and operating systems. Testing a product before committing to purchase it is a prudent approach when acquiring a PC data communications package.

Many PC/LAN configurations use CSMA/CD (802.3) or token ring (802.5) protocols. These techniques are explained in earlier sections of this chapter. However, due to the extensive use of CSMA/CD and Ethernet in personal computer local networks (and large-scale computer systems), it is described in more detail in the following section.

OTHER LOCAL AREA NETWORKS

Many local networks are available today. All use either baseband, broadband, or both technologies, and the majority of the networks use some form of CSMA/CD, token passing, or the conventional polling/selection protocol. Several of the vendors have announced support for selected layers of the ISO Open Systems Interconnection (OSI) model such as X.25 and X.21. The networks discussed in this section are representative of what is available in the market today. These products have also been selected because they illustrate the major features of LANs that were discussed earlier in the chapter.

Ethernet

Ethernet is one of the better-known LANs and has one of the larger user bases of LANs. It was developed by the Xerox Corporation at its Palo Alto Laboratories in the 1970s and was modeled after the Aloha network. In 1980 DEC and the Intel Corporation jointly published a local area network specification based on the Ethernet concepts.[1]

The IEEE 802.3 Standard is quite similar to Ethernet, with some minor differences in encoding, formats, and terminology. We cover Ethernet in detail here due to its widespread use in the industry.

Ethernet's primary characteristics include the CSMA/CD protocol and baseband signaling on a shielded coaxial cable. The data rate is 10 Mbit/s, with a provision of up to 1,024 stations on the path. It uses a layering concept, somewhat similar to the low levels of the ISO model, and transmits user data in frames or packets. Ethernet uses Manchester encoding (see Chapter 8); at a 10-Mbit/s rate, each bit cell is 100 ns long (1 sec/10,000,000 bps = 0.0000001). Since the Manchester code provides for a signal transition within each bit cell, the Ethernet signal is self-clocking.

The network architecture is shown in Figure 11–9. It consists of the coaxial cable, terminators, transceivers, controllers, and workstations. The cable can be as long as 550 feet, with extensions of 1,650 feet using one or two repeaters. The terminators complete the electrical circuit. The transceivers transmit and receive signals, detect packet collisions, and maintain signal quality on the bus. The controllers provide for collision management, translation of signals (encoding/decoding), and other CSMA/CD tasks. The workstations are the end-user devices, such as word processors, computers, and terminals.

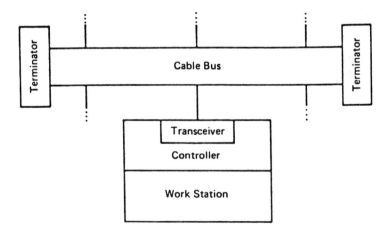

Figure 11–9. Ethernet architecture.

[1]*The Ethernet, A Local Area Network*, Version 1.0, September 30, 1980. Published by Digital Equipment Corporation, Maynard, Mass., Intel Corporation, Santa Clara, Calif., and Xerox Corporation, Stanford, Conn.

The Ethernet packet contains six fields (see Figure 11–10). The preamble is sent before the data to provide for channel stabilization and synchronization. The preamble is a 64-bit pattern of recurring 10s, with the last two bits coded as 11. The last bits indicate the end of the preamble and the beginning of the data. Upon reception of the double 1, successive bits are passed into the station.

The destination and source address identify the receiving and sending stations, respectively. Each address is 48 bits in length. The destination address can also be a multicast-group address (a group of logically related stations) or a broadcast address (all stations on the Ethernet).

The type field of 16 bits is used by end users (and not the Ethernet protocol) at a higher level in the local network. It is defined at the Ethernet level to provide for a uniform convention between higher levels. The data field contains user data with any arbitrary bit sequence allowed. The frame check sequence field provides for a cyclic redundancy value (CRC, see Chapter 7). The CRC field is 32 bits in length.

Ethernet is designed around the three layers depicted in Figure 11–11. The user or client layer is the workstation; the data link layer contains the data encapsulation and link management functions; the physical layer provides for data encoding/decoding and channel access. These layers will be used to illustrate how Ethernet transports packets and manages data flow.

Transmission of packet.   The client layer passes data to data encapsulation, which constructs the frame, calculates the frame check field, and appends it to the frame for error detection. The frame is passed to link management. This sublayer monitors the carrier signal on the bus and defers to passing traffic. When the channel is free, link management waits a brief period and sends a stream of bits to the physical layer. Data encoding first sets up and sends out the preamble to allow receivers and repeaters to synchronize clocks and other circuitry. It then translates the binary bit stream into Manchester-phase encoding. The encoder drives the transmit part of the transceiver cable. The channel access sublayer (transceiver) actually generates the electrical signals for the coaxial cable. In addition, it simultaneously monitors the bus for any collision.

Receiving of packet.   The receiving channel access detects the incoming signal and turns on a carrier sense signal for use by the data link layer. It synchronizes with the incoming preamble and passes the bits up to the next sublayer. Data decoding translates the Manchester code back to binary data, discards the preamble, and sends the data to the data link layer. Link management has detected the carrier sense from the trans-

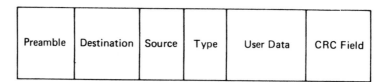

Figure 11–10.   Ethernet packet.

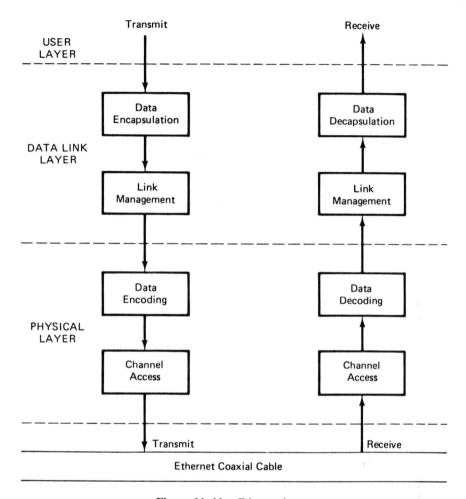

Figure 11–11. Ethernet layers.

ceiver (channel access sublayer). It receives the bits from the physical layer. Upon the carrier sense signal going off, it passes the frame to data decapsulation. This function examines the destination address field and, if appropriate, passes the frame to the client layer. It also checks the frame for damage and sends an error status code to the user station.

Handling collisions.   A station's signal can collide with another station. For example, if station A's signal does not reach station B before station B transmits a packet, then station B's link management sublayer has not activated its deferral logic. The signals collide. This period of vulnerability is called the *collision window* and is determined by the total propagation time on the channel.

A collision is noticed by the transmit side of the channel access sublayer. The transceiver "listens to itself" and, upon detecting the collision, turns on the collision detect signal. The collision detect signal is sensed by the transmit side of link management, which transmits a bit sequence called a *jam*. The jam ensures that all transmitting stations are aware of the collision (in case the collision is very short). Transmit link management then terminates the transmission and randomly schedules a retransmission. Excessively busy conditions will trigger exponential back-offs from the channel by the link management logic.

Receiving stations do not have their collision detection signal turned on by the collision. Rather, receive link management notes the fragmentary frames that resulted from the collision and simply discards these frames. A collision fragment is designed to be shorter than the shortest valid frame.

AT&T Information System Network

AT&T has also entered the LAN market with its Information System Network (ISN). Figure 11–12 illustrates the major components of ISN. The system employs three networks inside a central controller. One network, the contention bus, is dedicated to handling the access to the network. The other two subnetworks consist of a transmit and a receive bus. All three systems operate at 8.64 Mbit/s. The purpose of the transmit and receive buses is to provide a high-speed interface to remote components, such as multiplexers, or DTEs, such as computers. The two input/output modules utilize optical fibers for the transmission media. The central controller directs the traffic into and out of the system through the use of a multiplexing arrangement. The DTEs are attached to ISN through conventional interfaces such as EIA-232-D. The contention bus and its associated logic provide the assignment of transmission time slots to the attached DTEs. The actual allocation of the traffic depends on the nature of the request from the DTE and the amount of traffic to be handled.

The multiplexing controller allocates 50-ms (0.050-sec) time slots. These short data bursts interleave many packets in a short period of time, thereby diminishing the chances of contention. AT&T states that an ISN can switch up to 48,000 of these small 180-bit packets per second. This equates to the 8.64-Mbit/s rate of all three internal systems.

End-user DTEs are attached through plug-in modules into the system. Up to 42 plug-in modules representing 336 local devices are supported by a central controller.

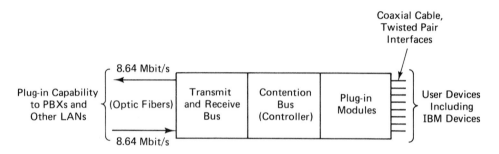

Figure 11–12.   AT&T's ISN.

Multiple controllers can be attached to each other. AT&T also states that a fully loaded ISN will support up to 1,680 end-user devices. The configuration with this capability would require one central controller with four remote concentrators attached to it.

AT&T has taken a major step into IBM's arena with the ISN enhancements to provide BSC or SDLC device attachment to its ISN. Another enhanced package supports the direct attachment of 3,270-family devices. AT&T provides these features, not only for the ISN, but for its System 75 and System 85 PBXs.

The AT&T product line also provides support into T1 digital trunks, Ethernet, DMI (digital multiplex interface), and the Dataphone digital service (DDS). Several special adapters allow a wide variety of other interfaces.

IBM Token Ring

In 1985 IBM finally announced its major entry into the LAN field with the IBM token ring. (The personal-computer-based LAN PC network was introduced in 1984.)

The IBM topology permits several rings to be attached through the bridges (see Figure 11–13). The bridges are then connected by a backbone ring. The bridge will provide a cross-ring network function by copying frames that are forwarded from one ring to another ring. The bridges also provide for speed translations if rings are operating at different data rates. Moreover, each ring still retains its own capacity and will continue operating in the event another ring on the bridge fails. Thus, the IBM token ring approach provides resiliency to station and link failure.

The backbone ring can be constructed with twisted pair cable operating with 4 Mbits/s or with optical fiber operating at 16 Mbits/s. In addition, the backbone ring can operate with a broadband channel such as a CATV cable, which would allow the ring to be connected into other networks or even video systems. The IBM token ring can use twisted pair, coaxial cable, or optical fibers. The combination of wiring schemes and the token ring access control allows the use of these media in the same local network. For example, optical fiber can be used along with twisted pair media.

The token ring uses a combination of star and ring topology. The physical ring provides for IEEE 802.5 unidirectional point-to-point transmission of signals to/from up to 250 workstations attached to one ring. The rings can be connected through several bridges that can also radiate through a building or office complex. IBM's principal reasons for developing this topology were (1) the ease in adding stations and links and (2) the simplification of troubleshooting problems on the links.

Each station attached to the ring is provided with a ring interface adaptor. This adaptor handles the basic line protocol and physical interface functions associated with any network. For example, the adaptor recognizes frames and buffer frames, generates and recognizes tokens, provides error detection, performs address decoding, and also provides for link error detection.

Workstations can be in any location throughout a building. The stations are connected to the network through wiring lobes. These lobes are really nothing more than two pairs of conductors for the send and receive channels, and they are connected to wall outlets for each of the workstations. In turn, the connectors are attached to wiring concentrators, which can also be located throughout a building.

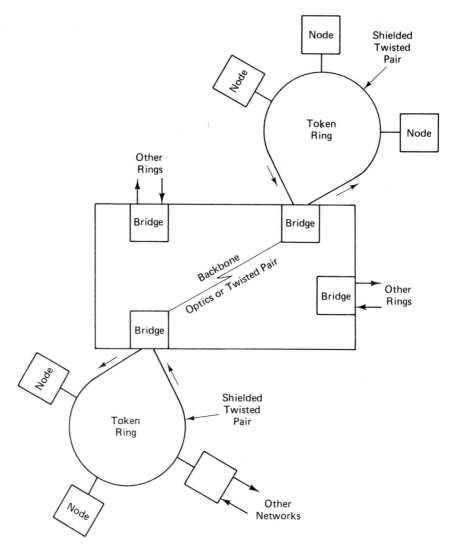

Figure 11–13. IBM token ring.

The announcement of IBM's use of twisted pair cable for its token ring has created some confusion in the industry. IBM does indeed support the conventional telephone-type unshielded twisted pair. The token ring permits each node to utilize this technology. This can be attractive for small business or users who wish to use the wiring already installed in a building. It should be noted, however, that unshielded telephone twisted pair cable is subject to more problems than other kinds of media. Consequently, IBM (while supporting unshielded twisted pair) also offers a higher-quality cable connection, which is called a *data grade cable*. If the user chooses the conventional telephone wiring, the maximum number of stations that can be attached to the ring is 72. In addition, no mix is permitted on the individual ring.

All stations must use the same type of media. However, this does not preclude two rings using twisted pair connecting to each other through the wiring closet from which the wiring concentrators could use the higher-grade cable themselves. Bear in mind that the twisted pair is more subject to noise, clocking, jitter, and decay problems, but the reduced cost may lead the user to choose twisted pair cable. It should also be noted that the use of the twisted pair limits the distance of the devices of no more than 45 meters to the wiring closet.

IBM has chosen to replace its synchronous data link control at the link level. In place of SDLC for the token ring network, IBM uses the IEEE 802.2 standard logical link control. This change was necessary because SDLC uses the HDLC subset normal response mode (NRM). With this technique, no peer-to-peer communications is provided on the channel. Rather, a primary station is responsible for maintaining traffic control with other stations. However with LLC, the asynchronous balanced mode (ABM) is established, which allows peer-to-peer communications between any stations on the local channel. This means that any station can send traffic at any time, independently of any commands coming from any other station.

Examples of Personal Computers and Local Area Networks

Several personal computer LANs are available today. In this section, we discuss several well-known LAN PC products (PC is used in the generic sense). They are chosen because they are representative of the offerings in the industry.

Three Com provides several Ethernet-type products called EtherSeries for personal computers. Etherlink is the data communications products of the Etherseries and uses a CSMA/CD protocol. Ethershare is a file server support package. It manages disks at the disk volume level and provides for multiple use into the files.

Ethershare provides other functions such as print support. This support package is called EtherPrint. EtherPrint is a powerful print serving function, and it allows users to perform multiple printing simultaneously without interfering with one another. The server keeps separate buffers on the disk and interleaves the various users onto the printer as they close their files.

Several LAN PC vendors have adopted the ARCNET System from Datapoint. For example, ARCNET-PC is offered by Standard Microsystems Corporation. It operates at 2.5 Mbit/s and connects to an ARCNET LAN. The network supports 255 personal computers as well as numerous options for sharing disks and printers. Nestar offers another ARCNET-like system called The PLAN 4000. It also operates at 2.5 Mbit/s and supports 255 workstations. PLAN 4000 has extensive server support for disk, printers 3778, 3270, SNA, and Telex. It also provides a gateway server to allow one PLAN 4000 network to communicate with another PLAN 4000 network. In addition to these two vendors, other organizations provide an ARCNET system. Davong provides the multi-link LAN and 3M provides LAN/1. These systems operate at 2.5 Mbit/s over coaxial cable and support 255 workstations.

PCnet is another widely used LAN for personal computers. PCnet was developed by Orchid Technology; however, the product is available from other vendors as well. They are all basically the same system. In addition to Orchid, AST Research and Santa Clara Systems offer a PCnet product. PCnet is very similar to the Ethernet and IEEE 802.3 CSMA/CD systems discussed earlier in this chapter. Unlike the Three Com system just discussed, the PCnet requires an external Ethernet transceiver. Three Com offers its transceiver on the Three Com personal computer board. PCnet is offered as a baseband product; however, the broadband version of the system is available and is named the NET/1 Personal Connection.

IBM entered the personal computer LAN market with the introduction of the Cluster Network. The network was introduced in 1983 but has not achieved much success. A more notable IBM entry into the LAN arena is its PC Network system. The product uses coaxial cable and operates at 2 Mbit/s. It uses a CSMA/CD protocol and supports file, print 3270, and gateway servers. It operates with the MS-DOS operating system. PC Network uses a broadband approach that permits a more flexible operation than most of the other LAN PC systems utilizing the CSMA/CD baseband technology. The IBM PC Network was developed by Sytek. It also manufactures some of IBM's local PC Network boards. Sytek also leases this protocol to other vendors and users. As mentioned before, PC Network will interface into IBM's token ring.

A widely used product is IBM Netbios (Network Basic Input/Output System). Working with the personal computer operating system MS-Dos 3.1, Netbios allows the interfacing of any LAN, regardless of the hardware used. Netbios is destined to become an industry standard.

SUMMARY

Local area networks have become the preferred technology for supporting the distribution and sharing of resources in the office and campus environment. With few exceptions, vendors are using the IEEE and ANSI standards for their products.

As LANs grow in use, technologies, such as 802.6 and switched multimegabit data service (SMDS) (and in the not too distant future, SONET), will provide the wide area backbone between the LANs.

12

Managing Distributed Systems

INTRODUCTION

This chapter examines the pros and cons of distributed networks and describes a model for managing distributed resources.

Distributed Systems

Distributed systems have become commonplace today. Vendors regularly announce products that support distributed processing and user applications are rapidly adopting distributed techniques. Several years ago, the idea was viewed with considerable skepticism, considered by many to be too complex for practical implementation. However, the changing data-processing environment has created attractive costs and benefits for distributed processing and has provided the impetus for both user and vendor to support the concept. In today's environment, the question is becoming less of "Should we distribute?" and more of "How do we distribute?"

Distributed data processing (DDP) is defined as follows:

- In contrast to the conventional single, centralized site, processing is organized around multiple processing elements (PEs). A PE is a computer or other device capable of performing automated, intelligent functions.
- PEs are organized on a functional and/or geographic basis.
- Distributed elements cooperate in the support of user requirements.

- Connection of processing elements is through common carriers or private links.
- It entails the dispersion of hardware and/or software and/or data to multiple PEs.

Distribution is *not* decentralization. The latter connotes dispersion with no integration of the parts to the whole. Distributed processing provides functional or geographic dispersion, yet the dispersed parts are integrated into a whole coherent system. One of the greatest pitfalls an organization faces in dealing with DDP is the mistaken belief that decentralization is the same as distribution. Decentralized systems make good sense for certain organizations; for others, the approach can be very disruptive and expensive. Both are viable options as long as it is recognized which approach is being implemented. This point will be emphasized throughout this chapter.

WHY GO DISTRIBUTED?

Given the definition of a distributed system, one might question why an organization would choose the distributed approach. After all, its description seems to imply increased complexity. The seeming anomaly can be answered by an examination of certain events that have taken place in the industry during the past decade.

Several years ago, the idea of economies of scale encouraged the industry to develop large, centralized computers. All processing for user departments was performed by one or a few large mainframe machines. Grosch's law held that the cost of an executed machine instruction was inversely proportional to the square of the size of the machine. Hence, the larger the system, the better the economies of scale.

Grosch's law seemed to hold for some time but other factors were at work. For example, the increased complexity of the large centralized computers resulted in diminishing returns in using the larger systems. It is quite easy to see the diminishing returns problems in operation today. The large-scale centralized systems are indeed powerful; some machines execute more than 80 million instructions per second (mips). These systems have been generalized to accommodate a wide variety of user needs and applications. Yet the machines are often overkill for many user systems. The large-scale systems have elaborate and complex operating systems designed to perform many functions, but not many of them in an optimum manner. A simple user inquiry (transaction) may require the execution of tens of thousands of instructions on these machines. The resulting overhead negates or diminishes much of their raw processing power.

The large centralized systems suffer from overgeneralization—they do many things but none of them very well. The revolutionary microelectronic age has given genesis to the notion that specialized machines can perform fewer functions in a cost-effective manner and perform them very well. These machines are being used increasingly for dedicated applications. The issue of generalization versus specialization was partially resolved by the extraordinary cost and performance benefits of small, inexpensive computers. Moreover, auxiliary storage costs such as disks have also been decreasing significantly. Redundant data and duplicate data bases are not so much a cost issue today as they are an issue of coordination and control. Consequently, local storage of data is a very viable option today, especially if large-scale disk units are used.

Another major reason for the growth of distributed processing has been pressure from users to gain control of some of the computing power in the organization. In many organizations, the users are not satisfied with the services received from the applications development staff. Projects are often late. Typically there is a backlog of applications to be developed and, in many instances, the backlog is increasing. The maintenance costs for applications running on large-scale systems are truly extraordinary. One would be amazed at the amount of time a programmer must spend in simply keeping the applications system synchronized with the changing mainframe environment. Weekly and sometimes daily changes are made to job control language, data-base control blocks, job streams, and software libraries. Users do not understand the environment and do not understand why a programmer must spend so much time in system maintenance. (The smaller and simpler minicomputers and personal computers require less of this kind of maintenance.)

Users have become disenchanted with the closed-shop approach. The *closed shop* means the users are given limited personal access to the large computer. (It is too complex for them to operate anyway.) More important, in a closed shop the user has little input to or control of the data-processing department. It is believed by many that the centralized data-processing department is not appreciative of user needs nor responsive to their requirements. Consequently, many users believe the large centralized environment militates against taking full advantage of the real power of the computer.

Financial factors are also at work within the organization. There are increasing cost-related and profit-related pressures to gain more control of information systems management by user departments. The users of today are much more knowledgeable and sophisticated than they were several years ago. They understand that information is power and that control of the information resource is important to their performance and even their bottom-line profit. Many users believe their professional destiny is greatly dependent on the computer and they want more control over their destiny.

Nowhere is the distributed processing trend more evident than in the use of the personal computer. Some organizations are literally bringing hundreds of these machines into their daily operations. These machines are quite powerful and flexible and are seen by many as a revolutionary automation tool.

Perhaps it appears as if centralization and the supercomputer have been failures, but that is not the case. The large-scale centralized computer is absolutely essential for many applications today. In fact, the industry needs even more powerful computers to solve many of its problems and they are needed to increase productivity of many of our offices. Large mainframes will also play a major role in the DDP arena by managing large complex data bases. The point to be made is that the supercomputer and large-scale mainframes are not needed nor suited for many applications that are currently running on them.

The personal computer has provided the foundation for a significant transformation in the data-processing industry. Distributed data processing will be one end result of this transformation. DDP is affecting practically everyone. Just witness the effects of advances in microelectronics and data communications. Hardly a day goes by without our using a computer or a computer network. The use of an electronic game, the telephone request for a hotel reservation, the inquiry for a bank balance, the entering of a manuscript on a word processor—all use computers and some use networks. As the industry matures (as the required high-level software is designed to provide end-user access to data), more people will begin to use and acquire the systems. Computers and supporting networks are being distributed into practically every aspect of our lives.

However, certain organizations are not reaping the benefits of DDP. These companies' managers are not managing or controlling the move to DDP. The companies experience spiraling applications software costs, redundant and conflicting data bases, and incompatible data communications protocols. This point will be emphasized throughout the chapter: DDP requires unified coordination within the organization if it is to succeed. It requires top management involvement, active user participation, and strategic planning, especially with the increasing use of the personal computer. In essence, problems in DDP usually stem from the lack of top management control and commitment.

PROS AND CONS OF DISTRIBUTED PROCESSING

The Disadvantages

Practically speaking, distribution may not be for everyone. And, if it is, it offers some potential dangers.

Loss of control.   The most serious potential problem with DDP is the loss of control over the organization's automated resources. This includes the inability to provide proper audits among all the departments, the emergence of multiple standards within the organization, and the lack of cost control measures over the distributed departments. The loss of control stems from the problems cited next.

Duplication of software resources.   The personal computer users are often tempted to develop their own automated systems to fit perceived specific needs. Consequently, departments that have the same requirements may develop duplicate software systems that have the same or nearly the same functions. This often results in unduly high software costs.

Duplication of data.   Independent distributed facilities are also prone to develop their own version of a corporate data base. This can occur for several reasons: (a) The corporate data base is designed to optimize efficiency for all users. The individual site will "spin off" a portion of the data base and optimize the data to its specific needs. (b) The distributed site wishes to add data to the corporate data base; again, it duplicates the data base and then appends its unique source data to the duplicate copy. (c) The distributed site wishes to use special software (a different data-base management system or data dictionary) that is not suited to the corporate data base.

It should be emphasized that redundancy, per se, is not necessarily a poor approach. However, uncontrolled redundancy creates problems. When the same data are presented in a variety of ways, it is often difficult and expensive to resolve the differences. This topic is covered in more detail later.

Hardware problems.   Independent acquisition of hardware by autonomous managers will likely result in the inability to share the computers among the sites because of incompatibilities among the vendors and models. Different vendors' machines often have different word sizes, varying instruction sets, and conflicting compilers. This problem is especially evident today in the different personal computer architectures from various vendors.

Reversion to past inefficiencies.   The data-processing profession has made great strides during the past several years. Project control, programming techniques, and data management have become more disciplined and more productive. Data-processing professionals are usually highly skilled and highly trained. The placement of personal computers and other automated resources under the responsibility of untrained and inexperienced users (or other personnel) can lead to the same inefficiencies that existed in earlier years. The uninitiated user tends to ignore sound programming techniques. Documentation is often not prepared under this environment. At a minimum, budget and cost control problems may become severe because the data-processing labor to produce systems may not be accountable when the systems are developed in the user department. The resulting inefficiencies can lead to escalating complexities in the system.

Maintenance of the remote sites.   Those sites that are located in remote areas may have difficulty in obtaining timely response to technical problems. Vendor support personnel and the organization's technical support staff may not be readily available, and maintaining a trained staff at each site is often prohibitively expensive.

Incompatibility of hardware and software.   Unless the acquisition of automated resources is controlled and coordinated, the departments may develop hardware and software systems that are incompatible and that cannot communicate with one another. This problem often surfaces in the communications protocols, personal computer application software packages, and operating systems that are acquired from different vendors. As a consequence of this independence, a considerable amount of time and effort may be spent in developing emulation software or protocol conversion packages. This is not to say one should go sole source (that is, one vendor for everything), but the organization cannot allow the distributed sites complete independence in choosing the product.

The Advantages

While the potential dangers of distributed processing are real and can be serious, the offsetting advantages of a *properly implemented* system are quite significant:

Reduction of costs.   In many instances, DDP saves the organization money. Local processing can reduce the amount of traffic across a communications line. Data can be entered and edited for errors at the distributed sites. In several actual cases, the author knows where DDP paid for itself solely by local data entry and editing. Distributed systems can provide opportunities for cost reductions in other areas: (a) use of less expensive and less complex computers, (b) decreased complexity for certain applications (for example, payroll, accounts receivable) that run in the simpler, small computer environment, and (c) better utilization of personnel that use the system (more on this subject later).

Response time improvements.   The lengthy delays encountered in a centralized system often stem from an overloaded CPU and slow communications lines. Local processing of a transaction eliminates the relatively slow common carrier lines in favor of high-speed channels. It also eliminates the lengthy waiting queues that accumulate at the single-server, centralized host. Local processing can also shorten the time for an application to complete the processing of its cycle.

Distributed processing can improve response time for certain applications that can be partitioned (or divided) into pieces for simultaneous execution. Therefore, instead of the serial processing approach, the functions are executed in parallel on multiple functionally distributed computers. This technique decreases the lag that is inherent with a serial process (see Figure 12–1). Parallel processing techniques are increasing in the industry and will likely become a dominant method of DDP implementation.

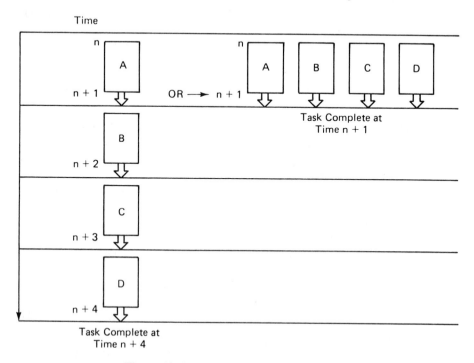

Figure 12–1.   Serial and parallel processing.

User control.   Earlier it was stated that users wish to have more control over the critical data-processing resources that largely determine their profit or loss. Distributed processing can provide the user with this control. However, the point should be reemphasized that unregulated user autonomy and control will surely do more harm than good. Later discussions will provide guidelines on delineating user independence and user control.

Without question, users need to participate more in the development and selection of automated resources. To do so would decrease the tension and political infighting that often occur between the user community and the data-processing department. The impression that the users are getting more tailored support and, to an extent, are controlling their information systems can have very high payoffs, both in terms of morale and productivity.

Backup.   If one wishes to provide backup to a large-scale centralized machine, one must acquire another large-scale centralized machine. Some organizations attempt to acquire services from other companies or time-sharing facilities to provide backup of critical applications. However, this approach is quite cumbersome in keeping the two organizations' systems compatible with respect to operating systems releases, compiler enhancements, and myriad other daily ongoing chores. If the organization can use two maxis, then coupling the machines together properly will allow for one machine to back up the other.

On the other hand, distributed systems can provide very flexible and cost-effective backup. Since the system has its parts integrated to a whole, a failed processing element can have its work transferred to another site. We see this technique being refined today; it is available in several vendor offerings at the present time.

DISTRIBUTED DATA BASES

Since the purpose of computers is to process data and to manipulate the data into something meaningful (information), the issue of data in a distributed environment is very important. Distributed data represent one of the more interesting and challenging problems of DDP, and considerable care must be taken in implementing distributed data bases if the potential benefits of a distributed system are to be realized.

Reasons for Distributing Data

The reasons for distributing data are similar to the rationale for DDP discussed at the beginning of this chapter:

- Placing data at the organization's departments on personal computers can reduce the amount of data transferred among the host computers, resulting in reduced communications costs.
- Local access of data can improve the response time to obtain the data, since delays of remote transmission are eliminated.

- Distributed data bases can give increased reliability to a system because the data are located at more than one site. The failure of a node need not close down all operations of data access in the network.
- The provision for local storage gives users more control over the data.
- Distributed data bases present a challenging technical problem. While this statement is made somewhat tongue in cheek, the author knows of instances where organizations allowed technicians to move to the distributed data environment because the technicians wanted to "make it work." To be sure, this is not a very good reason and it once again points to the need for management control of the process.

Types of Distribution

Three basic types of data distribution can be implemented. The first type is centralized data [see Figure 12–2(a)] and is not really distributed, but will be used for purposes of comparison. In this approach, all data reside at one site; all data queries and updates from the remote sites are transmitted to the central site.

Figure 12–2(b) illustrates the partitioned data-base approach. In contrast to the centralized scheme, the data are split into pieces or partitions and assigned to selected departments or sites in the network. The partitioned data bases all may be of the same data structure, format, or access method, in which case the system is a homogeneous partitioned data base. If the partitioned data consist of different structures, formats, or access methods, the system is a heterogeneous partitioned system.

Replicated data are the third approach [see Figure 12–2(c)]. This type stores multiple copies of the same data at different departments or different sites in the network. The same data structures among the replicated data are called *homogeneous replicated data*. Replicated data bases may be classified as heterogeneous replicated systems if the duplicate data are reformatted or placed under a different access method to fit local needs.

Distributed data bases are further classified as being vertically or horizontally distributed. The vertical system exhibits the form of the vertical topology where data are distributed in a hierarchical manner. Detailed data may be stored locally and general, aggregated data or less detailed data stored farther up in the hierarchy. Horizontally

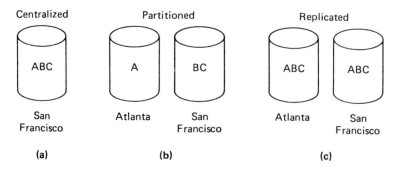

Figure 12–2. Types of data-base distribution.

distributed data exhibit the form of the horizontal topology wherein data are distributed across departments or peer sites in the network.

In summary, data bases can be placed in the network in various combinations of

- Centralization
- Partitioning
- Replication
- Homogeneity
- Heterogeneity
- Vertical distribution
- Horizontal distribution

Distributed Data Terms and Concepts

To follow the subsequent discussion on distributed data systems, several basic terms and concepts should be understood. Many different names are attached to these concepts, and different vendors or designers may use their own term to describe the same concept.[1]

Consistent state.   All data in the network data bases are accurate and correct. The replicated copies contain the same values in the data fields. Two examples illustrate the idea: (1) A customer's total bank deposits reflect the sum of his checking deposits and savings deposits. If check deposits = \$100 and savings deposits = \$250, total deposits must contain the value \$350 if the data are to be consistent. (2) A department in an organization has its monthly sales data stored on a personal computer file. The data are also stored in the corporate data base, yet both copies contain the same values.

Transaction.   A transaction is a sequence of operations transforming a current consistent state to a new consistent state. For example, transferring funds from a customer's bank account to another customer's bank account involves more than one operation and also involves moving the data base from one consistent state to another consistent state.

Some data-base systems permit a transaction to create an undefined number of operations or even another transaction. These systems are usually difficult to control and often create loading problems on the network computers. The transaction sets off a chain reaction to multiple data bases or programs, often resulting in a chaotic environment. This practice, called a *multifunction transaction*, is to be avoided.

Temporary inconsistency.   This term describes the state of the data during the execution of a transaction. The state occurs in between the operations. For example, an applications program that transfers \$100 between two customers will inherently create a

---

[1]Upon review of many variations, the author has settled on the terms and definitions found in *ACM Computing Surveys*, 13, no. 2 (June 1981). I also am indebted to the Association for Computing Machinery (ACM) for its examples in this particular issue.

temporary inconsistency because the program's instructions are executed sequentially. For example, transaction 1 (T1) is processed by the following program:

Coding Example 1: Code to Transfer Funds

```
      Sequence of Operations
          BEGIN
T1 - 1          Read Customer A Account
T1 - 2          Read Customer B Account
T1 - 3          Write Customer A Account — $100 to Customer A
                Account
T1 - 4          Write Customer B Account + $100 to Customer B
                Account
          END
```

The program transfers $100 from the customer A account to the customer B account. After the execution of the first WRITE instruction, the data are temporarily inconsistent by $100. Only with the full completion of the transaction do the data move from one consistent state to a new consistent state.

Conflict.   Upon the completion of an operation or a series of operations, the resulting state is inconsistent. Conflict usually occurs when two or more transactions are involved in an update of the same data. The following code depicts two transactions executing simultaneously on a host computer or a personal computer file server. The code in Coding Example 1 is used for both transactions, so processing the two transactions interleaves the instructions of the two copies of the same code. As in the first example, transaction 1 transfers $100 from customer A to customer B. Transaction 2 transfers $75 from A to B. The code shows the sequence of instructions involved for the two transactions and the values in the customer's account after the execution of each instruction.

Coding Example 2: Code to Transfer Funds

```
          BEGIN
T1 - 1          Read Customer A Account
T2 - 1          Read Customer B Account
T1 - 2          Read Customer B Account
T1 - 3          Write Customer A Account — $100 to Customer A
                Account
T2 - 2          Read Customer B Account
T1 - 4          Write Customer B Account + $100 to Customer B
                Account
T2 - 3          Write Customer A Account — $75 to Customer A
                Account
T2 - 4          Write Customer B Account + $75 to Customer B
                Account
          END
```

The result is a conflict. The data are inconsistent. The total deposits of the two customers should be $600, with $125 in customer A's account and $475 in customer B's account. Due to the overlapping of operations between the two transactions, customer A has $225 and customer B has only $375 for a total deposit of $600. The initial $100 transaction was undone. A careful analysis of the program and the work space of transactions 1 and 2 shows how this problem occurs (see Table 12–1).

The transactions are using separate work spaces for the reading and writing of the data base. Notice that, upon execution of T1-3, the transaction 1 A Account work space is reduced by $100 and the value written to the data base. *However*, transaction 2 A Account work space remains at $300. Later, with the execution of T2-3, transaction 2's A Account work space is reduced by $75 and the value is written to the data base. The conflict has occurred with one copy of the data base. Later discussions show how distributed copies further complicate the problem.

Schedule. A *schedule* is an ordering of events or instructions within multiple transactions. The events in Coding Example 2 represent a schedule, but not a very good one. Conflict can be avoided by running each transaction individually until it is completed. However, this approach is not effective due to resulting performance problems.

Serializable schedule. The effect of interleaving the operations of multiple transactions is the same as running the transactions serially; that is, the result is a consistent state. A serializable schedule can be obtained in Coding Example 2 by issuing both WRITEs for transaction 1 before issuing the READs for transaction 2. However, this then becomes a straight serial process, so other methods must be used to achieve the effect of serial processing.

Locking. The locking of data ensures the inaccessibility of the data while they are in a temporarily inconsistent state. Locking is used to prevent multiple transactions from creating a conflict in the data base. The data-base management system or a personal

TABLE 12–1 CONFLICT OF TRANSACTIONS IN A DATA-BASE UPDATE

| | Results in | | | | | |
| | Transaction 1 Work Space | | Transaction 2 Work Space | | Data Base | |
Execution of	A Account	B Account	A Account	B Account	A Account	B Account
T1-1	300	—	—	—	300	300
T2-1	300	—	300	—	300	300
T1-2	300	300	300	—	300	300
T1-3	200	300	300	—	200	300
T2-2	200	300	300	300	200	300
T1-4	200	400	300	300	200	400
T2-3	200	400	225	300	225	400
T2-4	200	400	225	375	225	375

computer disk or file server is usually responsible for locking the affected data, typically at a record or segment or byte level. Each application that has WRITE code to a data base must be defined to the DBMS prior to execution. Thereafter, when the application code is executing, a READ instruction will signal the DBMS to disallow other applications from obtaining the data that were accessed by the READ. The lock is released after the application completes the transaction, and the other waiting applications are given access to the data. For example, in Coding Example 2, the initiation of transaction 1 locks the data from transaction 2. The next chapter discusses locking in more detail and points out some potential problems with personal computer locking mechanisms.

Resiliency.   The dictionary defines *resiliency* as the ability to return to original form. The term aptly describes a critical characteristic of a distributed or shared data base: The failure of a computer system should not affect the operations of another system. A down site should not evoke a "sympathetic failure" at other computer sites. An incomplete transaction (for example, a hardware failure during the execution of the update code) should be completely backed out at all sites and the data restored to their original form.

The Challenge of Distributed Data

A distributed or shared data system is deceptively complex. This section will describe the complexities and problems, as well as techniques to avoid some of the possible pitfalls. Figure 12–3 is a guideline for decisions on distributing data. Generally, the

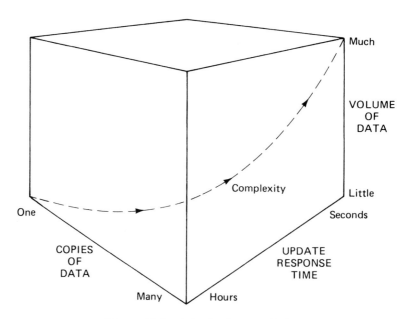

Figure 12–3. Distribution complexity.

figure shows that as an organization moves to (a) larger data bases with (b) multiple copies of data and (c) shorter response time on updates, the organization also moves to an increasingly complex distributed environment. If possible, complexities should be avoided because of the increased risk of system failures, data inconsistencies, and increased costs. If the organization needs this type of environment, it should recognize the trade-offs.

An example of the complexities and problems is provided in Figure 12–4(a). Users A and B simultaneously update an item in the data base. In the absence of control mechanisms, the data base reflects only the one update; the other update is lost. This happens when both users retrieve the data item, change it (add or subtract from the value), and write their revised value back into the data base. In the illustration, the revised value should have been 250 instead of 150. This example is similar to the problem encountered in Coding Example 2.

The problem is compounded in Figure 12–4(b). At a later time, user C retrieves the data and stores them in a replicated local data base (for example, in a local file of a personal computer). The organization now has a rather serious consistency problem and it is not a temporary inconsistency. The data bases are in conflict. This is only one example of many possibilities.

Coding Example 2 represents the problem with only one copy of the data; as multiple copies are distributed the problem becomes more complex. For example, personal computer users often off-load data from a central data base and store multiple copies on the PCs. The data may be corrected or updated by the local users without the resulting changes finding their way back to the host data base and the other PC users.

Lockouts and the deadly embrace.   The most common solution to this problem is preventing sites A and B from simultaneous executions on the same data. Through the use of lockouts, for example, site B would not be allowed to execute until site A had completed its transaction [see Figure 12–4(c)].

Lockouts work reasonably well with a centralized data base, although some personal computer systems have rather crude lockout mechanisms. However, in a distributed environment, the sites may possibly lock each other out and prevent either transaction from completing its task. *Mutual lockout*, often called *deadly embrace*, is shown in Figure 12–5. Users A and B wish to update base items Y and Z, respectively; consequently, user A locks data Y from user B and user B locks data Z from user A. To complete their transactions, both users need data from the other *locked* data bases. Hence, neither can execute further and the two sites are locked in a deadly embrace. Clearly, the deadly embrace is an unacceptable situation and the system must be able to detect, analyze, and resolve the problem. We address this problem in the next chapter.

Lockouts and sharing with personal computers.   Personal computer networks also provide lockout capabilities to allow multiple, distributed personal computers to use the same data base or file. The better PC networks provide two valuable functions: *file sharing* and *user query redirection*.

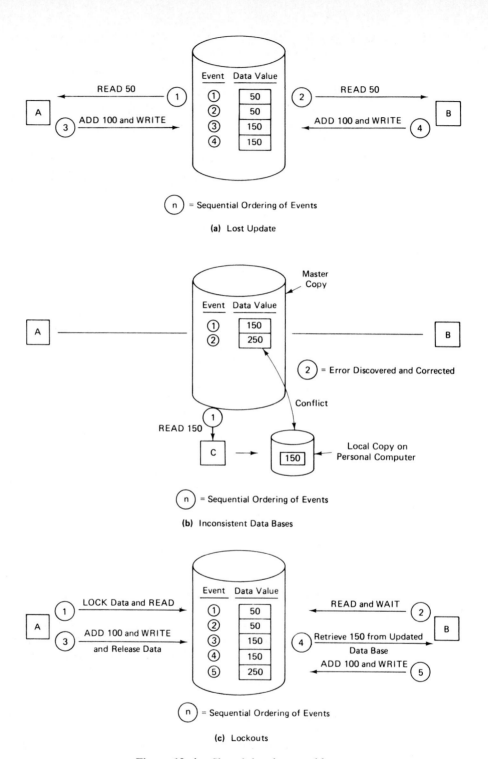

Figure 12-4. Shared data-base problems.

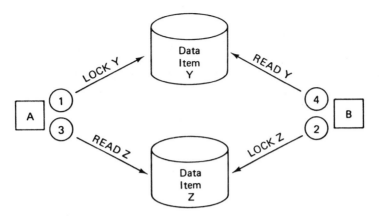

Figure 12–5. Deadly embrace.

The share function allows an initial user to stipulate that a data base can only be read by any user who subsequently attempts to access the data. This technique is called "read/write access with deny write sharing mode." The reader is cautioned that older PC applications were not written to use the share function and must be changed to use this capability.

The second function, user query redirection, can reroute a user transaction over the network to a data base at another computer. This capability is essential if an organization is to have true distributed data-base operations.

Update and retrieval overhead. The use of locks for both personal computers and large-scale computers (mainframes) is a widely accepted method for achieving consistency. When properly implemented with serialized scheduling, locks provide a very valuable method for maintaining data-base integrity. However, consistency of the distributed data does not come without cost. For example, in Figure 12–6 the site in San Francisco issues a transaction to update two replicated data bases in New York and Atlanta. The following communications messages must be exchanged over the network among San Francisco and the two other sites:

Event 1: San Francisco sends lock request messages to New York and Atlanta.

Event 2: New York and Atlanta send lock grant messages to San Francisco (if the request is acceptable).

Event 3: San Francisco transmits the update transaction.

Event 4: The receiving sites update the data bases and transmit to San Francisco the acknowledgment of an update completion.

Event 5: San Francisco receives the acknowledgment and transmits messages to release the lock.

A typical locking algorithm requires $5 (n - 1)$ intersite messages to manage an update transaction among *n* distributed sites. This could be considered an extreme ex-

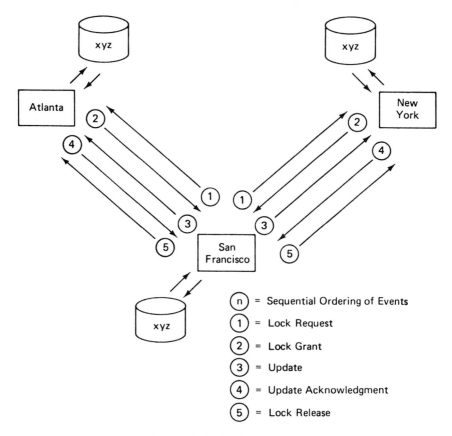

Figure 12–6. Update overhead.

ample. The messages in events 1 and 3 can be piggybacked onto each other. The update portion of the message would only be used after an established time had elapsed and San Francisco had not been sent a revoking message indicating one of the sites had sent San Francisco a lock denial. However, the $5 (n - 1)$ algorithm is simpler and more reliable.

This overhead is the tip of the iceberg; each of the messages requires data link control (DLC) messages to ensure that the data-base messages are properly received. A DLC might require four DLC control messages to every user data message. The number varies from three to nine, so the number four is conservative. Consequently, the locking algorithm is actually $D [5 (n - 1)]$, where D is the number of overhead messages needed to manage one user message flow. In the example in Figure 12–6, assuming a communications overhead factor of 4, the calculation reveals that 40 messages are transported through the system to accomplish *one* update at two sites: $40 = 4 \times [5 \times (3 - 1)]$. Finally, the example did not calculate the additional costs of environments that have heterogeneous topologies and/or data systems. Protocol conversions and data structure translators consume additional overhead. It takes little imagination to recognize that the proper placement of replicated data in a system is a very important task.

Figure 12–6 depicts the transmissions across remote sites. However, be aware that communications overhead, data-base software efficiency, and machine processing power are also factors, because they can reduce throughput on the channel with the consequent delay in response time to the individual users. To illustrate, a 4-Mbit/s token ring LAN typically provides only 60 to 190 kbit/s of throughput for a file-to-file transfer.

Retrieval overhead presents problems also, especially in a partitioned data base. A data retrieval request may require the "rounding up" of the needed data at several data bases in the network, since the data have been partitioned into subsets and assigned to different locations. The DLC, protocol conversion, and data structure translation data-base software execution, operating systems efficiency, and machine processing power are important considerations in the decisions of how to partition the data bases.

Failure and recovery. The efforts to achieve resiliency in a distributed system are quite different from efforts in a conventional centralized environment. The centralized approach assumes the availability of much information about a problem or failure. The operating system can suspend the execution of the problem program and store and query registers and control blocks, during which the problem component does not change.

In a DDP system, the time delay in gathering data for analysis may be significant; in some cases, the data may be outdated upon receipt by the component tasked with the analysis and resolution. The problem may not be suspended as in a centralized system, since some distributed systems have horizontal topologies and autonomous or near-autonomous components.

Referring again to Figure 12–6, one can gain an appreciation of the situation. Let us assume the update executed successfully at New York but the Atlanta site experienced problems due to a hardware or software failure. The update must be reversed in the New York copy. All items must be restored, transactions eventually reapplied, backup tapes made, and log files restored to the preupdate image. In the meantime, other transactions must be examined to determine if they were dependent on the suspended transaction. Of course, one has the option of maintaining the New York update, continuing subsequent updates, and bringing the Atlanta data up to date at a later time. Nonetheless, the affected nodes cannot independently make these decisions; all must be aware of one another if the data bases are to be properly synchronized.

A key question must be answered: Does the organization need timely data at the expense of consistency? Stated another way, must all copies be concurrent with one another? Practically speaking, certain classes of data (such as historical data) may be allowed to exhibit weak consistency: Data are not kept concurrent. On the other hand, other classes of data (real-time data, for example) may need strong consistency. The designers must examine the user requirements very carefully. The benefits of strong consistency must be weighed against the increased costs of additional complexity and overhead.

Major factors in distributed data decisions. The discussion in this chapter has focused on more general guidelines for deciding how to distribute the data in the network. The determining factors are summarized as follows:

1. Frequency of use at each site
2. User control of data
3. Real-time update requirements
4. Backup requirements
5. Class of data
6. Cost to store locally versus cost to transmit remotely
7. Security considerations
8. Time of use of the data
9. Volume of data accessed
10. Retrieval response time requirements
11. Location of data users
12. Retrieval access versus update accesses

Loading Factors

Loading.   The term *loading* refers to the assignment of resources to a distributed site. The resources can be data or software. In most cases, loading is accomplished in a non-real-time mode. This approach can simplify the distributed environment considerably. Loading can be accomplished within the vertical or horizontal topology in three ways: downline loading, upline loading, and crossline loading (see Figure 12–7).

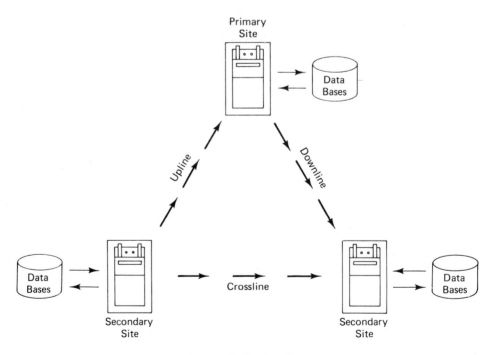

Figure 12–7. Loading.

Downline loading. Resources are transmitted from the primary or master site to the secondary or slave site(s). Downline loading is often used to transport copies of software developed and tested at the centralized site. The programs are then placed at the secondary sites for execution. This approach avoids staffing the distributed sites with programming personnel. Data are frequently downline loaded as well. For example, data are updated at one site; the one copy greatly simplifies the update process. At selected times, the data are sent to the secondary sites and copied into the files. This approach works well for small data bases, but a large data-base copy transmission creates considerable traffic on the network. An alternative approach is transmitting only the segments of the data base that have been altered since the last downline load. Another very useful technique is the downline loading of tasks, in which the master station receives transactions and decides which processing elements are available and/or have the proper resources for the particular transaction. This concept is also called *workload partitioning* or *transaction downloading.*

Upline loading. This technique is used when the secondary site, such as a personal computer, needs a larger computer to accomplish its task. It transmits work ''up stream'' to the master site for processing. Upline loading is also used to transmit data. The data can be detailed items but are frequently summarized or aggregated data. Upline loading is also used to accomplish distributed system development. Each secondary site is responsible for the development of a part of the system (that is, the development is partitioned). At prearranged times, the subsystems are transmitted to one or two sites (usually the master site) for integration testing. The completed system may then be downline loaded for execution at the other modes. Distributed system development has several advantages, but must be approached carefully if its full benefits are to be realized.

Crossline loading. The horizontal network components can accomplish the same functions discussed above. The term to describe peer-to-peer exchange is *crossline loading.* As in downline and upline loading, the technique of crossline loading is often used to share resources, partition work, and provide backup for the peer processing elements.

What are some candidates for off-loading? The following list provides some examples. It is not all inclusive but serves to show the potential value of off-loading:

- *Edits.* Data editing is performed locally. Edit criteria can be developed at the central site and downline loaded.
- *Formats.* Screen and print formats stored locally.
- *Error processing.* Any error condition software is loaded to the local elements.
- *Protocols.* Certain processing elements are designated as protocol handlers. The protocol overhead is off-loaded from central host.
- *Audit-trails.* Approach this area with caution; distributed audit trails can become complex.
- *Data bases.* Selected data are assigned to the remote sites.
- *Addressing.* Address resolution and message routing are off-loaded from the primary station.
- *Processing programs.* The applications themselves are off-loaded to remote sites.

TABLE 12–2 LOADING FACTORS

Determine functions, processes, data, programs to be off-line loaded

How often
Time of day
Volume of data to be transmitted
Rotation of line load sequences
Procedures for use if operator functions changed
Verification of transmission and load
Controls over what happens at up/down/cross line site
Line load and analysis
Transmission method

Candidates for offloading

Forms
Formats
Edit criteria
Security/privacy screens
Master data bases
Processing queues
Address capability
Error processing
Protocol handling
Diagnostics
Processing programs
Routing controls
Audit trail storage

The values of off-loading are resource sharing, distribution of peak load, relieving the primary site from certain specialized activities, and backup. The reader is encouraged to examine this idea further; it can be very effective. Table 12–2 provides other points that should be considered when establishing an off-loading system.

MANAGING THE DISTRIBUTED RESOURCES

The advances in distributed data processing during the past few years have been remarkable. Many fully tested hardware and software components are now available commercially. Distributed networking concepts have been refined, and strides are being made in managing dispersed data bases. If computing costs continue to decline relative to transmission costs, the number of DDP networks will increase.

Yet, while the technical matters are being solved, many management issues are not. Ironically, some of the more attractive features of DDP present the most vexing management problems. For example, distributed network architecture is conducive to load leveling, or resource sharing, among the sites. Although this can lead to more effective use of the network's computers, resources dispersed at these sites are not easily managed. Distributed data processing appeals to some organizations because it lets them move computerized resources to various departments and divisions throughout the organizational structure. But this movement may lead to uncontrolled proliferation of conflicting or redundant software and data.

The primary challenge to DDP management is to effectively administer the hardware, software, and data resources that exist throughout the network. This task is especially difficult if the organization has acquired or merged with other companies that have different computer architectures and network protocols. Moreover, many large organizations have separate departmental budgets that often allow managers to develop unique information systems. The resulting incompatibilities can be costly and difficult to manage.

If one fundamental principle were to guide management in the use of DDP, it would be that the organization requires strong unified management control and guidance. At first this might seem contradictory but, in fact, DDP requires a stronger management structure than the traditional centralized approach.

A distributed system may have millions of source statements (such as computer program instructions), hundreds of programs, thousands of data items, and scores of data bases residing in many geographically dispersed sites. Because of performance considerations and communications costs, many of these resources will be duplicated at various network sites and departments in the organization.

Typically, the different departments develop, maintain, and update their own data files and programs. It is not uncommon for a site to develop programs or create data files for its own needs and informally pass these resources on to other sites. Some organizations permit users to modify the code or data files that were originally developed for general use, resulting perhaps in several versions of the same program or data file. Companies do not always track and record these changes. Even worse, they may allow different departments to develop redundant programs that perform similar functions, which usually occurs when departments or subsidiaries of a company have enough political clout to establish their own versions of an information system.

Figure 12-8 illustrates the problem caused by lack of control in an evolving distributed environment. Site I develops a program or data base [Figure 12-8(a)] and, to share resources, passes it to site II. To meet its specific needs, site II modifies the core program [Figure 12-8(b)]. At a later date, site I changes its version of the program [Figure 12-8(c)] and then passes the modified program to site II.

However, the altered program does not fulfill site II's needs and, in some instances, may not function in II's environment [Figure 12-8(d)]. Site II is then faced with the difficult choice of modifying its version of the program to accept the change or rejecting the change and expanding its staff to maintain permanently both the core program and the enhanced program.

It is not difficult to see how an organization's distributed information system can become unsynchronized and inaccurate. Disorganized distributed systems have cost companies considerably in dollars and credibility. In addition to paying an inordinate

(a)   (b)

Site I Develops a Program and Passes it to Site II,
Which Makes Changes.

(c)   (d)

Site I Later Changes the Program and Passes it to Site II,
Which Cannot Use it.   **Figure 12–8.**   Control problems.

overhead for supporting this kind of environment, these companies experienced system failures and data errors when changes were made to supposedly identical copies of code or data files.

As a company's DDP network grows in size and complexity, the impact of a poorly conceived coordination and control policy becomes more severe. Unfortunately, many organizations begin the initial move to DDP without an awareness of the pitfalls of having no centralized control. The ideal solution is to give the distributed sites the freedom to manage their resources and develop information systems under the general supervision of a companywide entity. This benefits staff morale and productivity and ensures the best use of a distributed network.

Management Model

Distributed automation management (DAM) is a management and control model for a distributed network. Essentially, DAM is an architecture containing detailed information about the automated (computerized) resources existing throughout the organization. It can be applied to an organization with distributed departments or to subsidiaries that perform similar automated functions or, to a more limited extent, to an organization with widely varying data-processing needs. The advantage of DAM is that all dispersed sites can participate in the decisions and implementation of a developing system, while management can monitor the process.

If a company chooses to use the distributed automation management approach, it must establish well-defined, companywide standards for structuring all information subsystems and software modules. Modules should have clearly defined interfaces and functions. Without such definitions, system integration and testing will be extremely difficult and time-consuming. If each subsystem and module is relatively self-contained, several development teams located at various distributed sites can work on different components, which should prevent major integration problems as the project nears completion.

The distribution of the program development process has more risks than a centralized effort. For example, the distributed modules will usually require more complex interfaces and, therefore, are subject to a higher probability of error. Moreover, DAM entails additional overhead for project coordination among the sites, so the travel budget will most likely increase. Nonetheless, if the network is properly controlled, it will be more efficient.

Figure 12–9 depicts the elements and structure of the architecture. At its most general level, DAM contains information on project management, data/data-base administration, software inventory, equipment inventory, and sources and uses of the company's reports. These responsibilities are broken down into functions, which are handled by the individual elements and subelements (see Table 12–3).

An uppermost element in the DAM architecture, system-life-cycle management (SLC), is similar to the conventional centralized approach in which systems development is performed in phases such as analysis, design, testing, and cutover. The primary difference between SLC and the centralized method is that the SLC process involves all the distributed departments and sites. SLC includes milestones, due dates, exception reports, descriptions of end products, commitments for equipment installation, testing plans, and other project-management information. It may also contain relationships between the development-cycle phases and the other architecture components.

In addition, SLC identifies the acceptance sites for the software development projects; that is, it assigns an impartial group with testing new or revised programs. Since acceptance-site personnel are unbiased toward the program, test data are usually better structured and more fully exercise the program logic.

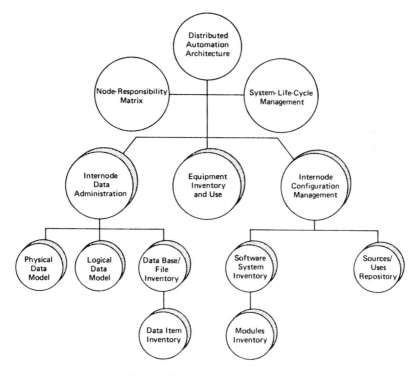

Figure 12–9. DAM architecture.

TABLE 12–3 DAM ELEMENTS

Elements and Subelements	Functions and Stored Information	Elements and Subelements	Functions and Stored Information
System-life-cycle management (SLC)	Identification of project phases Designation of site responsibility for project deliverables Descriptions of end products Milestones, due dates for deliverables Exception-reporting procedures Description of post-implementation review milestones Designation of site for acceptance testing	Data base/file and data item inventories (DFII)	Description of files and data bases for distributed sharing Description of data groupings Relationships among data items over time Description of unique data characteristics Relationships between data items and data bases and files
		Equipment inventory and use (EIU)	Description of network hardware components Repair history of components
Node-responsibility matrix (NRM)	Designation of site responsibility for ongoing operations Identification of sites' security responsibilities Description of rules for change to common components Designation of audit sites and milestones for audits	Internode configuration management (ICM)	Vendor information Maintenance statistics and dates Financial information
		Software systems and modules inventories (SSMI)	Information on available programs General description of program functions

Term	Description
Internode data administration (IDA)	Information on organization's data files, data bases, and data items across all distributed sites
	Description of data
	Node awareness of and access to data
	Description of identifier schemes and naming conventions
	Data relationships between local and remote sites
Physical data model (PDM)	Physical location of data
	Physical device view of data
	Internal representation of data
	Access methods to data
	Data-usage statistics
Logical data model (LDM)	Application program view of data
	Description of program interface to physical data model
	Identification of which sites use program
	Detailed description of each module's functions
	Descriptions of hardware architecture, compilers, and job-control language used to run software
	Listing of parameters for module use
Sources/uses repository (SUR)	Description of input forms (sources)
	Description of output reports (uses)
	Relationships between data sources and uses and the distributed software and database components

The node-responsibility matrix (NRM), closely related to system-life-cycle management, identifies the sites' ongoing responsibility for the distributed programs, equipment, and data files. In certain instances, an organization may assign specific custodianship for key data bases or programs and define an authorization procedure for altering these automated elements. The node-responsibility matrix is a logical tool for this function, since it contains rules for the changes and identifies the sites that are to receive the altered components. Subsets of the information in the system-life-cycle are moved to the node-responsibility matrix as network nodes are placed in production mode.

NRM also contains technical audit information—an important component of the DAM architecture—to assist review teams in assessing node design and project control. It identifies the dates, participants, and status of the audits of the distributed components, as well as the personnel responsible for implementing the auditors' findings and recommendations.

A company can place security-related entries in the node-responsibility matrix. For example, certain network data, software, or hardware may require limited-access restrictions. Although an operating system and a data-base management system usually provide for passwords and other user identification measures, NRM offers a higher level of security, perhaps with additional identifier codes or some form of encryption access for each node.

Internode Data Administration

Internode data administration (IDA) can assist management in organizing the company's data files and data items across all departments and sites, and in determining both the effects of data changes in the network's data bases, where the data should reside, and how to control the partitioning and replication of data bases. IDA and its subelements, the physical data model, the logical data model, and the data-base file and data item inventories, include data descriptions, data definitions, types of data bases, plus the home location of data—where the data reside and which sites have access to them. IDA also provides identifier schemes and naming conventions for data items and data bases. Though this portion of the architecture is similar to a conventional centralized data administration model, it includes the additional vital information pertaining to the various departments' use of the data.

One IDA subelement, the physical data model (PDM), provides the data's actual physical storage characteristics: the data's location and format, the physical record layouts, the data-item relationships (as implemented by "pointers"), and the access methods. These aspects of the model closely resemble portions of a data base management system.

The physical data model also contains important data-usage statistics, one of which, the hit ratio, is vital for managing distributed data bases. The hit ratio, calculated as total data obtained at a node divided by total data items requested at that node, can be used to determine the appropriate data locations. For example, the prevalence of low hit ratios may indicate that the data are mislocated or should be replicated at those sites experiencing low hits. Be aware that replicating the data usually leads to decreased communications costs.

Since data directories often mask the problem of mislocated data in the network, the physical data model's usage statistics are critical to determining data-base replication/partitioning alternatives and data use of network communications lines. Yet usage statistics should be gathered at selected intervals, not continuously, since this is too costly.

The logical data model (LDM) provides an end-user (subschema) view of the data and the interfaces of the software programs to the physical data model. It also enables virtual access to data from local or remote sites.

For example, if an application issues a request for data, the program need not be aware of where the data are located. The logical data model passes the request to the physical data model, which examines the home locator information and initiates requests to network protocols for the data. The required data are located, passed to the logical model, formatted to the application's view, and then given to the application. A change in the physical location of the data will not affect the application-program logic or the logical model. Rather, the physical model can be modified to reflect the data file movement. The approach closely resembles that of layered network protocols and has similar advantages.

The data-base/file and data item inventories are closely related sub-elements that contain the relationships between data items and other data items, data bases, data files, and the distributed nodes. Their descriptions of the data elements can be used during the initial stages of a system life cycle to determine if the company has either the needed data or data that are very similar to the required data. Recent experience has shown that organizations can decrease data management costs by establishing a data inventory and passing all new data requirements through it prior to initiating expensive data-acquisition and data-reporting endeavors. This approach can be especially important if data are distributed and managed (perhaps created) at various locations in the organization.

The data item inventory contains standardized names for the many data elements in the distributed network. A distributed network whose components use common data element names offers several advantages: Communicating and disseminating data changes to all sites is simplified, distributed development teams can more easily read and comprehend code, and, since learning curves are reduced significantl by this approach, code is more easily maintained.

Naming standards also facilitate the use of end-to-end protocols by allowing user programs to exchange data that are commonly understood. Moreover, layered protocols sometimes examine data elements emanating from other layers to invoke certain editing or routing algorithms. Common names allow the various layers to more easily interface with one another. Moreover, variable-length records from the application program or the data base are more easily implemented if standard names precede the data content.

If an organization has limited resources and cannot afford to implement all aspects of DAM, then, at a minimum, it should establish the data item inventory by defining its data elements and establishing company data names for them. The benefits will be significant.

The item inventory of the DAM architecture can handle derived data and time-dependent data. Derived data reflect the manipulation or calculations of other data items. It is often aggregated from individual data items. For example, a company's liquidity position, sometimes called *current ratio,* is calculated, or derived, from current assets and current liabilities. As the company grows and as financial instruments (such as investments and loans) change over time, the elements that constitute the ratio may also change.

The automated systems' data inventory can aid management in comparing the company's liquidity positions in current and previous planning periods by calculating the ratios as economic factors change and by storing the time-dependent relationships. It can also help a firm's distributed subsidiaries track and use the meaning of financial indicators across disparate systems by storing time-dependent and derived data.

Equipment Inventory

Another element in DAM, equipment inventory and use (EIU), describes the network's hardware components and holds information on vendor names, model numbers, service dates, unique characteristics, and repair history. The EIU is of paramount importance for those organizations that have a wide array of personal computers, since these machines are often acquired without any centralized control. The EIU can serve to "keep tabs" on the PC proliferation.

Internode Configuration Management

Internode configuration management (ICM) is a vital part of the architecture, because it links several DAM components together—primarily the software resources at the distributed sites. Properly implemented, it provides an overview of the organization's software resources and allows for companywide coordination of software development, acquisition, and maintenance.

Two of ICM's subelements, the software systems and modules inventories, describe the network's available programs, including their major functions. They also show which sites use what software, a vital point for coordination of distributed-network maintenance and acquisition of conversion packages.

The modules inventory provides a detailed description of an individual program's functions and the input and output parameters in the modules. It allows the distributed sites to access the descriptive information and browse through the functional descriptions. The sites may then choose to use a particular module instead of developing or purchasing a redundant capability. As with the data inventory, new applications program requirements should pass through the software inventory in order to avoid redundant development. If the site uses the component, it can then examine the inventory to find information such as compiler language used, architecture-specific features, and job-control language.

The sources/uses repository (SUR) provides the final link between the organization's reports and its distributed network. It details the input-data forms (for example, a division's balance sheet) and which applications accept them. Further, it indicates the site responsible for preparing the forms. The repository also contains an inventory of output reports (for example, a stockholders' report) and their relationships to the automated programs that produce them.

SUR also provides information on the data files and data items that are used for the input forms (sources) and the output reports (uses). The data element names that are maintained in the data inventory identify specific sources and uses of the company's data flows.

As a simple example, an inventory data base at a warehouse in St. Louis might use form ABC containing a data element named WIDGET.6A.B. If an order-entry system in Chicago uses the same data for output report XYZ, it will likewise use the same WIDGET. 6A.B. The DAM identifies that St. Louis and Chicago use this data item respectively in report ABC, the inventory data base, and in report XYZ, the order-entry file. Consequently, the DAM facility would alert management that a possible alteration to form ABC used in St. Louis might affect some of the automated operations and management reports in Chicago. The changes could then be coordinated with full knowledge of the effects. Many companies have little idea of the impact or cost of making even such a simple change.

Using Distributed Automation Management

The complete architecture could function as follows. A company decides it needs a new automated system. The functional requirements, data needs, and output report requests are reviewed by a coordinating group, which examines DAM to determine if the new requirements can be partially or completely fulfilled by existing automated resources.

The data base/file inventory determines if some of the data are already available. The software system inventory provides the planner with the option of selecting existing code for use or modification to support the new system. The sources/uses repository determines which of the company's many reports will be affected.

DAM provides information on all forms, reports, files, software modules, hardware components, and sites that will be altered by the new system. If the change affects hardware performance, DAM contains statistics and information that help management determine how to reconfigure the equipment and perhaps shift computing to other resources.

Consequently, DAM helps management make cost-benefit judgments in solving the problem, thereby controlling undesirable ripple effects into the distributed components. It also provides a means to integrate the revised and new components, determine the sites that are responsible for the implementation, and manage the progress of the effort.

Substantial resources are required to maintain the many elements in the distributed information automation management facility, especially for a large organization that has widely dispersed components. Therefore, an organization may choose to implement only those aspects of the architecture that appear practicable and cost-effective to its environment.

DIVISION OF RESPONSIBILITIES

This chapter has emphasized the need for unified and central direction if an organization is to use distributed processing successfully. Of equal importance is the realization that the departments and distributed sites must be given some responsibility and control over

TABLE 12-4 DIVISION OF RESPONSIBILITIES

Centralized		Distributed
Definition of central and local responsibilities	⇨	Activity participates in definition, but policies established at headquarters
Selection and design of applications to serve multiple locations	⇨	Participation in selection and design of applications to serve multiple locations
Maintenance of corporate data dictionary. Review of local sites input to dictionary	⇦	Input of local data to corporate dictionary
Choice of network standards, data description language, and data-base software	⇨	Participation in selection of standards, data description language, and data-base software
Maintenance of master data bases	⇦	Input to local copies of data bases, and upline loading to master data bases
Selection of applications for intersite use	⇨	Development of intersite applications
Review of intersite application for adherence to standards	⇨	Follows up on review findings
Review of local application development trends	⇦	Local application development, within standards
Review of local data base trends	⇦	Design of local data bases, within standards
Review of local subschemas	⇦	Design of subschemas for system-wide data bases
Review of equipment selection trends	⇦	Selection of locally used equipment, within standards
Consulting services	⇨	Receives consulting services
System security policies	⇨	Participation in development of security policies
Auditing policies and procedures	⇨	Participation in development of auditing procedures
Coordination of operational reviews	⇨	Conducting operational reviews

TABLE 12-4   (*cont.*)

Centralized		Distributed
Coordination of secondary site testing	⇨	Secondary site testing
Personal Computer acquisition policies	⇨	Participation in formation of policy
Global data-base administration with design review authority	⇨	Local data-base administration functions

many of their resources. The managers at the distributed sites must feel a sense of participation with the undertaking. Simply stated, a successful distributed environment has strong centralized direction with considerable well-defined delegation to the distributed departments. Table 12-4 provides a list of responsibilities that are assigned either to the distributed sites or central headquarters. The arrows point to the staff that is affected by the initiating site; that is, the site that begins or initiates the actions or tasks.

MANAGING DISTRIBUTED NETWORKS WITH THE X.500 DIRECTORY

The X.500 Recommendations could be used to support DAM. These recommendations describe the operations of the *directory*. For distributed networks, it is designed to support and facilitate the communication of information between systems about *objects* such as data, applications, hardware, people, files, distribution lists, and practically anything else that the organization deems worthy of "tracking" for management purposes. X.500 is intended to allow the communication of this information between distributed systems, which can include OSI applications, OSI layer entities, OSI management entities, and communications networks.

   X.500 actually encompasses eight recommendations, collectively known as the X.500 Recommendations. They are listed below:

X.500	The directory—Overview of concepts, models, and services
X.501	The Directory Models
X.509	The directory—Authentication framework
X.511	The directory—Abstract service definition
X.518	The directory—Procedures of distributed operation
X.519	The directory—Protocol specifications
X.520	The directory—Selected attribute types
X.521	The directory—Selected object classes

Key Terms and Concepts

Our task in this section of the chapter is to come to grips with several key terms, concepts, and definitions used by the X.500 specifications (see Figure 12–10). The information held in the directory is known as the *directory information base* (DIB). The DIB

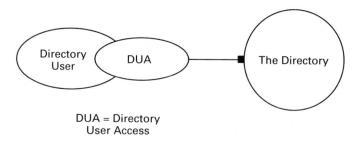

DUA = Directory
User Access

Figure 12-10. Functional view of the X.500 directory.

contains information about objects, and is composed of entries. Each *entry* consists of
a collection of information on one object only. Each entry is made up of *attributes*, and
each attribute has a *type* and one or more *values*.

The DIB is accessed by the directory user through the *directory user agent* (DUA),
which is considered to be an applications process. The DUA is so-named because it acts
as an agent to the end user *vis-à-vis* the DIB.

Figure 12-11 shows that the entries in the DIB are arranged in a tree structure
called the *directory information tree* (DIT). The vertices in the tree represent the *entries*
in the DIB. These entries make up a collection of information about one *object* (such as
a person, a data element, a piece of hardware, a program and so on). The *alias* is also
permitted (not shown in the tree); it points to an object entry.

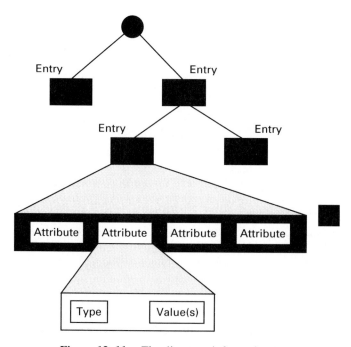

Figure 12-11. The directory information tree.

As we just learned, each entry in the DIT consists of *attributes*, and each attribute is made up of a *type* and one or more *values*. The attribute type specifies the syntax and the data type of the value (such as, integer, Boolean, etc.).

Directory names.   A fundamental concept of X.500 is user-friendly naming. Names are stored in the directory, and the directory provides the services of verifying names, and uses a name to retrieve addresses. These addresses could be any type of address, such as an ISDN address, an X.25 address, an X.121 address, and so on. The directory uses the name for verification, retrieval of addresses, searching/browsing, and so forth.

Perhaps a good analogy to the use of the X.500 directory can be made with the telephone system's white and yellow pages. For example, when using the white pages, a user-friendly name such as John Brown can be accessed through the white pages to obtain a telephone number and perhaps an address. This same idea holds true for the X.500 directory services. Taking the analogy a bit further to the yellow pages, the user can browse on trade names or functional names and the yellow page "directory" will yield the telephone number, address, and of course the user-friendly name.

Distinguished names are a fundamental part of the X.500 directory service. X.500 imposes no rules on what the distinguished names may be, but some examples of distinguished names could be an individual's name, a telephone number, a FAX number, a distribution list, an OSI network address, and so on. However, a distinguished name must uniquely identify a directory entry. It must not be ambiguous.

X.500 uses the term *schema* in a different context than other directory and database systems. A schema is a rule to ensure the DIB maintains its logical structure during modifications. It prevents inconsistencies in the DIB such as incorrect subordinate entries' class, attribute values, and so on. It is the responsibility of the directory to ensure that any changes to the DIB are in conformance with the directory schema. Furthermore, controls are present to prevent a user from exceeding thresholds such as the scope of a search, the time spent on a search, the size of the results, and so on.

The DIB may return a request using more than one entry. To do so, X.500 uses a *filter*. Many network control systems use the concept of filters. A filter is an assertion or a set of assertions about the attributes of a resource (in OSI terms, a managed object). In its simplest terms, it is a way to select tests for the selection of operations. The filter operations can be coded into C, ASN.1, and so on, to select operating parameters from the directory. Filters use the conventional Boolean operators of AND, NOT, and OR.

Directory services.   At the broadest level, the X.500 Recommendation defines the following operations:

SERVICE QUALITY

- *Controls:* Establishes the rules for access and modification to the directory.
- *Security:* Defines the authentication, password, and other security procedures for directory use.

- *Filters:* Rules that define one or more conditions that must be satisfied by the entry if it is to be returned in the result to the user.

INTERROGATION

- *Read:* Obtains the values of some or all the attributes of an entry.
- *Compare:* Checks a value against an attribute of a specific entry in the DIB.
- *List:* Obtains and returns a list of subordinates of a specific entry in the DIB.
- *Search:* Using a filter, a certain part of the DIT is returned to the user.
- *Abandon:* Causes the directory to cease processing a prior request from a DIB user.

MODIFICATION

- *Add entry:* Adds a new leaf entry to the DIT.
- *Remove entry:* Removes a leaf entry from the DIT.
- *Modify entry:* Changes a specific entry, including the addition, deletion for replacement of attribute types and attribute values.
- *Modify relative distinguished name:* Changes a distinguished name of a leaf entry in the DIT.

OTHER

- *Errors:* Rules that describe how and why errors are reported.
- *Referrals:* Procedures for referencing other resources.

X.500 Services and Ports

The directory is organized around the concept of ports. As discussed in earlier chapters, a port represents the service seen by the user of a CCITT protocol.

The X.500 ports are organized as depicted in Figure 12–12. Three ports are defined: read, search, and modify.

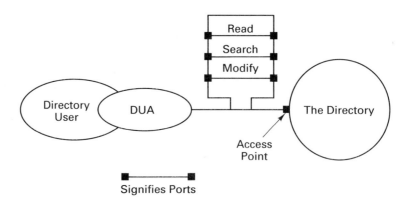

Figure 12–12.   The X.500 ports.

The *read* port consists of three operations: (1) read, (2) compare, and (3) abandon.

The purpose of the *read* operation is to extract information from a directory entity. The operation must contain the identity of the entry from which the information is to be extracted. It must also contain an argument that identifies what information is to be extracted from the named object. The result of this operation contains an entry parameter that holds the information that was obtained as a result of the request. There are also several fields in this operation for listing status indicators and error reports in the event of problems.

The *compare* operation is used to compare an argument value in the request of the operation to an attribute type in the directory. As with all operations to the directory, the name of the object must be provided, as well as the arguments used to perform the compare.

The last operation for the directory read port is the *abandon* operation. Its purpose is self-descriptive: It is used to abandon a previous operation. Although listed with the read port, it is also applicable to the search port (specifically, the list and search operations of the search port).

The *search* port, as indicated in Figure 12–12, consists of two operations: (1) list and (2) search. As its name implies, the *list* operation obtains a list from the directory. It is used to access the directory for the immediate subordinates of the identified entry. A distinguish name or relative distinguished name is used to identify what set is to be accessed in a directory. Also, the list operation contains time and size limits that, if exceeded, will cause the list operation to stop. If the list is not finished, partial results will be made available.

The *search* operation is used to browse through the DIT and to return information from the entries. This operation identifies the node in the tree where the search begins. It could possibly be the root of the DIT. In addition, the search operation allows the user to define the searches to be applied to subordinates above or below a node.

The *modify* port consists of the following operations: (a) add entry, (b) remove entry, (c) modify entry, and (d) modify RDN (relative distinguish name). *Add entry* allows the addition of a leaf entry to the DIT. The arguments for this operation define the entry that is to be added, as well as providing information about where the entry should reside in the directory tree.

The *remove entry* simply performs the reverse operation of the add entry; it removes a leaf entry from the DIT.

The *modify entry* operates on an existing entry in the DIT. It is used for a number of modifications that could be made to the directory: (a) removing an attribute, (b) adding an attribute value, (c) adding a new attribute to an existing entry, (d) removing an attribute value, (e) modifying an alias in the directory, and (f) replacing attribute values.

The *modify RDN* is used to change an RDN of a leaf entry. It may be either an object entry or an alias entry in the directory.

Operating a Distributed Directory

X.500 assures the directory can be distributed across a wide geographic area. To support this environment, the directory system agent (DSA) provides access to the DIB from the DUAs or other DSAs. Figure 12–13 shows the relationship of the distributed directory.

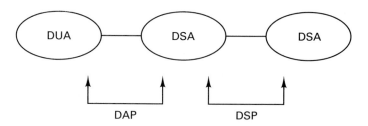

Figure 12–13. Distributed operations.

A DUA is permitted to interact with a single or multiple DSAs. In turn, the DSAs may internetwork with other DSAs through referrals to satisfy a request. The DSA is considered to be an OSI application process.

The DUAs and DSAs communications are governed by two protocols:

- *Directory Access Protocol* (DAP): Specifies actions between DUA and DSA in order for the DUA to have access to the directory.
- *Directory System Protocol* (DSP): Specifies actions between DSAs.

The directory is administered by the *directory management domain* (DMD), which consists of a set of one or more DSAs and zero or more DUAs. The DMD may be a country, a PTT, a network, or anything designated to manage the DIB.

The distributed directory model uses the read, search, and modify ports of the directory and also extends them to three other ports, called chained service ports. They are as follows: *chained read*, *chained search*, and *chained modify*. The purpose of the chained operations is to pass a request to another DSA because the passing DSA knows that the other DSA has knowledge about the operation.

AUTHENTICATION PROCEDURES FOR DIRECTORY ACCESS

It is reasonable to expect an information repository as important as an information resource directory to have security features to prevent unauthorized access. In turn, a secure directory might contain the authentication names and passwords to support other applications. The directory includes these types of support features in X.509. Presently, two types of authentication are defined. *Simple* authentication uses a simple password authentication scheme, and *strong* authentication uses public key cryptographic techniques. The user may choose between simple and strong authentication, depending upon the need for secure services.

Simple Authentication

Simple authentication is supported only within a simple directory domain and is restricted to use between one DUA and one DSA or two DSAs. The procedure for simple authentication operates as follows (see Figure 12–14):

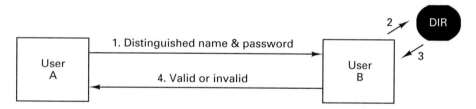

Figure 12–14.　Simple authentication.

　　　User A sends to user B its distinguished name and password (step 1). This information is then forwarded to the directory and the password is checked against an appropriate password in the directory (step 2). The directory then informs B that A's credentials are valid or invalid (step 3). Finally, B informs A about the results of the directory authentication operation (step 4).

　　　Other procedures are also supported. For example, it is possible for B to check the distinguished name and password. Another approach is to use a random number or a timestamp with the distinguished name and password.

Strong Authentication

The CCITT has adapted the public key crypto system (PKCS) for the directory strong authentication operations. The public key concepts were developed in the early 1980s and are now widely used throughout the industry.

　　　The use of public keys has been in existence for just a few years. The advantage that public keys have over private keys is the ease of their administration and the ease of changing of their values.

　　　The concept of public keys is illustrated in Figure 12–15. As noted, the user A has, in its possession, the public key for user B and A's private key. In turn, user B has

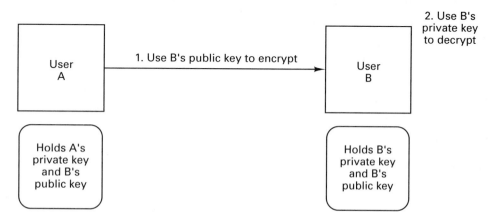

Figure 12–15.　Public keys.

in its possession the private key for user B, and the public key for user A. It is essential that both A's and B's private and public keys be derived from the same function.

As shown in the figure, A can use B's public key to encrypt the data to be transmitted to B. In turn, B uses its private key (which is not available to any other user) to decipher the traffic. The reverse process occurs by B using A's public key for encryption before transmitting the data to A, which then applies its private key for decrypting the traffic into clear text.

Digital signatures. This previous example shows the use of the public key for enciphering data and a complementary secret key used for deciphering the data. This process can be reversed to provide a very powerful authentication procedure, known as a *digital signature*.

A digital signature operation is illustrated in Figure 12–16. User A employs its private key to encipher a digital signature (for example, a password or some other form of identification). This is transmitted to user B, which has possession of user A's public key. Any user that has possession of the public key can decipher the data, but only A can perform the complementary encryption because it alone has the private key.

User A first informs B that it is indeed A. Next it sends the encrypted traffic. Then B uses A's public key to decipher the protocol data unit. If A stated it was someone else, it would not have the proper private key to create the digital signature. In this manner, a user can be authenticated and the source of the information can be verified. Of course, since some of these concepts are new, most systems do not employ authentication and digital signatures. Notwithstanding, they are very powerful and flexible techniques and the OSI Model and the X.500 Directory employ digital signatures for authentication.

X.509 requires that both the private key and the public key be used for encryption and decryption in the following manner:

- *Public key used to encipher:* Secret key used to decipher
- *Secret key used to encipher:* Public key used to decipher

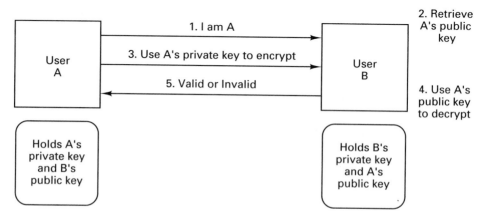

Figure 12–16. Digital signatures.

A specific encryption/decryption algorithm is not defined by the directory. As long as the users involved in the authentication process use the same system, and each possesses a unique distinguished name, the directory will support the authentication process.

SUMMARY

The challenge of managing distributed networks is as much a managerial challenge as it is a technical one. Without firm management control, an enterprise runs the risk of duplicate and possibly redundant information services. The concepts of distributed automation management provide an effective tool to manage the distributed environment.

13

Design Considerations

INTRODUCTION

This chapter discusses the basics of communications systems design. The design problems and solutions are relatively simple and straightforward. Consequently, the material should be used as a vehicle for developing a general understanding of the process. A portion of the chapter uses a case study to explain certain concepts. The chapter is organized into three major sections: (a) communications line loading and network configuration, (b) software design, and (c) network data-base design.

Chapter Structure

Several calculations are included, and the case study is structured around the calculations. The reader may choose not to examine the calculations in detail, but it is recommended they be reviewed in order to better understand the accompanying explanations. The calculations can be very useful; it is the author's experience that organizations that use a disciplined approach (such as the one described herein) find themselves more knowledgeable of the many factors that determine the network's traffic and, therefore, are in a better position to discard or accept the implications of the calculations. Their greatest benefit is to provide an inexpensive, rapid, and manual method to estimate an approximate size and number of the network components.

The calculations are described in four parts: (a) a formula, (b) a brief explanation of the formula, (c) a description of the application data, and (d) the actual calculation.

356

Some of the calculations do not pertain directly to the case study and do not contain parts (c) and (d).

Calculations 1 through 7 exemplify a very basic line-loading analysis. Subsequent calculations and discussions take the reader into more involved problems and considerations.

COMMUNICATIONS LINE LOADING

Case Study Background

A manufacturing company has decided to off-load some of its centralized automated functions to its plants, warehouses, and sales offices throughout the United States. In the past, the company has relied on centralized processing at its corporate site in New York. Presently, leased lines and dial-up lines are used to connect remote points to the central New York computer facility where several computers provide support to over 40 sites in the country.

Figure 13-1 depicts the current network structure of this company. The four regions have headquarters located in relatively large cities. Intradistrict distribution points are also located at the regional headquarters. The sales offices within the regions use leased lines to access the New York computers. The central facility processes inventory queries and sales transactions and sends pertinent data to the sales offices, plants/warehouses, and regional offices.

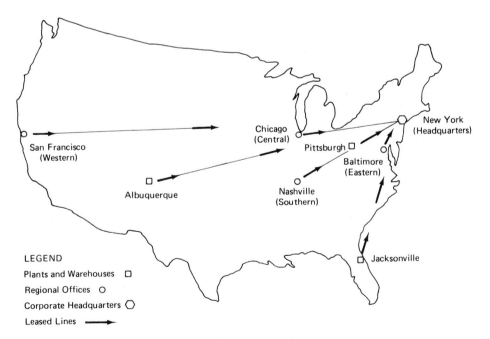

Figure 13-1. Current network structure.

Figure 13–2 shows the southern region, which will be used for this study. The southern headquarters in Nashville, Tennessee, is responsible for 13 sites. The sites for this region consist of sales offices and local distribution facilities. The company's policy is to keep frequently ordered components near the customer due to the time-critical nature of the customer's needs for the material.

The company intends to install computers at the four regional headquarters. These computers will provide support to the offices in the respective regions. This impetus comes from the fact that local personnel are tasked with much of the data entry and validation. The company's personnel need to be near the sales offices and customer locations. In addition, the central host computers in New York have become bottlenecks during the periods of heavy traffic, and communications costs and response time delays have increased. An analysis (discussed in the data-base design section of this chapter) reveals that the company should locate computers and data bases away from the New York site.

During the business day, the sales representatives and inventory personnel at the local offices will be using the regional computer to access data on parts inventories, order components, and keep the regional data bases current. During the evenings, selected data will be transmitted to company headquarters in New York to update the corporate files. Transactions will also be transmitted to the company's manufacturing plants and major warehouses in Jacksonville, Albuquerque, and Pittsburgh in order to replenish the regional distribution points.

Approach to the Analysis

The decision of how to configure a network can be accomplished in part by a typical analysis of user needs and a design to support the user applications (requirements identification, specification, software and data-base design, etc.). Additional refinements necessary for the network are explained in this section.

Figure 13–2. Southern region.

One of the more difficult aspects of designing a network to support applications is determining the actual requirements of the applications. For example, each application will send/receive a certain volume of data across the network and will process these data under response time constraints. The data and response time requirements will provide a traffic pattern from which the communications lines, terminals, and computers can be configured. However, these data are often not readily available and may be subject to some "best guessing." Users may not know how they will use the network until they have gained some actual experience.

If the applications (such as inventory and sales in this study) are not yet automated, the design team must work closely with the end user to develop the requirements. The task is made easier if a system is already automated. The designers can then analyze the activity of the system and develop statistics for use in configuring the network according to the traffic pattern of the applications and growth pattern of the company. One should not rely on statistics alone, however; there is no substitute for close work with the user.

Traffic pattern.   User requirements should be gathered into a traffic pattern showing the number of messages and amount of data that must be transmitted and received. The traffic pattern is derived from a detailed analysis (a) of each application's input and output traffic, (b) at each site, (c) during the peak period of activity. For example, in a sales order entry system, a sales clerk may be able to handle 15 customer calls per hour. If a typical call generates eight inputs and eight outputs to/from the computer (queries and updates), then during a peak period of one hour the clerk will generate 240 pieces of activity (transactions) onto the network (1 hour $\times$ 15 calls per hour $\times$ 16 input/outputs per call $=$ 240 transactions). The network must be able to service this amount of activity, or management must accept degraded service in order to reduce costs.

It may be difficult to determine detail to this level. Nonetheless, the failure to develop some kind of traffic pattern may lead to an "underdesign" of the network resulting in poor performance or an "overdesign" with unnecessary high costs and unused capacity.

As stated earlier, the data from which to develop a traffic pattern simply may not be available. The users and the designers may not know what the traffic will be. Since the baseline for a design is the amount of applications data to be passed through the network, the designers and the users must knowingly establish boundaries pertaining to (a) the most likely amount of data, (b) the most likely peak period, and (c) an expected response time. Management should review these boundaries in order to make cost-performance trade-off decisions. The goal of the organization should be to meet the user requirements with a minimum cost design.

Cost-performance trade-off analysis can be very valuable. For example, network costs can often be reduced substantially by offering a longer response time for selected messages and applications. Extended response time can decrease the costs of communications lines, processing computers, and the network software. In addition, low-priority traffic can sometimes be delayed until the nonpeak traffic hours. This will also reduce costs, since the traffic can be "smoothed" over a 24-hour period, and costs to implement a high-capacity, peak-hours network can be reduced.

The number of input and output messages is dependent on the amount of data needed by the user and the format of the messages or transactions that flow into and out of the application. Due to efficiency and buffering considerations, it may be necessary to create more than one message from an input/output activity (that is, the 16 transactions in the sales order entry example could be broken into smaller units on the communications path). The total traffic is stated in volume of characters. The volume is determined by the number of messages and the number of characters in each message.

Protocol overhead.   The length of the messages will also be determined by line and protocol control characters [such as end of transmission indicator (EOT)], and these characters must be included in the total amount of traffic during the peak period. The design team must know the data link controls (DLCs) that are to be used, and they must be able to calculate the ratio of overhead control characters to the applications data.

The data link control method and modem will also influence the ratio of applications usage to that of protocol and overhead usage. For example, if a half-duplex protocol is used, the line will not be available while the receiving modem is "turning around" and resynchronizing itself for transmission in the other direction. On an aggregate basis, these modem turnaround times can become significant. Moreover, the manner in which the protocol controls the message flow will determine the ratio of applications data to overhead data. An acknowledgment of every message (IBM's bisync) will require more overhead than inclusively acknowledging every one to seven messages (IBM's synchronous data link control).

The number of errors that occur is likely to affect total traffic throughput, since messages that are received in error will probably be retransmitted. The design team must factor probable error rates into the total traffic load. The manner in which errored messages are retransmitted requires that the design team understand how the data link control handles the errors. As we shall see, a go-back-N DLC will give a traffic throughput figure different from a selective repeat DLC.

Performance.   The performance of the system is of paramount importance to the design team. Performance analysis entails the balancing of response time (or delay) and throughput. Response time to individual users must be weighed against total throughput for all users. Fast response time requires that minimum delay be encountered in moving the message through the network. Small delays rely on relatively short messages in order to reduce the time required to receive and check all bits of the message. Fast response time also benefits from short message queues, since the shorter queues will decrease the aggregate waiting time for message processing.

On the other hand, high throughput requires longer messages in order to reduce the ratio of overhead characters to applications-specific characters. High throughput also benefits from long queues in order to smooth the traffic load. During periods of peak network activity, the lower-priority messages can be placed on queues and processed later when the traffic decreases. In this manner, overall line utilization is improved.

It should be recognized that excessive optimization of response time to each user reaches a point of diminishing returns, and overall response time to all users will eventually suffer. Obviously, an increased line speed and powerful computers will improve both response time and throughput, but the design team must still make trade-offs between these two important elements.

Finally, the network support functions must be considered carefully. Certain functions may extend response time (security provisions, code translation, providing for different terminal types, protocol conversion), while others may reduce throughput (adding department, data base, terminal or user identifiers to the message header). Yet these functions may be essential in meeting the user requirements. Without question, reliability is a major function of any network, and certain reliability functions will decrease response time. For example, redundant data bases and audit trail logging will increase delays to the network users.

Consequently, the designers will find themselves facing trade-offs between the factors of throughput, response time, and support functions (sometimes called the DDT, or designer's dilemma triangle, see Figure 13-3). It is usually not possible to provide optimum results at one point of the triangle without degrading results at the other two points. There are exceptions (the support function of data compression will increase throughput), but the DDT should be uppermost in the minds of the design team.

The managers and users of the network should participate in decisions that affect the location of the point on the DDT. It is the responsibility of the design team to act as a catalyst for the decisions; it is *not* the function of the team to make these decisions.

Applications requirements.   The company's technical personnel have performed an extensive analysis of each site within the four regions. The analysis has led to the following requirements for the southern region:

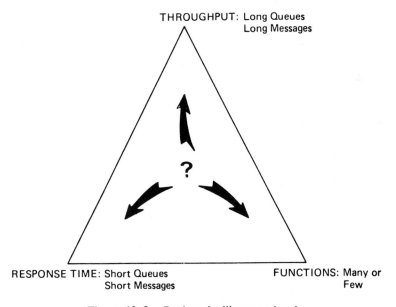

Figure 13-3.   Designer's dilemma triangle.

TABLE 13-1 TRAFFIC DURING PEAK PERIOD

Sales Offices in Southern Region	Number of Transactions During Peak Period
Lubbock, Texas	1,688
Austin, Texas	1,864
Dallas, Texas	3,916
Houston, Texas	4,736
Little Rock, Arkansas	2,016
New Orleans, Louisiana	2,500
Jackson, Mississippi	1,000
Birmingham, Alabama	1,544
Gainesville, Florida	1,568
Miami, Florida	3,664
Atlanta, Georgia	4,008
Charleston, South Carolina	4,620
Raleigh, North Carolina	2,572
Nashville, Tennessee	4,712
	40,408

The peak traffic load occurs once a day for 60 minutes from 10:15 to 11:15 A.M. Since timeliness is an important requirement, the network must accommodate to the peak period and the network must be designed to handle the traffic during the one-hour peak period.

The analysis team conducted studies at each sales office and tabulated the transactions for the peak hour traffic load (see Table 13-1). A *transaction* is defined for this study as consisting of one application input to the host and one application response from the host. Several transactions are usually needed to process a full applications query. This transaction activity during the peak period provides valuable input to the traffic pattern calculations.

The offices use sales and marketing information during the peak period. (Generally, other traffic is not allowed during this time—personnel, administrative, etc.) The marketing representatives use terminals or personal computers for entering sales orders and querying of orders. Inventory personnel use the system to provide component-availability information to company personnel and to customers.

The terminal and personal computer market was examined and the company has selected devices with an EBCDIC 8-bit character set. The terminals use buffered memory and will input and output with the modems selected at 2,400 bits per second (bit/s).

The team has designed the message formats for the communications system. Figure 13-4 illustrates the format and applications data content of the messages for the sales and inventory applications. Since a transaction is defined as an input to the host and a response from the host, the sales application will require 100 characters and the inventory 130 characters for each complete transaction.

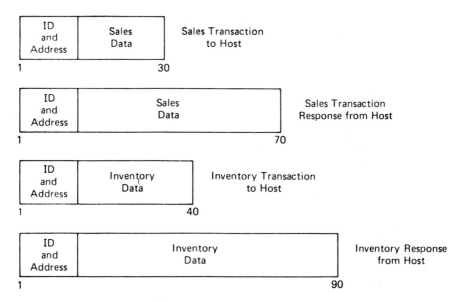

Figure 13–4. Message formats.

The workstation user should not be required to key in the complete 30/40 characters for the two applications. The terminals and personal computers can be programmed to accept abbreviated input from the user and expand the input to a full transaction. In this manner, fewer personnel are required to input the traffic to the host (we return to this issue later in the chapter).

The design team estimates that the processing time at the regional computer(s) will be 100 milliseconds (ms) for each transaction. The decision to acquire faster or slower machines will be based on the effect of the 100-ms delays on line throughput, response time, and computer capacity. This study will determine these effects. The design team will use the 100-ms figure for the initial calculations. A processing time estimate may be difficult to obtain with any assurance of accuracy. However, a rough figure can prove very useful for the first iteration of the calculations. We will cover this topic in more detail later in the case study.

The sales transactions currently comprise approximately 70% of the workload and the inventory transactions account for 30%. It is anticipated that this ratio will remain consistent for the foreseeable future.

Company management projects an annual growth rate in sales of 6% for the next five years. Obviously, this growth will affect the use of the network. Based on the estimated growth and a turnpike effect of 15%, the traffic volume is projected (Table 13–1). The *turnpike effect* is simply a "margin of safety" factor to help ensure that the system is not underdesigned. Its name is derived from the experiences that turnpike designers had several years ago. The first turnpikes were designed to carry long-haul traffic. The designers did not think a local driver would use the facility due to the trouble of getting on and off the turnpike. However, local traffic did indeed use the turnpikes and they were underdesigned.

The turnpike effect need not be just a guess. Some organizations develop scenarios that estimate a linear growth rate of traffic and then factor other contingencies, such as offering new products or altering the organization's mission. These contingencies would be part of a turnpike factor.

Some organizations find it too expensive to configure the system for five years in advance. A sound alternative is to configure for present needs, and design the system to accommodate growth by planning for the expansion of communications capacity, additional workstations, and more processing power at the host computer(s).

Leased versus dial-up lines.   Leased lines have been selected to support the sales and inventory applications in this network. Several trade-offs exist between dial-up and leased facilities, and the design team must consider both options. For example, dial-up lines provide for a flexible backup: If a line is lost, the operator simply redials into the network. Dial-up facilities are also attractive for low-volume users.

If the dial-up option is chosen, response time is lengthened due to the operator's time in dialing and connecting to the computer (perhaps 8 to 13 seconds). An alternative is for the computer to dial the terminals and communicate with the terminals' interface logic (or a transmission control unit) and *not* the human operator. Computer-generated dial-ups are, in effect, a form of polling. They offer three significant advantages over operator-generated dial-ups:

1. Delay is not dependent on the manual keying in of the data. The data are entered into a buffer and, upon a dial-up connection, transmitted onto the communications line at a much faster rate than the operator typing speed. The data are ready for transmission when the connection is made (or the dial-up is terminated by a "hang-up" and disconnect).
2. The operator does not experience delays in performing the dialing.
3. Since the operator does not dial, he or she does not get a blockage (that is, a busy signal).

Leased lines are cost-effective for the transmission of larger volumes of data for extended periods. Moreover, since leased-line arrangements permit the permanent connection of the communication path within the telephone system, the lines can be monitored and "conditioned" for better service than is available on switched, dial-up facilities. Some applications require leased facilities if the delay involved in dialing numbers presents a problem. Our case study shows a great amount of activity during a critical peak hour and, therefore, warrants the leased lines. (One is now faced with what to do with the expensive lines during the nonpeak hours.)

The costs of leased lines are based on (1) line distance measured in air miles, (2) rate schedules, (3) local loop costs (termination charges), and (4) installation charges. AT&T uses a Cartesian grid coordinate system for this purpose (see Figure 13–5). The

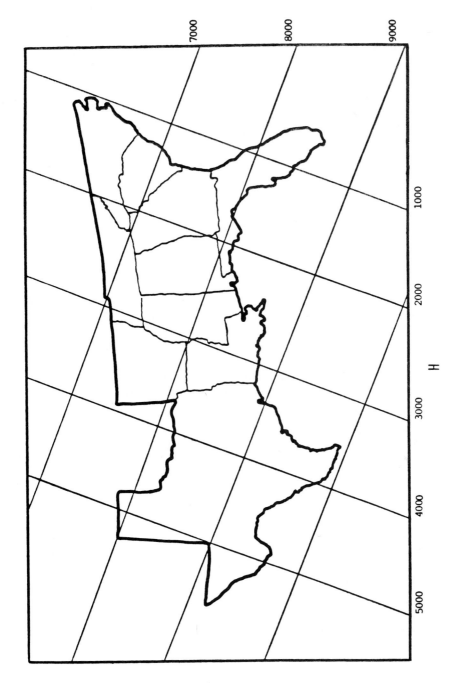

Figure 13-5. V-H grid map of the southern region.

grid establishes air mile distance between sites and applies the following formula to compute the distance between two points:

$$\text{Distance} = \sqrt{\frac{(V_1 - V_2)^2 + (H_1 - H_2)^2}{10}}$$

The cost for line distance, installation, and termination stations is readily available from the carriers. However, be aware that varying line rates from city to city will affect network layout decisions. Some cities' interconnections will cost more than others.

Line data link control (or protocol). The line protocol will be half-duplex with line turnaround time (TAT) of 110 ms. The line turnaround allows for the sending modem to resynchronize itself to receive and the receiving machine to "turn around" to send. The rationale for half-duplex is due to the relatively simple and low-capacity requirements of the system (and to explain its effects to the reader!). Moreover, an organization usually has existing communications facilities with certain types of protocols. In many cases, the selection of a different protocol (for example, full-duplex) may require extensive software and hardware changes. Consequently, a company may choose to use an existing protocol in order to reduce development conversion costs.

The protocol is a conventional bisync-type polling/selection, stop-and-wait system and handles a terminal conversation in the following manner (we examine full-duplex protocols later):

1. Poll to terminal from host
2. Message sent by terminal
3. Acknowledgment by host
4. End of transmission from terminal; process the transaction
5. Address the terminal from host
6. Acknowledgment by terminal
7. Message sent by host
8. Acknowledgment by terminal
9. End of transmission from host

These nine elements will require additional characters for line control (polling, selection, EOT) and line and device synchronization. As stated earlier, the design team must add the overhead characters to the application characters in order to determine a total message length. Figure 13–6 provides an illustration of the relationship of the nine elements and the overhead and applications data.

The nine elements, as well as the number of characters (bytes) associated with each element, are shown in Figure 13–6. The sales application will require 65 overhead characters and 100 data characters; the inventory applications will require 66 overhead characters and 130 data characters. (The longer inventory message requires an extra

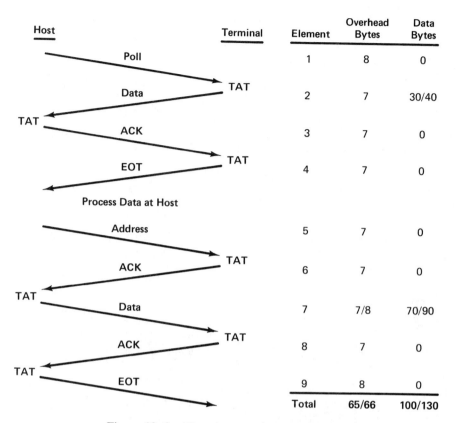

Host	Terminal	Element	Overhead Bytes	Data Bytes
Poll		1	8	0
Data	TAT	2	7	30/40
TAT ACK		3	7	0
EOT	TAT	4	7	0
Process Data at Host				
Address		5	7	0
ACK	TAT	6	7	0
TAT Data		7	7/8	70/90
ACK	TAT	8	7	0
TAT EOT		9	8	0
		Total	65/66	100/130

Figure 13–6. Nine elements of the transaction.

synchronization character.) Consequently, the total data sent through the network to complete one full transaction are 165 characters for sales and 196 characters for inventory.

Line-Loading Calculations

Block error rate.   As previously stated, the design will account for some frames containing errors. These frames must be retransmitted and will affect total frame throughput. The communications line can be tested and monitored to determine a probable error rate. The common carrier can also provide probable error statistics based on the type of line and the level of conditioning. The engineers can provide data on bit test patterns, from which the design team can calculate a probable block error rate (BLER).

The size of the frame block is an important design consideration. For example, during noisy periods on the line, longer blocks are more likely to be retransmitted, since bit errors occur more often in a longer bit stream. Yet shorter blocks decrease overall throughput due to the additional control headers and trailers required for each frame.

For purposes of simplicity, assume the tests have been performed on bit patterns and on the actual message block lengths that were established by the design team.

Calculation 1: Block Error Rate

Formula: $$BLER = \frac{TBE}{TBR}$$

Where: BLER = block error rate
TBE = total blocks received in error
TBR = total blocks received

Application data: Technical team conducted random tests on lines and ascertained the following:

TBE: 1000
TBR: 100,000

Calculation: $$BLER = \frac{1000}{100,000} = 0.01$$

Throughput.   Throughput is a very important design consideration. The term refers to the amount of data that can be sent over a communications channel during a given time period. Throughput is described in bits per second (bit/s) and is usually calculated on a one-way transmission. There are a number of methods to calculate throughput. The following approach is commonly used and is based on ANSI Standard X3.44.

Calculation 2: Throughput

Formula: $$TP = \frac{M(1 - P)}{M/R + T}$$

Where: TP: throughput
M: applications message length (in bits)
P: probability of one or more bit errors in block
      (see Calculation 1)
R: line speed in bits per second (bps)
T: time between blocks in seconds

Application data: M = 920 avg.
Sales: 100 × 8 =   800
Inv: 130 × 8 = 1040
                                    1840

1840/2 = 920

P = 0.01
R = 2400
T = 0.110

Calculation: $TP = \dfrac{920\,(1 - 0.01)}{920/2400 + 0.110} = 1846$

The parameter M is derived by calculating an average message length of the sales and inventory messages. Be aware that an average might skew the throughput figure if one application's message is significantly longer than others and has considerably more traffic on the line. For purposes of line loading, tuning, and simplicity, fixed message lengths for all applications should be considered. This approach requires that a logical user message be segmented into pieces (packets) and transmitted separately, but it greatly simplifies the design, implementation, and operation of the system.

The formula illustrates the importance of the message block length on network performance. For example, very long block lengths will increase the significance of probability P because longer messages increase the probability of receiving an erroneous bit in a message. The parameter T will be less a factor with longer messages because the time between message blocks decreases as messages increase in length. On the other hand, T assumes more significance with short messages, since the relative amount of time between blocks increases.

It is very important to understand that the time between blocks may be determined by the turnaround time if the line is configured as half-duplex. As a worst-case approach, Calculation 2 computes time between blocks and Calculation 5 adds in the TAT values. However, in a half-duplex arrangement, the T parameter is somewhat masked by TAT.

The parameter T depends to a great extent on the data link control logic that manages the flow of messages between the host and secondary sites, the capacity of the host to service the line regularly, and the rate at which data are entered at the workstations. For example, the delay between blocks rests on the efficiency of the polling/selection routines and how well they keep the line "busy." The modem and DLC vendors should be consulted before computing the T factor. This calculation assumes only the delay between the blocks; later calculations will include modem turnaround time.

Utilization factor.   The utilization factor is a number indicating the applications' actual use of the line's stated throughput capacity. In this study, the 2,400-bit/s line would not allow 2,400 bit/s of sales and inventory data to be passed over the line due to the overhead characters, line turnaround, errors, and polling. In some applications, such as a tape file transfer or a remote job entry (RJE), response time is not an important component and the line utilization factor is used for capacity planning. Response time calculations must also be used if responsiveness is a user requirement. Interactive applications must be given careful consideration in relation to response time.

In simple systems, the utilization factor is not calculated but is derived from subjective evaluations and the experiences of the designers. The actual utilization usually ranges from 40% to 95%. The wide variation results from factors such as switching technology, queueing delays, multipoint complexities, and the need for low utilization to enhance response time.

The utilization factor can also be used to account for the overhead of unsuccessful polls, in which a terminal is polled and has nothing to send to the host. The design team must account for unsuccessful polls, call setups, and call clearings for some protocols, since this type of overhead may use a significant amount of the available line capacity. Calculation 3 is a simple illustration of determining the utilization factor. Be aware that many elements can influence the actual line utilization.

Calculation 3: Utilization Factor

Formula: $\quad UF = \dfrac{TP}{R}$

Where: UF: utilization factor
           TP: throughput (see Calculation 2)
           R: line speed in bps (theoretical maximum
                capacity)

Application data: TP = 1846 (see Calculation 2)
                  R   = 2400

Calculation: $\quad UF = \dfrac{1846}{2400} = 0.77$

Message line time.   This calculation determines the time required to transmit a message across the 2,400-bit/s channel. The reader should note that Calculation 4 includes the applications characters and the overhead characters. Returning back to Calculation 2, it can be seen that overhead data were not used in the throughput computation. Several methods exist to factor in overhead data; the important point is not to overlook it. The 300 characters per second (cps) is derived from the 2,400-bit/s line using 8 bit characters (2,400/8 = 300).

Calculation 4: Message Line Time

Formula: MLT = TC × CLT

Where: MLT: message line time
            TC: total characters transmitted in complete poll
                  and address (to complete a full transaction)

CLT: character line time (how long it takes for one character to move through the line)

Application data: TC   sales: 165 characters
inv: 196 characters
CLT = 3.33 ms per character
(1000 ms/300 cps)
Note: 1000 is used because
1000 ms = 1 second

Calculation: MLT (sales) = 165 × 3.33 = 550 ms
MLT (inv)   = 196 × 3.33 = 653 ms

Network transaction time.   The next calculation provides the time required to process a complete transaction. This includes the computer processing time, line turn-around time (only on half-duplex lines), and the time required to move the complete transaction (that is, the nine elements previously discussed) from start to finish.

The processing time parameter (PT) will not be a factor in line loading if the line is released for other transactions while the computer is processing the ongoing transaction. This *released-line* discipline is commonly found in the larger systems. Typically, a front-end processor handles the held-line or released-line tasks. Chapter 4 contains additional information on this topic. Also, Chapter 4 discusses the processing time parameter in more detail.

Calculation 5: Network Transaction Time

Formula: NTT = MLT + PT + TAT

Where: NTT: network transaction time
MLT: message line time (see Calculation 4)
PT: processing time
TAT: line turnaround time (*Note*: Do not use on full-duplex line calculations)

Application data: MLT = sales: 550 ms
inv: 653 ms.
PT   = 100 ms for both applications
TAT = 770 ms (7 TATs × 110 ms each, see
Figure 11-6)

Calculation: NTT (sales) = 550 + 100 + 770 = 1420 ms
NTT (inv.) = 653 + 100 + 770 = 1523 ms

Weighted average transaction time. The sales and inventory applications will not use the network equally, since sales will comprise 70% of the traffic and inventory the remaining 30%. Therefore, weighting factors must be applied to compensate for this uneven use.

Calculation 6: Weighted Average Transaction Time

Formula:

$$\text{WATT} = \sum_{N=1}^{K} (\text{TPCT(n)} \times \text{NTT(n)})$$

Where:

WATT:	weighted average transaction time
TPCT:	total percentage of network traffic for this application
NTT:	network transaction time (see Calculation 5)
K:	number of applications

Application data:

TPCT = sales: 70% of traffic
        inv: 30% of traffic
NTT = sales: 1420 ms
        inv: 1523 ms

Calculation:

WATT (sales) = 0.7 × 1420 ms = 994 ms
WATT (inv.) = 0.3 × 1523 ms = 457 ms

994
457
‾‾‾
1451 ms or 1.451 seconds

Line capacity for applications. The next calculation determines how many transactions can be accommodated on a 2,400-bit/s line during the peak period. Since previous calculations have shown how long a full transaction occupies the line, it remains now to divide the applications line time into peak period time to determine the line capacity for the one hour.

The utilization factor is also applied. This may appear to be doing "double accounting" for overhead (since overhead was part of Calculations 4 and 5). However, as stated earlier, multipoint lines with queuing delays, polling delays, and unsuccessful polls introduce additional overhead. The utilization factor is one method to include these factors.

Unsuccessful polls occur when the host scans of polling table, obtains an address of a terminal, and issues a poll without obtaining a response because the terminal has nothing to send. The terminal operator may be keying in data or simply thinking. Whatever the case, unsuccessful polls can account for a substantial amount of the total network traffic (As we shall see shortly, a common approach to this problem is the utilization of multiplexers or cluster controllers.) In some instances, the network overhead also consumes a substantial portion of the computer capacity. It should be noted that an actual situation may require the substitution of the utilization factor calculations with data derived from the queueing formula and polling models discussed later in this chapter.

Calculation 7: Line Capacity for Applications

Formula: $LC = \dfrac{LENPP}{WATT} \times UF$

Where: LC: capacity of a line to handle traffic
LENPP: length of peak period in seconds
WATT: weighted average transaction time (see Calculation 6)
UF: utilization factor (see Calculation 3)

Calculation: $LC = \dfrac{3600}{1.451} \times 0.77 = 1909$

Therefore, 1909 transactions can be accommodated per line per peak period.

Total number of lines.   We now have sufficient information to determine how many lines will be required at each branch office in the southern region. Calculation 8 shows that the two applications will require 18.703 communications lines. It is very unlikely that 40,408 transactions an hour can be handled by a small computer. The design team must develop the loading profile and response times (both discussed shortly) in order to size the proper computer(s) in the work load.

The design team must also make evaluations on where to place the computers within the southern region. (This study has assumed that the host is situated at regional headquarters.) The section on distributed system design will discuss this issue in more detail.

Calculation 8: Total Number of Lines

Formula: $TL = \dfrac{TV}{LC}$

Where: TL   = Total lines required
TV: = Total volume
LC: = Capacity of a line to handle traffic (see Calculation 7)

Application data and calculations:

Site	TV	/	LC	=	TL
Lubbock	1,688		1909		0.884
Austin	1,864		1909		0.976
Dallas	3,916		1909		2.051
Houston	4,736		1909		2.481
Little Rock	2,016		1909		1.056
New Orleans	2,500		1909		1.309
Jackson	1,000		1909		0.523
Birmingham	1,544		1909		0.808
Gainesville	1,568		1909		0.821
Miami	3,664		1909		1.919
Atlanta	4,008		1909		2.100
Charleston	4,620		1909		2.420
Raleigh	2,572		1909		1.347
Nashville	4,712		1909		2.468
	40,408		1909		21.171
			(Nashville)		−2.468
					18.703

The total volume of 40, 408 transactions for the southern region represents a sizable work load for the region computer(s). The reader may have surmised by now that an average processing time of 100 ms for each transaction means the peak-hour traffic cannot be effectively accommodated on a computer or computers of this capacity. Theoretically, the 100-ms window allows 36,000 messages per hour to be processed if the messages arrive at a fixed rate (100 ms: 10 transactions a second $\times$ 60 seconds $\times$ 60 minutes = 36,000 transactions per hour). However, the traffic represents a greater than 100% utilization of one computer's CPU cycles, which *cannot be obtained*. Moreover, the 100-ms processing time assumes all resources function without further delay and without error, which is rarely the case.

In other words, the hypothetical machine capacity may not suffice. As noted earlier, the design team used the figure for preliminary calculations and, in order for the line-sizing data to make sense, the computer capacity (processing time) should be evaluated with response time calculations (see Calculations 14 and 15) to permit the full effect of the traffic load to be analyzed.

Practically speaking, an organization faced with this type of problem has several options:

- Examine the market for machines of greater capacity.
- Consider installing additional machines, with a front-end processor to route the traffic among the computers.
- Off-load work from the regional site by locating small computers at some of the sales offices.

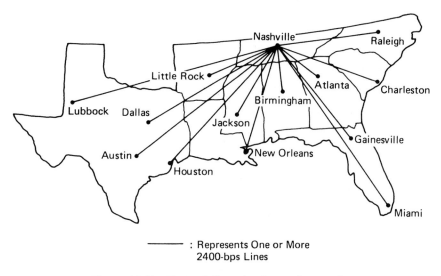

: Represents One or More
2400-bps Lines

Figure 13-7. Network lines for the southern region.

- Downgrade the system response time by allowing fewer transactions during the peak hour (for example, only critical inquiries) and transmitting less important traffic at a later time.

Whatever the options chosen, the decision will affect line sizing and will require another iteration of Calculations 1 through 8.

Other Considerations

Choice of network topology. The line layout for the southern region is illustrated in Figure 13-7. The line layout shows several locations configured with multiple lines. For example, the traffic volume from Houston will require three (2.48 lines, rounded to 3) lines to satisfy the peak load throughput requirements.

The design team's job is not yet complete, however, because the present arrangement is not the most cost-effective approach. The lines may now be configured to give a minimum-cost network topology that satisfies the performance objectives. For example, the New Orleans and Jackson branches will need 1.307 and 0.523 lines, respectively, to satisfy their requirements. Full line capacity must be given to these branches, since it is not possible to lease a part of a line. Consequently, the two sites have unused line capacity.

The region can be reconfigured to provide the same service with fewer lines. This is accomplished by placing a line from New Orleans to Jackson and moving 0.309 of the New Orleans traffic to the partially used line of 0.523 at Jackson [see Figure 13-8(a).] The route of the altered data flow means leasing a line of shorter distance. As indicated earlier in this study, line costs are based on the air mile distance of the line,

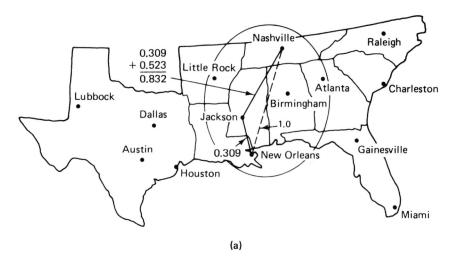

$$\begin{array}{r} 0.309 \\ +\ 0.523 \\ \hline 0.832 \end{array}$$

(a)

Figure 13–8. Alternate topology example

and the line from New Orleans to Jackson will cost less than from New Orleans to Nashville.

This approach would entail installing multiplexers on the New Orleans–Jackson–Nashville links. Indeed, the introduction of multiplexers into our design opens the door to another attractive alternative.

One alternative is shown in Figure 13–8(b). The 0.309 traffic at New Orleans is sent to an input port at a multiplexer in Jackson where it is multiplexed onto the line to Nashville. (A multiplexer is also needed at the Nashville and New Orleans sites.)

A topology analysis must examine the performance and cost trade-offs in reconfiguring the other New Orleans traffic (that is, its full-line requirement). Figure 13–8(b) illustrates a rather awkward arrangement with two 2,400-bit/s lines emanating from New Orleans. This alternative requires two multiplexers at New Orleans and Nashville to service the New Orleans traffic. Moreover, the user devices at New Orleans are permanently attached to the multiplexers, which yields an inflexible arrangement. If MUX A's ports are all busy, a device wired to MUX A cannot use MUX B, even though MUX B may have spare capacity at the time. A better alternative is to acquire a Nashville–Jackson–New Orleans link of greater capacity (higher-speed modems and multiplexers and leased lines with better conditioning). This approach is shown in Figure 13–8(c). All traffic from New Orleans is now routed through Jackson.

The design team must also consider other alternatives. For example, what are the trade-offs of routing the New Orleans traffic through other intermediate nodes, such as Birmingham? Our simple analysis has focused only on Jackson, yet many of other network topology alternatives exist. (We return shortly to some multiplexer calculations.)

The design team could possibly perform the network configuration analysis by hand but, with 13 sites involved, the task would involve hundreds of combinations. Computer models are available to perform programmatically the configuration. The common carriers provide this service as part of their product, and consulting firms have

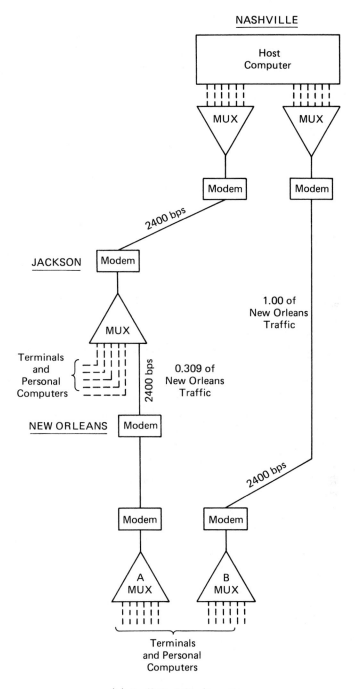

(b) Inefficient Configuration

Figure 13–8. (*cont.*)

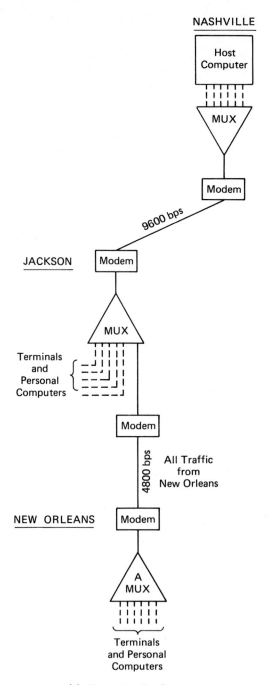

(c) Alternative Configuration   **Figure 13–8.**   (*cont.*)

the capability. IBM and other companies also have network configuration models. The IBM model is called the Communications Network Design Program (CNDP). This program accepts input parameters of site-to-site distances and rates. Network paths are "grown" from the farthest node toward the host. CNDP repetitively adds a node to a link, reevaluates the change in relation to previous configurations, and compares costs. The detailed explanations of Esau-Williams, the Prim approach, and others are available from vendors.

The Network Analysis Corporation (NAC) uses a product called MIND (Modular Interactive Network Designer) for line configuration, cost analysis, and topology layout.[1] The MIND user inputs parameters describing each node (ID, telephone company location [area] codes, input and output traffic, number of terminals at each node, certain node termination costs, and other parameters). MIND then provides the following information:

- Network costs based on current tariffs
- Assignment of terminals
- Effect of possible use of multiplexers
- Analysis of multipoint versus point-to-point
- Line load
- Analysis of effect of increasing/decreasing line speed and/or traffic and/or terminals
- Reliability indicators
- Waiting and response time reports
- Simulation of different data link controls

Improving the Network

The addition of multiplexers provides considerable flexibility to the design team. However, to effectively use the components, a more efficient line protocol is required. The protocol depicted in Figure 13–6 entails excessive overhead in (a) the turnaround times and (b) the requirement to acknowledge every block transmitted.

Protocols are available other than the half-duplex, stop-and-wait method that was selected by the design team. Two full-duplex protocols frequently used are go-back-N and selective repeat. The use of full-duplex protocols requires that the communications line provide for two-way, simultaneous transmission. This capability is usually provided by two separate lines attached to full-duplex modems.

The T parameter used in Calculation 2 greatly diminishes the actual throughput on a channel, and is especially evident on a high-speed facility. Calculations 9 and 10 illustrate the throughput using full-duplex components, such as multiplexers, and 9,600-bit/s lines.

[1] Network Analysis Corporation, 130 Steamboat Road, Great Neck, NY 11024.

The reader will note that these calculations eliminate the T factor (see Calculation 2) because a full-duplex protocol does not experience a significant delay in time between blocks. Moreover, the TAT values in Calculation 5 are irrelevant on a full-duplex circuit because no line turnarounds are needed. Also, the selective repeat formula does not contain the N factor (probable number of retransmissions of correct messages) that is in the go-back-N calculation.

Calculation 9: Throughput with Go-Back-N

Formula: $$TPGB = \frac{M \times (1 - (N \times P))}{(M/R)}$$

Where: TPGB: throughput
M: applications message length (see Calculation 2)
P: probability of one or more bit errors in block (see Calculation 1)
R: line speed in bits per second (bps)
T: time between blocks in seconds (not used)
N: probable number of retransmitted messages

Application data: M = 920
P = 0.01
R = 9600

N = 3 (assumption for purposes of this example)

Calculation: $$TPGB = \frac{920 \times (1 - (3 \times 0.01))}{920/9600} = 9312$$

Calculation 10: Throughput with Selective Repeat

Formula: $$TPSR = \frac{M \times (1 - P)}{M/R}$$

Where: See Calculation 9

Calculation: $$TPSR = \frac{920 (1 - 0.01)}{920/9600} = 9504$$

The improvement in throughput for selective repeat is generally not much better than go-back-N if line conditions are reasonably good and the protocol does not allow a great number of messages to be outstanding before a NAK or ACK is required. However, the throughput rates of 9,312 and 9,504 bit/s are better than the rate for a half-duplex protocol. The differences become more evident on higher-speed lines. For example, Calculation 2 reveals that a 9,600-bit/s, half-duplex protocol yields only 4,425 bits in throughput due to the T factor.

Multiplexer capacity.   Now that we have established a basis for evaluating the full-duplex protocols' throughput, let us return to the subject of multiplexers. The use of a conventional frequency-division multiplexer (FDM) or time-division multiplexer (TDM) would prove useful if the workstations (terminals and personal computers) are continuously busy, with little or no idle time between transmissions.

To illustrate the use of these multiplexers, another calculation is available to provide an approximate estimate of the number of lines or/and the speed of the required multiplexer. Let us again suppose the New Orleans traffic is routed to Jackson and tied into the multiplexer at the Jackson site. The multiplexer must support the 1.309 and 0.523 loads of the two sites, which were calculated for a 4,800-bit/s capacity. Is a 7,200-bit/s output sufficient? Do we need a 9,600-bit/s multiplexer? Calculation 11 provides us a quick and simple approximation of the load requirements. Notice the calculation is now assuming the use of 9,600-bit/s lines from Jackson to Nashville.

Calculation 11: Multiplexer Capacity (FDM or TDM)

Formula: $A \times 0.97: \sum_{I=1}^{K} (N(I) \times C(I) \times L(I))$

Where: A: aggregate capacity in bps of output side
N: number of input channels at this speed and code
C: speed of input channels in characters per second: 4800/8 = 600 and 2400/8 = 300
L: length of character set (in bits)
K: total number of input channels

Application data: A: 9600 bps
Jackson   (0.523 lines)
N: 1
C: 300 CPS
L: 8
New Orleans (1.309 lines)
N: 1

C: 600 CPS
L: 8

Calculation: 9600 × 0.97: (0.523 × 300 × 8) + (1.309 ×
                    600 × 8)
                9312: 7538

Thus, the output side is of greater capacity than the input side.

While Calculation 11 provides an easy method to size the MUX, it should be used with caution, since it included the use of partial line load factors (0.523 and 1.309). It does not allow for the fact that "partial lines" or various multiples of line speeds are rarely available. Therefore, this calculation is often used by rounding the 0.523 and 1.309 to 1.0 and 2.0, respectively. As in the previous calculations, the reader is encouraged to experiment with the parameters in the formula and talk with the multiplexer vendors on their specific line loading calculations.

Moreover, the FDM and TDM use fixed allocations of frequency and time, respectively. This approach can lead to wasted line capacity when the terminals are idle (for example, an operator pausing for think time). The line capacity is still reserved for the terminal regardless of whether the terminal is using the line.

The use of statistical time-division multiplexers (STDM) can increase the actual use of the line. The STDM does not provide fixed allotments of time for each station. Rather, the time slots are dynamically allocated to active terminals only. In a sense, the STDM plays the odds that all terminals will not be operating at the same time, because the sum of all input rates to the STDM are greater than the output rate.

While STDMs are valuable devices, their use requires a more detailed analysis in order to obtain proper performance and sizing. For example, the design team must examine the following areas for inclusion into STDM configuration planning:

Call rate per terminal: Frequency of terminals' use of the communications system

Message arrival distribution: Frequency of receiving and transmitting messages at each terminal and the amount of data in each message

Acceptable blocking or increased response time: Possibility that STDM must queue up traffic

STDM techniques add overhead with each additional active terminal in order to properly identify data from those terminals on the line. Be aware that the addition of overhead causes a nonlinear (exponential) effect on the line. Notwithstanding, STDMs have virtually captured the market supporting terminals with bursty transmission characteristics. Consequently, let us consider another calculation that provides a better method for sizing the lines and the supporting multiplexers.

To do this, the design team must answer two questions: (1) What is the probability that a workstation has data to send or receive? (2) Given (1), how many of these devices can be expected to be busy at the same time? The first question must be answered by actual observation of the people using the devices or from an analysis of statistical data on the system. We will address question 1 in Calculations 13 and 14. The second question is answered by Calculation 12.

Let us assume the design team models the New Orleans site with 16 workstations/devices to handle the peak-load traffic. Furthermore, the analysis reveals that a 25% probability exists that N devices have data to process.

Calculation 12: Multiplexer Capacity (STDM)

Formula: $P(N) = N^cM \times P(ON)^n \times (1 - P[ON])^{m-n}$

Where: P(N):   probability of N devices being active at the same time

N^cM: number of possible combinations, taken N at a time *Note:* N^cM represents the total number of combinations in which N devices of M total could be active at a time. This figure is calculated from the formula $N^cM = M!/(N!(M - N)!)$, where ! means factorial (e.g., 4! = $1 \times 2 \times 3 \times 4$). The BASIC program listing following Calculation 14 should help the reader apply the formula.

P(ON):   Probability of N devices having data to send

N: Number of devices with data to send

M: Total number of devices

```
500 REM STATEMENTS 520-780 ARE FOR STAT MUX LOADING AND QUEUING
        ESTIMATIONS
510 REM STATEMENTS 790-860 ARE FOR WORKSTATION LOADING
520 INPUT "DO YOU WISH STAT MUX CALCULATIONS? YES OR NO";YESNO$
530 IF YESNO$ = "NO" THEN GOTO 790
540 INPUT "TOTAL NUMBER OF DEVICES AT THIS MUX";M
550 INPUT "TOTAL WITH DATA TO SEND, IF FINISHED ENTER -1";N
560 IF N = -1 THEN GOTO 720
570 PON = .2
580 FAC=M
590 GOSUB 740
600 MFAC=TOT
610 FAC=N
620 GOSUB 740
630 NFAC=TOT
```

```
640 FAC=M - N
650 GOSUB 740
660 MNFAC=TOT
670 NOM=MFAC / (NFAC * MNFAC)
680 PROB = NOM * (PON^N) * ((1 - PON)^(M-N))
690 LPRINT "PROBABILITY FOR "M" DEVICES WITH "N" OF THEM WITH DATA &
        BUSY "PROB
700 TOTPROB = TOTPROB + PROB: LPRINT "RUNNING TOTAL PROBABILITY = "
        TOTPROB
710 GOTO 550
720 LPRINT "SUM OF P(0) THROUGH P(N) = " TOTPROB
730 STOP
740 TOT = 1
750 FOR I=2 TO FAC
760     TOT = TOT * I
770 NEXT I
780 RETURN
790 INPUT "DO YOU WISH WORK STATION LOADING? YES OR NO";YESNO$
800 IF YESNO$ = "NO" THEN GOTO 860
810 INPUT "INPUT WORK STATION TRANSACTION CAPACITY PER PEAK
        PERIOD";WCS
820 INPUT "TOTAL VOLUME FOR SITE, IF FINISHED ENTER -1";TV
830 IF TV = -1 THEN GOTO 860
840 TWS = TV / WCS
850 LPRINT "TOTAL VOLUME AND TOTAL WORKSTATIONS FOR THIS SITE ARE
        "TV" "TWS
860 STOP.
```

Application data: N^cM: see program listing

P(ON):   0.25

N: 1 through 16

M: 16

Calculations: The formula is repeated, varying N from 0 to 16.
The calculations provide the following
data:

Devices with Data to Send		Percentage of Time	Cumulative Percentage of Time (Rounded)
P(0)	=	0.010	0.010
P(1)	=	0.053	0.063
P(2)	=	0.133	0.197
P(3)	=	0.207	0.404
P(4)	=	0.225	0.630
P(5)	=	0.180	0.810
P(6)	=	0.110	0.920
P(7)	=	0.052	0.972
P(8)	=	0.019	0.992
P(9)	=	0.005	0.998
P(10)	=	0.001	0.9997
P(11)	=	0.0002	0.9999
P(12)	=	0.00003	0 9999
P(13)	=	0.000003	0.9999

Devices with Data to Send		Percentage of Time	Cumulative Percentage of Time (Rounded)
P(14)	=	0.0000002	0.9999
P(15)	=	0.00000001	0.9999
P(16)	=	0.0000000002	0.9999

The calculations enable the designers to make the following conclusions: 63% of the time, four or fewer devices will have data to send. If the workstations are operating at 2,400 bit/s, and sharing a multiplexed line of 9,600 bit/s, then queuing occurs when five or more devices have data to transmit. The queuing occurs approximately 37% of the time, and during these periods the workstations will notice decreased throughput.

Each active device beyond three will further degrade the throughput. To illustrate:

Five or more: 9,600/5 = 1920 bit/s

Six or more: 9,600/6 = 1600 bit/s

Seven or more: 9,600/7 = 1371 bit/s

If the P(ON) can be reduced to 20%, then four or fewer devices will have data to send about 80% of the time, and queuing would occur approximately 20% of the time. Of course, reducing P(ON) means reducing the activity of the devices.

Regardless if queuing occurs at 37% or 20% of the time, either is unacceptable. The figure is too high. One solution is to reduce the number of devices that contend for the use of the multiplexer. We address this issue in the next calculation.

Number of workstations required. In the previous discussion, terminals and personal computers are configured to handle the 2,500 transactions at the New Orleans site. How do we determine this number? Often, by actual observation of the personnel and their working style (keying speed, amount of think time required to complete a transaction, etc.).

Another helpful approach is to add the results of Calculation 5 to (a) the operators' think time, (b) rate of data entry, and (c) speed of workstation output (printer or screen). This determines the *total* time the device is busy for each transaction.

To illustrate the concept of workstation loading, let us assume the design team has observed the workstation users' activity. The observations reveal that a typical transaction requires approximately 20 seconds. The programmable devices require the user to key in only a few characters; the software then builds the complete transaction.

Calculation 13: Work-Station Capacity

Formula: $WSC = \dfrac{LENPP}{WSTT}$

Where: WSC: work-station capacity to handle transactions

LENPP: length of peak period in seconds
WSTT: work-station transaction time in
             seconds

Application Data:

LENPP: 3600
WSTT: 20

Calculation: $WSC = \dfrac{3600}{20} = 180$

Therefore, each workstation can accommodate 180 transactions per hour.

Total number of workstations required.   It is now possible to determine the number of workstations needed at each of the sites in the southern region. Bear in mind that factors such as operator efficiency and fatigue will influence the number of personnel and devices needed.

Calculation 14: Total Work Stations

Formula: $TWS = \dfrac{TV}{WSC}$

Where: TWS: total work stations required at each site
TV: total volume at each site (transactions)
WSC: work-station capacity (see Calculation 13)

Application data and calculations:

Site	TV	WSC	=	TWS
Lubbock	1,688	180	9.3	10
Austin	1,864	180	10.3	11
Dallas	3,916	180	21.7	28
Houston	4,736	180	26.3	27
Little Rock	2,016	180	11.2	12
New Orleans	2,500	180	13.8	14
Jackson	1,000	180	5.5	6
Birmingham	1,544	180	19.3	20
Gainesville	1,568	180	8.7	9
Miami	3,664	180	20.3	21
Atlanta	4,008	180	22.2	23
Charleston	4,620	180	25.6	26
Raleigh	2,572	180	14.2	15
Nashville	4,712	180	26.1	27
		Total work stations		249

It is readily apparent even to the uninitiated that 249 work stations and transaction clerks present a formidable resource to support (financially and technically). In such a situation, management often looks for alternatives to decrease the magnitude of the problem. The following questions should be addressed by the organization:

- Can the workstations' programs be improved to decrease the transaction clerks' time required to process a transaction?
- Can the line (if half-duplex) be released between line turnarounds in order to allow other devices to use the otherwise idle line? (Using full-duplex multiplexers, this is a moot question.)
- Can more powerful host computers improve response time?
- Can the workstation users be trained better to increase their transaction processing efficiency?
- Are *all* the sales and inventory applications of equal priority? Can some of the traffic be deferred to a later time?
- Can the peak period of one hour be extended? Such a decision would dramatically decrease the size and costs of all components (communications lines, modems, multiplexers, workstations, personnel, etc.).

Let us examine the effect of extending the peak period (assuming it is possible) from one hour to two hours. In effect, each site's transaction load is cut in half. As a consequence, when the formula parameters are changed, Calculation 7 shows the line capacity during the peak is doubled from 1,909 to 3,818. The final effect in Calculation 8 shows that New Orleans now needs only 0.65 of a 2,400-bit/s line instead of 1.30. Jackson's requirements have gone from 0.52 to 0.26.

Moreover, since the length of the peak periods is also a factor in workstation capacity (Calculation 13), the extension of the period to two hours decreases the requirements for workstations by one-half.

This decrease in the number of devices also has a dramatic effect on throughput and queuing (Calculation 12). A reduction to eight workstations at New Orleans would result in experiencing queuing delays less than 2% of the time.

Of course, this scenario assumes the traffic load can indeed be spread over a longer period. If spreading is not feasible, the organization should continue to look for other possibilities. Then the parameters to the calculations should be changed and the calculations can be run again to provide a fast, simple, and inexpensive "first-cut" to determine the magnitude of the problem.

Satellite links.   Satellite links are available from a number of specialized common carriers, and the small-volume user can purchase voice-grade lines at a reasonable price. However, satellite circuits entail additional problems for the designer. A primary consideration results from propagation delay. This delay is the time required to move the message from the sending terminal to the host. A typical propagation delay from the San Francisco office to the New York site would be around 20 to 30 ms using a land circuit. Satellite transmission must traverse a greater distance, since the satellites are usually located 22,300 miles above the equator. A San Francisco–New York one-way satellite transmission would require about 240 to 270 ms, plus additional time for delays at earth stations and the user's site.

The propagation delay poses a number of problems for the design time. First, the data link protocol may be affected. Typically, a polling/selection protocol polls a station and waits a given time period for a reply. If the polled terminal does not respond within the time period, the protocol logic usually repolls and eventually executes some error routines. The delay on a satellite link would result in protocols spending much of their time in the timeout and error logic because many protocols are designed for the faster terrestrial links.

The second problem relates to response time. The longer delays on a satellite link may not be acceptable for some applications (for example, real-time applications) and the design team must be aware of the user's response time requirements. However, a propagation delay of less than 0.5 second is not a problem for many applications and several satellite carriers have developed techniques for dealing with the delay problem.

Computer capacity considerations.   Calculation 5 includes a parameter for the computer time required to process a transaction. The computer processing time is often quite difficult to calculate precisely, especially if the host is multiprogrammed, multiprocessed, or coupled to other hosts. It is possible to determine the sequence of operations (and instruction set) of the applications programs that will be used to process a transaction, and these data can be very useful for performance tuning and analysis of the possible impact of increased traffic. However, the processing time is dependent on factors that vary from period to period, such as transaction load and job mix. Moreover, the operating systems and data-base management systems vendors may not provide the instruction sequences for those packages. The designer should be aware of these factors.

The processing time parameter is often influenced by disk I/O channel capacity. Many smaller machines have a single I/O bus that does not permit overlapping I/O transfer. Other systems use I/O for fetching instructions on disk and, again, this approach can add many variables to the situation.

The software can contribute to the wide range in the processing parameter. For example, an operating system that performs time slicing on an applications transaction may build up large execution queues. On the other hand, an operating system that allows tasks to go to completion could also present queuing problems, but of a different nature.

It is naive to think the vendor's specifications will provide a definitive guideline. The machines' power measure in (a) memory fetch time, (b) instruction time, (c) millions of instructions per second (mips), or (d) thousands of operations (ADD, MOVE) per second (kops) are useful figures but measure internal processing speed and must be evaluated in view of many other considerations.

One approach to sizing a work load for a transaction-based system is depicted in Figure 13–9. With this technique, the various processes to service a transaction are measured. The factors (such as number of instructions, number of data-base I/Os) are translated into times and computer work loads. The designers can then determine approximate delays at the serving processes and calculate a processing time for the trans-

LOADING PROFILE

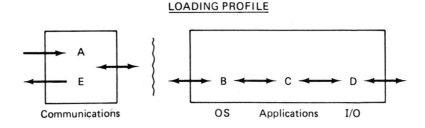

SERVERS	TASKS	SIZING FACTORS
A	Network Input	Message Size; Line Speed; Delay
B	OS Process	Number of Instructions
C	Applications Process	Number of Instructions
B	OS Accepts Request	Number of Instructions
D	I/O Access (Directory)	Peripheral I/O Rate; Block Size
D	I/O Access (Data)	Peripheral I/O Rate; Block Size
B	OS Accepts I/O	Number of Transactions
C	Applications Process	Number of Instructions
E	Network Output	Message Size; Line Speed; Network Delay

Figure 13–9. Work load sizing.

action. As previously stated, this task is complicated by lack of knowledge of O/S and DBMS instruction sets, multiprogramming, and time-sharing operating systems, but the exercise can be helpful in understanding more about the traffic work load.

Moreover, the simpler personal computer and minicomputer is being used increasingly in data communications systems, such as distributed systems and local area networks. These machines, often tailored to operate with specialized software and limited instruction sets, permit a more exact calculation of the sizing factors. In any event, sizing is an absolute necessity for systems requiring fast response time and efficient execution.

Standard work unit. An additional tool for designing an on-line transaction-oriented environment is the standard work unit (SWU). The SWU is used to regulate and predict the resources consumed by each on-line transaction in the network. The SWU concept requires that each transaction consume a limited amount of computer and data resources. For example, the SWU could define (a) a maximum number of data-base calls, (b) a maximum of machine cycle executions for each transaction, or (c) a maximum amount of CPU time.

The idea behind SWU is illustrated in Figure 13–10. The nonstandard work unit imposes unpredictable loads on the computer, resulting in unanticipated peak-load saturation and long-range computer resource planning. In contrast, the SWU provides for a more stable operating environment and a better ability to predict the implication of adding systems to the network. The SWU is particularly useful in view of the nonlinear

STANDARD WORK UNIT CONCEPT

Purpose: Attempt to Regulate Resources Consumed by Each Execution
of on-line Transactions.

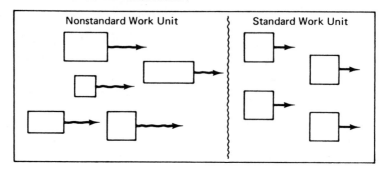

CAPACITY PLANNING

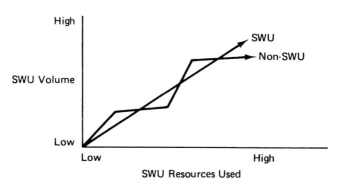

Figure 13-10.   Standard work unit.

relationship between increased work load and response time. The standard work unit is also very useful for a design technique called *dimension analysis*, which is discussed later in this chapter.

Benchmarking and modeling.   The use of benchmarking or modeling is a practical approach in determining an appropriate computer architecture. These techniques allow the designers to examine a number of alternatives before committing to a configuration to support the network traffic.

Modeling has long been a popular method of computer capacity sizing. It attempts to represent the performance of a computer through the use of programs that accept and process known or assumed patterns of behavior on work load. Modeling can be expensive, and the programs can become large and complex. Nonetheless, the technique is a powerful tool and should be considered by the designers.

Use of queuing models.   Many data communications systems designs are based on providing fast response time, in contrast to obtaining consistent, high throughput or providing ''just enough'' capacity to meet the traffic demands. Regardless of the design objectives, it is quite important to examine response time as part of the analysis and design process.

Queuing formulas are quite helpful in this analysis and have seen increasing use for designing transaction-based data communications systems. The formulas are integrated into computer programs to provide models for sizing response time.

Queuing analysis is quite important because of the nonlinear relationship between work load and response time. This occurs because response time is a function of processor time and the waiting time in queues. The waiting queues exist at several points in the process. For example, in Figure 13–9, servers A and E usually have significant queues and the other servers may also have waits associated with them.

The important point to remember about this discussion is that the time a message spends in a queue depends on the arrival rate of messages into that queue and/or the service time for that queue. Consider the following response time formula:

$$R = E(ts)/(1 - E(n)E(ts))$$

where R = response time
$E(n)$ = message arrival rate
$E(ts)$ = service time at server

Since $E(n)$ is a denominator in the formula, $E(ts)$ is not a linear function of $E(n)$. Therefore, as service time or message arrrival rate increases, response time increases nonlinearly, as shown in Figure 13–11.

Queuing models do not obviate the systems analysis and user requirements study. Indeed, the formulas are only as valid as their input parameters, which are based on the applications' traffic pattern. The following user data are the primary input parameters to the response time calculations:

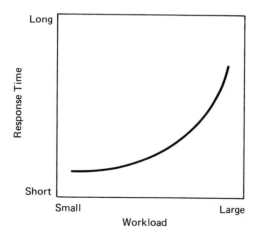

Figure 13–11. Work load and response time.

- Average arrival rate of applications messages at computer site
- Time between arrival of messages
- Number of queues (the messages' waiting lines)
- Time in the queue
- Number of messages in queue
- Number of servers (for example, computers to service the message)
- Average service time

Given these data, the queuing formula can then be used to calculate an expected response time. A design should use and substitute various parameters and repeat the formula calculations. In this manner, sizing and cost trade-offs can be compared against the response time requirements and adjustments can be made as dictated by user needs and the company's budget.

Summary of Line-Loading Analysis

The reader should now have an awareness of the basic elements in data communications line loading and topology design. This section introduced the subject; it is a discipline and profession unto itself. Nonetheless, you should have a sufficient background to understand the process. The next two sections on network software design and data-base design round out the material in the first section.

PARTITIONING AND ALLOCATION

One common approach to network software design is the partitioning/allocation method (PAM). The object of PAM is to divide and distribute the automated resources to the proper nodes in the network. PAM can be used to achieve more consistent load leveling, higher throughput, and faster response time at sites in the network. For example, as depicted in Figure 13–12, code can be partitioned (divided) into parts so that each part can be executed in parallel. The subcomponents can then be loaded to separate processors for simultaneous or parallel processing, thus decreasing the overall processing wait time that would be encountered by using one computer. By placing the program on four processors, the time required to execute the code is reduced from T + 4 to T + 1.

Network software partitioning requires more computers, which of course is an added expense to the system. However, the rapidly declining cost in hardware has provided the impetus to develop parallel processing systems. The trend is toward distributed parallel processing using machines and software tailored for specific functions.

Partitioning involves the initial description of the design at a very general and narrative level. The design moves to more detail as the requirements are refined and described in greater detail. Eventually, the partitions are realized in the form of source code (see Figure 13–13).

Since the partitions may be allocated to separate or remote machines, the partitioning design is an important part of the design process. The partitions must be as

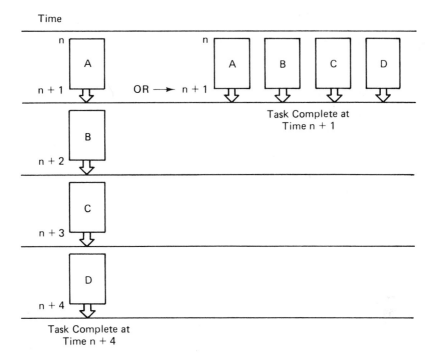

Figure 13–12. Parallelism.

independent and self-contained as possible yet contribute to the overall system goals as an integral part of the whole. The partitions should have few connections to one another in order to minimize complexity and error propagation. Each module should have only one entrance into its code and one exit and should connect (couple) only to modules directly above and below it. The ideas are illustrated in Figure 13–14. The multiple connections in Figure 13–14(b) greatly complicate the system and lead to excessive traffic across the communications lines. For example, if modules C and E were loaded into computers in Nashville and Dallas, respectively, execution of code in module C could affect module E. This kind of connection results in transactions and messages being transmitted between the two sites. Obviously, message flow among computers is inevitable, even desirable. But the code must be organized into modules to avoid inter-nodal dependency.

To achieve simple connections, the partitions should exhibit strong logical cohesiveness. The goal of cohesiveness is achieved when the elements (or code) within the partition perform one function or a set of closely related functions. Once the instructions in the partition are executed, the process *should not require* other sites to complete the task. The objective is to partition programs into efficient and self-sufficient modules.

Systems that exhibit strong cohesiveness within modules are said to have tight logical binding. Tightly bound modules provide the added effect of loosely coupled modules. This means that the software modules executing in the network computers do not depend on other modules, since the functional code is located locally.

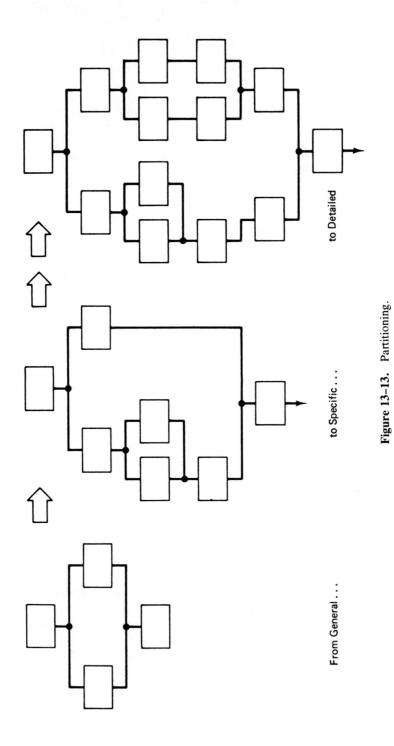

From General . . .　　　to Specific . . .　　　to Detailed

Figure 13-13. Partitioning.

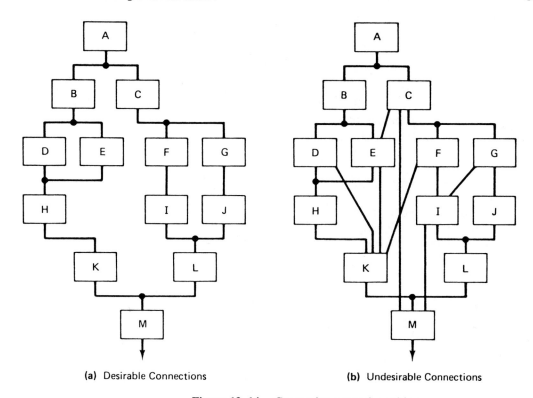

(a) Desirable Connections   **(b)** Undesirable Connections

Figure 13–14. Connecting network partitions.

Figure 13–14 also illustrates another critical aspect of PAM: keeping the scope of effect within the scope of control. This simply means that the execution of an instruction should affect only its own module and the modules connected directly below it. Figure 13–14(a) achieves this goal; Figure 13–14(b) does not. The danger of the connection in Figure 13–14(b) is the initiation of undesirable and unpredictable ripple effects throughout the network.

Partitioning and allocation work best when adhering to the principles of atomic actions.[2]

- An action is atomic if process X is not aware of the existence of other active processes and the other processes are not aware of process X during the time process X is performing the action.
- An action is atomic if the process performing the action does not communicate with other processes while the action is being performed.
- An action is atomic if the process performing the action can detect no changes

[2]B. Randall, *Operation Systems: An Advanced Course* (New York: Springer-Verlag, 1979) pp. 282–391.

except those performed by itself and if it does not reveal its state changes until the action is complete.

Upon the completion of the partitioning, resource allocation can be accomplished. Figure 13–15 depicts how the system modules in Figure 13–13 are allocated to sites A, B, and C. In this example, site A initiates the action by accepting the message and routing it to the proper site for processing. It could go to sites B and C for parallel execution. The results of the processing at C and B are transmitted back to A for final execution.

Data Flow Systems

To further illustrate partitioning and allocation, we will examine an actual example of software.[3] The following code is a series of FORTRAN arithmetic assignment statements. FORTRAN code is read as follows: The value of the variable on the left side of

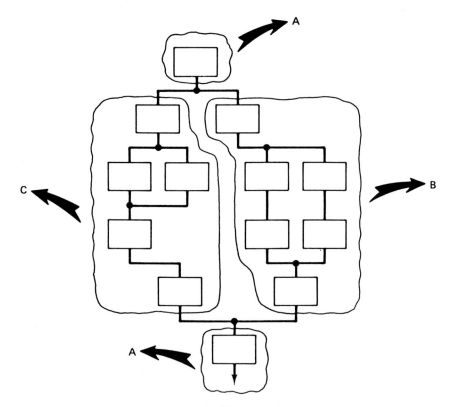

Figure 13–15. Allocation.

[3]The partitioning of individual instructions within a software module is a complex undertaking. It is explained here briefly to give the reader an appreciation of the process. A user application would rarely partition down to this level, but today's operating systems are evolving toward this process.

the equals sign is replaced by the calculation on the values of the variables on the right. That is, in statement 1, A is replaced by the division of B by C:

Statement Number	Program Instruction
1	A = B/C
2	D = A + E
3	F = P − Q
4	R = G * S
5	T = W * D
6	V = R/T
7	X = D + F

The code need not be executed sequentially from statements 1 through 7. Several different sequences of execution are possible; for example, 1; 2 and 3 simultaneously; 7; 4 and 5 simultaneously; 6. Another: 1 and 4 simultaneously; 2 and 3 simultaneously; 5, 6, and 7 simultaneously. The alternate sequences permit the program to be processed on multiple execution units.

Most large-scale mainframes provide this function in the form of look-ahead decoding, pipelining, and parallel processing. The important point to note here is that applications, telecommunications, and data-base code can be designed to execute within a network on different processing elements. The technique should be examined in view of cheaper processors and the resulting benefits of load leveling and decreased delay.

These ideas require a different design mentality, since many people in the applications programming area have become accustomed to thinking in terms of sequential code execution, sequential module execution, and sequential job dependencies. Consequently, the PAM technique will require training for the software staff.

The FORTRAN program might be partitioned and allocated as shown in Figure 13–16. The first option is a conventional sequential processing [Figure 13–16(a)]. As an alternative, in Figure 13–16(b), statements 2 and 3, 4, and 5 are executed simultaneously to cut down overall delay from T + 7 to T + 5. In Figure 13–16(c), additional parallelism gives a response of T + 4.

The FORTRAN coding example illustrates the concept of data flow systems. In contrast to the classical von Neumann approach of a single program counter and memory addresses, data flow systems execute instructions *only* if all required values to the instruction have been computed and are available. The instructions compute a value, and the value is passed to subsequent instructions for further processing. All sequencing is based only on data dependencies.

Data flow ideas are attractive for several reasons: (a) Partitioning to achieve parallelism is simplified; (b) data flow programs are very modular; (c) the software achieves tight binding and loose coupling; and (d) the scope of effect of an instruction or module execution is quite limited. All these points are important to a communications network containing computers that share resources such as data bases and CPU processing.

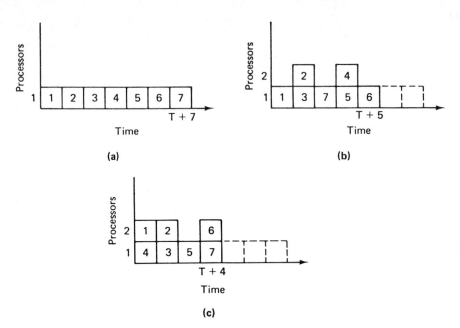

Figure 13–16. Partitioning for parallelism.

The code on page 383 presents data conflicts because the sequencing of its operations are (a) not based on data dependencies and (b) use duplicate work spaces for the same data value. Data flow concepts could improve the code by ordering instruction execution by data availability. Obviously, this would require rethinking and redesigning computer systems that are sequentially bound and allow independent transaction execution. The system would be required to provide for complete integration of all transactions running on the computer. Data flow systems for multiple transactions on partitioned/replicated data bases would be very complex but very powerful. We will eventually see commercial implementation of the concepts. Recent research on distributed data-base systems is pointing toward increased use of these ideas.

The PAM concepts must be approached carefully (and data flow systems have not seen extended commercial application). Excessive partitioning will consume inordinate delay and overhead in transporting the data between the processing elements. It should be remembered that a common carrier path operates in a milliseconds world and the local area network path in microseconds, whereas the processors operate in nano- and picoseconds. The relatively slow paths between the processors should be used to shift work load and move transactions only if the rules of binding, coupling, atomic actions, and scope of effect/control are followed. Otherwise, the network will spend needless time in managing excessive traffic and the resulting delays.

Dimension Analysis

Dimension analysis is used to determine how many processors should be used for the allocation. It is also used to determine the load on each processor. The concept is shown in Figure 13–17. The system is described by its logic width and logic depth.

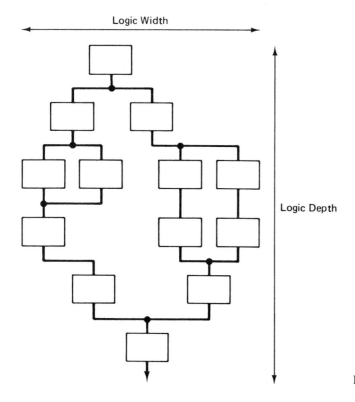

Logic Width

Logic Depth

Figure 13-17. Dimension analysis.

The depth of the logic determines the time required to execute a process and depends on the number of modules that are executed sequentially and on the number of instructions that are executed in each module. The depth of the logic is also dependent on the data depth (amount of data), since recurring instances of data may result in the interactive execution of instructions. Obviously, varying the data depths from transaction to transaction creates ambiguity and problems in obtaining an accurate logic depth assessment. Consequently, an accurate dimension analysis should use the ideas of a standard work unit discussed previously.

The width of the logic determines the number of concurrent executions of modules that can be executed simultaneously. Logic width is an especially important consideration for local area networks in which multiple computers share a task or in applications where parallelism and equal work distribution on computers is important.

Partitioning Resources in the Southern Region

Once the software is partitioned according to the concepts of binding, coupling, scopes of effect and control, dimension analysis, and atomic actions, it can then be allocated effectively to the computers in the network. To illustrate this point, let us assume in the case study that the Houston and Dallas volumes grow to the extent that the computer in Nashville cannot handle all the traffic of the region. For purposes of response time and communications costs, the decision is made to add a computer in Dallas to process sales

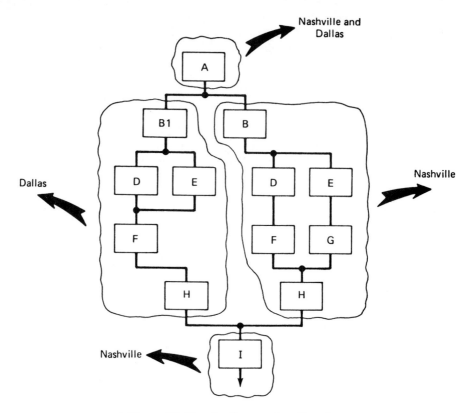

Figure 13–18. Southern region allocation.

and inventory data for the Houston–Dallas offices. If the system has been designed according to PAM conventions, the tasks of further partitioning and allocation are greatly simplified. Figure 13–18 shows why.

The software system to process the sales and inventory transactions is allocated to the computers in Nashville and Dallas as shown in Figure 13–18 and Table 13–2. Note that the adherence to PAM conventions allows module G to be used only at the regional computer. Since G deals only with the warehouse/plant function, the Dallas site is not concerned with this function. This code is *not* embedded into other modules. Moreover, modules A, D, E, F, and H are shared because they are designed to perform specific tasks relating to customers' sales and inventory functions. Typically, modules must be modified for local needs, so module B was changed to accommodate Dallas' unique requirements, giving module B1. As the network continues to grow, dimension analysis may reveal other opportunities for further PAM distribution. For example, at the Nashville office, modules D-F and E-G are candidates for additional partitioning.

Our case study does not exhibit the complex and sophisticated parallelism discussed earlier. However, it does exhibit load leveling, resource sharing, and distributed processing. It exhibits another characteristic of utmost importance: It is a simple solution to the problem.

TABLE 13–2

Module	Location	Functions
A	Nashville, Dallas	Accepts input transactions from either sales or inventory. Edits transactions. Sends data to B1 or B.
B1	Dallas	Modification to B to satisfy Dallas' local environment.
B	Nashville	Performs housekeeping chores. Obtains specific customer profile from data bases. Passes data to D and E.
D, F	Nashville, Dallas	Performs functions for sales application.
E	Nashville, Dallas	Performs functions for inventory application.
G	Nashville	Performs tasks to send component ordering data to warehouses and plants in Jacksonville, Albuquerque, and Pittsburgh.
H	Nashville, Dallas	Posts updates to files. Formats data for I.
I	Nashville	Performs regional summaries. Formats data for N.Y. headquarters. Transmits data to plants and warehouses.

Finally, the ability to downline load program modules to the Dallas site depends on the compatibility of Nashville's and Dallas' information systems. The nodes must have the same hardware architecture, communications protocols, DBMS, compilers, and operating systems.

NETWORK DATA-BASE DESIGN CONSIDERATIONS

Chapter 5 contained introductory information on data bases and their role in communications networks. Chapter 12 expanded the discussion, focusing on distributed data bases. This section continues the discussion and provides additional guidelines for designing data bases for a distributed network.

Ratio Analysis

Ratio analysis is often used to configure data bases for a network. It is based on an examination of the frequency of use of the data by each userat each site in the system. Data-base decisions regarding centralization, partitioning, and replication are based on the analysis. The process is based on five ratios:

1. Interest ratio
2. Miss ratio
3. Update/retrieval ratio
4. Site update/total update ratio
5. Precision ratio

Interest ratio.   This is a useful preimplementation tool to determine where data bases should reside. The interest ratio is derived as follows:

$$IR = \frac{TNI}{ANI}$$

where   IR = interest ratio
TNI = this node's interest in the data
ANI = all nodes' interest in the data

TNI represents a node's probable frequency of use of a data base or a segment of the data base. A typical user/customer requirements analysis is used to obtain the interest statistics. TNI is divided by ANI to obtain an indicator of one node's interest relative to all nodes' interest. Ratios heavily weighted toward one node are an obvious sign favoring the location of the data at that site. Thus, the interest ratio provides a "home location" indicator.

The ratio is only as valid as the analysis that produces the TNI and ANI parameters. It is often impossible to predict data usage, and the formula's parameters may be "best guesses." On the other hand, if the data are already automated and stored in a data base, interest and usage statistics can be obtained fairly easily.

In most instances, it is not practical to perform a data interest analysis to the level of an individual data item. Rather, the design team usually groups similar or common items together for the interest ratio calculation. This approach, called *clustering,* is widely used for general design decisions. The grouping can also serve to evaluate the clustering of data at the distributed sites and to relate the clustering to the users' subschemas.

Figure 13–19 provides an example of the data interest worksheet. The data obtained from the analysis and recorded in this sheet were used to justify the earlier decision in our case study to place computers and data bases in the four regions and three plants. For example, the Nashville analysis indicates a total of 40,812 sales and inventory transactions against the data bases during the peak period. These data are used operationally at Nashville more often than at the New York headquarters site. Figure 13–19 shows 12,244 transactions against the sales system (30% of 40,812) and 28,568 against the inventory system (70% of 40,812). In marked contrast, the New York site has 950 and 470 transactions against these two data bases (total 1,420). The interest ratio shows:

$$IR = \frac{TNI}{ANI}$$

New York: 3%

Site Data	New York	Pittsburgh	Albuquerque	Jacksonville	Nashville	Chicago	Baltimore	San Francisco	
Price	U: 250[1] R: 700[1]				U: 3917 R: 8337				Sales = 12,244
Inventory Location	U: 170[2]				U: 18,269				Inventory = 28,568
Stock Deletion Date	R: 300[2]				R: 10,299				
Personnel									
Payroll									
Market Trend Analysis									
Corporate Sales MIS									
Corporate Inventory MIS									
Southern Sales MIS	U: 0 R: 16,200	U: 2720 R: 5900	U: 400 R: 520	U: 3600 R: 2000	U: 6400 R: 15,200				
Southern Inventory MIS									
Central Sales MIS									

NOTE: Blank Entries in Worksheet are Not Required for Examples.

U = Frequency of Update Transactions
R = Frequency of Retrieval Transactions
* = Accessed During Peak Period Hour
** = Accessed During 24-hour Period
[1]Sales = 950
[2]Inventory = 470

Figure 13–19. Data interest worksheet.

$$0.03 = \frac{1,420}{40,812 + 1,420}$$

Nashville: 97%

$$0.97 = \frac{40,812}{40,812 + 1,420}$$

The Nashville site interest ratio is 97%; New York's ratio is only 3%, an obvious reason for home locating the data bases in Nashville.

This illustration, while a bit simple, serves the purpose of showing how the interest ratio is used. Its value is greater in circumstances where several sites have interest in the data, and the usage magnitude differences may be less obvious. For instance, after the Nashville site has processed the peak-period work load, it transmits sales and inventory data to the three plants in Pittsburgh, Albuquerque, and Jacksonville and to the headquarters computers in New York. The data are aggregated with accounting information (accounts receivable, accounts payable), parts invoices, and other data to form the Southern Region Inventory MIS (management information system). Five sites have need of the inventory MIS base. The activity against the southern region MIS data entails 58,000 transactions during a 24-hour period as depicted in Figure 13–19. The interest ratios reveal the following:

New York: 27.9%
$$0.279 = \frac{16,200}{58,000}$$

Pittsburgh: 15.0%
$$0.15 = \frac{2,720 + 5,960}{58,000}$$

Albuquerque: 1.6%
$$0.016 = \frac{400 + 520}{58,000}$$

Jacksonville: 18.3%
$$0.183 = \frac{3,600 + 7,000}{58,000}$$

Nashville: 37.2%
$$0.372 = \frac{6,400 + 15,200}{58,000}$$

Nashville has greater usage of the data at 37.2%; New York follows with a 27.9% usage ratio; next Jacksonville (18.3%) and then Pittsburgh (15%). Albuquerque does little support work with the southern region (1.6% ratio).

The designers now have some data to use for rational design decisions. Several options are available. First, the Southern Region Inventory MIS could remain centralized at the Nashville site. However, this means about 63% of the transactions would have to be transmitted across the expensive communications path to the Nashville computer. Second, all sites could be loaded with a replicate of the data base. However, this approach would be wasteful in view of the fact that Albuquerque and Pittsburgh do not have much interest in the data. Third, replicated copies could be placed at the Nashville and New York sites, giving 65% of all transactions a local access capability. The three plants would then transmit transactions to Nashville and New York to fulfill the remaining 35% of the total traffic. As we shall see when the update/retrieval ratio is examined, the third alternative is particularly attractive from the standpoint of simplicity.

The interest indicators are useful analysis tools. Once a system has been implemented, the data and software used at each site must be reexamined frequently in order to determine if the distributions still make sense. Data usage does not ordinarily remain stable in growing and dynamic organizations. Data flow changes as the company introduces new products, changes its mission, and acquires or divests itself of subsidiaries. Consequently, the interest ratios should be examined periodically to determine if the initial analysis is still valid.

Miss ratio. The miss ratio is useful for this purpose. The ratio can be used to relocate data bases—in essence, to determine if the home locations are still appropriate. The ratio indicates how frequently data are requested at a local site but obtained elsewhere.

$$MR = \frac{TDNO}{TDR}$$

where MR = miss ratio (at the local site)

     $TDNO$ = total data not obtained (at the local site)

       TDR = total data requested at the local site

Obtaining data for the TDNO and TDR parameters will probably require the writing of software that "traps" these statistics. For example, all outgoing transactions must be logged, with information on where the transaction is being transmitted. The statistics should be gathered periodically, not continuously. The overhead to collect the data can become quite expensive.

Interest and miss ratios should be evaluated with other factors. They should not be used to provide the "final answer," but as a tool to be used with other considerations:

- *Frequency of use versus need for timeliness:* A site may not use data often but may need the data immediately upon its infrequent request. In such a situation, it may make sense to keep redundant data at the sites that use it regularly *and* at the sites that need it rapidly.

- *Frequency of use versus vested interest:* A site that accesses data frequently may not necessarily be the site that considers the data most vital to its operations. Corporate headquarters in New York could have vested interest in certain data, yet actually use them infrequently.

- *Update versus retrieval:* The design team must make decisions on how to provide optimum performance for users who retrieve information and for users who update the data bases. It is difficult to provide ideal performance for both types of users, especially if the data are dispersed to multiple sites. We examine this problem with the next ratio.

Update/retrieval ratio.   The decision to replicate a data base in the network depends to a great degree on the frequency of updates versus retrievals that occur. The case study worksheet in Figure 13–19 provides an example.

Chapter 10 explained the complexity and potential problems of updating replicated data, especially in a real-time mode. As a general rule, real-time updates should be confined to centralized or partitioned data. The Southern Region Inventory MIS update/retrieval ratio is calculated as follows:

$$URR = U/R$$

where URR = update/retrieval ratio
      U = number of updates against a data base
      R = number of retrievals against a data base

The formula reveals that the sites have these URR ratios: New York = 0%; Pittsburgh = 45%; Albuquerque = 76%; Jacksonville = 51%; Nashville = 42%. We examine the significance of these ratios after examining the next ratio.

Site update/total update ratio.   In many situations, the total number of updates created at each site relative to the other sites is another important consideration. Consequently, the site update/total update ratio is also used:

$$UUR = TUTS/TUAS$$

where UUR = update/update ratio
    TUTS = total number of updates at this site
    TUAS = total number of updates of all sites

$$TUAS = 0 + 2,720 + 400 + 3,600 + 6,400$$

$$= 13,120$$

The UUR formula gives the following results: New York = 0%; Pittsburgh = 20%; Albuquerque = 3%; Jacksonville = 27%; Nashville = 50%.

The URR and UUR data provide a basis to make the following conclusions:

- New York presents no update complexity problem, since it has no update traffic. Moreover, the interest ratio reveals New York has 28% of the total transaction traffic. These two factors support the decision to replicate a copy of the data at the New York site.
- The Pittsburgh, Albuquerque, and Jacksonville plant sites have 45%, 70%, and 51% update/retrieval, respectively. At first glance, perhaps the high incidence of updates warrants replicated data at these sites. *However*, the total update traffic revealed by the update/update ratio is much smaller for the plants: 20%, 3%, and 27%, compared to Nashville's 50%. Nashville has primary update interest, a factor favoring the location of data at that site.

- Moreover, and most important, since the three plants do generate update traffic, replicating the data at those sites may create the timing and synchronization problems.

Consequently, the decision to replicate the data at New York and Nashville keeps all updates at the one data-base location in Nashville. The three plants will transmit their relatively small number of updates and retrievals to Nashville. (Pittsburgh could reasonably use the New York copy for its retrieval as well.) At some point in the 24-hour processing cycle, Nashville will downline load a fresh copy of the data to New York (practically speaking, perhaps using air express). Thereafter, New York's 16,200 average load will be done locally.

Precision ratio. We return to the problem of physical layout on the disk discussed in Chapter 5. Retrieved requests from remote sites in the network should create responses containing the exact data needed—nothing more and nothing less. For example, let us assume the inventory MIS has 200 separate items or fields stored in a physical block on the data base. The five sites' subschemas vary; some need certain fields within the record and not others. Moreover, the sites have different subschemas depending on a specific retrieval requirement.

The precision ratio is an ongoing analysis tool used to ensure that the physical data-base storage accommodates the total user community. This is especially important if an organization's system transmits and receives disk blocks without reformatting into smaller more precise messages. The precision ratio is calculated as follows:

$$PR = \frac{RIR}{TIR}$$

where PR = precision ratio
RIR = relevant items retrieved
TIR = total items retrieved

The ratio is used to analyze each user logical view (subschema) and determine how concisely the data base is structured to satisfy the request. For example, a user at the New York site has a subschema to view items 1–30, 78, 100–175 of the 200-item block, and the precision ratio is 53% (0.53 = 106/200). The 53% figure means that 47% of the data in the disk block was read, sent across a channel into a computer buffer (and perhaps even transmitted across a communications link), and not used. Is this a reasonable ratio? The answer is that it depends on the ratios of *all other* users. If a precision ratio aggregate reveals that users at several sites in the network are receiving low ratios, it is quite likely that the physical data bases need to be reformatted and reorganized. Precision ratio analysis is especially important for data bases with a large community of users in the network. They must be as precise as possible for the entire user community, or individual users will "spin off" data and create their own data structures. Such actions can create wasteful redundancies and data conflicts in the organization.

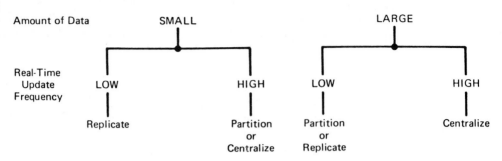

Figure 13–20. Decision tree.

Data-Base Design Decision Trees

In addition to the ratios, decision trees are useful design aids. The graphic nature of their structure can be used as a briefing tool design aid. Figure 13–20 shows a simple decision tree based on two factors: amount of data and real-time update frequency. Each organization should determine the specific parameters for the two variables. The decisions to centralize, replicate, or partition are general guidelines and certainly subject to change as individual circumstances warrant. Figure 13–21 shows a more involved tree. The update/retrieval ratio has been added to the structure. Finally, Figure 13–22 is an example of a tree developed for postinstallation analysis based on the amount of data, the miss ratio, and the real-time update frequency. The miss ratio might indicate a restructuring of the network data bases. While not illustrated here, the precision ratio can also be used with the decision tree. The reader is encouraged to draw a tree using the precision ratio as it relates to his or her organization.

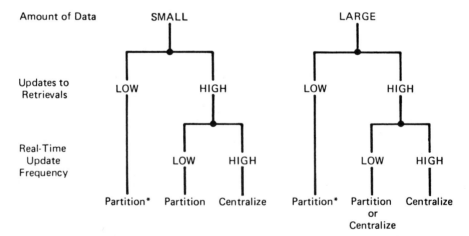

*CAUTION: "Round-up" Overhead and Delay.

Figure 13–21. Decision tree.

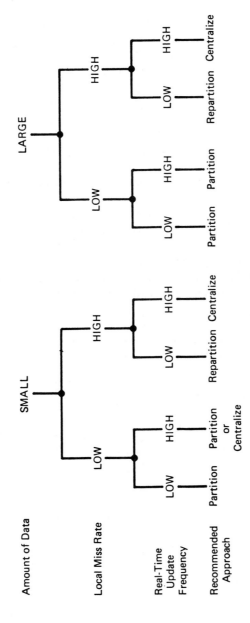

Figure 13–22. Decision tree.

Each organization should design the trees and the final recommended approaches based on its specific requirement. Since the three trees presented here are approaches that have been substantiated by the experiences of network and data-base designers, the reader can use them as the initial working assumptions.

Synchronization of Network Data Bases

In many instances, ratio analysis and the decision tree will lead to the decision to partition and replicate data bases. This section examines methods to keep the segmented and copied data concurrent and consistent across the nodes.[4] The subject is covered with four discussions: (a) system architecture, (b) serialized scheduling, (c) conflict analysis, and (d) network data management.

As discussed previously in the case study and data-base ratios, distributed data bases should provide strong locality of references: storing data items where they are most frequently used. To achieve this goal, it is often desirable to replicate data bases at multiple sites.

System architecture.   The network data base system is organized around the transaction manager or module (TM) and the data manager or module (DM). Each site has a computer running the TM and DM software (see Figure 13–23). The TM supervises transactions and *all* network action to satisfy the user's transaction request. The DM manages the data bases and the DBMS. In a sense, the DM is a back-end data-base

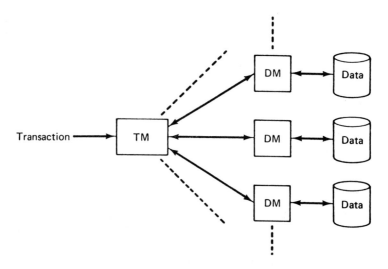

Figure 13–23.   TM/DM architecture.

[4]The approach discussed here is based on the research by the Computer Corporation of America (4 Cambridge Center, Cambridge, MA 02142), which led to their Distributed Database Manager (DDM). The material is also based on an earlier version of DDM called SDD-1 (a system for distributed data bases).

processor, and it is conceivable that DM functions could be placed in a separate back-end computer. The architecture functions through four operations at the transaction—TM interface:

1. BEGIN: TM sets up work space for the user transaction (T). It provides temporary buffers for data moving into and out of the data bases.
2. READ(X): TM looks for a copy of data X in T's work space. It returns it to T. If the data are not in the work space, it issues a dm-read(x) command to one of the network DMs, which accesses the data and returns them to T's work space.
3. WRITE(X): TM looks for a copy of X in T's work space. If found, it updates the ''old'' copy with the current value of X. If the data are not in the work space, a copy of the current value is placed into it.

Notice that no changes have yet been made to the network data bases. That is, no dm-write(X) commands have been issued by the TM to the DMs. The system uses a two-phase commit procedure to assure (a) restart/recovery integrity, (b) adherence to atomic commitment, and (c) resiliency across nodes.

- *Restart/recovery:* The DBMS can restart a transaction at any time before a dm-write(x) is executed.
- *Atomic commitment:* Two-phase commit keeps all nodes' data-base actions related to one transaction isolated from each other.
- *Resiliency:* Failure of a component during a Write does not lock up or bring down other components in the network. In other words (and using another term), a component failure does not produce *sympathetic failures* of other components executing the affected transaction.

4. END: For the first phase of the two-phase commit, TM issues a *pre*Write(x) to each DM in the network. The DM copies X from T's work space onto some form of secure storage. A DBMS failure at this juncture does no harm. After all DMs have executed the preWrite, the second phase of the commit begins by the TM issuing a dm-write(x) to the DMs. The DM then updates the data base from T's secure storage.

The preWrite commands specify all DMs that are involved in the two-phase commitment. Consequently, if a TM fails during the second phase, the DMs timeout, and check with other DMs to determine if a dm-Write(x) had been received. If so, all other DMs use it as if it were issued by the TM. Moreover, in the event of a DBMS failure during the Write, secure storage is used to recover data.

Serialized scheduling. Network data bases using partitioned or replicated copies are increasingly using the concept of serialized scheduling, wherein the effect of executing multiple, interleaved transaction executions is the same as running the transactions serially. Figure 13–24 shows the effect of serialized scheduling of three trans-

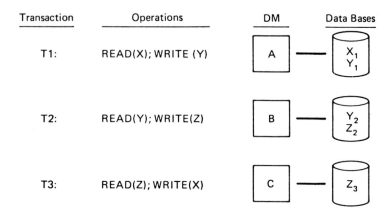

Transaction	Operations	DM	Data Bases

Figure 13–24. Serialized scheduling. (From "Concurrency Control in Distributed Database Systems" by Philip A. Bernstein and Nathan Goodman. *ACM Computing Surveys*, Vol. 13, No. 2, June 1981, p. 196.)

actions executing across three sites. The activity logs of the three DMs reveal the following order of operations [$R_i(X_j)$ means transaction i evokes a READ of X data base at DM_j]:[5]

1. DM A: $R_1(X_1)$ $W_1(Y_1)$ $R_2(Y_1)$ $W_3(X_1)$
2. DM B: $W_1(Y_2)$ $W_2(Z_2)$
3. DM C: $W_2(Z_3)$ $R_3(Z_3)$

The scheduling establishes transaction 1 to precede transaction 2, which precedes transaction 3. The schedule has the same effect of running each transaction serially. The DMs process all of transaction 1 actions before executing transaction 2, and the transaction 2 Write is executed at DM C before transaction 3.

Serialized scheduling is accomplished through the use of timestamps and message classes. Timestamps are placed on each transaction in accordance with a systemwide logical clock. The universal clock provides rules for keeping all sites at approximately the same logical time. The timestamp is made unique by the placement of a node identification within the timestamp. The transactions are divided into classes. The class is predetermined, based on the network data the transaction reads and writes. Since some transactions access the same data, their executions can possibly interfere and cause an inconsistent state in the data base. Consequently, transactions arriving at a node with conflicting classes must be processed in timestamp sequence. Since the transaction classes are predefined, all nodes know of potential conflicts.

Conflict analysis.   The analysis of class conflicts using timestamps involves two types of conflicts: Write/Write and Read/Write. Each type is based on class scheduling, wherein nodes will not process a Read with a conflicting class until all affected

[5]Philip A. Bernstein and Nathan Goodman, "Concurrency Control in Distributed Database Systems," *ACM Computing Surveys*, 13, no. 2, (June 1981) 196.

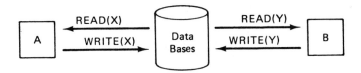

Figure 13–25. Conflict analysis.

earlier Writes have been processed. Figure 13–25 provides an example of Write/Write conflict analysis.

Site A transmits a Read transaction for a data base. Let us assume that the Read(X) transaction has a time stamp of t6. The node DBMS knows that classes X and Y may conflict. Since no class Y transaction with a t equal to or greater than t6 has arrived, site A's transaction is held.

Site B transmits a Read to the data base with a time stamp of t4. Since t4 < T6, B could possibly send a Write (say, at t5), *and* since B's timestamp is earlier than A, site B's Read is executed.

Site B obtains data, and then issues a Write (Y) with a timestamp of t5. Its Write is executed since site A's time stamp is t6. Site B then sends a timing message with a timestamp of t6. Since A's t is equal (or less than B's t), its Read and subsequent Write can now be executed.

Network data management. A network data base must do much more than scheduling and conflict analysis. SDD's TM provides many other functions, some of which are illustrated in Figure 13–26.[6] The relationaldata bases are stored at the nodes in pieces called *fragments*. (Ratio analysis would be a good tool for deciding how to fragment the data.) The data fragments are accessed and provided to the end user through the following sequence of events:

1. The transaction is analyzed by the request parser to determine if the requested data are available and the user has authority to access. The parser obtains this information from a systemwide directory.

2. The request is translated into relational access language. The directory is used to obtain fragment definitions, and the fragment query generator transforms the access language to match the fragments.

3. The access planner obtains the site locations of the fragments from the Directory. The cost estimator establishes how many data are to be moved to satisfy the user request. The planner develops an access plan for obtaining the data. This process is critical; the plan must provide for efficient and fast data movement. ''Roundup'' overhead must be kept as low as possible.

4. The move manager executes the access plan and generates requests to the affected DMs in the network.

[6]James A. Martin, *Design and Strategy for Distributed Data Processing* (Englewood Cliffs, NJ: Prentice Hall, 1981), p. 337.

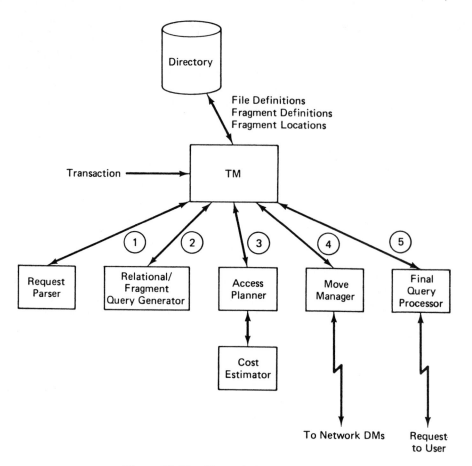

Figure 13–26. Network data management.

5. Data are moved to one site, assembled by the final query processor, and presented to the user. During this process, other activities such as serialized scheduling and conflict analysis are also taking place.

Additional Considerations on Using Personal Computers

A typical personal computer data-base network manages distributed systems by one of two methods: (a) as a disk server or (b) as a file server.

The disk server is a more limited approach and does not have sophisticated capabilities such as serialization scheduling and conflict analysis. A disk server user perceives that a remote data-base is local and dedicated to that one user. The disk server software coordinates the requests from multiple users without their knowledge. Each user's personal computer maintains a file allocation table (FAT), which keeps track of the used and unused portions of disk. However, the multiple FATs require rather extensive coordination and synchronization, and it is not uncommon for inconsistencies to develop in the various FATs. Disk servers frequently handle this problem by assigning specific disk sectors on the shared file to the different systems, not a very flexible approach.

The personal computer file server utilizes a redirector program that receives *all* user transactions, examines the active and pending transactions, and performs the actual data-base operations. Only one FAT is maintained, which decreases inconsistencies and errors. The file server approach is found in practically all mainframe computers as part of the data-base management system software. Personal computers have now incorporated these techniques into their systems. Notwithstanding, the reader who is accustomed to the powerful mainframe environment should be aware that the personal computer data-base offerings are more limited in scope and function.

Summary of Network Data-Base Considerations

Network data bases can be cumbersome to use and complex to update. As discussed previously, if multiple copies of one file exist at several sites, an update requires rather extensive coordination among the sites to keep all copies concurrent and identical.

The problems with updating multiple copies are reduced substantially by batching updates and processing them during a nonpeak period; the software complexity is reduced and the possibility of a site's "down" data bases does not pose as big a danger during an off-hour. This is a popular and well-proved approach.

Of course, the advantage of multiple copies for local retrieval may outweigh the problems with the updates. Using local queries, the transaction is processed on site, thereby providing opportunities to reduce communications costs. The potential bottleneck problems are relieved by having multiple service points, and the backup copies provide for failure recovery.

The use of partitioned data bases presents different considerations. In this case, the single copy is divided (partitioned) and placed at more than one location. This approach provides a simpler environment for updates; the update request is sent to the proper site, and the data base is locked out, updated, and released. The one copy eliminates many of the overhead and delay problems associated with multiple copies.

A possible disadvantage of partitioned data bases called *roundup overhead* arises when a data retrieval request requires data from several of the data-base partitions. The data request must be transmitted to all sites where the data reside, sent to the requestor and assimilated into a logical request, and presented to the user. The data retrieval could experience inordinate delay and overhead. Nonetheless, if the data are partitioned based on valid home location indicators, multiple retrievals to the distributed sites can be reduced.

The segmentation of the data files will affect line usage, since the duplication of data could decrease the transaction rates during the peak period. For example, as was suggested in the case study, the larger offices in the southern region might acquire their own machines and data files due to the findings of the distributed systems analysis. In a practical sense, several offices in the southern region could likely benefit from local computing capacity. This means fewer transactions at the Nashville regional headquarters. Consequently, an organization must periodically and frequently reevaluate the traffic flow because the network topology will be affected.

The ripple effect must be evaluated with *each change* to the network. If duplicate data are created, the replicated data bases will require additional transactions during the peak period in order to keep the data consistent across sites, thus creating additional overhead. Response time and throughput must then be reevaluated. Again, the ripple effect must be uppermost in the minds of the design team.

The distribution of data presents significant opportunities yet must be approached carefully. The environment should be kept as simple as possible. As an organization moves to multiple copies of data, fast response time requirements, and larger data volumes, the distributed systems become more complex and subject to synchronization problems.

SUMMARY

Some enterprises choose not to perform a detailed analysis of traffic patterns and data usage. These organizations simply purchase the bandwidth and file capacity to handle their operations. Other enterprises take the approach that bandwidth and storage are too expensive to allow such an approach.

While it may not be possible to know the exact usage and requirements of each application running on the network, some type of quantitative approach will place the enterprise in the position of knowing what effect the applications may be having on the network performance. Otherwise, the network manager is "running in the dark" . . . a risky way to travel.

Index

W

X

BIRKBECK COLLEGE
Malet Street, London WC1E 7HX
0171-631 6239
If not previously recalled for another reader;
this book should be returned or renewed
before the latest date stamped below.